MW00761859

ISRAEL

FODOR'S TRAVEL PUBLICATIONS

are compiled, researched, and edited by an international team of travel writers, field correspondents, and editors. The series, which now almost covers the globe, was founded by Eugene Fodor in 1936.

OFFICES
New York & London

Fodor's Israel:

Area Editor: Mike Rogoff
Editorial Contributors: Robert Brown, Jan Chilwell, Lisa Marrongelli, Ira Mayer, Haim Shapiro
Editor: Thomas Cussans
Executive Editor: Richard Moore
Illustrations: Lorraine Calaora
Maps: Swanston Graphics

SPECIAL SALES

Fodor's Travel Publications are available at special discounts for bulk purchases (100 copies or more) for sales promotions or premiums. Special editions, including personalized covers, excerpts of existing guides, and corporate imprints, can be created in large quantities for special needs. For more information, write to Special Marketing, Fodor's Travel Publications, 201 East 50th St., New York, NY 10022.

FODOR'S

ISRAEL
1988

FODOR'S TRAVEL PUBLICATIONS, INC.
New York & London

Copyright © 1987 by Fodor's Travel Publications, Inc.

All rights reserved under International and Pan-American Copyright Conventions. Published in the United States by Fodor's Travel Publications, Inc., a subsidiary of Random House, Inc., New York, and simultaneously in Canada by Random House of Canada Limited, Toronto. Distributed by Random House, Inc., New York.

No maps, illustrations, or other portions of this book may be reproduced in any form without written permission from the publisher.

ISBN 0-679-01527-2
ISBN 0-340-41796-X (Hodder & Stoughton)

MANUFACTURED IN THE UNITED STATES OF AMERICA
10 9 8 7 6 5 4 3 2 1

CONTENTS

FOREWORD

Israel, indeed the Middle East as a whole, is in so constant a state of flux that it can be hard for a daily newspaper to chart the myriad shifts and changes of this volatile region, let alone an annually revised guide book. We have provided as much essential background information and color as we can, but any visitor would be well advised to check with their travel agent and the Israel Government Tourist Office before making their trip to bring themselves up to date with the latest situation. Similarly, with an inflation that has sometimes soared into three figures, all prices quoted, even though in dollars, should be taken as indications only. Be sure to double check to get the latest figures.

We would like to stress that the hotel and restaurant listings are selections. We do not profess to provide a complete listing for accommodations and eating places. We select those we feel would interest our readers, changing the listings year by year to include new places that have surfaced. Space alone prevents us being more comprehensive and there could well be twice the number of acceptable places in any given town or area than we have been able to list.

***

The task of creating this edition would not have been possible without the help of many friends both in Israel and in tourist offices abroad. We would especially like to express our gratitude to the Israel Government Tourist Office in London, and to Swanston Graphics, who have provided the maps for this edition. But above all, we would like to thank Mike Rogoff, our Area Editor and prime mover behind this guide. Without his tireless efforts and expertise, this book would not have been possible.

We greatly appreciate letters from our readers, telling us of their experiences and giving us that "traveler's eye view" of things, which is not always the same as that of our professional editors. Hotels and restaurants are liable to drop from being thoroughly pleasant, friendly places to stay to become rip-off joints by a change of ownership or even the temporary illness of the manager. Highways are extended, museums are closed, buildings suddenly wrapped in sheets of plastic for essential renovations, new archeological sites open. . .all the confusion of modern life can affect the contents of a travel guide.

Our addresses are:

In the U.S.: Fodor's Travel Publications, Inc., 201 East 50th St., New York, NY 10022.

In the U.K.: Fodor's Travel Guides, 9–10 Market Place, London W.1.

MAP OF ISRAEL

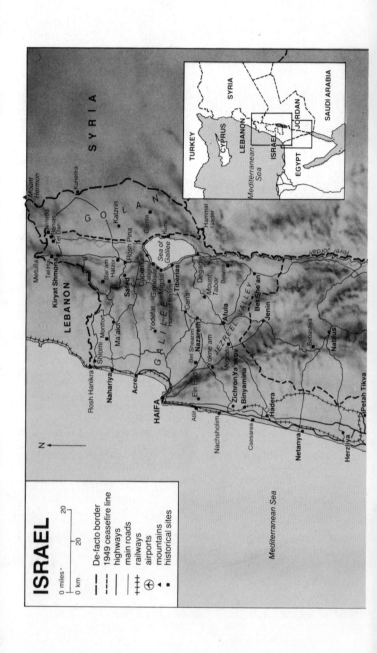

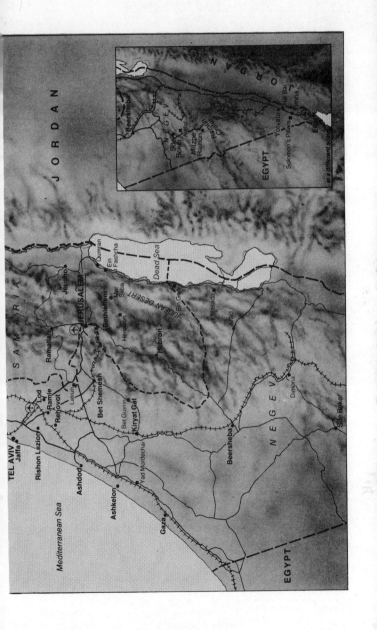

FACTS AT YOUR FINGERTIPS

FACTS AT YOUR FINGERTIPS

Planning Your Trip

NATIONAL TOURIST OFFICE. The major source of information for anyone planning a vacation in Israel is the Israel Government Tourist Office (I.G.T.O.). They can supply information on all aspects of travel to and around Israel, much of it free and all of it useful.

Their addresses are:

In the U.S.: 350 Fifth Ave., New York, N.Y. 10118 (212–560–0650); 5 South Wabash Ave., Chicago, IL 60603 (312–782–4306); 6380 Wilshire Blvd., Suite 1700, Los Angeles, CA 90048 (213–658–7462); 4151 Southwest Freeway, Houston TX 77027 (713–850–9341); 420 Lincoln Rd., Miami Beach, FL 33139 (305–673–6862); 3514 International Dr. NW, Washington, D.C. 20008 (202–364–5699); 220 Montgomery St., Suite 550, San Francisco, CA 94104 (415–775–5462).

In Canada: 180 Bloor St. West, Suite 700, Toronto, Ont. M5S 2V6 (416–964–3784).

In the U.K.: 18 Great Marlborough St., London W.1 (01–434 3651).

TOURS. Israel is in many ways almost by definition a specialist destination, with a premium on religious and cultural holidays. Even a simple sightseeing vacation will involve a good deal more concentrated and varied touring than in most other countries. In much the same way, you will also find enormous numbers of activity holidays—sailing, climbing, hiking, golfing, and so on—all taking full advantage of an ideal climate and varied landscape. But those after nothing more demanding than a beach, a bar and nightlife into the small hours will not be disappointed, though they will find themselves in a minority.

Prices are generally very competitive, a reflection of the large number of tour companies after the tourist dollar and shrewd management by the tourist authorities. For up-to-the-minute information on prices and schedules, contact any Israel Government Tourist Office (see above), your travel agent, or tour operators themselves. We give a representative list of operators below. If you need further information on any tour operator, contact either the *American Society of Travel Agents,* 4400 MacArthur Blvd, NW, Washington D.C. 20007, or the *British Association of Travel Agents,* 53 Newman St., London W.1.

Art and Archeology. Visitors have long been welcome to lend a hand at the numerous excavations throughout the country, though fairly spartan living conditions and the need to stay for at least two weeks make this preeminently a younger person's vacation. But if you want no more than a taste of what it's all about, plus a seminar on archeology, the aptly-named *Dig for a Day,* 11 Shonei Halachot St., Jerusalem (tel. 02–273515), or any I.G.T.O. office, will point you in the right direction. *Command Travel,* among a host of others, also offer in-depth historical and archeological tours, as does *Heritage Travel* in the U.K.

1

Cruises. A substantial number of luxury liners call in at Haifa and Ashod for stays of up to 48 hours—easily enough time to get to at least two or three of the major areas—on cruises around the Mediterranean. For those who want the convenience and comfort of modern ship-board life, plus the opportunity to sample a number of other Mediterranean destinations, this can provide an ideal introduction to Israel. *Cunard, P&O* and *Chandris* are among the major operators.

Pilgrimages. The Israel Ministry of Tourism's *Pilgrimage Committee,* Box 1018, Jerusalem (tel. 02–237311), offers lectures, forums, fellowship sessions, special certificates for pilgrims and lists of religious sites. An equally helpful source of information is the *Christian Information Center,* Jaffa Gate, Jerusalem (tel. 02–282621), run by the Franciscans. They can also supply tickets (free, but very limited) to Christmas midnight mass in Bethlehem; write as far in advance as you can. Jewish organizations such as the American Jewish Congress, United Synagogue, the United Jewish Appeal and others offer tours geared to Jewish visitors. In addition, any I.G.T.O. can also help arrange for a service at the Western Wall or at Masada.

Roughing It. For those eager to see the country at close range, on foot, horse back, even by camel, or keen to get to grips with the expanses of the Negev, contact the *Society for the Protection of Nature in Israel,* 4 Hashefela St., Tel Aviv (tel. 03–335063). Desert safaris are the specialty of *Neot Hakikar,* 36 Keren Hayesod St., Jerusalem (tel. 02–699385 and (Tel Aviv) 03–463111); *Johnny's Desert Tours,* Box 261 Eilat (tel. 059–76777); or *Metzoke Dragot,* D.N. Bikat Yericho (tel. 057–90802 or 02–228114/5/6). *Adventure Center,* in Oakland, California, run a tour for lovers of the great outdoors which covers Israel from top to bottom. In the U.K., these tours are operated by *Explore Worldwide.*

Spas. Though as yet not as well known as European spas, Israel has two main spas, at the Dead Sea and Sea of Galilee, where those suffering from rheumatic pains and other ailments can bathe in natural hot sulfur springs under the supervision of qualified physicians. In addition, the Dead Sea area provides natural treatments—largely the result of its very low elevation—for sufferers of psoriasis. Information on health cures is available from any I.G.T.O.

Summer Camps. Families visiting Israel may like to investigate summer camps for children. General information is available from *Neve Hanofesh,* 44 Hibat Zion St., Ramat Gan (tel. 03–793550). Families spending all or part of a summer in Israel may want to place their children in a day camp. Camps, many with English-speaking counselors, can be found in community centers throughout the country. Again, any I.G.T.O. can help.

Sports. We give details of sports in the *Practical Information* sections at the end of every chapter. But among the many sporting vacations available in Israel, scuba diving in the Red Sea has proved particularly popular. It's one of the richest areas for tropical fish and corals in the world, and special underwater archeology and photography courses spice up the mixture. *Aqua Sport,* Box 300, Coral Beach, Eilat (tel. 059–72788) is about the largest company offering diving holidays. Other water-borne activities in the Red Sea are yacht cruises, either for divers or those who merely want to get away from it all; contact *Fantasea,* Box 420, Herzlia Bet (tel. 053–96482).

U.S. Tour Operators

Adventure Center, 5540 College Ave., Oakland, CA 94618 (415–654–1879).

American Express, 822 Lexington Ave., New York, N.Y. 10021 (212–758–6510).

Arkia Israel Airlines, 630 Third Ave., New York, N.Y. 10017 (212–687–0615).

El Al Israel Airlines, 850 Third Ave., New York, N.Y. 10022 (212–486–2600).

Kwik Travel Services, 5834 N. Lincoln Ave., Chicago, IL 60659 (312–989–1100).

Maupintour, 1515 St. Andrews Dr., Lawrence, KS 66046 (800–255–4266).

Travel Plans International, Box 3875, Oak Brook, IL 60522 (312–573–1400).

TWA Getaway Vacations, 28 South 6th St., Philadelphia, PA 19106 (215–925–7885).

Unitours, 60 East 42 St., New York, N.Y. 10165 (212–949–9500, or, from outside New York State, 1–800–223–1780).

Wilcox World Tours, 1705 Northwestern Plaza, Asheville, NC 28801 (704–254–0746).

U.K. Tour Operators

Club Méditerranée, 106–108 Brompton Rd., London S.W.3 (01–581 1161).

Enterprise Holidays, Box 100, Hodford House, 17–27 High St., Hounslow, Middx. (01–572 7373).

Explore Worldwide, 7 High St., Aldershot, Hants. (tel. 0252–319448).

Inter-Church Travel Ltd., 13–17 New Burlington Pl., London W.1 (01–734 0942).

P&O Cruises, 29–55 Middlesex St., London E.1 (01–283 8080).

Serenissima Travel Ltd., 2 Lower Sloane St., London S.W.1 (01–730 9841).

Speedbird Holidays, 152 King St., London W.6 (01–741 7348).

Thomson Holidays, Greater London House, Hampstead Rd., London N.W.1 (01–387 9321).

Twickenham Travel, 84 Hampton Rd., Twickenham (01–894 5500).

WHEN TO GO. The answer to this is simple: any time at all. There is hardly a winter day when it is not blissfully warm somewhere in Israel or a summer day when you can't feel a cool evening breeze (though the summer can be blisteringly hot). Rain falls only during the winter, and even then it's more often sunny than not. Perhaps the most important thing to remember is to be prepared for anything in the way of weather. Snow can and does fall once or twice a year in the mountains. And even in early spring or late fall there can be hot dry desert winds that Israelis refer to by the Arabic name *hamseen,* which means "fifty," ostensibly because its potential season totals 50 days, though in fact it usually doesn't last more than three or four at a time.

If you're looking for bargain rates, the best time is probably December, January and February (but not, of course, during the Christmas holidays) for most of the country, while Tiberias and Eilat drop their prices in summer. If you are not bound by school schedules, the best time of all is probably the spring and the fall, when the weather is warm but not yet too hot.

Average temperatures in degrees fahrenheit and centigrade:

	Jan.	Feb.	Mar.	Apr.	May	June	July	Aug.	Sept.	Oct.	Nov.	Dec.
Jerusalem												
F°	53	57	61	69	77	81	83	85	82	78	66	56
C°	11	14	16	20	25	27	28	30	28	25	19	14
Tel Aviv												
F°	65	66	68	72	77	83	86	86	89	84	76	66
C°	18	19	20	22	25	28	30	30	31	29	24	19
Eilat												
F°	70	73	79	87	95	99	103	103	97	92	83	74
C°	21	22	26	31	35	37	40	40	36	33	28	23

 NATIONAL AND RELIGIOUS HOLIDAYS. Israelis have to keep at least three calendars in mind. The first is the regular calendar used in most of the world. Then there is the Jewish calendar, which has 12 lunar (moon) months of 28 days each, with a complicated system of leap years during which there is an extra month. (1988 is actually the year 5748 according to this reckoning). The Muslim calendar also has 12 lunar months, but no leap years, so holidays move slowly from season to season. And just to complicate things a little more, the Orthodox Christian churches follow the old Julian calendar, which is 12 days behind Western calculations.

The most important event occurs every week: the Jewish Sabbath, which begins on Friday at sunset and ends on Saturday night. Orthodox Jews do no work. Lighting fires, smoking, driving, and cooking food are all forbidden. Stores and bus service shut down in most of the country and many restaurants, cafes and places of entertainment also close. Most hotels serve food which has been cooked in advance and kept warm. In some Orthodox sections, especially in Jerusalem and Tel Aviv's Orthodox suburb of Bnei Brak, no traffic is allowed at all and barriers are put up to keep cars out. But Sabbath observance varies widely throughout the country. In Jerusalem, where the rules tend to be the strictest, Israelis and tourists alike head for Arab East Jerusalem and the Old City. In Tel Aviv the cafes do their biggest business on Friday night, and in Eilat the only way you know it's the Sabbath is because the beaches are jammed with local residents. As a result of a longstanding compromise, there are bus services, albeit somewhat restricted, in Haifa and much of the north on Saturday. Most Jewish religious holidays are bound by rules similar to those of the Sabbath.

The Jewish year begins with *Rosh Hashanah,* a two-day holiday which falls in September or October, marked by the blowing of the ram's horn, or *shofar,* in the synagogue.

Yom Kippur, the Day of Atonement, a fast day and the most important holiday in the Jewish year, falls ten days later and this is one time the country really shuts down. Traffic comes to an almost complete standstill and even hotels usually give box lunches to guests who are not fasting.

Sukkot, the Feast of Tabernacles, is a week-long harvest festival, a few days later. Many families build a small booth, covered with leaves, in which they eat during the festival. A popular sports event, the March to Jerusalem, is usually held at this time and tourists may participate. The last day, Simhat Torah, marks the completion of the reading of the Five Books of Moses, the Torah, in the synagogue, and worshippers sing and dance with the Torah scroll both there and, the following night, in public parks and streets.

Chanukah, the Feast of Lights, which falls in December, commemorates the victory of the Maccabees over Antiochus Epiphanes, who outlawed Jewish religious practices in the 2nd century B.C. Candles or oil lamps are lit for eight days.

Tu B'Shvat, the New Year of the Trees, in late January or February, is a jolly time when everyone—including tourists, if they wish—goes out to plant trees.

Purim, the Feast of Esther, in March or April, celebrates the rescuing of the Jews of Persia by Queen Esther. Children and even adults dress up in costumes and there are sometimes parades and carnival-like events in the large cities.

Pessach, Passover, also in March or April, is the festival of the exodus of the Israelites from Egypt, when most Jews eat only unleavened bread, or matza, for a week. The first night of the holiday is marked by a festive meal and service, called a *seder,* and visitors should try, if at all possible, to find a way of spending this evening with an Israeli family or on a kibbutz. (The I.G.T.O. can sometimes arrange this, as it can a visit to the Samaritan Passover sacrifice on Mt. Gerizim.)

Two days of mourning, Holocaust Memorial Day, for Jews killed by the Nazis, and the Day of Remembrance for soldiers killed in Israel's wars, fall in close succession. The latter is followed by Independence Day, a time of general merrymaking, singing and dancing in the streets, picnics and bonfires.

Lag Ba'Omer, between Passover and Shavu'ot, historically recalls the momentary relief from the string of national disasters which occurred in this period. It is often marked by the lighting of bonfires.

Shavu'ot, Pentecost, seven weeks after Passover, is a harvest festival, with the symbolic offering of first fruits by school children and on kibbutzim.

Tisha B'Av, a fast day which falls in mid-summer, marks the destruction of the First and Second temples.

For Christians, Christmas and Easter are of particular importance. Visitors at Christmas time should try to visit Bethlehem where the festivities begin on December 24 with a procession at noon and continue in the evening with appearances by choirs from all over the world in Manger Square. Midnight mass is broadcast, for those unable to get into the church, on a giant TV screen in the square. Festivities take place for the Greek Orthodox on January 6 and for the Armenians on January 17.

Easter festivities begin with processions on Palm Sunday from the Mt. of Olives and continue throughout Holy Week, culminating in the Procession of the Cross along the Via Dolorosa on Good Friday. Especially moving are the Orthodox rites, attended by thousands of black-clad pilgrims from Greece and Cyprus, who jam into the Church of the Holy Sepulcher on Holy Saturday for the Ceremony of the Holy Fire, in which fire emanates from the Tomb of Christ and is spread within seconds from candle to candle throughout the church. Several Protestant sunrise services are held in Jerusalem on Easter Sunday.

The most important time for Muslims is the month of Ramadan, when they fast from sunrise to sunset. In Jerusalem a cannon blast marks the beginning and end of the fast and special foods and cakes are sold in the streets every evening. The completion of the fast is a three-day festival, Id el-Fitr.

In addition to the religious holidays, the Israel Festival, with concerts, theater performances and street events, is held in Jerusalem and Caesarea every spring. And Jerusalem Day marks the 1967 reunificiation of the city.

1988 Dates. Tu B'Shvat Feb. 3; Purim Mar. 3; Passover Apr. 2–8 (first and last days holy days); Holocaust Day Apr. 13; Day of Remembrance Apr. 20; Independence Day (public holiday) Apr. 21; Lag Ba'Omer May 5; Shavu'ot (holy day) May 22; Tisha B'Av July 24; Rosh Hashanah (holy days) Sep. 12–13; Yom Kippur (holy day) Sep. 21; Sukkot Sep. 26–Oct. 3 (first and last days holy days); Channukah Dec. 4–11.

WHAT TO PACK. Travel light is the watchword. Try not to take more than you can comfortably carry yourself and you'll be far happier than if you had taken that extra dress or jacket. Generally, Israel is a very informal country. Even in the fanciest hotels and restaurants you only need a jacket and tie if you feel more comfortable that way. In winter, be sure to bring a warm, rainproof coat and sturdy shoes, and even in Eilat be prepared for chilly nights. In summer, cotton garments are far more comfortable than synthetics, though a windbreaker or heavy sweater is needed for cool nights. A bathing suit is a must for winter and summer. Shorts are fine for touring except in religious sites, where women are sometimes also expected to cover their arms. Men must cover their heads in synagogues. But religious sites of all religions will usually help you out with a scarf, cloth or other covering to hide offending legs, shoulders or heads.

COSTS IN ISRAEL. In a country beset by economic problems, and with an inflation rate that has sometimes soared to three figures, Israel might appear to be one of the most expensive countries in the world. In fact, when prices are not frozen by government decree, the value of the dollar keeps abreast of price rises, and the tourist hardly feels a thing. A typical day in Jerusalem or Tel Aviv might cost a couple traveling comfortably anywhere from $120 to $250, including hotel, meals, tours and drinks, depending on the level of service, but budget travelers can get along on far less by staying in smaller hotels, hostels or similar accommodations, using public buses and eating in cheap restaurants.

In contrast to many other countries, package tours, with hotels and some meals included, are generally cheaper than doing it on your own. So even if you don't like being with a group, it is often worthwhile to find a package that suits you. Even within Israel, if you are planning an excursion of a few days, it's a good idea asking a travel agent if any special deals are available.

Israeli Currency. In 1986 Israel changed its currency to the New Shekel, represented in Hebrew by a logo of the initials of "shekel hadash," and in English NIS. One New Shekel is equivalent to 1,000 old ones. To avoid confusion, and to cope with changing rates of exchange, all prices quoted here are in dollars, as they are in any case in hotels and many restaurants and shops catering to tourists.

Changing Money. Banks are unquestionably the best bet. Hotels will suffice in a pinch, but their rates tend to be less attractive than the official one. Banks are generally open 8.30 A.M. to 12.30 P.M. (12 on Friday), and 4 P.M. to 5.30 P.M. They are closed Mon., Wed., Fri. afternoons and, of course, all day Saturday. Bank branches within major hotels often have different and more convenient hours. For departing travelers, the banks in Ben Gurion Airport's departure area are always open.

If your're traveling with the widely accepted U.S. dollars, there is little reason for changing large amounts into local currency. You will need some shekels, of course, for smaller "on the street" needs. But if the current government controls end and the shekel again begins to slide against the dollar, it will become even more necessary to change prudently small amounts, preferably every day, to take advantage of changing rates of exchange.

TAKING MONEY ABROAD. Traveler's checks are still the standard and best way to safeguard your travel funds; and you still usually get a better exchange rate in Israel for traveler's checks than for cash. In the U.S., many of the larger banks issue their own traveler's checks—just about as universally recognized as those of American Express, Cook and Barclays/Visa. In most instances there is a 1% charge for the checks; there is no fee for Barclays/Visa checks. Some banks also issue them free if you are a regular customer. The best-known British checks are Cook's and those of Barclays, Lloyds, Midland and National Westminster banks.

It is also always a good idea to have some local currency upon arrival, though dollars go a very long way in Israel and open many doors. Some banks will provide this service.

Credit Cards. Major credit cards are generally, but by no means universally, accepted in larger hotels, restaurants and shops. As a result of inflation, many medium priced restaurants which once accepted credit cards no longer do so. Accordingly, you would do well to check carefully which cards are accepted, particularly in hotels and restaurants, before checking in or ordering a meal.

Our hotel and restaurant listings in the *Practical Information* sections at the end of every chapter give details of the four major cards—American Express, Diner's Club, MasterCard (incorporating Access and Eurocard) and Visa, listed under the abbreviations AE, DC, MC and V—accepted in each hotel and restaurant we carry. But as we say, double check.

PASSPORTS. Americans. Apply in person at U.S. Passport Agency Offices, local county courthouses or selected Post Offices. If you have a passport not more than eight years old you may apply by mail; otherwise you will need:

—proof of citizenship, such as a birth certificate.

—two identical photographs, two inches square, either black and white or color, on non-glossy paper and taken within the past six months.

—$35 for the passport itself plus a $7 processing fee if you are applying in person (no processing fee when applying by mail) for those 18 years and older, or, if you are under 18, $20 for the passport plus a $7 processing fee if you are applying in person (again, no extra fee when applying by mail).

—proof of identity that includes a photo and signature, such as a driver's license, previous passport, or any governmental ID card.

Adult passports are valid for ten years, others for five years; they are not renewable. Allow four to six weeks for your application to be processed, but in an emergency, Passport Agency offices can have a passport readied within 24–48 hours, and even the postal authorities can indicate "Rush" when necessary.

If you expect to travel extensively, request a 48- or 96-page passport rather than the usual 24-page one. There is no extra charge. When you receive your passport, write down its number, date and place of issue separately; if it is later lost or stolen, notify either the nearest American Consul or the Passport Office, Department of State, 1425 K St. NW, Washington DC 20524, as well as the local police.

Canadians. Canadian citizens apply in person to regional passport offices, post offices or by mail to Passport Office, Bureau of Passports, Complexe Guy Favreau, 200 Dorchester West, Montreal, P.Q. Canada H2Z 1X4. A $21 fee, two photographs and evidence of citizenship are required. Canadian passports are valid for five years and are non-renewable.

Britons. British subjects should apply for passports on special forms obtainable from main post offices or a travel agent. The application should be sent or taken to the Passport Office according to residential area (as indicated on the guidance form) or lodged with them through a travel agent. It is best to apply for the passport four to five weeks before it is required, although in some cases it will be issued sooner. The regional Passport Offices are located in London, Liverpool, Peterborough, Glasgow and Newport. The application must be countersigned by your bank manager or by a solicitor, barrister, doctor, clergyman or justice of the peace who knows you personally. You will need two full-face photos. The fee is £15; passport valid for ten years.

 HEALTH AND INSURANCE. The different varieties of travel insurance cover everything from health and accident costs, to lost baggage and trip cancellation. Sometimes they can all be obtained with one blanket policy; other times they overlap with existing coverage you might have for health and/or home; still other times it is best to buy policies that are tailored to very specific needs. Insurance is available from many sources, however, and many travelers unwittingly end up with redundant coverage. Before purchasing separate travel insurance of any kind, be sure to check your regular policies carefully.

Generally, it is best to take care of your insurance needs before embarking on your trip. You'll pay more for less coverage—and have less chance to read the fine print—if you wait until the last minute and make your purchases from, say, an airport vending machine or insurance company counter. If you have a regular insurance agent, he or she is the person to consult first.

Flight insurance, which is often included in the price of the ticket when the fare is paid via American Express, Visa or certain other major credit cards, is also often included in package policies providing accident coverage as well. These policies are available from most tour operators and insurance companies. While it is a good idea to have health and accident insurance when traveling, be careful not to spend money to duplicate coverage you may already have . . . or to neglect some eventuality which could end up costing a small fortune.

For example, basic Blue Cross-Blue Shield policies do cover health costs incurred while traveling. They will not, however, cover the cost of emergency transportation, which can often add up to several thousand dollars. Emergency transportation is covered, in part at least, by many major medical policies such as those underwritten by Prudential, Metropolitan and New York Life. Again, we can't urge you too strongly that in order to be sure you are getting the coverage you need, check any policy carefully before buying. Another important example: Most insurance issued specifically for travel does not cover pre-existing conditions, such as a heart condition.

Several organizations offer coverage designed to supplement existing health insurance and to help defray costs not covered by many standard policies, such as emergency transportation. Some of the more prominent are:

Travel Assistance International, the American arm of Europ Assistance, offers a comprehensive program providing medical and personal emergency services and offering immediate, on-the-spot medical, personal and financial help. Trip protection ranges from $35 for an individual for up to eight days to $220 for an entire family for a year. Full details from travel agents or insurance brokers, or from *Europ Assistance Worldwide Services, Inc.,* 1333 F St., N.W.,

Washington, D.C. 20004 (800–821–2828). In the U.K., contact Europ Assistance Ltd., 252 High St., Croydon, Surrey (01–680 1234).

Carefree Travel Insurance, c/o ARM Coverage Inc., 120 Mineola Blvd., Box 310, Mineola, NY 11510 (516–294–0220) offers insurance, legal and financial assistance, and medical evacuation arranged through Inter Claim. Carefree coverage is available from many travel agents.

International SOS Assistance Inc., Box 11568, Philadelphia, PA 19116 (800–523–8930) has fees from $15 a person for seven days, to $195 for a year.

IAMAT (International Association for Medical Assistance to Travelers), 417 Center St., Lewiston, N.Y. 14092 (716–754–4883); 188 Nicklin Road, Guelph, Ontario, N1H 7L5 (519–836–0102).

The British Insurance Association, Aldermary House, Queen St., London E.C.4 (01–248 4477) will give comprehensive advice on all aspects of vacation travel insurance in the U.K.

Another frequent inconvenience to travelers is the loss of baggage. It is possible, though often complicated, to insure your luggage against loss through theft or negligence. Insurance companies are reluctant to sell such coverage alone, however, since it is often a losing proposition for them. Instead, it is most usually included as part of a package also covering accidents or health. Remuneration is normally determined by weight, regardless of the value of the specific contents of the luggage. Should you lose your luggage or some other personal possession, be sure to report it to the local police immediately. Without documentation of such a report, your insurance company might be very stingy. Also, before buying baggage insurance, check your homeowners policy. Some such policies offer "off-premises theft" coverage, including loss of luggage while traveling.

The last major area of traveler's insurance is trip cancellation coverage. This is especially important to travelers on APEX or charter flights. Should you get sick abroad, or for some other reason be unable to continue your trip, you may be stuck having to buy a new one-way fare home, plus paying for space on the charter you're not using. You can guard against this with trip cancellation insurance, usually available from travel agents. Most of these policies will also cover last minute cancellations.

STUDENT AND YOUTH TRAVEL. All student travelers should obtain an International Student Identity Card, essential for getting student discounts, youth bus passes, etc. It is available for $10 from the *Council On International Educational Exchange* (see below for addresses). Canadian students should apply to the *Association of Student Councils,* 187 College, St., Toronto, Ont. Canada M5T 1P7. The Canadian card is $5. The following organizations can also be helpful in finding student flights, educational opportunities and other information. Most deal with international student travel generally, but materials for those listed cover Israel.

American Youth Hostels, Box 37613, Washington D.C. 20013 (202–783–6161). Members are eligible for entree to the worldwide network of youth hostels. The organization publishes an extensive directory to same.

Council on International Educational Exchange (CIEE), 205 East 42 St., New York, N.Y. 10017 (212–661–1414); 312 Sutter St., San Francisco, CA 94108 (415–421–3473) provides information on summer study, work/travel programs and travel services for college and high school students and a free *Charter Flights Guide* booklet. Their *Whole World Handbook* ($7.95 plus $1 postage) is the best listing of both work and study possibilities.

Institute of International Education, 809 United Nations Plaza, New York, N.Y. 10017 (212–883–8200) is primarily concerned with study opportunities and administers scholarships and fellowships for international study and training. Among the leaders in youth and student travel are: *Arista Student Travel Assoc.,* 11 East 44th St., New York, N.Y. 10017 (212–687–5121); *Bailey Travel Service,* 123 East Market St., York, PA 17401 (717–854–5511); and *Campus Holidays,* 242 Bellevue Ave., Upper Montclair, NJ 07043 (800–526–2915).

The Israel Student Travel Association (ISSTA) offers low-priced tours and special programs of interest to student travelers. They may be contacted at 109 Ben Yehuda St., Tel Aviv (03–247164) or 5 Elissar St., Jerusalem (tel. 02–225288).

HINTS FOR HANDICAPPED TRAVELERS. *Access to the World: A Travel Guide for the Handicapped,* by Louise Weiss, is an outstanding book covering all aspects of travel for anyone with health or medical problems. It features extensive listings and suggestions on everything from availability of special diets to wheelchair accessibility. Order from *Facts On File,* 460 Park Ave. South, New York, N.Y. 10016 ($14.95).

Tours specially designed for the handicapped generally parallel those of the non-handicapped traveler, but at a more leisurely pace. For a complete list of tour operators who arrange such travel write to the *Society for the Advancement of Travel for the Handicapped,* 26 Court St., Brooklyn, N.Y. 11242. *Moss Rehabilitation Hospital,* 12th St. and Tabor Rd., Philadelphia, PA 19141, answers inquiries regarding specific cities and countries as well as providing toll-free telephone numbers for airlines with special lines for the hearing impaired and, again, listings of selected tour operators. Also helpful is the *Information Center for Individuals with Disabilities,* 20 Park Plaza, Room 330, Boston, MA 02116.

The *International Air Transport Association* (IATA) publishes a free pamphlet, *Incapacitated Passengers' Air Travel Guide,* explaining the various arrangements to be made and how to make them. Write IATA, 2000 Peel St., Montreal, Quebec H3A 2R4.

In the U.K., contact *Mobility International,* 43 Dorset St., London W.1; the *National Society for Mentally Handicapped Children,* 117 Golden Lane, London E.C.1; the *Across Trust,* Crown House, Morden, Surrey (they have an amazing series of "Jumbulances," huge articulated ambulances, staffed by volunteer doctors and nurses, that can whisk even the most seriously handicapped across Europe in comfort and safety). But the main source in Britain for all advice on handicapped travel is the *Royal Association for Disability and Rehabilitation* (RADAR), 25 Mortimer St., London W.1.

Wheel chairs may be obtained by tourists from *Yad Sarah,* 49 Haneviim St., Jerusalem (02–244242). This is a philanthropic organization devoted to providing medical and para-medical equipment to those who need it. There is no fee, but they do ask for a deposit and contributions are welcome.

LANGUAGE. The official languages in Israel are Hebrew and Arabic, but English is taught from elementary school on and it is rare to be in a situation where no one speaks English. Indeed many Israelis speak it fluently. For that matter you can usually also find someone speaking French, German, Yiddish or Russian as well.

ISRAELI TIME. Israel is seven hours ahead of Eastern Standard Time, eight hours ahead of Central Time, nine hours ahead of Mountain Time and ten hours ahead of Pacific Time. It is two hours ahead of Greenwich Mean Time. The recently introduced Summer Time in Israel is one hour ahead of the regular clock, but its permanent annual dates have not yet been fixed by law.

Getting to Israel

From the U.S.

BY AIR. Flights from major departure points in the U.S. to Israel's Ben Gurion airport are frequent and generally easy to arrange. El Al, the Israeli national airline, has four non-stop flights a week from New York to Israel (six in summer), T.W.A. have one (two to three in summer) and Tower Air have two. El Al and Tower Air's other flights stop in Europe, but without a change of aircraft. Most other flights change planes at a major European city. Flying time from New York to Tel Aviv is from nine to 11 hours. Flying via London, for example, from New York, the total journey time is around 14 to 15 hours.

Expect very thorough security checks at the airport before you leave, with bag searches and in-depth quizzing about your trip. You can also count on only slightly less of a grilling when you leave Israel.

Fares. For up-to-the-minute information and advice, contact your travel agent and get him to explain the confusing and complex array of fares available. Generally, however, you'll find that APEX (Advance Purchase Excursions; always round trip) represent the best value, with only minimum inconvenience: you must book and pay for your fare at least 14 days in advance, and can stay for no less than six days and no more than two months; tickets are non-transferable and cancellation charges high; one stopover is allowed. First class, Business and the misleadingly named Economy, though giving maximum flexibility, are all expensive and frankly not worth it.

You might also find it worth while investigating package tours, even if you don't want to go on the tour itself. Tour operators can get such discounts on air fares that the total cost of a package can work out less than the normal airfare. But the amount of investigating you'll have to do to save no more than a handful of dollars means this is not usually worth the bother.

If you're prepared to wait until the last minute, which can take a certain amount of nerve, you can sometimes benefit from the last minute sales tour operators hold in order to fill unsold pre-booked seats. A number of brokers specializing in these heavily discounted seats have sprung up. Among them are: *Stand-Buys Ltd.,* 311 West Superior, Suite 414, Chicago, Il 60610 (312–943–5737); *Moments Notice,* 40 East 49th St., New York, N.Y. 10017 (212–486–0503); *Discount Travel Intl.,* 114 Forest Ave., Narberth, PA 19072 (215–668–2182); *Worldwide Discount Travel Club,* 1674 Meridian Ave., Miami Beach, FL 33139 (305–534–2082). All charge an annual membership fee, usually about $35–45.

Typical fares as of early-1987 for New York–Tel Aviv were: first class, one way $2,211; economy, one way $699; APEX, round-trip $779–989 depending on season; excursion and youth fares $979–1,189 round-trip but without the APEX restrictions.

Airlines serving Israel from the U.S.:
British Airways, 530 Fifth Ave., New York, N.Y. 10036 (212–687–1600).

El Al, 850 Third Ave., New York, N.Y. 10022 (212–486–2600).
Pan Am, Pan Am Building, New York, N.Y. 10166 (212–687–2600).
Tower Air, 200 Park Ave., New York, N.Y. 10166 (718–917–8500).
T.W.A., 605 Third Ave., New York, N.Y. 10016 (212–290–2141).

From the U.K.

BY AIR. Flights from London (Heathrow) to Tel Aviv, operated by British Airways and El Al, are frequent, with at least one every day (except Friday). Flying time is around four-and-a-half hours. El Al also operate a flight between London (Heathrow) and Eilat once a week, via a quick connection in Tel Aviv.

Fares. Scheduled fares are very high (see below), but the wide range of discount and off-peak fares mean that you should shop around carefully before booking. A large number of charter flights are also available to both Tel Aviv and Eilat. Check the classified ads in the *Standard, Times* and *Sunday Times.* But make a point of checking prices thoroughly as airport taxes and fuel surcharges mean that flights may not always be as cheap as they first appear. Similarly, it can be well worth searching out the bucket shop ads in the Sunday papers and magazines like *Time Out* and the *Business Traveller* (the latter an excellent source of information on low-cost flying). Bucket shops—some more reliable than others, so don't hand over all your money until you have the ticket(s)—offer seats at rates significantly below the so-called official ones. But they often operate at short notice and may not be suitable for anyone hoping to book their flight some time in advance.

Typical fares as of early-1987 for London–Tel Aviv were: Club class return £924, Excursion return £519–£709 depending on length of stay; APEX, round-trip, no stopover, around £259 depending on season.

CUSTOMS ON ARRIVAL. Those over 17 may import duty free into Israel: 250 cigarettes or 250 grams of tobacco products; plus, two liters of wine and one liter of spirits; plus, a quarter of a liter of eau de cologne or perfume; plus, gifts totaling no more than $125 in value. Fresh meats may not be imported.

Non-residents may bring any amount of foreign currency and shekels into Israel, but may take out no more foreign currency than was imported and no more than the equivalent of US$5,000 for an adult (over age 18), or $2,000 for a child. The reconversion must be done during your stay and only with the bank receipts proving the original conversion. In addition, up to US$100 worth of shekels can be reconverted at an airport bank on departure (without the need for receipts).

A large deposit is sometimes required at Israel Customs on expensive and/or professional quality equipment brought into the country. This is to ensure that they are not being imported under the guise of personal accessories. This applies to large video-recorders, computer hardware, etc; regular cameras and small tape-recorders are unaffected. The deposit is completely refundable in the original currency on departure, and can be paid in cash, traveler's checks or Visa credit card.

Staying in Israel

HOTELS. Hotels in Israel run a very wide gamut from the very luxurious to the small and simple, though there are relatively few of the small, simple hotels which one might be used to finding in Europe. But practically all hotels are clean and comfortable and a room without a bath or shower is hard to find. For those seeking luxury, the large American hotel chains are well-represented, but many local chains and independent hotels are extremely comfortable.

The Tourism Ministry regulates and supervises all hotels which it recommends, which include the vast majority of hotels in the country. It has graded these hotels from one to five stars, although many of those in the tourist industry have questioned the criteria for this grading system and there are wide divergencies within each category. Many guided tours of the country will guarantee accommodations in hotels of a certain category or better and this does give the tourist a degree of assurance he is getting what he is paying for.

Prices. We have divided all the hotels we list into four categories—Deluxe (L), Expensive (E), Moderate (M) and Inexpensive (I). These grades are determined solely by price. Two people in a double room can expect to pay

Deluxe	$90 and up
Expensive	$60 to $90
Moderate	$30 to $60
Inexpensive	under $30

All prices include service, taxes, and usually a very large and filling Israeli-style buffet breakfast.

KIBBUTZ GUEST HOUSES. These are among the most interesting accommodations in Israel, but if you had any ideas of roughing it on the farm, forget it. They are usually very comfortable, if functional, with new modern dining rooms and spacious lawns. Most have swimming pools and offer regular lectures and tours to give the guests a small taste of what kibbutz life is all about. For those looking for peace and quiet in a rural setting, they can't be beat. Moreover, they are ideal bases for touring with a car. They range in price from $30 to $50 for two, including breakfast, service and taxes.

HOLIDAY VILLAGES. Also occasionally run by kibbutzim, they offer very simple facilities, usually sleeping from four to six people, with cooking facilities in each unit. Often located near beaches or in resort areas and with other sports facilities, they provide an inexpensive alternative for families.

CHRISTIAN HOSPICES. Some 30 Christian hospices, located mainly in Jerusalem and Galilee, provide lodging and sometimes meals at bargain rates. Preference is usually given to pilgrimage groups, but when space is available almost all will accept the general tourist, Christian and non-Christian alike. Their facilities range from almost luxury to truly bare and rates fluctuate accordingly, although it is not uncommon for them to offer room and three meals for $20 to $30 and a bed only for about $5. A full list of such hospices is available from the I.G.T.O.

YOUTH HOSTELS. There are over 30 youth hostels in Israel, which are open to all, regardless of age. Some provide family rooms, in addition to the usual dormitories. Some are airconditioned and all provide some meals, while some offer cooking facilities. The Israel Youth Hostel Association also has a super-bargain touring plan that includes stays of from 14 to 21 days at youth hostels, travel on public buses, some tours and entry to parks and sites. Rates for members of a national Youth Hostel Association run from $4.50 per person for those under 18, to $6 per person in family rooms, slightly higher for non-members. For information or membership contact the Youth Hostel Associations in the U.S., Canada, and the U.K. or *Israel Youth Hostel Association,* Box 1075, 3 Dorot Rishonim St., Jerusalem, (tel. 02–222073).

CAMPING. With at least nine months of sunshine, Israel is an ideal country for camping. Some 15 camping sites throughout the country belong to the Israel Camping Union. All are extremely well organized and offer everything from space for a tent or mobile home to a bungalow or tent for rent, complete with beds, linens and cooking facilities. Many have pools or are located near beaches. Most have shops that sell camping supplies and groceries and all have toilets, showers, electric outlets, telephones and first aid. All campsites are guarded and lighted at night. Advance reservations are necessary for July, August and Jewish holidays. Information is available from the I.G.T.O. or the *Israel Camping Union,* Box 53, Nahariya (tel. 04–923366).

Also ask for the Israel Camping Union's special package programs which offer excellent low-cost holiday plans for a minimum of 14 days, complete with optional car rental or a minibus and tent, mobile home or other accommodations, to be used in campsites around the country. The I.C.U. even provides a 24-hour welcome service at Ben Gurion airport and free transport to their camping reception center 8 kms. (5 miles) away.

RESTAURANTS. Israel offers a wide variety of eating opportunities, from quickie streetside snackbars, to truly elegant dining establishments, and everything in between, with prices to match. Many restaurants, especially those catering to tourists have menus and prices outside so that you can judge before walking in, and even in the very simple and cheap restaurants, menus in English (albeit sometimes very strange English) are the rule rather than the exception. Even hotels have begun serving moderately priced full-course meals, with controlled maximum prices for drinks and other extras.

Prices. We have divided all the restaurants we list into three categories—Expensive (E), Moderate (M) and Inexpensive (I). As with hotels, these grades are determined solely by price.

Prices, per person and excluding drinks, are:

Expensive	$20 and up
Moderate	$10 to $20
Inexpensive	under $10

Food in cafes is generally reasonably priced, but a cup of coffee or bottle of beer will cost about $1. A bottle of wine in a restaurant will cost from $5 up, with special vintages or imported wines coming to much more. In restaurants, water is often not put on the table unless you ask for it.

BUDGET EATING TIPS. A vast variety of fast food is available in the center of every town and city, with the local felafel competing with pizzas, sandwiches and hamburgers. Burger Ranch, and the pointedly named McDavid's, have become national hamburger chains.

Remember, if you're staying in a hotel, you will no doubt be starting the day with an Israeli breakfast, a buffet spread of rolls, cheeses, eggs, pickled fish, fruit and vegetables, all usually included in the price of the room. For picnics, many Israeli supermarkets have a wide selection of hot and cold ready-to-eat food, often with plastic plates and cutlery provided.

TIPPING. In the good old days, Israelis were too proud to take tips. Now the practice has spread, largely due to the influence of the tourists themselves. In medium and high priced restaurants, a 10 to 15 per cent service charge is often added. If not, it normally says so on the bill, and the waiter will in any case also usually hasten to tell you so. Again, 10 to 15 per cent is the usual tip. You may give a little more if the service was good.

Hotel rates include a service charge, but porters and chambermaids expect a little extra, depending on the service. The porters at Ben Gurion Airport are not supposed to receive tips and there are signs that say so, but we wouldn't suggest trying not to tip them. Barbers and hairdressers also expect about 10 per cent. It is acceptable to tip a taxi driver—though most Israelis would not—if his service has been good, including the operation of his meter as required by law. If he does not use his meter, the chances are he has already built a healthy tip into his suggested fee.

MAIL. The symbol of the Israeli post office is a white deer on a blue background and the common joke is that it ought to be a turtle. Mail is slow and letters sent home often arrive after you do. In addition, frequent increases in the price of stamps make hotel concierges occasionally unwilling to stock stamps. To contact friends in the country, call or send a telegram a few days in advance. Philatelists, on the other hand, will find lots of beautiful stamps and there are special counters selling them at the main post offices in Jerusalem, Tel Aviv and Haifa.

TELEPHONES. While not quite as problematic as the mail, telephones are also not entirely reliable. Often you have to dial many times to get a number. Many shops and cafes have phones for public use for about 30 cents, something that comes in handy when you can't find a public phone in the area. The pay phones take a special token (*asimon*), which may be purchased for about 12 cents at the post office, in some shops and at some hotels. The phone directory is published in Hebrew, the latest English directory being long out of date, but information (dial 14) has listings in English and most information operators speak English. Direct dialing is available to most Western countries, but hotel guests should check very carefully about rates before calling from their hotel room. For special overseas calls, the international operator is obtained by dialing 18. Overseas calls can also be made from the main branches of the post office in large cities, where telex facilities are also available.

 CLOSING TIMES. For bank hours, see "Changing Money," p.6. Shops are generally open from 8.30 A.M. to 1 P.M., and again from 4 to 7 P.M., but department stores, restaurants and many tourist-related enterprises stay open all day. The I.G.T.O. is open 8 A.M. to 6 P.M. Remember, Saturday is the Jewish Sabbath and Sunday is a regular working day. Shops usually close on Friday and the day before any major holiday by 1 or 2 P.M. and the buses stop running about an hour before sunset, and resume service on Saturday night.

Museums have shorter hours on Friday and Saturday, usually from about 10 to 2. Officially, most museums don't sell tickets on Saturday, but there is usually a little man near the entrance selling tickets.

Warning: Laundries and cleaning shops close for the week-long holidays of Pessach and Sukkot.

 ELECTRICITY. The current is 220 volts, but some hotels have plugs (always clearly marked) for shavers which run on 110 volts. Transformers for 100v appliances such as hair driers are sometimes available.

 NEWSSTANDS. These are plentiful and well stocked with periodicals from all over the world. The *International Herald Tribune* and many British papers are flown in daily. *The Jerusalem Post,* Israel's only English paper, appears daily except Saturday.

 LAVATORIES. Be prepared for a shock. If at all possible use the rest rooms in large hotels (even if you're not staying there). Always carry tissues and wash-and-dry towelettes; toilet paper and towels are often lacking. In restaurants ask for the toilet or W.C. and look for a "00" sign. Outside of the hotels and restaurants, the best lavatories are usually at national parks and nature reserves, the worst at gas stations. Public conveniences do not abound, but are usually fairly reasonable when found.

Getting Around Israel

 BY AIR. Arkia, Israel's inland airline, flies mainly from Tel Aviv, Jerusalem, Haifa and Ben Gurion airport to Eilat. Its main office is at Sde Dov, Tel Aviv's local airport, (tel. 03–413222).

 BY TRAIN. Rail links cover a relatively small part of the country, but the service between Tel Aviv and Haifa is frequent, fast and comfortable. The ride from Haifa to Jerusalem is slow, on the other hand, but very picturesque and especially nice for children. There is one class only, but seats may be reserved, a good idea if you're going on Friday, the day before a holiday or during school vacations.

BY CAR. Roads in Israel are fairly good, if not quite up to the standard of the U.S. and Western Europe. But Israeli drivers tend to drive aggressively and badly and it is well to be very careful. Still, a car is one of the best ways of seeing the country, because distances are short and many sites are difficult to get to by public transport. Maps are available from the I.G.T.O. and many stationery shops. Highways in Israel are numbered according to a recently introduced system and the numbers appear on interurban road signs and on the better maps, although most Israelis won't know what you're talking about if you ask, say, for highway number 10.

Traffic signs are similar to those used in Europe. Directional signs are clear and frequent on the highways, but often hard to find in cities. Traffic drives on the right. Fuel is sold in 91 and 96 octane for about 70 cents a liter (about $2.50 a gallon) and service stations are frequent.

All the major car rental firms are represented and will have a car waiting for you at the airport if you wish. Local firms are harder to find, but tend to be cheaper. (See the *Practical Information* for Jerusalem, Tel Aviv and Haifa for addresses). Some fly-and-drive packages are available abroad and are usually good buys.

Car hire companies accept International driving licences, or those of any country with whom Israel has diplomatic relations (and provided the licence is printed in English or French), and all arrangements can be made as smoothly and easily as at home. The minimum age for car rental varies from 21 to 23, depending on the company. Rates also vary, but the daily rate with unlimited mileage for a car rented for at least a week would range from about $25 a day on a small car, such as a Fiat 127, to $70 for a large car, say a Volvo 244.

Conversion Chart

If you want to convert from miles (m) to kilometers (km), read from the center column to the right; if from kilometers into miles, from the center column to the left. Example—5 miles = 8 kilometers, 5 kilometers = 3 miles.

m		km	m		km
0.6	1	1.6	12.4	20	32.1
1.2	2	3.2	18.6	30	48.2
1.8	3	4.8	24.8	40	64.3
2.4	4	6.3	31.0	50	80.4
3.1	5	8.0	37.2	60	96.5
3.7	6	9.6	43.4	70	112.2
4.3	7	11.2	49.7	80	128.7
4.9	8	12.8	55.9	90	144.8
5.5	9	14.4	62.1	100	160.9
6.2	10	16.0	124.2	200	321.8

BY BUS. Egged, the Israel bus cooperative, covers virtually the whole country with comfortable, cheap and frequent service. Buses are often airconditioned. It is sometimes possible to reserve seats for long rides, a good idea on Friday, or before a holiday, when the buses can be very crowded. In any case, it is wise to arrive more than a few minutes before your bus is due to leave. There are no buses from late Friday afternoon to Saturday night, except in Haifa and areas with a large Arab population.

For information about bus schedules ask at the information booth in the central bus station of any town of city or call 03–432414 in Tel Aviv, 02–528231 in Jerusalem, 04–535276 in Haifa, and 059–75161 in Eilat.

Egged Tours and a few other companies also run regular tours, varying in length from half-a-day to a week, to tourist sites around the country. They are conducted by expert, licensed guides. Even those who never take tours might consider them for sites which are difficult to get to by public transport. They range in price from about $12 for half-a-day to over $400 for a week-long tour of most of the country, including hotels and some meals. Most such tours will pick you up and drop you off at your hotel. You can book these tours at your hotel or with any travel agent, where you can also arrange for a private tour of your own with a licensed guide-driver, who will have a car or minibus bearing the official Israel Tourist symbol. Egged Tours is located 15 Frishman St., Tel Aviv (03–244177).

 BY TAXI. All taxis are required to have meters and to use them in town. An average fare in town would come to about $2–$4. Controlled rates from Ben Gurion airport to all large cities are listed on signs at the airport. To go between other cities or for an hour or two of driving around, negotiate the price in advance. Since there have been numerous complaints about taxis from tourists, it is well to remember that if you do think you have been overcharged, you should have the taxi's number and, if possible, a receipt, together with other details, such as the day, time and place. Address such complaints to the I.G.T.O. and if justified you should receive a refund.

Sherut Taxis. These are shared taxis which run along some bus routes in town and on highways and charge a set fare, slightly higher than the bus fare. They are especially popular on the Sabbath when the buses stop running. Sherut stands for interurban travel are usually located near the central bus stations.

 VISITING EGYPT. Since the Egypt-Israel peace treaty in 1979, many tourists have taken the opportunity to visit Egypt proper, or the eastern shore of Sinai. There is daily air service to Cairo, and U.S., British, and Canadian nationals can get a visa at Cairo airport. The bus from Tel Aviv to Cairo takes about ten hours and you must have a visa in advance, obtainable at the Egyptian Embassy, 54 Basel St., Tel Aviv (03–224151). To go from Eilat to Sinai *only* (i.e. returning to Eilat) for up to one week, you need a valid passport (from a country with diplomatic relations with Egypt); but no visa is necessary. In addition, there is an Israeli departure tax of $11, payable in shekels or dollars (at time of writing), and an Egyptian entry tax of $6 payable in dollars. Several package tours of Sinai and Egypt proper are available in Israel, details from travel agents.

Leaving Israel

 AIRPORT TAX. An airport tax of $11, payable in shekels or dollars (at time of writing), is levied on all passengers leaving Israel. It may not have been included in your air fare, though at time of writing such an inclusion was being considered.

CUSTOMS ON RETURNING HOME. Americans.

U.S. residents may bring in $400 worth of foreign merchandise as gifts or for personal use without having to pay duty provided they have been out of the country more than 48 hours and provided they have not claimed a similar exemption within the previous 30 days. Every member of a family is entitled to the same exemption, regardless of age, and the exemptions can be pooled. For the next $1,000 worth of goods a flat 10% rate is assessed.

Included in the $400 allowance for travelers over the age of 21 are one liter of alcohol, 100 non-Cuban cigars and 200 cigarettes. Only one bottle of perfume trademarked in the U.S. may be brought in. However, there is no duty on antiques or art over 100 years old. You may not bring home meats, fruits, plants, soil or other agricultural products.

Gifts valued at under $50 may be mailed to friends or relatives at home, but not more than one per day of receipt to any one addressee. These gifts must not include perfumes costing more than $5, tobacco or liquor.

If you are traveling with such foreign-made articles as cameras, watches or binoculars that were purchased at home or on a previous trip, either carry the receipt or register them with U.S. Customs prior to departure.

Canadians. In addition to personal effects, and over and above the regular exemption of $300 per year, the following may be brought into Canada duty-free: a maximum of 50 cigars, 200 cigarettes, 2 pounds of tobacco and 40 ounces of liquor, provided these are declared in writing to customs on arrival. Canadian customs regulations are strictly enforced; you are recommended to check what your allowances are and to make sure you have kept receipts for whatever you may have bought abroad. Small gifts can be mailed and should be marked "Unsolicited gift, (nature of gift), value under $40 in Canadian funds." For other details, ask for the Canada Customs brochure *I Declare*.

British Customs. There are two levels of duty free allowance for people entering the U.K.; one, for goods bought outside the EEC or for goods bought in a duty free shop within the EEC; two, for goods bought in an EEC country but not in a duty free shop.

In the first category you may import duty free: 200 cigarettes or 100 cigarillos or 50 cigars or 250 grammes of tobacco (*Note* if you live outside Europe, these allowances are doubled); plus one liter of alcoholic drinks over 22% vol. (38.8% proof) or two liters of alcoholic drinks not over 22% vol. or fortified or sparkling wine, or two liters of still table wine; plus two liters of still table wine; plus 50 grammes of perfume; plus nine fluid ounces of toilet water; plus other goods to the value of £28.

In the second category you may import duty free: 300 cigarettes or 150 cigarillos or 75 cigars or 400 grammes of tobacco; plus 1½ liters of alcoholic drinks over 22% vol. (38.8% proof) or three liters of alcoholic drinks not over 22% vol. or fortified or sparkling wine, or three liters of still table wine; plus five liters of still table wine; plus 75 grammes of perfume; plus 13 fluid ounces of toilet water; plus other goods to the value of £207 (*Note* though it is not classified as an alcoholic drink by EEC countries for Customs' purposes and is thus considered part of the "other goods" allowance, you may not import more than 50 liters of beer).

In addition, no animals or pets of any kind may be brought into the U.K. The penalties for doing so are severe and are strictly enforced; there are *no* exceptions. Similarly, fresh meats, plants and vegetables, controlled drugs and firearms and ammunition may not be brought into the U.K. There are no restrictions on the import or export of British and foreign currencies.

ISRAEL AND THE ISRAELIS

Charm and Chutzpa

by
HAIM SHAPIRO

Israel is one of those countries that seem to begin the minute you step on the plane, especially if you happen to be travelling on El Al, the national airline. Within minutes of fastening your seat belt, you will probably learn that your seatmate is a nurse from Herzlia; that she has been visiting her son who is studying abroad; that she has another son who lives on a kibbutz; and a daughter who is in the army.

By the time you are off the ground, she will tell you that her daughter's boyfriend's parents are from Morocco. But, she will add quickly, he is a very nice boy. It's just, she might say confidentially, she doesn't like the kind of music he listens to. Still, she might muse, it could be worse. Her daughter could get mixed up with someone from the far right, or the far left, or worse still, become intensely religious.

And now that she has gotten to know you, she will proceed to plan your itinerary in Israel, making sure that you miss no ancient column, no historic wall, indeed no pile of rubble, during your stay. Of course she will insist that you visit her in Herzlia and meet her husband; you will probably find yourself actually planning your tour around a visit to her home.

And during all this, you might notice that a religious service seems to be taking place at the back of the plane. At the same time, everyone else seems to be strolling about, joking, speculating whether the customs men will find that video set in the hand baggage, and drinking an endless round of soft drinks.

As the plane prepares to land, about half of your fellow passengers will be wiping the tears from their eyes. They're the tourists. The Israelis will be gathering their bundles together, ready to dash down the aisle the second the plane lands. No red-blooded Israeli would sit and wait just because a stewardess told him to.

As for your neighbor from the plane, she was quite serious when she asked you to visit her. By all means do so. It is one way of really learning about the country. When you do go to see her, she will probably serve three different kinds of cake, all home made, and insist you try each one. You're on a diet? Don't be silly. One little piece won't matter. If you happen to be unmarried, you can be sure that your new found friend will have someone of the opposite sex for you to meet.

Meanwhile, just in case you imagine that the flow of information will have been one-sided, she has asked about your home, your family, your job, your car, your religion and how much you paid for your jacket. She might also have a small wardrobe trunk ready with things she would like to send back with you for her son. If you can't take them, don't be embarrassed about turning her down. What are friends for if they can't be honest with each other? Israelis are generally warm, friendly, generous people. They can also be prying, rude and exasperating. But you can be sure, they will never be boring.

Facing the Unknown

If there is any one trait that can be said to typify the Israelis, it is summed up in the word *chutzpa,* a Hebrew word which has found its way into English by way of Yiddish. It might be translated variously as daring, audacity, aggressiveness or effrontery. It is the quality that has made the Israeli army almost legendary in its accomplishments. It is the source of confidence that has made it possible for Israel to forge ahead in agriculture and technology. Without a good measure of *chutzpa,* it is doubtful if the leaders of Israel could even have contemplated taking in hundreds of thousands of homeless refugees.

But it also means that Israelis won't wait their turn, be it at a bus stop, in the bank or at the supermarket. Nor is the daring of the battlefield very welcome on the highway. Israelis are notoriously bad drivers and much of their lack of driving skill may be traced to the unwillingness to wait your turn and a readiness to take chances.

On the other hand, much of the attraction of Israel lies in its spontaneity, a willingness to improvize and a readiness to face the unknown. Of course the spontaneity sometimes leads to trouble. The improvization doesn't always come off, and the unknown can be worse than that which we know. But all in all, Israelis have found that taking chances usually does pay. After all, if they weren't willing to take a risk, they would never have created the State of Israel.

The Price of an Umbrella

Ask an Israeli what Israelis are like and he will probably come up with the magic word "sabra." A sabra, literally a prickly pear, is the word used to describe the native born Israeli. And in a country of immigrants, the native born is a rare and valuable commodity. Your informant will probably go on to tell you that just as the fruit of the cactus is hard and prickly on the outside and soft and sweet on the inside, so the Israeli is difficult to get to know. But get past the tough outer layer, and he will do his all for you.

Sabras, according to the local mythology, are everything that the Jews of the Diaspora are not. Proud and straightforward, with their heads held high, they are a nation of pioneers, not shopkeepers. If that is so, you may well ask, who runs all the shops in Tel Aviv? Some of the shopkeepers must have been born in Israel. You may also, especially if you are Jewish, question the Israeli stereotype of the Diaspora Jew as a cringing, ingratiating type. Go right ahead and make your point. There's nothing an Israeli likes better than a good argument.

One area where the myth of the sabra is certainly amiss is in its characterization of Israelis as strong silent types. As a people there are few who are more garrulous and friendly. All you have to do is board a public bus and start asking directions and you will probably find people confiding their family history to you, then getting off the bus to take you exactly where you want to go. Even taxi drivers, one group of which the tourist is well advised to beware, have been known to take tourists home to their mother after a tourist asks them the best place to eat in town. If you like to talk to strangers, Israel is the country for you.

But the myth does tend to be valid insofar as Israelis often do say what they think to an extent that visitors sometimes find embarrassing. Nothing is taboo, including religion and politics. But happily, people are capable of engaging in raging arguments and then, for the most part, parting on the best of terms.

This tendency toward verbosity is also seen in a habit that many Western visitors find startling, to say the least. Israelis are frankly curious and they are particularly interested in comparing their lifestyles, and standard of living, with that of other countries. They have little hesitation in asking all sorts of questions that would be taboo elsewhere. Nor are they likely to believe you when you tell them you do not remember how much you paid for your umbrella.

Just try to remember that such questions are not motivated by ill will. If they do embarrass you, fend them off as best you can. After all, most Israelis had a very tough time of it, by Western standards, until a very few years ago. They are proud of their achievements in the material sphere and your friend from Herzlia is as likely as not to show you every appliance in her kitchen. The fact that this rise in the average Israeli's standard of living has apparently come at the expense of the national economy just doesn't seem to bother most people.

The swift rise in living standards for most Israelis might also provide some explanation for what is probably the country's most worrisome problem, the fact that many Israelis, often those who haven't made it in Israel, have chosen to live abroad. While the estimates vary wildly, they go as high as 400,000. Known as *yordim* (those who go down) by their countrymen, these emigre Israelis mostly seem to be driving taxis in New York. A few have become millionaires and return on visits as benefactors, but most seem to be eking out a living. Israelis will often tell you that having gone abroad to get rich, the *yordim* are ashamed to return no better off than when they left. Many of those living abroad will swear that in just a year or two they will be going back, just as soon as they save a little more.

A Mid-East Melting Pot

Naturally, any talk about the typical Israeli is bound to be a bit of an over-generalization. Israelis come in all sizes, shapes and colors. At one time, when you spoke about sabras, for example, it was assumed that their families originally came from Europe. Now, as a result of the massive immigration of the '50s, over 60 per cent of all Jewish Israelis trace their lineage to the countries of the Middle East. The largest such ethnic group is North African, particularly Moroccan, but there are also large groups from Iraq, Iran, Syria, Turkey and Egypt.

Perhaps the most singular of these immigrants are from Yemen, at the southern tip of the Arabian peninsula. Largely cut off from other Jewish communities for thousands of years, they nonetheless maintained a high level of scholarship. And despite the discriminatory and often demeaning regulations which were forced upon them by a regime that was medieval in outlook, they never seemed to have lost their self-pride.

Though groups of Yemenite Jews made the arduous journey on foot to the Holy Land over the centuries, it was only when the State of Israel was declared that they came en masse. For many, the airplanes which brought them were the first they had ever seen. It was as if the prophecy that they would be gathered up "on the wings of eagles" was being literally fulfilled.

And despite their almost total unfamiliarity with the technological society into which they were thrust, they made great and rapid strides in advancing themselves in the arts and sciences, even in politics. Their cultural heritage has also made a deep and lasting impression on Israeli cultural life. Much Israeli folk dancing, for example, is largely based on Yemenite forms. In fact, there is one professional dance company, Inbal, which was originally formed specifically to popularise Yemenite dancing. Only now, many years later and after much success, has Inbal branched out and begun to include other dances in its repertoire.

Pride or Prejudice?

For many Israelis the absorption of the Yemenites, with their very dark skins, also serves to prove that whatever difficulties some groups of immigrants may experience, Israeli society on the whole is far from racist. True, they admit, the immigrants from the Islamic world, and their children, do lag behind their fellow Jews of European origin educationally and economically, and their entry to the upper levels of society and politics is still the exception rather than the rule. But most Israelis will argue that this is due to cultural factors, rather than inborn prejudice.

The question of possible Israeli racial prejudice recently assumed an even greater importance in connection with the immigration of several thousand Jews from Ethiopia. This community, far more cut off from the mainstream of Judaism than even the Yemenites, had long asked to be brought to Israel. But the vast divergence of their customs from those of normative Judaism caused some rabbis to question whether they were Jews at all. It was only because the famine in Ethiopia threatened them with starvation that they were finally brought into the country. Were the doubts about their Jewishness racially motivated? The average Israeli will deny it. The spontaneous enthusiasm with which this community was welcomed by everyone, including most religious institutions, tends to confirm this view.

A Community of Immigrants

For purposes of convenience, the two major groups of Jews are known as Ashkenazim and Sephardim. Technically, the Ashkenazim are the descendants of those Jews who originally went to Germany (Ashkenaz in medieval Hebrew) and later spread out throughout Central and Eastern Europe. They spoke Yiddish, a language largely derived from German, but with many Hebrew and Slavic words and written in Hebrew letters. Later, they formed the major Jewish communities in Western Europe and the U.S.

The Sephardim, strictly speaking, are the descendants of those Jews who were exiled from Spain (Sepharad in Hebrew) in the 15th century and who mostly found refuge in the then more tolerant Muslim East. They spoke Ladino, a language close to medieval Spanish and also written in Hebrew letters. But just to make things confusing, some Sephardim settled in England, Holland, the Americas and even Germany. And to make it even more confusing, in Israel today all Jews of Middle Eastern origin are known collectively as Sephardim, even though their ancestors never stepped on Spanish soil.

Within these two subdivisions, the ethnic mixture is almost infinite. There are Kurdish Jews, who, in addition to speaking the Arabic and Kurdish of their non-Jewish neighbors, spoke Aramaic among themselves, the language of the Jews at the time of Jesus. There are Georgian Jews, not from the American South, but from the Asian Soviet republic. (In Jerusalem there's a community of Jews from Boukhara, also in Soviet Asia, who in the last century were known for their wealth. Men and women dressed in gorgeously embroidered robes. Then Soviet Russia conquered Boukhara and they were suddenly cut off from their source of income, leaving them impoverished, but still boasting their fine robes and, often as not, palatial homes.) The small Indian Jewish community traces its origins back thousands of years. Like the rest of Indian society, the Jews of India were divided into several sub-groups.

When they arrived in Israel in the early '50s, one group would barely speak to the other.

Each community of immigrants has its own traditions, customs, dress and foods. But even in less than four decades these have often become confused and intermingled. Thus, the Moroccan Jews have a popular holiday at the end of Passover, the *Mimouna*. In Morocco families would go out together for a day in the countryside. Now, in Israel, the day has evolved into a huge outdoor picnic attended by Israelis of every background.

Nor should it be thought for a moment that all Jews of European origin are alike. The Hungarians are known for their distinctive accent, and their prowess in cake making, the Germans for their cultural and academic distinction, and the fact that despite this many of them seem incapable of learning Hebrew. The early pioneers from Russia still hold the upper hand, politically, while those who have come from Russia in the last few decades are often ready to dismiss other Israelis, including the earlier immigrants from Russia, as "uncultured primitives." And if you meet someone of Romanian origin, he will no doubt happily tell you that all (other) Romanians are thieves.

Meanwhile, in recent years yet another ethnic group has made its presence felt. These are immigrants from the English-speaking world. Semites they may be, but they are generally somewhat startled on arrival to hear themselves described as "Anglo Saxons." Nonetheless, this is how they are commonly known in Israel. (To be fair, a representative sample of these "Anglo Saxons" will often as not include the odd Dutchman or Scandinavian). Many of these English-speakers, used to the more delicate social courtesies of their countries of origin, are often put out by the more abrasive approach in Israel. Some adapt, many never do—but some of those nice "Anglo Saxon" manners have begun to rub off on the natives as well.

Tuning In

Meanwhile, the argument of whether there is prejudice or discrimination in Israel continues, with the Ashkenazim, who are usually the ones accused of practicing such discrimination, stoutly maintaining there is no such thing. In recent years, the question of cultural discrimination has risen to the fore, with many Jews of Middle Eastern origin claiming that their music, for example, has not been given its just due.

In fact, for some years there have been a number of performers whose style seems to fall somewhere between Arabic, Turkish, Greek and Spanish music. It is, in short, typically Mediterranean. They appeared at weddings, and cassettes of their songs were sold at open stands around the central bus station in Tel Aviv. But the record companies ignored them, as did radio and television. They were, in fact, known as "singers of the central station" and only in recent years, as a result of much protest, are they being heard more and more over the airwaves. If you take a public bus, you have a good chance of hearing them on the driver's radio, while the average sherut driver is sure to have a cassette or two to play for the enjoyment of his passengers. It is quite different from the Israeli music of the '50s, with its Russian themes, but it is no less Israeli.

Popular music occupies a very important role in the country. Do not be surprised if your Israeli friends take it for granted that you know that Israel won the Eurovision Song Contest two years in succession. For those so lacking in knowledge, the contest is sponsored by the European television networks with entries from every country in Western Europe and, of course, Israel. Each country enters a song and, in a program broadcast throughout Europe, votes on the other songs. Israel's entries are most often presented by performers of Middle Eastern extraction and they always seem to do well, even if they don't win every year. For most Israelis such a victory is of far greater significance than any on the battlefield and it is a toss-up whether Israel's greatest moment in the last decade was the rescue at Entebbe, winning the Eurovision Song Contest or the time that the Tel Aviv Maccabi basketball team won the European championship, with a breathtaking, last-minute defeat over a team of Russian giants.

It is such accomplishments, going beyond ethnic or political lines, that serve to unite the entire country. They also serve to form a bridge between Arab and Jew, just as the music of the "singers of the central station" has had something of a black market success in the Arab states, and form a common point between Israel's 3.5 million Jews and the over 650,000 non-Jews, not to speak of about a million Arab residents of the West Bank and Gaza.

The Non-Jewish Population

Like the Jews, Israel's non-Jews, though mostly Arab, are far from one ethnic unity. About 80 per cent are Muslim Arabs, but even among them there is a sharp differentiation between those who live in cities and villages and the Beduins, many of whom still wander through the wilderness with their flocks. In political terms, many of the Israeli Arabs identify with Arab nationalism, while the Beduins have no qualms about expressing their support for a Jewish state and often volunteer to serve as trusted and valued members of the Israeli army.

Distinct from the Muslims, although their religion is said to be an offshoot of Islam, are over 50,000 Druze, a fierce group of mountain dwellers in the Galilee, part of a larger community spread through Syria and Lebanon. Known for their bravery on the battlefield, their men are drafted, like Jews, into the army and often serve with distinction. But their firm allegience to the State of Israel has been tested in recent years as a result of the war in Lebanon when Druze soldiers from Israel sometimes found themselves in confrontation with the Druze of Lebanon.

Intriguingly, the Druze religion, which apparently began in the 10th century A.D., is secret and only chosen members are introduced to all its mysteries. What is known is that they revere Jethro, the father-in-law of Moses, and make a yearly pilgrimage to his tomb in the Galilee. With sweeping mustaches for the men and gauzy white headscarves for the women, they make up one of Israel's more colorful groups.

Nor can we forget the Circassians, Muslims from the Caucasus Mountains. They settled in two villages in the Galilee in the 19th century, after their country had been conquered by Russia, yet retain their language and much of their Slavic tradition. Here, too, a martial tradition is expressed through service in the army. Though a minuscule community within Israel, the Bahais have their world center in Haifa, on the slopes of Mount Carmel, where the "Bab," their "prophet herald" martyred in Persia in the 19th century, is buried.

Local Christians make up a relatively small part of the population, but their importance is far greater than their numbers as a result of the historic links of Christianity with the Holy Land. Most are either Roman Catholic, Greek Catholics or Greek Orthodox. However, as a result of the fact that missionaries from abroad, especially in the last century, suffered a singular lack of success in converting either the local Jews or the local Muslims, they turned their sights instead on the indigenous Christians, some of whom are today Protestants.

As elsewhere in the Middle East, there has been a tendency on the part of local Christians to emigrate to the West. This caused the utmost concern to local church leaders. Even the Vatican has expressed the fear that without local believers the Christian shrines of the Holy Land will become empty museums, devoid of meaning. It was thus with some satisfaction that the Israeli government noted recently that for the first time in many years there had been an increase in the number of local Christians.

In addition to the major branches of Christianity, there are at least small numbers of virtually every Christian community and sect. For the student of religions, the country presents a virtual gold mine, especially with the presence of such Eastern churches as the Assyrians and the Armenians, the Copts and the Ethiopians.

A Fragile Peace

As well as their religious significance, the churches also have political importance. Israel takes great pride in guaranteeing freedom of worship to all and freedom of access for all to the holy places. Sometimes, however, this can be more difficult than it might appear. Thus an altercation between the Ethiopian and the Coptic churches over the possession of a collection of structures on the roof of the Church of the Holy Sepulcher in Jerusalem assumes all the characteristics of a diplomatic incident, with the active participation of the Egyptian and Ethiopian governments. A few years ago, the police had to stop the annual symbolic cleaning of the Church of the Nativity in Bethlehem when an argument over who was to clean a certain column evolved into a brawl, with monks hitting each other over the head with chairs and broomsticks.

Officially, matters of religious jurisdiction are regulated according to the status quo. That is, they are left the way they were at the end of the Turkish rule in 1917. The status quo determines where a religious procession can go, and when, who owns what stone in what church and who has the right to fix the roof. There is even a status quo, albeit of more recent vintage, for religious practice, and the absence thereof, by

Jews. Thus, though buses all over the country stop running on the Jewish Sabbath, they continue operating in Haifa. On the other hand, an attempt by the mayor of Petah Tikva, a suburb of Tel Aviv, to open cafes and movie theaters on Friday nights almost caused a national government crisis.

On a more serious level, according to the status quo, each religious community is in charge of matters of personal status for its members, including marriage, divorce and even inheritance. Thus, there is no civil marriage or divorce in Israel and it is often difficult for members of two different religions to marry each other. For Jews, there are other marital restrictions as well. A woman whose husband has disappeared may not remarry. Nor may a *cohen,* or member of the Jewish priestly caste, marry a divorcee. The most common solution in such cases is for the couple to go to nearby Cyprus, where there is civil marriage.

Another aspect of the status quo which offends some is that only Orthodox Judaism is recognized, creating a situation in which, according to some, there is religious freedom for everyone in Israel except Jews. Though there are a number of Conservative and Reform Jewish congregations throughout the country, mainly made up of immigrants from the West, their rabbis may not, for example, perform marriages. Conversion too is a cause for dissension. One of the first laws passed by the State of Israel, the Law of Return, gives every Jew the right to emigrate to Israel. But what about someone converted to Judaism by a Reform or Conservative rabbi abroad? At the time of writing, such converts were included under the Law of Return, although they, and even their children, might find it difficult to marry in Israel. But for several years, the religious parties have been trying to put through an amendment to the law which would, in effect, make only Orthodox conversions recognised. Generally, although the majority of Israel's Jews tend to be non-observant, it is Orthodoxy which they choose not to observe.

The strictures of Jewish religious law are particularly irritating to the country's feminists. Thus, it is a man who must divorce his wife, and not vice versa. In cases where a rabbinical court orders a man to divorce his wife and he refuses to do so, it can have him imprisoned until he agrees. But the decision is still the man's.

An Orthodox Revival

All this has been made more complex by the fact that there is a growing movement, especially among young people, to become newly religious. Possibly reflecting a worldwide trend toward religious fundamentalism, many Israelis from entirely secular backgrounds have adopted ultra-Orthodoxy, complete with such paraphernalia as long black coats for the men and head scarves or even wigs for married women. Numerous yeshivot, or religious schools of higher learning, exist for such *baale teshuva* (returnees) and often they actively proselytise, especially among young tourists. The movement has also been felt in the country's prisons, with some rabbis calling for an early release for those who become religious.

At one time, the ultra-Orthodox community was content to isolate itself in a few parts of Jerusalem and the Bnei Brak suburb of Tel Aviv. Many rejected, and still do reject, the State of Israel on the grounds that a Jewish State can only come into being when the Messiah arrives. Others argue that they cannot favor a Jewish state which does not accept Jewish religious law as the final authority in all areas.

Such views, which most Israelis simply dismiss as bizarre, have achieved increased importance as a result of the growing political strength of the ultra-Orthodox, both from a growth in their electorate and an increased sophistication by their leaders in playing coalition politics. Naturally, such phenomena result in a reaction, with a broad coalition of groups, ranging from Reform and Conservative Jews, to the Israel Humanist Association to a group which calls itself Concerned Parents Against Return to Religion, joining together to fight the influence of the ultra-Orthodox.

Rather unlikely partners in this coalition are the country's archeologists, who suffer from attempts by some rabbis to enforce stringent religious rules against disrupting any Jewish burial ground for eternity. Archeologists have naturally resisted such restrictions of their scientific freedom to unearth the past, especially since burial sites so often provide finds of great interest. But in tackling the archeologists, the rabbis perhaps took on more than they could handle, for archeology is something of a sacred cow in itself. An exhibit of tiny, barely discernable clay figures and some strands of woven materials can and does attract vast crowds to the Israel Museum. For many, a day off is an excuse to go and do a bit of amateur digging. Israel's most famous general, for example, the late Moshe Dayan, was the proud owner of a vast collection—which critics claimed was the fruit of years of illegal private excavating. (The collection is now in the Israel Museum.)

The most intense clash between the rabbis and the archeologists was at a dig in Jerusalem, the site of the biblical City of David, which the rabbis said was the site of a medieval Jewish cemetery. Every day delegations of men with long beards and long black coats would go out to demonstrate against the diggers. Their pressure resulted in the introduction (but not the passage) of an "archeology law" which would have made it necessary to get rabbinical approval for any archeological dig.

Museums and Mothers

But if archeology can be said to be a national pastime, such cultural activities as painting, literature and the theater tend to remain the preserve of Ashkenazim and a small group of educated Sephardim. True, the theater companies make a concerted effort to go to outlying towns and villages. But even when they do it is usually the village teachers and social workers, or the members of neighboring kibbutzim, who make up a large part of their audience.

One successful attempt to break the culture barrier was that of the Israel Museum. It ran a series of special shows on the life of Jewish communities from areas such as Morroco and Kurdistan. Items for the exhibits came from all over the country, and to some extent the show provided concrete proof, especially for the children, that their parents' cultural heritage was of value. Museum curators were delighted by the crowds of people, many of whom had never set foot in a museum before. The curators didn't even get excited when some visitors spread out their picnic lunches on the museum floor.

Nonetheless the cultural dichotomy continues to exist and it even affects family life and behavior. In families originally from the Middle East, for example, women are traditionally subservient to men and, in some cases, even women with doctorates or with successful business careers would not dream of letting their husband get a glass of water for himself, or go out to a film without asking his permission.

Despite this, one would still get very different answers concerning the question of the position of women in Israeli society, depending on whom one asked. The average man, and many women as well, would tell you that women are quite equal to men. Women serve in the army (although not for quite as long as men), their rights are protected by law and there are women in the top ranks of virtually every profession. Indeed, one of the country's best known prime ministers was the late Golda Meir.

Other women, those concerned about women's issues, would probably say that Golda Meir was the exception who proved the rule and that a pitifully small proportion of women serve in the Knesset, Israel's parliament, and even fewer become cabinet ministers. There are no women generals and indeed most women soldiers end up as secretaries. They will point to the refuges for battered women in the major cities and tell you that the police almost always side with the man in cases of wife-beating.

Still, even they will admit that the wind of social change is blowing, although they were less than enthusiastic about the tone of a recent campaign by the women's section of the Histadrut, the general labor federation, which featured the slogan, "Be a man, give her a hand." It is true that many men who could barely hold their first child a decade ago, have been finding that with their second or third child, they could even change dirty diapers as well as any woman.

Nonetheless, it remains true that many women are far from happy with their position in society, even in the most "progressive" of Israel's communities, the kibbutzim. Though kibbutz women once went out into the fields with the men in the pioneering days, today they are more likely to stay closer to home in such places as the kitchen, the laundry and the nursery.

Kibbutzim and Moshavim

The kibbutz is, of course, the communal settlement for which Israel is justly famous. The members, without coercion, work together, share all their property and eat their meals together in a communal dining hall. Each member is assigned a home in the kibbutz and often the children live apart in separate children's houses.

Many of the more difficult questions, such as who does what work, who gets which house, or who is allowed to go off to study, are decided by a general meeting of the entire kibbutz. But everyone, even kibbutz members who are cabinet ministers, have to take their turn cleaning the dining room.

Since Degania, the first kibbutz, was founded in 1909, they have grown in number and in wealth. Now it is not just food and clothing that is shared out, but computers, theater tickets, even trips abroad. Over the years, the kibbutzim have added industry to the agriculture which was once their mainstay. Kibbutz homes have become more comfortable and roomier. And in many the children now sleep at home with their parents.

For many young people from abroad, the kibbutz represents a fascinating challenge, and many come to Israel to spend a few months living and working in a kibbutz as volunteers. Some fall in love with the kibbutz and its way of life; others are disappointed. This is to some extent a result of the volunteer's own attitude, but it is also in some measure dependent on the kibbutz as well. Some kibbutzim are known for the friendliness and openness of their members, while others have acquired a very different reputation. Most kibbutzim will assign each volunteer to "kibbutz parents" and often very close relationships develop.

But for all their fame and influence, the kibbutz members make up only a small part, about four per cent, of the population. Far more prevalent are the country's agricultural villages, the moshavim, where many of the immigrants who came after the establishment of the State settled. In the moshav, each family lives in its own home. Sometimes they hold and work all or part of the land communally, sometimes each family works its own plot of land. Today, in fact, many a moshav near a large city has become a virtual suburb, most of its residents working in town and doing a bit of farming on the side.

The Political Line Up

Practically all the kibbutzim and most of the moshavim are affiliated with organizations which identify with one or another of Israel's political parties. This is to some extent a legacy of the pre-State period when much of the country's development was carried out through political groupings. Such power, once acquired, is usually given up grudgingly and much of Israeli life is colored by politics.

Thus, for example, the sports organizations, and thus the leading soccer and basketball teams, are identified with political groups. Betar represents the Herut or Revisionist branch of the right wing Likud party, while Maccabi is identified with the Liberal, or General Zionist, faction of the same party. Hapoel is sponsored by the Histadrut, which is in the firm control of the Labor party, also known as the Alignment. While not all fans of a team vote for the party it represents, a good many will.

The Histadrut, by the way, is far more than a labor federation. It has the country's largest health care system. Its subsidiaries also own one of the country's largest banking systems, Bank Hapoalim, and one of the largest building contractors, Solel Boneh. (It's not unheard of for Histadrut workers to go out on strike against one of the Histadrut-owned companies).

Officially, the country's political life is carried out in the single chamber Knesset, or parliament, which has 120 members, chosen on the basis of nationwide elections. But rather than vote for a candidate, Israelis must choose from among lists of candidates, drawn up by the various parties. While scrupulously fair in making sure that even small groups of voters are represented, this system tends to encourage political instability.

Thus in addition to the two major blocs, the Alignment, or Labor, and the right-wing Likud, there are numerous small parties: the left-wing Socialists; the ultra-nationalist Tehiya party; a number of Arab parties; and a flurry of small religious parties. The Communist party is legal in Israel and receives almost all of its support from Arab voters for whom it represents a legal outlet to aspirations of Arab nationalism. (Any party which openly advocates the destruction of the State of Israel is illegal).

But the political group that worries most Israelis is at the other end of the political spectrum, the frankly racist Kach party, led by an immigrant from the U.S., Rabbi Meir Cahana, who preaches disenfranchising the Arabs and encouraging them to leave the country. Cahana, who recently won a seat in the Knesset, seems to enjoy making appearances at Arab villages and fomenting the clashes that inevitably develop with such appearances. It is due to him that the Knesset has felt called upon to limit its members' traditional immunity and unlimited freedom of movement. Even those whose strongly nationalistic outlook might seem to make them his allies consider him outside the pale of accepted political action.

Despite continued efforts toward electoral reform, it appears that the same small parties which presently benefit from the system will keep it from being changed. The small religious parties in particular have made an art of extracting every last ounce of influence for every vote they add to the coalition. After all, with the Knesset so evenly balanced between the two major parties, it is not surprising that the small parties, who often find themselves with what, in effect, is the casting vote, should enjoy such an apparently disproportionate influence.

Soldiering On

One area which has remained almost entirely free of political influence has been the army. This is perhaps an indication of just how important the army is in Israeli life. Practically every Israeli enters the army for three years at the age of 18 and for many, army service is a highpoint of their lives. For most youngsters, not being accepted into the army, even for a legitimate cause such as a physical disability, is a major tragedy. In fact, the army has a regular program of special training and classes for delinquents and illiterates to enable them to serve.

The few who do not serve include most Arabs (although they can volunteer, and some do) and the ultra-Orthodox, who officially enjoy a deferment on the grounds that they are yeshiva students. Religious girls are also exempted if they wish, but many choose to volunteer for a year or two of alternative "national service" in schools, hospitals or social service agencies.

Training in Israel's army is hard and exacting, and living conditions often at subsistence level, especially for new recruits. But there is definitely an esprit which is lacking in most armed services throughout the world. Part of this spirit comes from a tradition that precedes the establishment of the State in which officers do not command their men to go forward. Instead, the order is "After me." An easy camaraderie reigns between officers and men, with almost a complete absence of spit and polish.

But if the average youngster looks forward to becoming a soldier, most Israelis view with dread their annual army reserve service, which can amount to over 30 days a year (more for officers) up to the age of 55. True, some reserve soldiers have a fairly easy time of it, patrolling the streets of the main cities. But others find themselves suddenly plucked away from their daily routine and thrust into hard physical work, marching for miles on end, sleeping in tents and eating barely edible food. While most Israelis accept the fact that the country's security situation makes such reserve service a necessity, they still resent it.

The security situation also means that Israelis, and visitors, have to put up with other measures. Because of the predilection of terrorists for placing bombs in public places, it is common to have a guard who examines all packages and purses at the entry to supermarkets and even concert halls. Visitors also find it surprising to see many young people in the streets with weapons casually slung over their shoulders. Again because of the threat of terrorists, for whom even small children are game, every school trip must be accompanied by a certain number of adults with weapons. Others are simply soldiers on leave who must carry their weapons with them if they are stationed in dangerous areas.

For all this, Israel is a surprisingly peaceful country. True, in recent years it has shown some of that disturbing tendency towards violent crime you see throughout the Western world. But compared to the large cities of, say, the U.S. or the U.K., the country is still far behind in its violent crime rate. Even the purse snatchers—and there are some—seem far more gentle. Most visitors take a particular pleasure in being able to stroll about after dark in Tel Aviv or Jerusalem, though they would fear to do so at home.

But if someone walks up to you, don't be afraid. The chances are that, like most Israelis, he just wants to talk.

ISRAEL'S EARLY HISTORY

A Tapestry of Time and Place

by
MIKE ROGOFF

There can be few countries in the world where the regional location and the lie of the land—in short, the geography—are as finely interwoven with the course of human events as in Israel. Understand the geography, wrote a Victorian explorer of the Holy Land, understand the country as a whole, and "you will hear through it the sound of running history."

First, it is vital to picture Israel as a sort of slender continental bridge, the *only* land bridge between Africa to the west, and the vast mass of Asia (and Europe) to the east and north. Israel's rich prehistorical finds, some dating back three-quarters of a million years and more, bear witness to primitive man's use of the "continental bridge." Much of that immeasurably long Stone Age remains clouded in mystery, but with the dawning of the historical era, the era of written records that is, say about 5,000 years ago, the clouds begin to lift a little. Two dominant civilization centers emerge, each rooted in the fertile valleys of a great river: Egypt on the Nile; and, on the Tigris and Euphrates of Mesopotamia (modern Iraq), the ancient empires of

Sumer and Accad, Babylon and Assyria. The natural road between Egypt and Mesopotamia lay across Israel—the famous Via Maris, as it was later to become known—and for millenia the armies and embassies of rival powers rushed up and down it.

All coveted this little but strategically placed sliver of land. It was equally useful to Egypt as a buffer zone against invasion from the north, and to Assyria as a spring-board for an attack on the Land of the Nile. In either case the local inhabitants usefully provided the invader with produce and taxes to fuel his campaign, and a sort of practice-run in the well-developed arts of destruction, pillage, slaughter and slavery. Cities were destroyed or abandoned, often to be rebuilt on the same site until the next army came through.

The Lay of the Land

Israel's history has been shaped as profoundly by the country's topography as by its position on the land bridge between continents. It has been said, perhaps with much truth, that if you take a good topographical map of Israel, and erase the modern features—cities, roads, railways—leaving only the mountains, the valleys, and of course the water sources, you could guess the location of half the ancient cities. Some, like Megiddo or Hatzor, dominate critical passes; others, like Acre (Akko) or Jaffa were port cities; and others again, like Jericho or Dan, while strategically located, owed much of their importance to the abundant springs next to which they were built.

Furthermore, the mountainous nature of the country created natural pockets, somewhat isolated from each other. The result was often fierce regional or tribal loyalties which prevented the unification essential to empire. In fact, throughout its history, Israel has only been united three times under *native* rule: under David and Solomon in the 10th century B.C.; by the Jewish Hasmonean dynasty and Herod the Great in the 2nd and 1st centuries B.C.; and in the modern State of Israel since 1948. At all other times the country was either politically fragmented (the period of the Canaanites, and of the Tribes of Israel under the Judges, for example), or under the foreign dominion of, variously, the Egyptians, Assyrians, Babylonians, Persians, Greeks, Romans, Byzantines, Arabs, Crusaders, Mameluks, Turks and Britons. The list seems endless.

This picture is in vivid contrast to the conditions prevailing in Egypt and Mesopotamia. The huge empires of the time were all founded on the wide fertile plains of great rivers which allowed large-scale *irrigated* farming and large concentrations of population. Under such circumstances not everyone needed to work the land. Farmers could produce more than they needed just for themselves, and energies were thus released which found expression in cultural and material advances: writing, arts and crafts, engineering, architecture, and so on. In Israel, on the other hand, the more rugged terrain and lack of water tended to produce subsistence farming instead, "each man under his grapevine and under his fig tree."

The Land of Milk and Honey

In addition to location and topography, one other important geographic factor has had an impact on Israel's history, its climate. Israel is long and narrow, about 415 kms. (260 miles) from north to south and 110 kms. (70 miles) wide at its maximum width. Yet it is no larger than Wales or New Jersey. It lies between the desert to the east and south, and the Mediterranean Sea to the west, and the never-ending struggle for influence between these two great natural forces accounts to no small extent for the astonishing diversity of the country's climate and landscape.

Take the Biblical phrase, "a land flowing with milk and honey." It is common wisdom among scholars today that "honey" in this phrase means not bee-honey, but date-honey, a sort of jam made from the fruit of the date-palm. God's promise to bring the Children of Israel to "a land flowing with milk and honey" carried no hint of some great health-food store. Rather, by contrast with both the harsh wasteland of the desert *and* with the irrigated gardens of the Nile, the Promised Land "is a land of hills and valleys which drinks water by the rain from heaven" (Deuteronomy 11). Obedience to God will bring the reward of "the rain for your land in its season" to provide "grass in your fields for your cattle" (the milk), and to irrigate crops and orchards (the honey) (compare Deut. 8:8).

These poetic Biblical passages mean just this: besides the townsfolk who engaged in trade and crafts, most people in that essentially agrarian economy were either herders (sheep, goats, cows) or cultivators (fruit or grain). The former, like David, were to be found in the hill-country and the edge of the desert. The latter, like Naboth, the owner of the vineyard coveted by King Ahab, worked the fertile and better-watered valleys.

And more. Throughout history there existed an on-going confrontation between the half-starving, always-thirsty desert nomads, and the landed settlers. Drought often drove the nomads to seek water and pasturage in the cultivated valleys and hills. Where the settlers were strong and united they were able not only to stop the incursions of the nomads, but drive them off and reclaim parts of the desert. Where the settlers were weak and divided the nomads could penetrate, leaving devastation behind them. "And so it was, when Israel had sown, that Midian and Amalek and the children of the east [the desert] came up against them, and they encamped against them, and destroyed the produce of the earth as far as Gaza." (Judges 6).

The Spade and the Book

If an understanding of the geography of Israel illuminates the stage, so to speak, on which the events of the country's past were enacted, how can we now reconstruct those events themselves?

The vast jigsaw puzzle that is ancient history draws its clues from two sources: the written word, and archeological evidence. Although some inscriptions on clay, pottery or stone have been found which shed light on places or events in Ancient Israel, the Bible remains our main written source for the 1,200 years or so from Abraham to Ezra the Scribe. Valuable though their observations are, however, the Bible's authors and editors had no intention of compiling a comprehensive guide book to the country, or a text book of its history. Rather, their purpose was fundamentally religious; that is, to reinforce the idea of the unity of the people of Israel faithfully walking in the ways of their One God. Through prescription, parable, prophecy and psalm, they followed this purpose. *Events* are important only insofar as they serve the purpose, and are used to illustrate the twin themes of the rewards of faith and the wages of sin.

With the above reservation in mind, we can still reap an immense harvest of historical and geographical detail from the Bible. Once it was fashionable to treat much of this detail as unreliable; today archeological finds are constantly confirming Biblical accounts. The process is not without its problems, of course. Some Biblical books have clearly been lost (like "the book of the Kings of Israel" referred to often in Kings or Chronicles). Then again, the Bible is selective of its material; many towns and events known from other sources go unmentioned. And, in some cases, archeology has simply refused to confirm a Biblical account, as in Joshua's conquest of the cities of Jericho and Ai.

But, when archeology and the Bible are in tune, they thrill the thoughtful visitor. One example will suffice. In 701 B.C. the Assyrian King Sannacharib invaded Judah. Complementary accounts are found in the Bible on the one hand (II Kings 18, II Chronicles 32, Isaiah 36), and in Assyrian inscriptions and wall-reliefs found at Nineveh on the other. Excavations of ancient sites like Lachish in the Shefela confirm the accounts. In Jerusalem King Hezekiah of Judah prepared for the expected siege by building new fortifications and an ingenious water tunnel. Both have been discovered: the former in the shape of a wall 23-feet thick, in today's Jewish Quarter of the Old City of Jerusalem; the latter, a 577-yard long water tunnel under the City of David, complete with wall-plaster, chisel marks and an ancient inscription describing the work, the latter now in a museum in Istanbul.

For centuries the Holy Land has fired the Western imagination as the stage of many of mankind's great ancient dramas. Soldiers and adventurers, pilgrims and scholars have strained to hear the echoes of those dramas. Since the middle of the last century they have also begun looking for physical traces. The systematic search for remains of the distant past in order to better understand it is what archeology is all about.

Once the success of an archeological expedition would have been judged by the spectacular nature of its finds. The temples and tombs of ancient Egypt, Mesopotamia and Greece are awe-inspiring and their wondrous treasures of jewels, vessels, art and inscriptions fill the galleries of Western museums. But in Israel such spectacular finds are rare. In a country which seldom rivalled the *material* culture of the ancient supercultures, and which, furthermore, was trampled over thoroughly and often by foreign armies, the scope of excavations has been more subdued, the joys of discovery more subtle.

Israel is freckled with historical sites. Some have been positively identified with known ancient towns, others not. Many have been excavated in the last 100 years, others remain tantalizingly untouched. How they are found (not all are obvious), and how, where possible, they are identified, is the first step of the treasure hunt.

Cities, as we have said, were often built on a particular site for a good reason—a strategic highway, defensible location, water supply, etc.—and when a city had been destroyed or abandoned, later resettlement would often take place on the exact same site, for the same good reasons as before. This superimposition of one layer of civilization upon another eventually formed a "tel," an artificial mound, a sort of archeological layer-cake. Typically, a tel looks a bit like a flat-topped loaf of bread. The aim of the archeologist is to cut into it in a systematic manner to expose the strata, and read off a historical profile of the site. Of course it's not nearly as simple as that. Strata are not always readily distinguishable, and part of the *art* of archeology, if one may put it that way, is being able to tell where one level ends and the next one begins. The *science* of archeology is concerned with dating those levels.

To begin with only one thing is certain: the lower the level, the older the period to which it belongs. If an inscription or some distinctive artifact or architectural style allows us to date a particular level exactly, we then move from *relative* dating of the strata, to *absolute* dating of at least the level concerned, and thus often of the others above and below it.

Only occasionally will the trowel bring to light some real treasure, however modest. But one thing is found in abundance: pottery. One of the great advances in archeology came at the end of the 19th century when it was realized that the debris of ancient cities had its own story to tell. By now a cross-referenced dossier of pottery types is so well-developed, that an expert walking over the top and sides of a tel can usually learn from the potsherds on its surface in which periods the site was used without turning a single clod of earth.

By the Hellenistic and Roman periods the limited area of the tel had become insufficient for the more spacious urban plan then in vogue, and the ancient sites were abandoned. Obviously much more remains of these later periods, say from the 3rd century B.C. on, since they have had less time to be ravaged by the forces of nature and of man. Often at least the outlines of the buildings of such a site are easily visible, as they were at Qumran and Masada even before their excavation.

A Word About Names

It *is* confusing, to be sure. Once called Canaan, then the Land of Israel (Eretz Yisra'el), then Israel. Later "Israel" meant just the Northern Israelite Kingdom, including Samaria and Galilee, while the south was called "Judah." Judah became the Greek form "Judea," applying only to a small part of the country centered on Jerusalem. In order to obscure the Jewish identification of the country, and indeed of Jerusalem itself, the Roman Emperor Hadrian, having just had to put down yet another Jewish revolt, changed Judea to "Palaestina," and Jerusalem to "Aelia Capitolina." Palestine later became the name of this tiny district in a huge Near-Eastern Muslim empire, though more often the local district was named after its principal town. To Christians it was always the Holy Land, to Jews still Eretz Yisra'el.

The use, therefore, of the form Israel in the following Chronological Tables does not always imply any specific set of borders, today or in yesteryear, but the country as a whole, the ancient Land of Israel

DATE TABLE—Pre-Biblical and Old Testament Periods

B.C.

c. 3200– Early Canaanite Period (Early Bronze Age). Writing is developed 2150 in Mesopotamia (beginning of "history"). Many major cities are built for the first time: Megiddo, Hatzor, Jerusalem, etc.

c. 2150– Middle Canaanite Period (Middle Bronze Age). Amorite (Semitic) 1550 invasions from Mesopotamia in the northeast cause destruction and upheaval. Later stability and the Age of the Patriarchs: Abraham, Isaac and Jacob.

c. 1550– Late Canaanite Period (Late Bronze Age). The country is divided 1250 into independent and often mutually hostile city-kingdoms, all subjects of the powerful Egyptian pharoahs. This is the time of the Hebrews' sojourn in Egypt. Eventual decline of Egyptian power and the Exodus from Egypt of the Hebrews under Moses. The nation receives the Torah (the "Law") at Mount Sinai.

This is the most profound moment in Jewish history, from which all else flows. The Hebrews are finally melded into the "Children of Israel;" the foundation of their code of ethics and religious practices is laid, and the special contractual relationship with God established: "You keep my Commandments, and I will bring you to the Land which I promised to your forefathers." But 40 years of wandering in the wilderness still separate the Israelites from their Promised Land. (Incidentally, there is no Jewish tradition as to where Mt. Sinai is, the significance of the event being more important than the actual spot. The peak shown and climbed in the southern Sinai Desert is a Byzantine and Beduin tradition.)

c. 1200– Period of the Judges (Deborah, Gideon, Samson, etc.), charismatic 1025 regional leaders. The Israelite spiritual center is at Shiloh. Philistines invade from the Aegean across the Mediterranean and establish a league of city-states in the southern coastal plain. The Israelites, needing strong leadership to counter the Philistine threat, and influenced by neighboring traditions, appeal to Samuel the Prophet to give them a king.

1025   Saul, of humble origin, first King of Israel.

1006   Saul and three sons, including Jonathan, are killed fighting the Philistines. David rules Judah.

1000   David conquers Jerusalem, a Jebusite enclave, and makes it the national capital of a now completely unified Israel. He brings the Ark of the Covenant to Jerusalem, establishing the city as the new religious center as well as the political capital. The kingdom is greatly expanded and a census taken (c.980).

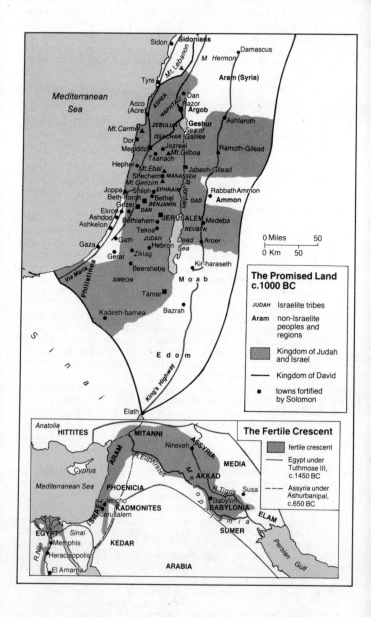

The Promised Land c.1000 BC

JUDAH Israelite tribes

Aram non-Israelite peoples and regions

Kingdom of Judah and Israel

Kingdom of David

towns fortified by Solomon

The Fertile Crescent

fertile crescent

Egypt under Tuthmose III, c.1450 BC

Assyria under Ashurbanipal, c.650 BC

968   Solomon becomes king and consolidates David's kingdom with administrative and military centers and an extensive bureaucracy. He builds the First Temple to the Lord on Mount Moriah in Jerusalem (c.950).

928   Division of the Monarchy after the death of Solomon. The Northern Tribes under Jeroboam break away to form the Kingdom of Israel with its capital at Shechem (now Nablus, in the West Bank). The Southern Tribes, now known as the Kingdom of Judah with its capital at Jerusalem, are ruled by Rehoboam, Solomon's weak son.

c. 865   Ahab (871–51) King of Israel, Jehosophat (867–43) King of Judah, and peace between the sister kingdoms. Ahab's wife Jezebel introduces pagan idol-worship, wrathfully opposed by the prophet Elijah. Shomron (Samaria) now the capital of the Northern Kingdom.

c. 800–   A time of expansion and prosperity under Jeroboam II of Israel
750 (785–49) and Uzziah of Judah (786–58). The resulting moral laxity is condemned in fierce terms by the prophets Amos and Hosea.

722   Destruction of the Kingdom of Israel by the Assyrians (now the super-power of the region), and the exile of the bulk of its population, a historical oblivion from which it never returned (the Ten Lost Tribes). The Kingdom of Judah comes under the Assyrian yoke.

701   Hezekiah, King of Judah, revolts against Assyria, and is rewarded by a full-scale Assyrian invasion. After ravaging the countryside the Assyrians lay siege to Jerusalem, the capital. Hezekiah's brilliant engineering—huge new fortifications and a superb water system— and the inspiration of the prophet Isaiah help the city withstand the siege.

697   Menasseh King of Judah (697–640), vassal of Assyria. Pagan cults are re-introduced to Jerusalem.

609   Josiah, the last great king of Judah (640–609) and an important religious reformer, is killed at Megiddo trying to block the northern advance of an Egyptian army. Jeremiah prohesies the approaching national catastrophe.

587   The end of Judah. The Assyrians have been defeated by the new Babylonian power whose king, Nebuchadnezzar, conquers Judah, captures Jerusalem, and destroys the Temple. Of those that survive the devastation, large numbers (and especially the leadership) are exiled to "the rivers of Babylon," there to weep as they "remembered Zion."

The catastrophe is as much a religious trauma as a national one. The Temple ritual is no more; and there is a crisis of faith. But the message of the Prophets simultaneously rationalizing the tragedy and promising redemption, and the influence of Josiah's religious reform a generation earlier, create a moral resilience that assures survival. This is a major watershed in Jewish history: neither the nation nor its faith will be quite the same again. There is a return to strict observance of non-Temple commandments (Sabbath, purity, etc.), and, with the Temple and sacrifices gone, the idea of the synagogue and prayer is born.

538–   The Babylonians are soon swallowed up by a new rising force.
515 Cyrus the Persian founds the greatest empire of the Ancient East, and issues an Edict allowing those Jews who wish to to return home. A

few do, many do not. The "Zionists" of yore begin rebuilding the Temple in Jerusalem, though, when it is completed in 515 B.C., it is but a shadow of its glorious predecessor. Beginning of the Second Temple Period.

The Second Temple Period

B.C.

515   Completion of the Second Temple in Jerusalem.

c. 457   Ezra "the Scribe," returning from Babylon, wins trust in his spiritual leadership and undertakes thoroughgoing religious reform.

445   Nehemiah sent by the Persian king with authority to rebuild and rule Judah. In face of continual hostility and harassment he completes the rebuilding of Jerusalem's walls (Neh. 2).

333   Persian Empire is defeated by Alexander The Great. All the Near East including Judea (as it soon becomes known) comes under Hellenistic sway.

323   Death of Alexander and a period of struggle for control of his empire. Ptolemy in Egypt, Seleucus in Syria and Mesopotamia.

301   Ptolemy establishes his control over Judea. The now Greek-speaking Jewish population in Egypt grows greatly. The Bible is translated into Greek: the Septuagint.

198   The Seleucids (of Syria) defeat the Egyptian Ptolemies at Banias, the headwaters of the Jordan, annex Judea, and establish good relations with the Jewish community.

167   Antiochus IV outlaws all Jewish religious practices. At Modi'in (near Lod) the priest Mattathias assassinates a royal officer come to enforce the decrees and a fellow-priest prepared to obey. Beginning of the Maccabean Revolt.

165   After four decisive victories over Hellenistic armies, Mattathias' son Judah the Maccabee enters the desecrated Temple in Jerusalem, purifying and rededicating it (an event celebrated in the festival Hannukah).

142   Simon, last of Mattathias' five sons, achieves political independence for Judea, taking for himself the title of High Priest. Establishment of the Hasmonean Dynasty.

135   John Hyrcanus, High Priest. He expands Judean territory and converts the Idumeans to Judaism.

103   Alexander Jannai, King as well as High Priest. Judea extends "from Dan to Beersheba" as in Biblical days.

63   Pompey, the Roman general, enters the country to settle a civil war between the last Hasmonean princes, but annexes it as a Roman province, introducing four centuries of Roman rule.

This tempestuous period in Jewish history is characterized by deep divisions among the Jews themselves according to how they perceive their own religion and their relationship to the Hellenistic world around them. Sadducees draw their strength from the priesthood and upper classes, practising their religion in literal Biblical terms (Temple and sacrifice), yet accepting where convenient certain elements of the attractive Hellenistic culture. Pharisees add to the authority of the Bible that of "Oral Law" (rabbinic interpretation) and develop such beliefs as life after death and

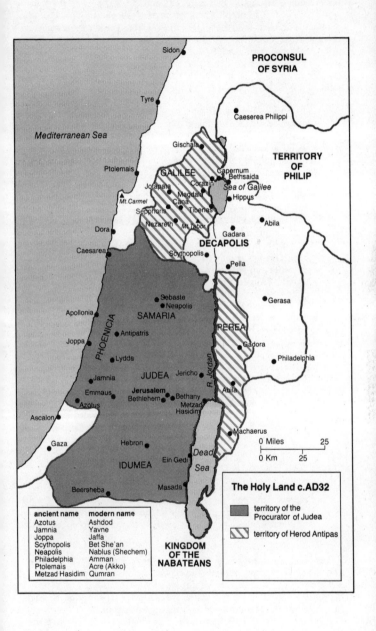

PROCONSUL
OF SYRIA

Sidon

Tyre

Caeserea Philippi

Mediterranean Sea

Gischala

TERRITORY
OF
PHILIP

Ptolemais

GALILEE

Capernum
Bethsaida

Jotapata

Corazin

Sea of Galilee

Magdala

Mt.Carmel

Cana

Hippus

Sepphoris

Tiberias

Nazareth

Abila

Dora

Mt.Tabor

Gadara

Caesarea

DECAPOLIS

Scythopolis

Pella

Sebaste

Gerasa

Neapolis

Apollonia

SAMARIA

PEREA

Antipatris

Gadora

Joppa

Philadelphia

Lydda

Jamnia

JUDEA

Jericho

Emmaus

Jerusalem

Abila

Azotus

Bethlehem

Bethany

Ascalon

Metzad
Hasidim

Gaza

Hebron

Machaerus

0 Miles   25

Ein Gedi

Dead

0 Km   25

IDUMEA

Sea

Beersheba

Masada

The Holy Land c.AD32

territory of the
Procurator of Judea

territory of Herod Antipas

ancient name	modern name
Azotus	Ashdod
Jamnia	Yavne
Joppa	Jaffa
Scythopolis	Bet She'an
Neapolis	Nablus (Shechem)
Philadelphia	Amman
Ptolemais	Acre (Akko)
Metzad Hasidim	Qumran

KINGDOM
OF THE
NABATEANS

R. Jordan

resurrection of the dead. They reject any accommodation with the pagan world. A party of the people, they give birth to other groups: the Essenes, religious extremists who isolate themselves from what they consider a corrupt and doomed society; the Zealots, who translate their anti-Hellenism into armed revolt; and, later, the followers of Jesus of Nazareth, who see in him the realization of the Pharisees' Messianic dream. The intensity of these divisions splits the country and lays it open to the disasters that follow.

48   Pompey's murder in Egypt. Julius Caesar's campaign in the area is assisted by the Hasmonean prince and high-priest Hyrcanus II and his minister Antipater, a converted Idumean. Rewarded with greater political influence, Antipater appoints his sons, among them Herod, to key administrative positions.

40   Mark Antony appoints Herod King of the Jews.

37   After fighting his way through the country, Herod claims his throne in Jerusalem. Hated by the Jews he seeks to legitimize his reign by marrying a Hasmonean princess (whom he later murders), but builds a series of desert refuges as well (Masada, Herodion, etc.) . . . just in case.

31   Antony is defeated by Octavian, now the emperor Caesar Augustus. Herod pays homage to Augustus in Rome and is confirmed in his titles and territories. Later he names the cities of Caesarea and Sabaste (Augustus) in honor of his new patron.

The climax of Herod's building achievements, and perhaps the one that earns him the title "the Great," is the rebuilding of the Temple in Jerusalem on a grand scale. He builds it as a sop to his oppressed Jewish subjects (and as some long-term occupational therapy for them, no doubt); but, always mindful of his reputation, he erects this "wonder of the world" more as a monument to his own glory than to God's. This is the Temple (number IIb, if you like) seen by Jesus and later destroyed by the Romans.

c. 5   Birth of Jesus in Bethlehem.

4   Death of Herod the Great. His kingdom is divided among three sons. Archelaus ruling in Jerusalem is exiled ten years later and replaced by direct Roman rule of Judea by Procurators based in Caesarea.

A.D.

27   Beginning of Jesus' Galilean ministry: he calls the disciples, teaches, heals and performs miracles, mostly around the Sea of Galilee.

29   Jesus and his disciples celebrate Passover in Jerusalem. Arrest, trial and Crucifixion of Jesus by the Romans on orders of Pontius Pilate.

The New Testament relates that Jesus, as the climax of his divine mission, deliberately sacrifices himself to expiate the sins of mankind, is resurrected on the third day after his death, and ascends to Heaven 40 days later. Identification with this event as the way to personal salvation is what characterizes the community of faith that is Christianity.

For the priesthood in Jerusalem, the claim that Jesus is the divine Son of God is inconceivable. For the Romans the claim of Messiah ("the anointed one") with its implications of kingship is a direct challenge to the imperial authority of Caesar, and therefore high treason carrying a death sentence.

41 Agrippa I, grandson of Herod, reigns briefly as King of Judea (41–44).
66 After decades of Roman oppression and administrative abuses, the Great Revolt breaks out. The Romans are swept out of the country and for a brief and heady moment the Jews reassert their political independence.
67 Galilee falls to the Romans. The Jewish commander defects to the enemy. Romanizing his name to Josephus Flavius he follows the Roman campaigns, eventually recording them in *The Jewish War*.
70 After a long and terrible siege of Jerusalem, with the agony of its citizens intensified by internal factional fighting, the city falls to the Roman general Titus. The Temple is destroyed completely. Slaughter and slavery follow and the Revolt is officially at an end.
73 Masada, the last stronghold to resist the legions of Rome, finally falls. Rather than suffer the humiliation of surrender and the wrath of Roman vengeance, 960 defenders take their own lives.

From Bar-Kochba to Allenby

A.D.
c. 69 Before the fall of Jerusalem the sage Yochanan Ben-Zakkai leaves the city, settling with his disciples in the town of Yavne, by grant of Vespasian.
70 With the destruction of Jerusalem and the Temple, Yavne becomes the seat of the Sanhedrin, the Jewish High Court. Its sages find religious responses to the new reality of Judaism without the Temple, and the spiritual and legal authority of Yavne is established.
106 The Roman emperor Trajan destroys the desert civilization of the Nabateans in the Negev and Transjordan, creating the province of Arabia.
116 Revolt against Rome of Jews in the Diaspora (the "Dispersion," i.e. outside Israel), and possibly within Israel itself. Crushed by Trajan's general Quietus.
132 Against the background of the threat of the Roman emperor Hadrian to rebuild Jerusalem as a pagan city, a revolt breaks out led by Bar-Kochba, and supported by Rabbi Akiva. Secret preparations and a strong unified command distinguishes it from the earlier Great Revolt, and lead to spectacular initial successes.
135 Death of Bar-Kochba (near Jerusalem). The Revolt is finally suppressed with great brutality, but only after severe Roman losses and the arrival in huge numbers of Roman reinforcements. Hadrian plows over Jerusalem and builds Aelia Capitolina, a pagan city off-limits to Jews, changes the name of the country from Judea to Palaestina (after Philistines) to dissociate the land from its Jewish identity, and outlaws Jewish religious practice. The Sanhedrin relocates in the Lower Galilee.
c. 200 At Bet She'arim, Judah the "Nasi" (Patriarch), spiritual and political head of the Jewish community, compiles the Mishnah (summary of the "Oral Law," the rabbinic interpretation of Biblical laws, and thus the basis of Jewish jurisprudence). A period of peace and prosperity under the tolerant Severan emperors.

313 Emperor Constantine the Great recognizes Christianity, himself eventually converting. His mother, Helena, comes to the Holy Land in 326 and initiates the building of major churches.

330 Constantine transfers his capital from Rome to Byzantium, now renamed Constantinople. Beginning of the Byzantine Period. Judaism on the defensive.

351 Jewish revolt against the Roman ruler Gallus, primarily in the Galilee.

361 Julian the Apostate, Emperor (361–363), tries to reintroduce the pagan cults at the expense of Christianity. Favors the rebuilding of the Jewish Temple in Jerusalem, but the project is aborted on his death.

c. 400 Final codification of the "Jerusalem" Talmud (actually written mostly in Tiberias), comprising a century-and-a-half of rabbinic elaboration of the Mishnah. (The Babylonian Talmud, codified a century later, is regarded as more authoritative.)

527 Emperor Justinian (527–565). Many important churches built or rebuilt during his reign, among them the present structure of the Church of the Nativity in Bethlehem. The large number of synagogues from the Byzantine period discovered and excavated throughout the country attest to a vibrant Jewish community even at times of Byzantine persecution.

614 Persian invasion accompanied by wide-spread destruction of churches and monasteries.

622 Mohammed's "flight" *(hejira)* from Mecca to Medina in Arabia: beginnings of Islam.

628 Defeat of the Persians and restoration of Byzantine rule in Israel.

632 Death of Mohammed. The Arab Empire is now headed by a Caliph, the religious, political and military leader.

636 Arab invasion of the country.

638 Byzantine Jerusalem falls to the Caliph Omar.

660 The Ummayad dynasty moves its capital from Mecca to Damascus.

691 The Caliph Abd el-Malik builds the Dome of the Rock in Jerusalem.

Within ten years of his flight from a hostile Mecca, Mohammed's new religion, Islam (submission), has triumphed throughout Arabia. Among Islam's "pillars of faith" (including belief in One God, Allah, and Mohammed as his prophet; prayer; charity; the fast of Ramadan; and pilgrimage to Mecca) is the doctrine of *jihad,* Holy War, against any who stand in the way of the True Faith. This doctrine fuels the zeal of the Arab armies who, within a century of Mohammed's death, carve out an empire stretching from Spain to India. Their arrival in Israel is a less brutal affair, however, than that of some conquests before or after them. For the following four centuries Israel passes from one Muslim empire to another: the Baghdad-based Abbasids around 775, the Egyptian Fatimids in 969, the Seljuk Turks in 1071.

1099 Sworn to redeem the Christian holy places from Muslim control, the armies of the First Crusade, made up of some of the cream and much of the riff-raff of Europe, reach the Holy Land. Jerusalem is taken and most of its population massacred, Muslim and Jew alike.

1100 Establishment of the Latin Kingdom of Jerusalem with Baldwin

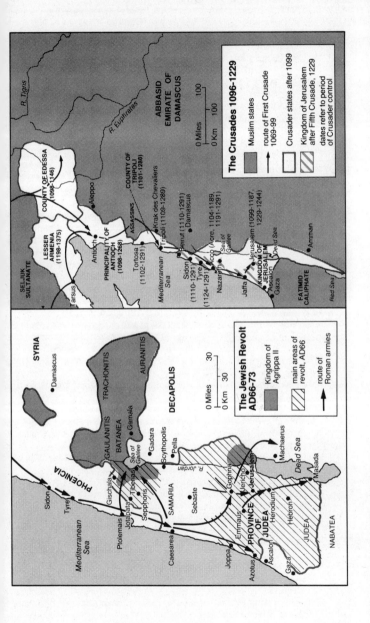

I at its head.

1110   Most coastal cities are now in Crusader hands, securing the lines
of communication and supply with Europe.

1187   The Crusader armies are decimated by the Arab general Saladin at
the Horns of Hattin near the Sea of Galilee. Crusader evacuation of
the country follows.

1191   The Third Crusade arrives, led by Richard the Lionheart of England and Philip II (Augustus) of France. The Emperor Frederick I
(Barbarossa) of Germany is drowned en route. The Latin Kingdom
of Jerusalem never regains its former size and glory, and the Crusaders must content themselves with the coast from Tyre to Jaffa, and
(later) with the Galilee. Acre is now the royal capital.

The Latin Kingdom is organized on feudal lines, with its hierarchical
system of rights and obligations, even purer in form than in Europe itself,
for the power of the Church as a mover in the affairs of men is felt far less
here in the East. Throughout the two centuries of the Crusades a major
problem of the "Franks" is that of manpower. Many a Crusader, knight
and peasant alike, having fulfilled his vows, returns home. The burden of
services and defence is borne by the monastic orders of the Hospitallers,
the Templars, the Teutonic Knights, and others. A later presence is that
of the merchant naval powers of cities like Venice, Pisa and Genoa. Many
Crusaders remaining in the country—as much to make a new life as for
pious reasons—gradually adapt to local ways, banking the fires of their
religious zeal, a disconcerting phenomenon for new arrivals from Europe.

1228   Jerusalem is gained by treaty but lost again in 1244.

1250   The militant Mamluk class take power in Egypt. The Crusade of
King Louis IX (St. Louis) against Egypt aborts. He is captured and,
on his release, comes to the Holy Land for several years.

1260   The Mamluks check the Mongol invasion at Ayn Jalout (Ein
Harod) in the Jezre'el Valley.

1265   Muslim reconquest of the land begins under the Mamluk sultan
Baybars.

1291   The fall of Acre and the end of the Crusader Kingdom. Mamluk
rule changes little, though commerce and trade apparently decline as
a result of the destruction of the coastal cities. Much fine architecture, especially in Jerusalem, survives from this period.

1492   Expulsion of the Jewish community from Spain. Many of these
Sephardic Jews later immigrate to Israel under the Turks.

1516   Mamluk armies defeated in Syria by the Ottoman Turks. Stable
conditions are established in the country. The Jewish community
throughout the country grows, and especially that of Safed (Zefat),
now a center of Jewish mysticism (Kabbalah).

1520   Suleiman the Magnificent (1520–66) initiates many building projects including the rebuilding of the walls of Jerusalem (1538 on-
wards).

1590   Revolt against the Turks by the Druze leader Fakhr al-Din, who
succeeds in capturing much of the country intermittently for several
decades.

1700   Arrival of substantial numbers of Ashkenazi (Eastern European)
Jews in Jerusalem.

c. 1740   Dahr el-Omar, tax collector in the Galilee, asserts independence
over much of the country. Assassinated in 1775 by Ahmad "al-

Jazzar" (the Butcher) Pasha who becomes Governor of Acre.

1799   The invasion of Israel by Napoleon Bonaparte founders on the ramparts of Acre.

1832   Egyptian nationalists under Muhammed Ali and Ibrahim Pasha take control of Israel. They are expelled in 1840 with the help of European nations which, in return, gain diplomatic, religious and economic concessions in the country.

1853   The Crimean War breaks out in Europe against the background of conflict between Catholic France and Orthodox Russia over the Christian holy places.

1869   Opening of the Suez Canal. Escalation of competition between the European powers for control of critical communication lines across the region.

1882   Arrival of first modern Jewish pioneers—the First Aliyah.

1914   Outbreak of World War I.

1917   Jerusalem falls to the British General Allenby. End of the Ottoman Empire.

FROM EXILE TO RETURN

The Story of Israel's Independence

Whether the State of Israel was born in a courtroom in Paris where a Viennese journalist by the name of Theodore Herzl was covering an espionage trial, or in a few hovels in the Galilee where a small group of idealists were trying to prove that Jews could be tillers of the soil, what remains beyond doubt is that the seeds of what is now the State of Israel were planted in the late-19th century.

True, there were and had been Jews in the land of Israel throughout the 2,000 years of dispersal, the Diaspora. True, Jews had prayed daily for a return to Zion. And true, small groups of Jews had from time to time returned to live in the country they had never stopped viewing as the Promised Land. But it was only at the end of the 19th century that the extraordinary and frequently tragic events that culminated in the foundation of the State of Israel in 1948 began slowly to develop.

Thinkers and Settlers

At the end of the 19th century, Palestine, the ancient Land of Israel, was a backwater of the Turkish Ottoman Empire, no more than an insignificant part of the Turk's Arab lands in the Middle East. It had a population of around 600,000 of whom only about 80,000 were Jews. The Turks had done little to develop the land and ruled through a combination of corruption and oppression. Disease and poverty were rife.

It was at about this time that Herzl, a successful author of popular newspaper articles and drawing-room comedies, came face to face with a series of events which were to stun European Jewry. These were the trial and subsequent retrials of Alfred Dreyfus, a Jewish captain in the French army, for selling military secrets to the Germans. The wave of anti-Semitism that swamped the trials came as a profound shock both to Herzl and many other European Jews, particularly as France had long been regarded as a home of liberalism. Even after Dreyfus' innocence had been convincingly established, a substantial portion of French public opinion, including the French General Staff, still condemned him, principally because he was a Jew.

Herzl's concern with the problems of the Jews in European society was not new. But whereas previously he had believed that Jews should assimilate into society, possibly by converting en masse to Christianity, now, in *Der Judenstaat*, "The Jewish State," which he published after the Dreyfus trial, he argued that the only solution to the Jewish question was for the Jews to have a state of their own. Even this was not a particularly radical view for the period. What was new was that this was the first time that it had been put forward by a respected Western European Jew. Hitherto, calls for a Jewish state had come only from the oppressed Orthodox Jews of Eastern Europe. Their appeals had not commanded a wide audience.

But while Herzl's arguments remained essentially in the realm of theory, it was these much-abused Eastern European Jews who took the first practical steps toward the establishment of substantial Jewish settlement in Palestine itself. Their motives were both idealistic and pragmatic. Idealistic in that they wished for a return to Israel not merely because it was the Promised Land, Zion, but because they wanted to work the land for themselves, with their own hands and by their own labor, literally *building* a Jewish state. This idealism is strongly underlined when one considers that they could in fact have gone elsewhere and indeed that at this period, while small numbers of Jews were arriving in Palestine, literally millions of others *were* going to another promised land: America. Pragmatic in that they needed urgently to escape from the real and ever-present danger of pogroms—massacres, to put it bluntly—in Eastern Europe in which mobs raced through the Jewish Quarters in towns and villages indiscriminately plundering, raping and killing. Their energy and determination was in striking contrast to the aims of the small numbers of ultra-Orthodox Jews already in Palestine, most living on charity sent from abroad, their lives passed in poverty and prayer, to whom the notion of a Jewish state was little short of blasphemous. For them, the Jews could return home and establish a state only when the Messiah came.

It was to such a society that groups of young people came from Eastern Europe at the end of the 19th century, establishing settlements like Petah Tikva, Zichron Ya'akov and Rosh Pina. Lacking all but the most rudimentary tools and equipment and desperately short of money, they faced tremendous hardship and great poverty. Indeed had it not been for the financial assistance of Baron Edmond de Rothschild of

France, there is no question that these early settlers would soon have dispersed. Not that the Baron's aid was without strings. Along with his money, he appointed administrators, many of whom were deeply out of sympathy with the aims of the settlers. The letters to Paris flew fast and furious. Prominent among the settlers' complaints was their objection to the use of hired Arab labor. Their determination to work the land themselves was not mere posturing.

It was against the background of these early pioneers in Palestine that Herzl organized the First Zionist Congress. It was held in Basle, Switzerland, in 1897 and launched the World Zionist Organization. "In Basle I founded the Jewish State," wrote Herzl in his diary. They were prophetic words. But for Herzl what was important was not so much colonization now as creating the right political climate for large-scale immigration and statehood later. To this end, he first attempted to meet the Turkish Sultan, Abdul Hamid II. Rebuffed, Herzl secured an audience with the German Kaiser, Wilhelm II. They met first in Constantinople and then later in Jerusalem during the Kaiser's visit to the Holy Land in 1898. Though the Kaiser himself seemed well disposed toward the aims of Zionism, and was said to have great influence with the Sultan, the Turks were less easily won over. Indeed, their reaction was one of fear and suspicion, and served only to reinforce their earlier ban on further Jewish immigration to Palestine.

The discouragement which Herzl felt at his inability to further his political aims was heightened in 1903 with the news of one of the most violent and widespread yet of the Russian pogroms against the Jews, at Kishinev. The Jews did not just need a national home. They needed a refuge from physical annihilation. It was at this moment that the British Government entered the fray with the suggestion—seemingly absurd, yet wholly sincere—that Uganda in East Africa be considered as the site of a Jewish national home. The Zionist Congress at least took them at their word, and passed a resolution that the scheme be given serious consideration. Nonetheless, the opposition from those who believed that only in the Land of Israel could the Jews build a homeland was such that the scheme was quickly dropped. Herzl healed the rift but died the following year, a broken man.

Attention was focused again on Israel by the Zionists, but this time with a slight shift of emphasis. Equal stress was to be put on political negotiation *and* the practical business of settlement. And indeed settlement by Jews was proceeding swiftly, particularly Jews from Eastern Europe. Nor were they the only ones. Thousands of Jews also came from Yemen on the southern tip of the Arabian peninsula, particularly in the years immediately before World War I. The question of what would happen to the substantial Arab majority in Palestine should the Jews succeed in their ultimate goal was, for the time being, tactfully left unasked.

As more Jews arrived, so they became better organized. Security, hitherto entrusted to hired Arab watchmen, was a particular problem. The formation of a Jewish watchmen's society, Hashomer, the forerunner of the Israel Defence Forces, whereby the Jews assumed direct responsibility for their own security, dates from this period. Similarly, Jewish workers also began to organize themselves into unions and cooperatives. Of equal significance, a group of Jews in Jaffa bought a stretch of sand dunes to the north of the city in 1909. Here they founded Tel Aviv, the country's first modern Jewish city. Other groups began to organize the communal settlements that later would grow into the kibbutzim.

This period of relative peace and expansion came to a sudden and brutal halt with the outbreak of World War I in 1914. Misery and hunger descended on Palestine. Cut off from its traditional sources of food, famine swept the country. In addition, many Palestinian Jews who had remained citizens of their own countries in order to escape the excesses of Turkish repression were deported or left of their own accord. In 1917 the pro-British Jewish spy ring, NILI, was uncovered. A number of its members, leading figures in the Jewish community, were executed by the Turkish authorities, and one at least was killed by Beduins.

Balfour Declares

Despite the setbacks brought about by World War I to the Zionist cause, 1917 nonetheless proved a crucial moment in its development, the turning point in the movement's history. In November of that year, as General Allenby's British army marched into Palestine, scattering the Turks before them, the British Government ringingly declared, in a document that came to be known after its author, Lord Balfour, the Foreign Secretary, that they would, "use their best endeavors to facilitate the establishment in Palestine of a national home for the Jewish people."

Much of the credit for the Balfour Declaration lies with Chaim Weizmann, later the first President of Israel, a scientist whose work had done much to aid the British war effort. But however persuasive, and valuable, Weizmann might have been, the British had other motives beyond a disinterested desire to further the cause of Zionism. To a large extent, the British Government viewed the Balfour Declaration as a means of winning over American Jewish public opinion, and thus gaining an ally in influencing the United States to enter the war on the side of the British. (Though in this the British Foreign Office was not as well informed as it might have been: many influential Jews in America, and Europe, too, for that matter, were opposed to Zionism, fearing that a Jewish homeland would threaten their own position).

At the same time the British were also nurturing Arab national aspirations, eager to foment an Arab rebellion against the Turks. Indeed it quite rapidly became clear that Britain's interests, both short and long term, lay much more with the Arabs in Palestine than with the Jews, whatever the Balfour Declaration might say. The predominantly Arab Middle East was of primary importance: strategically because the vital Suez Canal was the main route to India and the Far East; and economically because the oil-rich lands of the region were a prize far greater than the tiny underdeveloped territory of Palestine. Many Jewish critics of British policy in the Middle East have also felt that some British officials had a longstanding bias favoring the "picturesque" and "romantic" Arabs over the Jews, whom they viewed with disdain. But would the British Government actually go back on its word? The short answer was yes.

That tensions between Arabs and Jews were already rising was made clear by Arab attacks on Jewish settlements in the Upper Galilee in 1920, these despite an agreement, signed by Weizmann and the Emir Faisal, the most prominent Arab leader of the time and later King of Iraq, that Jew and Arab should live together as good neighbors. But despite their suspicion of Arab intentions the Jews were greatly encouraged by the decision of the League of Nations in July 1922 that confirmed the British presence in Palestine—gave Britain a mandate to rule Palestine—and charged her with the responsibility for "placing the country under such political, administrative and economic conditions as will secure the establishment of a Jewish national home." The appointment of Herbert Samuel, a Jew, as the first British High Commissioner boded equally well.

The '20s and '30s

The first blow to Jewish hopes came the same year. Britain gave her blessing to the establishment of an Arab emirate, ruled by Faisal's brother Abdullah, in Transjordan, the area to the east of the Jordan which had been included in the British mandate. Shortly afterwards, Samuel attempted to appease the Arabs further by the appointment of Haj Amin el-Husseini, a Muslim religious leader who had been sentenced for his part in inflaming attacks against the Jews, as Mufti of Jerusalem. Thus officially sanctioned, Husseini used his position to stir up violent opposition to the Jews. In a series of events that were to occur with depressing regularity, the Arabs would attack the Jews, and the British, ever mindful of their Arab interests and indeed of the conflict that would inevitably result from further large scale Jewish immigration, would react by curbing Jewish immigration and other rights.

Thus in 1922 the first of a series of British White Papers, official policy statements, was issued in which it was claimed that the Balfour Declaration had never intended all of Palestine to serve as a Jewish national home. A system of "certificates" for Jewish immigrants was devised, their number to be limited to the "economic capacity of the country."

Yet in spite of the continued threat of Arab attacks and the growing realization that Britain, caught between her contradictory promises to Jews and Arabs, had no intention of doing anything to make a Jewish national home possible, the Jews continued to consolidate their position in Palestine, much as the earlier settlers had consolidated the Jewish presence in Palestine before World War I. The acquisition of land was accelerated. The Jewish Agency, levying a voluntary tax, funded schools, hospitals and factories; a high point was the establishment of the Hebrew University on Mount Scopus overlooking Jerusalem in 1925. And the Jews were learning to fight back. The '20s saw the foundation of the Hagana, successor to the Hashomer, a clandestine Jewish self-defense force.

The Hagana grew rapidly after Arab riots swept the country in 1929 following a dispute over the right of Jews to pray at the Western Wall of the Temple. In Hebron in particular, holy to Jews and Arabs, mobs attacked and killed men, women and children, leading to the evacuation by the British of the entire Jewish population of the town. But though the Jews may have succeeded in defending themselves more effectively, the aftermath of the Hebron riots resulted in a further setback for the Jews. A Parliamentary Commission sent out from Britain to report on the rioting recommended that further restrictions be placed on Jewish immigration and that Jews be prohibited from buying Arab land on the generally spurious grounds that there was no more arable land in the country. Additionally, the British military authorities, accurately seeing the Hagana as a threat to British policy, vigorously attempted to suppress it. The British line was that they could hardly be expected to sit back while the Jews, still much in a minority, armed themselves against the Arab population. That they appeared to have no such qualms about Arabs carrying arms was noted with more than irony by the Jews.

Still, if the Arabs—backed by Britain—were continuing to resist further Jewish immigration, many of them were more than ready to take advantage of the economic growth the Jews sparked off in Palestine. Indeed a steady stream of Arab immigrants were attracted into Palestine from the surrounding Arab countries. Abdullah even held secret talks with the Jewish Agency over the possibility of Jews settling in Transjordan to act as a spur to development there. Nonetheless the essential enmity between the Arabs and Jews remained strong.

A new wave of Arab unrest, led by the Mufti, began with a six-month Arab strike in 1936, with intermittent attacks on Jewish settlements and random killings of Jews in the cities. It was in response to this strike that the port of Tel Aviv was hurriedly built to take the place of that in Jaffa. At the same time the first of a long series of partition plans—a plan to divide Palestine between the Jews and the Arabs—was proposed by a British Royal Commission in 1937. It was, however, swiftly rejected.

By the late '30s a new force had come into play that, while making the Jewish need for a safe refuge all the more urgent, simultaneously hardened British and Arab resistance to further Jewish settlement: the rise of Hitler's Germany. With the threat of war drawing near, Britain sought to appease the Arabs, fearing they might well support the Germans—as the Mufti was in fact to do—by placing ever greater restrictions on Jewish immigration at the very time that there was the greatest pressure from the threatened Jews of Europe to enter the country. As a result, the Jews of Palestine responded by making illegal immigration their official policy, as it were. A fleet of ramshackle, unseaworthy ships was pressed into commission to bring Jews to Palestine. More often than not they failed to make it. The British intercepted most, others even sank, but the refugees continued to trickle in. Their fate could hardly be worse running the blockade than at the hands of the Nazis. This hardening of attitudes also gave rise to more extreme forms of action by some Jews, who argued that violence could be met only with violence. The formation of the Irgun—a terrorist splinter group of the Hagana, which had hitherto concentrated only on defense —and later of the Lehi, an even more extreme grouping, added a new dimension to the terror and bloodshed.

Following the outbreak of war in 1939, the Jews committed themselves wholeheartedly to the Allied cause. "The great and pressing necessities of the time," as Weizmann put it, overshadowed the "differences"—Weizmann's word—that existed between the Jews and the British Mandatory authorities. Thousands of Palestinian Jews enrolled in the British armed forces almost overnight, and by 1943 two-thirds of the Jewish labor force in Palestine was occupied in direct defense-related work. Yet though the men of the Jewish Brigade played a distinguished role in the war, Palestine itself remained largely untouched by the terror sweeping Europe. It was in any case understood by all parties that the alliance between the Jews and Britain was nothing if not temporary.

Independence and War

By the end of the war the full extent of the Nazi Final Solution had become sickeningly clear. Six million Jews, together with millions more, had been systematically murdered by the Nazis and their henchmen all over Europe.

For many of the survivors, Israel, Zion, the Promised Land, seemed the only place to turn to. But while the sympathy of the world was now unquestionably with the Jews, sympathy alone was not going to advance the Jewish cause. The Arabs remained implacably opposed to the foundation of a Jewish state in Palestine, and Britain, the Mandatory Authority, facing an acute fuel shortage at home, was no more willing to risk its Arab oil interests than it had been before the war. Even though an Anglo-American commission in 1946 had recommended the immediate admission of 100,000 Jewish refugees, the gates of the Promised Land remained firmly barred to the Jews.

The period between the end of the war and the Declaration of Independence by Israel in 1948 was ugly and violent. Determined to press their case ever more strongly, the Jews continued to smuggle immigrants into Palestine though, as before the war, many more were captured than actually landed, most being sent to internment camps in Cyprus. Simultaneously Jewish and Arab terrorists began a campaign of random violence. In one of the most notorious acts of the period, the Irgun, led by Menachem Begin, blew up the offices of the Mandatory Government in Jerusalem which were sited in a wing of the King David hotel. 90 people—Jewish, Arab and British—were killed. To this day it is not clear whether the Irgun telephoned a warning, as its leaders claimed, only to be laughed off by the British. In another incident the British hanged seven Irgun and Lehi men. In retaliation, the Irgun hanged two British sergeants, booby-trapping their corpses (which duly exploded before they could be cut down).

By now pressure for a settlement to the increasingly intractable Palestinian problem was mounting worldwide. Prompted by active Jewish lobbying, especially in America, the United Nations stepped into the picture, much as the now defunct League of Nations had done after World War I. They voted to partition Palestine into two states, Arab and Jewish, with Jerusalem an international enclave. The vote, taken on November 29, 1947, was greeted ecstatically by the Palestinian Jews. This was the moment the Jews had prayed for during their long years of exile. The return to the ancient homeland was now surely at hand. The dreams of Herzl and the early settlers had come to pass.

In many important respects, however, the plight of the Jews was now even more desperate. Critically short of arms and ammunition, and denied by the Americans the right to buy them—America had agreed that if Britain would not arm the Arabs, they would not arm the Jews—they faced the wrath of an Arab world pledged to destroy them. Though disorganized and rent by serious internal divisions, the sheer numerical superiority of the Arabs made their victory seem inevitable. In addition, following the U.N. vote, Britain, by now desperate to extricate herself from a problem she had done so much to create, immediately announced she would withdraw from Palestine the following May. In the interval, the British troops were instructed to do no more than the minimum necessary to maintain order. In short, they washed their hands of the problem.

The vacuum seemed certain to be filled only by further fighting and lawlessness. The Arab attacks in fact began the day after the Partition Plan was voted in. The mounting spiral of violence accelerated quickly.

Jerusalem, prized above all other places in Palestine by both Jews and Arabs, suffered particularly. An Arab bomb blew up a large section of Ben Yehuda Street, one of the main thoroughfares of Jewish Jerusalem, with great loss of life. Another practically demolished the *Palestinian Post* building. The Arabs tightened their grip on the city, ambushing the inadequately armed convoys sent from the coast to relieve the beleaguered Jewish community. Even water was rationed. It was at this moment that the Irgun and Lehi, acting without the knowledge of the official leaders of the Palestinian Jews, hit back. They massacred large numbers of the population of Deir Yassin, an Arab village west of Jerusalem. Their intention—cynical but highly effective —was to so terrify the Palestinian Arabs that they fled the country. At the same time, they also raised the level of violence and bitterness significantly. A few days later, Arabs ambushed and killed a convoy of doctors and nurses making their way to Hadassah Hospital on Mount Scopus.

On May 14, as the last British troops were being evacuated, the Provisional Government, led by David Ben Gurion, assembled in Tel Aviv and signed Israel's Declaration of Independence. The new state had been born. That night, the Egyptian air force bombed Tel Aviv. The Arab invasion began the next day.

The story of Israel's War of Independence is too complex to relate here. Suffice it to say that by the time of the final ceasefire early in 1949, the Jews, to the amazement of the world, had not merely beaten off the Arab armies who had confidently boasted they would drive them into the sea within a week, but had expanded their own territories far beyond the original boundaries of the territories allotted them by the U.N. Israel was left with all the Galilee and the Negev, the coastal plain and a corridor leading to Jerusalem. The Egyptians held the Gaza

Strip, while the Transjordanians held Judea and Samaria and, bitterest blow of all to the Israelis, the Old City of Jerusalem, all of which they thereafter annexed as the West Bank of the renamed Kingdom of Jordan.

Statehood and Security

The two principal problems facing the new State were the security of her borders and the absorption of the enormous numbers of immigrants who had begun flooding into the country the moment the British left. Massive Jewish immigration was in fact a cornerstone of the fledgling State: the larger the Jewish population, the more permanent the Jewish State would become. At first the immigrants came mainly from the displaced-persons camps of Europe. Then they began arriving from the Arab and other Muslim states of the Middle East. In the first three years of statehood alone, 700,000 immigrants arrived, doubling the population. It was by no means an easy period. Most of the newcomers were penniless, hardly any spoke Hebrew, and few were trained for any productive work. At first they were housed in makeshift camps, often in tents, before being moved to temporary quarters known as *maabarot* and from these to new agricultural settlements around the country. A large number were given subsidized jobs planting trees.

It was, not surprisingly, a period of considerable deprivation. Food and clothing were rationed. Donations from Jews living abroad were vital to the continued survival of the country. Even so there was bitter opposition from many quarters when the government announced it had agreed to accept a payment of 715 million dollars from the West German government as partial compensation for the crimes of the Germans against the Jewish people. Nonetheless, it was these reparations, paid over 14 years in goods as well as cash, that to a large degree made possible Israel's early industrial development.

Israel's security problems were less easily dealt with. In truth, they have never been satisfactorily settled. Israel has made her borders secure since 1948, in the process becoming the dominant military power in the Middle East. But a resolution of the tangled and bitter problems of the region has never seemed more than a distant prospect at best, despite such major breakthroughs as the Camp David Agreement in 1979. It is not too great an exaggeration to say that the war the British observed with such detachment in 1948 has continued unceasingly to the present day.

Almost from the moment the Israeli War of Independence ended, Arab raiding parties began crossing into Israel. Equally regularly, the Israelis would retaliate. Since the Arab attackers were irregulars and the Israelis responded with regular army units, the United Nations would then censure Israel. This futile stalemate continued for many years. The Egyptians also refused to allow Israeli ships or goods to use the Suez Canal, and additionally attempted to blockade the Gulf of Akaba to prevent Israeli shipping from reaching Eilat on the Red Sea. Similarly, the Arab League boycotted companies with dealings with Israel. Like all economic sanctions, it proved only partially successful but did nevertheless scare off a number of large firms.

An equally sinister development that was to hold alarming implications for the future concerned the fate of the many hundreds of thousands of Palestinian Arabs who had fled the country during the War of Independence. The other Arab nations, resisting all attempts to re-settle them, herded the Palestinians into massive and squalid refugee camps where they subsisted on rations provided by the United Nations. The Arabs did this partly from fear of the Palestinians, who were generally better educated and more sophisticated than their Arab brothers, and partly from a desire to keep the Palestinian problem alive, an aim which proved tragically successful. These camps spawned a generation of embittered Palestinians, a generation that was to provide the nucleus of new terror groups dedicated to the overthrow of Israel.

In 1956 the abortive and in some respects pathetic Suez campaign launched against Egypt by Britain and France went some way towards alleviating Israel's immediate security problems. Convinced that Nasser, the new Egyptian leader, was a Hitler in the making and greedy to regain control of the newly-nationalized Suez Canal, Britain and France secretly persuaded Israel to invade Egypt across the Sinai while they attacked from the north. The invasion went ahead as planned and Israel rapidly pushed across the Sinai, taking the Gaza Strip in the process. Equally rapidly, and in considerable disarray, Britain and France then retreated in the face of overwhelming criticism from the United States, the United Nations and the Soviet Union. A few months later Israel too pulled out, but only after a U.N. Security Force had been stationed in the Sinai. This force did much to lessen tensions along the Egyptian border and to ease the Egyptian blockade on Eilat.

But the relief was shortlived. By 1967 a new wave of tension was forming, with repeated incursions into, and bombardments of, Israel along the Syrian border. In May, Nasser ordered the U.N. force out of Sinai, sending in large numbers of his own troops in their place. He announced a new blockade of the Gulf of Akaba. Jordan's King Hussein then placed his troops under Egyptian command. The Arabs were marshalling their forces for a Jihad, a Holy War. The threat to Israel had never been more real.

Unlike the War of Independence, this time Israel's victory was complete. In the six days from June 5 to June 10 the Israelis routed the Arab armies, transforming the political complexion of the Middle East. By June 10 Israel held the whole of the Sinai to the Suez Canal, the entire West Bank, including of course the Old City of Jerusalem, and the strategically vital Golan Heights on the Syrian border.

The Six Day War provided an enormous psychological boost to Israel. She had shown that she could more than hold her own against the Arabs. A new wave of immigration followed, while Israel basked in her new found self-confidence and assurance.

Yom Kippur and Camp David

Though Israel was now militarily secure, to some extent the Six Day War had raised more questions than it answered. Israel was in possession of the historic heartland of the ancient Land of Israel. Though only the Old City of Jerusalem was formally incorporated into the modern state, the acquisition of these lands, the West Bank in particular, led to immediate demands for permanent and extensive Israeli settlement there. The right wing Herut party, supported by a number of the religious parties, was in the forefront of this Land of Israel movement. And indeed, despite initial Government opposition, the settlement of the West Bank began shortly after the Six Day War, and has continued, gathering momentum all the while, to the present day.

To the defeated Arabs, smarting from their defeat, this served only to rub salt into an open wound. Many turned to acts of reprisal, the Jordanian-based P.L.O. and its later, more hardline splinter group, Black September, in the vanguard. Similarly, many Arabs on the West Bank likewise became more extreme and nationalist in their views. At the same time, it is also true that an equally large number of West Bank Arabs came to realize that the Israelis were not necessarily the monsters portrayed by their leaders. This view was further reinforced by the Open Bridges policy pursued by Israel which allowed free trade over the Jordan river and a measure of contact between West Bank Arabs and residents of other Arab countries. Certainly Israel itself was greatly changed by this first-hand contact with the Arab world. Nonetheless, what became increasingly clear was that the Six Day War had in no way brought nearer a solution to the problems of the Middle East.

The Yom Kippur war in October 1973 confirmed even the most pessimistic view of the situation. The Egyptian and Syrian armies attacked Israel simultaneously on Yom Kippur, the holiest day of the Jewish calendar, catching the Israelis entirely off guard. Predictably perhaps, the Israelis drove both armies back, but only after they had made deep inroads into Israel and inflicted exceptionally heavy casualties. The war may have made it clear for once and all that the Arabs were kidding themselves if they thought they could overcome Israel through military strength, but, in stark contrast to the aftermath of the Six Day War, it also produced a new mood of self-doubt and introspection throughout Israel. To some extent, self-confidence was boosted by the highly successful raid on Entebbe airport in Uganda in 1976 when Israeli forces dramatically rescued the passengers of a plane hijacked by the P.L.O. and flown to Idi Amin's blood-soaked Uganda. But the underlying questions remained.

Contrary to most expectations, the political and military climate changed dramatically and unexpectedly in the late '70s. Following the accession to power in 1977 of the Herut party, replacing a Labor party that had governed continuously since the foundation of the state, Egyptian leader Anwar Sadat expressed a genuine desire to make peace with Israel, (the irony that he was now dealing with a right wing Israeli government presided over by a former leader of the Irgun, Menachem Begin, was remarked by many). After almost 30 years of war it seemed inconceivable that any Arab leader would talk to the Israelis publicly, let alone journey to Israel and address the Knesset, the Israeli Parliament. That Sadat's action was one of great personal and political courage was made all too clear by his subsequent assassination by Muslim extremists in 1981. Nonetheless, under the auspices of the United States, Israel and Egypt hammered out a deal together—the Camp David accord—signed in 1979. Under the agreement, Israel would withdraw from Sinai; the Arabs of the West Bank and the Gaza Strip would be granted a loosely defined "autonomy"; and Israel and Egypt would normalize their relations.

Camp David unquestionably represented a major breakthrough in the long story of Arab-Israeli conflict and did much to relieve the near permanent tension of the Middle East. But that it signally failed to provide anything more than the temporary scaling down of the long term conflict can have come as no real surprise. Even as Israel completed the long-awaited hand-over of the Sinai in 1982, the violent protests of religious-nationalist extremists within Israel highlighted the growing determination of some sections of Israeli society to resist compromise with the enemy at any cost. Similarly, though Egypt may have made peace with Israel, other Arab nations, Syria and Iraq conspicuous among them, made very clear that they were not prepared to scale down their hostility toward Israel. The P.L.O., too, now based in Lebanon, had not in any way softened its position.

Lebanon and Beyond

In fact it was the bombardment by P.L.O. units in southern Lebanon of Israeli settlements in the Galilee that led to the next round of fighting when in June 1982 Israel invaded the Lebanon in an attempt to rout out permanently the P.L.O. bases there. Though initially successful, the Israelis rapidly found themselves embroiled in an enormously complex series of shifting alliances they could not hope to control, despite their military superiority. The assassination of Lebanese premier Bashir Jemayel, ostensibly a friend of Israel, and accession of his brother Amin, whose sympathies lay much more with the Syrians, signalled the final collapse of any hopes Israel may have had of emerging from Lebanon unscathed. Moreover, having taken the offensive for the first time in her brief history, and tainted by the massacre of Palestinian refugees in the Sabra and Shatilla camps by Lebanese Christians, Israel also found herself overwhelmingly condemned by the mass of world opinion. Withdrawal seemed the only option, though even this hardly went smoothly, with the Israelis under constant attack from Lebanese Shiite Muslims.

And here for the moment the story ends. Tracking the turbulent events of the Middle East is hard even for a newspaper, and lies well beyond the scope of a guide book. But there is scope for at least cautious optimism. Despite economic difficulties, Israel remains economically and militarily strong. And most important, the original spirit, vision and determination that guided the founders of the state, enabling them to return to an ancient homeland after 2,000 years of exile and establish a modern state, is still much in evidence. Nonetheless, the problems facing the country should not be underestimated: rampant inflation, a dangerous drop in foreign currency reserves, a greater willingness on the part of religious and nationalist extremists to employ violent means, and an ever-present threat from enemies in the Middle East and elsewhere.

FOOD AND WINE

Eat Your Way Around the World

Israel is perhaps the one country in the world that can be proud of the fact that it doesn't have a cuisine of its own.

Even as it reaches the ripe old age of 40, the State of Israel just hasn't had the time or the peace of mind to come up with one distinctive type of cooking that could be said to be Israeli. What you will find instead is a melange of cooking, representing the tastes of immigrants from all over the world. Every country that Jews have come from has contributed something. Add to that the cooking of the local Arabs, season it with the wonders of modern agriculture and you have the beginnings of something that no doubt will be Israeli cuisine in 100 years or so.

Meanwhile, for the visitor in particular, there is a strange and wonderful assortment of restaurants. Interestingly—if improbably (at first sight anyway)—this range of restaurants could almost be said to be a barometer of sorts of the international scene. Forget for a moment the cafes of Tel Aviv, with their mountains of whipped cream, seemingly transplanted from pre-war Vienna, let's take some more recent examples.

Take, for instance, Argentina, not a country you would generally think of in connection with Israel, let alone imagine had influenced her food. Yet before democracy was restored in Argentina, the repressive and anti-semitic military regime there sparked off a rapid increase in Jewish immigration to Israel. As a direct consequence, Argentinian grills, with leather-aproned gauchos presiding over thick steaks, have now become almost commonplace. An even more bizarre case stems from the chance discovery by an Israeli freighter of a small, overloaded boat in the open seas off Southeast Asia. On board were Vietnamese boat people, refugees with no place to go. The Israelis, remembering only too clearly a period when Jewish refugees found themselves in the same situation, offered to take them in. A number of them were ethnic Chinese, and a whole flurry of Chinese restaurants opened soon afterwards. Since then a substantial number of Chinese restaurants have sprung up in Israel, albeit with chefs from Hong Kong or Taiwan. Yet unquestionably it was the Vietnamese who originally introduced Israel to the delights of Chinese food.

Keeping Kosher

Yet though there may be no one body of cooking that can confidently be labeled Israeli, there are nonetheless a number of specific factors at play that influence food in Israel greatly. Foremost among them, of course, are the Jewish dietary laws, still widely observed. According to the Bible, several foods are forbidden, especially pork and such shellfish as shrimp or clams. But the restrictions don't stop there. There is also a Biblical injunction against cooking a kid in its mother's milk. Over the centuries, this has come to be interpreted to mean that observant Jews will not drink milk or eat any milk product with any meat, not even chicken: no veal in cream sauce, no pepperoni pizza, not even a cheeseburger. Milk and meat are not even served at the same meal, and though most Jews will eat meat shortly after milk, many wait up to seven hours after eating meat before they will touch so much as a drop of milk.

All this is called keeping kosher, and practically all of Israel's hotels are kosher, as are a good many of its restaurants. Usually, you won't even notice it, unless you're used to having cheese at the end of your meal, or until it's time for the coffee, which will either come black or with a cream substitute. What is interesting to remember is that many of the deluxe hotels have foreign chefs, whose first encounter with keeping kosher comes when they step into the kitchen of their new job. They usually start out by simply substituting; using margarine instead of butter, cream substitute for cream, smoked goose breast instead of ham. Then, the better chefs become a bit more creative. What happens, they wonder, if you use puree of avocado for a sauce? The influence of nouvelle cuisine, which in any case has often dispensed with butter and cream in the interest of making food lighter, has of course been a boon to this kind of creativity.

Yet another fundamental factor affecting Jewish cooking is the Sabbath, which begins on Friday at sunset and ends the following Saturday after sundown. No work, including cooking, may be done on the Sabbath; indeed Jews are not even allowed to light or tend a fire. There is even one Jewish sect, the Karaites, who eat only cold food on the Sabbath. But most Jews have evolved a sort of one-pot Sabbath casserole made up on Friday afternoon and left overnight in a low oven and then eaten for lunch on Saturday. Eastern European Jews called this a *cholent,* Middle Eastern Jews usually call it *hamin.*

Both the cholent or hamin nearly always include some sort of meat, starch and legume, but there the similarity ends, with Jews from different parts of the world adding their own touches. The Eastern Europeans usually use beef and potatoes with beans, and sometimes barley, while the Hungarians add a touch of paprika. North African Jews make it with chickpeas and mutton, sometimes adding steam grains of wheat. The Iraqis add a whole chicken, stuffed with rice; the Indians, hot pepper.

In the good old days, it was common to bring the dish to the village or neighborhood baker, who would keep it in his oven for you. There are many stories of mixups, in which a poor man would take home a rich man's cholent and feast on the choice cuts of meat, while the rich man would have to make do with the poor man's scraps of fat and bones. Today cholent is a regular part of the Saturday lunch time fare at most hotels in Israel and it is as often as not a melange of East and West, like much of the evolving Israeli cuisine.

There is yet another factor affecting the Jewish kitchen and that is the holiday of Pessach or Passover. Though it lasts only one week, it has a pervasive influence throughout the year. According to the Bible, when the Israelites left Egypt with Moses, they had no time to bake their bread, so they took the dough on their backs and the sun baked it into unleavened cakes. To this day many Jews eat only unleavened bread, flat, crackerlike cakes, called *matza,* instead of bread, for the entire week of the holiday. Indeed bread is usually available only in Arab areas. Hotels which keep kosher not only do not serve bread, but even ask guests not to keep bread in their rooms.

The laws of Pesach also forbid anything that might even be construed as leavening. The only cakes eaten are made with potato starch, or a flour made of ground-up matza, and eggs. Some Jews won't even eat rice or beans during the holiday. These restrictions have led to a special type of holiday cooking, generally making use of many eggs. Indeed, a number of these dishes have become popular year round. The most common are matza balls, a kind of light dumpling made with ground matza and egg and usually served in chicken soup. Many Jews pride themselves on their light matza balls, though others are said to produce a more robust variety, the kind that could injure your foot if it dropped from your spoon.

However, by no means all Jewish restaurants are kosher, and there are many that specialize in the shrimp that are found along Israel's Mediterranean and Red Sea coasts. Yet while Israeli restaurateurs are not shy about listing shrimp on their menus, they are usually more circumspect when it comes to pork. If your waiter asks if you want a "white steak," rest assured that he isn't talking about chicken.

Stuffing Your Fish

Though variety may be the key note of so much Israeli food, what is hard to find, on the other hand, are many of the dishes that Americans and Britons have come to think of as Jewish, especially things like corned beef and pastrami. True, you can find them if you look hard, but they usually aren't to be recommended. In fact, the owner of an Israeli delicatessen, asked whether his corned beef was any good, replied with a question.

"How long have you been here?" he asked. When told, "six months," he answered that this wasn't long enough. It was only after a year away from the real thing that his corned beef tasted any good. But to be fair, there have been improvements in recent years; the influence of English-speaking immigrants is making itself felt.

Other dishes found in "Jewish" restaurants in the United States and Britain are more readily available, although in far greater profusion in Tel Aviv than, say, Jerusalem. This is no mystery once you realize that the population of Tel Aviv is largely made up of descendents of the same Eastern European Jews who also went to England and the U.S. in the 19th century, while Jerusalem has a far greater percentage of Middle Eastern Jews, for whom *gefilte* fish is as foreign as a ham sandwich.

Gefilte fish (literally, stuffed fish) is, of course, one of the specialties of Eastern Europe where fish was a must for the Sabbath eve and poor Jews couldn't always afford enough for the whole family. The resulting product ranges from anything from a sort of boiled fish cake in which bread outweighs fish, two to one, to a very elegant dish in which the skin of an entire fish is emptied out, to be restuffed with a mixture of several kinds of fish, sometimes flavored with chopped almonds and gently poached in a broth made from the fish bones. Gefilte fish can be either "Polish," which means fairly sweet, or "Lithuanian," which is spicy. It is almost always served with a sauce of grated horseradish and beets which can be quite sharp at times.

Other typical Eastern European specialties include *kreplach,* the Jewish answer to ravioli or wontons, and *blintzes,* which are similar to crepes. These are often served with a sweet cheese or fruit filling, or chopped liver and roast goose and duck. Moving slowly west through Europe, we come to Hungary and dishes such as goulash and chicken paprikash, and to Vienna and, of course, schnitzel. It is only fair to warn the unwary, however, that a schnitzel in Israel is usually made from a slice of turkey breast rather than veal, unless the menu says otherwise.

Romania, too, has had quite an influence on Israeli cooking, and a visit to one of the country's many Romanian restaurants will be especially welcome to the meat lover. These are the places to try steaks, lovingly grilled over hot coals. Here a meal might start with a sour soup, or *chorba,* brimming with fresh vegetables and little meatballs, a bit of pickled carp, or the ubiquitous pickled herring. Another Romanian specialty is *irka,* a poor man's caviar made with herring roe.

Heading south again through Europe, the Balkan countries have had a very specific influence on Israel's cooking through the Sephardic Jews, many of whom settled in the Balkans following their expulsion from Spain in 1492. They preserved much of the medieval culture of Spain—and actually spoke an ancient form of Spanish, Ladino, until about a generation ago. Yet while some Sephardic dishes are clearly

Spanish in origin, others equally show the influence of Slavic Balkan food, while yet others are Turkish, a heritage of the Ottoman Empire that once spanned the region. You'll find salty cheese pastries, *bourekas,* on special stands throughout the country, while Sephardic restaurants specialize in vegetables stuffed with rice or meat and combinations such as chicken with prunes.

Middle Eastern Specialties

It is in fact difficult to distinguish between Balkan food, Middle Eastern Jewish food and that of the local Arabs. It's important to remember that until a little over 50 years ago the entire area was one political unit with much cultural interplay. Thus, many different kinds of Israeli restaurants serve *shishlik,* small pieces of lamb, beef or even turkey threaded on a spit and grilled over charcoal. A similar dish, kebab, is made with spiced chopped meat. Another dish common to the whole of the Middle East is *Majadra,* rice cooked with lentils and flavored with fried onions. In the more simple Middle Eastern restaurants it is not uncommon to see people making a lunch of rice, over which a few cooked beans have been poured for flavoring, with or without a few meatballs on the side.

With such a wide area of influence from which to draw, the variation of stuffed vegetables is virtually endless. Peppers, cabbage, vine leaves and zucchini squash are among the more common varieties, but you can also find stuffed carrots and radishes, not to mention artichokes, apples and pears. When well-made, a selection of stuffed vegetables is a true *tour de force,* each with a different filling and cooked in its own special sauce.

Nor, while considering Middle Eastern influences, should those two staples of any Israeli kitchen be omitted: felafel and houmus. Felafel consists of balls of ground chickpeas, deep fried and served inside pitta bread with a sauce of tehina, or ground sesame seed, plus a salad of chopped tomatoes and cucumbers, a pickle, and, if you like, hot pepper sauce. Indeed this is the perfect fast food lunch, a magnificently balanced vegetarian meal, with the chickpeas and bread providing the protein, the vegetables and tehina providing the vitamins, and no cholesterol to speak of. So popular is the felafel the P.L.O. once complained to the U.N. that the Israelis had stolen the Palestinian national dish. The Israelis just laughed and kept munching. Houmus, that other Middle Eastern favorite, is a thick paste made with mashed cooked chickpeas and served on a plate with a little tehina and olive oil. Just tear off a piece of the pitta bread and dunk it in the houmus.

A good Middle Eastern restaurant, Arab or Jewish, will often serve houmus as just one of about a dozen different little salad dishes, the whole comprizing a *meze* (from the Latin word *mensa,* meaning table), a delightful *hors d'oeuvre.* Other typical items are eggplant salad, with tehina, oil and lemon, or mayonnaise; cooked carrots flavored with cumin; pickled mushrooms; braised green peppers; tomatoes and cucumbers with *burghul,* a kind of cracked wheat; and Swiss chard, or spinach, in a lemon sauce.

Again, the cultural interplay goes beyond political borders and at least some of the items in a meze will be North African, even if the restaurant owner is from the Balkans or is a local Arab. Indeed Moroccan, Algerian and Tunisian foods are among the best in Israel, combining as they do Arabic, French and a dash of Sephardic cooking to boot. The staple North African dish is cous-cous, fluffy steamed grains of semolina, served with a thick soup of meat and vegetables poured over it. Other North African dishes worth trying are liver with olives, tongue in a raisin sauce and fish steak baked in a hot pepper sauce.

France has had a predictable influence on Israeli food, and you'll find a fair sprinkling of French restaurants here. They range in quality from the very poor to those whose proprietors make a valiant, and sometimes even successful, attempt to provide honest cooking. About the only thing the two have in common is the price, which is uniformly high. A few hints are all we can provide. Just remember that if goose liver pâté is on the menu, it will almost certainly be fresh. The asparagus will almost invariably come from a can, unless the waiter tells you otherwise. Generally, you can be sure that the fish will be good, as it will be almost anywhere in Israel, though some visitors seem to get upset by the sight of a whole fish staring up at them from their plate. If it bothers you, make sure in advance what sort of fish you're getting. Finally, remember that if the restaurant has a view this, and not the food, will be what you're paying for.

Local Specialties

Of course, not all Israeli food is the legacy of immigration, even if it can seem that way at times. The availability of locally-produced food is a vital factor in the development of any national cuisine. And in Israel this means above all fresh fruit, vegetables and dairy products. Looking down any listing of Israeli restaurants you will find at least some listed as "dairy" or "vegetarian." One reason for their popularity is the influence of the dietary laws (remember that kosher restaurants cannot serve meat and milk together). But equally important is that the Israelis themselves are exceedingly partial to light meals that make creative use of vegetables and cheeses, a preference made all the more reasonable by the country's long, hot summers. These two factors allied to the superabundance of fresh fruits and vegetables in Israel go a long way toward explaining the proliferation of salads, often with half the kitchen thrown in, in many restaurants and homes throughout the country.

Another Israeli product that deserves special emphasis is goose liver. In fact it is a badly kept secret that a large percentage of the goose liver sold in France comes from Israel. Fancier Israeli restaurants—and sometimes not so fancy—often make their own goose liver pâté, which, despite the cost, is worth trying at least once: it can be excellent. You'll also find that grill restaurants sometimes have a spit of cubed goose liver on the menu. But perhaps the best goose liver this writer has ever tasted was in a Hungarian restaurant, just lightly fried in goose fat, a true culinary delight.

The Israeli breakfast can also claim to be a genuine local specialty. It traces its origins back to kibbutzim, where members would sit down to breakfast at about eight having already put in a few hours' work in the fields. Hotel guests might find it wise to take a swim in the pool before facing a similar gargantuan feast.

It begins, of course, with orange juice (all but the cheapest Israeli hotels are required by law to serve fresh orange juice while oranges are in season). Usually there's grapefruit as well. Then you might like some hot or cold cereal and a few eggs, boiled, scrambled or fried. That's just the beginning. A full buffet awaits you, with perhaps two kinds of pickled herring and some sardines or smoked fish on the side. A blue cheese competes for your attention with Swiss cheese, but you might like some of that cottage cheese or that cheese and dill spread. And, for a change, why not some of those delicious, juicy sliced tomatoes or cucumbers, and a little helping of those grated carrots? With it, why don't you have some fresh rolls, or sweet roll or two, or some toast and some jam or honey? Don't miss the yoghurt, it comes in three flavors and you'd better try them all to see which you like best. It's no wonder that half the hotel guests walk out of the dining room with their pockets bulging. It's not that they want to save money on lunch, it's just that they haven't been able to taste everything.

Wine

Vastly underrated, Israeli wines have had to battle with an image that does them far less than justice. They have suffered principally because it is the country's sickly sweet wines, which many Jews the world over choose to drink on ceremonial occasions, that are most frequently sold abroad. But even if you can't get good, dry Israeli wines at home, there is no reason why you shouldn't enjoy the respectable, albeit less than vast, selection available in Israel itself.

Though many ancient grape presses are to be seen around the country, the modern Israeli wine industry dates only from the 19th century. It owes its beginnings to the Baron Edmond de Rothschild. As a Frenchman, he quite naturally thought that if the Jews were to become tillers of the soil, they should also press their own grapes. Accordingly, he sent the early Jewish pioneers some of his best stock.

It has been an uphill struggle though. Israel may have a near ideal climate for growing grapes, but the Israelis have never really taken to wine drinking. Even today in a good restaurant you can ask the waitress what red wine is available only to have a blank look appear on her face. She will come back, her face wreathed in smiles, as she tells you, "rosé."

Indeed, though Israeli rosé tends to be quite drinkable, it is served far more often than it might be simply because restaurateurs and hoteliers are often themselves not sure which wine to serve and have been told that, "rosé goes with everything." That doesn't make the wine any worse, but it has overexposed it.

As in many other countries, the better wines in Israel are labeled according to varieties, or the kind of grape from which the wine was made. Labels often also indicate the region where the grapes were grown. Among the common geographical descriptions are: Galil, meaning Galilee; Samson, indicating the foothills west of Jerusalem; and Dan, the coastal plain.

Among the varieties you are most likely to encounter is Cabernet Sauvignon, a rich, full-bodied red wine with a pleasant aftertaste. It is considered the best of the local red wines and some companies have put aside some of their best Cabernet Sauvignon to be sold under the label "special reserve."

Lighter than the Cabernet Sauvignon, but often with a pleasing bouquet, is the Carignan, a wine that many restaurants have chosen as their house wine, to be sold by the carafe or the glass. A newcomer on the market is the Petite Sirah. This is lighter still and could with impunity be chilled and savored with fish or chicken, although most restaurant owners will think you're committing blasphemy.

As for vintages, this is less of a factor in Israel than in most European countries where summers, specifically the amount of sunshine, are variable. Because there is sun all summer long, year in and year out, and because the grapes are in any case irrigated, wines are apt to be of an even quality every year. On the other hand, this surfeit of sun can affect grapes for white wine which can lose their aroma if they become overripe. It is only in more recent years that vintners have learned that they must pick their grapes before they are fully ripe if they want the best white wines.

The most common white wine is the Sauvignon, generally a very dry wine. Others prefer the Semillon, a little less dry and a little lighter, or the Chenin Blanc, which is a semi-dry wine and has a very full aroma. A fruity, almost sweet wine, which many enjoy, is the Emerald Reisling.

Carmel, the cooperative started by the Baron, is still going strong and is by far the largest in the country. But there are other labels worth looking for, among them Montfort, Ashkelon and Ben Ami. Two monasteries also produce wine, Cremisan and Latrun; their best red wines are worth trying.

Meanwhile, despite it all, we mustn't forget the rosé, the best of which is sold under the Grenache label.

Wine lovers should not miss a visit to the Carmel cellars either in Rishon Lezion or Zichron Yaakov, where a tour is combined with wine tasting. The Cremisan and Latrun Monasteries both have shops on the premises where you can taste the wine.

JERUSALEM

The Eternal City

"Jerusalem is the center of the world," declares a Renaissance Christian map showing the continents of Asia, Africa, and Europe as the leaves of a clover meeting in the Holy City. "The world is like a human eye," declaims a Jewish sage of the first century A.D., "the white is the ocean which girds the earth, the iris is the earth upon which we dwell, the pupil is Jerusalem, and the image therein is the Temple of the Lord." "The Rock of the Temple," a Muslim tradition relates, "is made of the stones of the Garden of Eden, and on the day of Resurrection the holy Kaaba stone of Mecca will come to Jerusalem to be joined with it." A source of inspiration for poets and prophets, and object of centuries' yearnings, Jerusalem is holy to one-third of the world's population.

Today it is a modern, upbeat city of almost half-a-million inhabitants. Its citizens are a fiercely patriotic breed looking down their collective noses at the "soulless" metropolis of Tel Aviv on the coast. The compliments are returned, of course. Tel Avivians disdainfully regard Jerusalem as a provincial town, interesting to visit as long as you're back where the action is by nightfall. Like many such generalizations, it is not without a kernel of truth. The city is never likely to rival the nightclubs, discos, bars, and restaurants of Tel Aviv, though it has some, of course, and good eating places in Jerusalem have multiplied greatly in recent years. But for sheer visual excitement, a heady surge of history, the powerful emotional vibrations of different religious groups, and, simply, a view of the human mosaic, Jerusalem is in a class by itself.

Since the reunification of the city in 1967, Jerusalem has been in a frenzy of development: spacious neighborhoods ring the city limits, commercial high-rises and luxury hotels abound, parks and gardens have proliferated. More than anything, Jerusalem has grown into its role as the capital of the modern State of Israel. And yet it remains intimate. Surprises await one around every corner in the Old City. 19th-century neighborhoods on the west side of town seem to have been left behind in the scurry towards the end of the 20th. Quiet moments under a pine or olive tree taking in a sweeping view from one of Jerusalem's many hills linger in one's memory long after the snapshots have become dog-eared.

A Glance at History

Recent archeological excavations give Jerusalem an age of about 5,000 years, making it one of the oldest continuously-inhabited cities in the world. By the 20th century B.C., it was important enough to be cursed in Egyptian "hate texts." Is it to be identified with the city of Salem of Abraham's time? We do not know for sure, but it was conquered by Joshua's tribes, and then made the capital of the Kingdom of a united Israel by David in 1000 B.C. Solomon the Wise built the Temple to the Lord in it. Following his death, and the division of the kingdom, it remained the capital of the south, the Kingdom of Judah, for three-and-a-half centuries. It saw days of glory and of degradation; it heard the thundering remonstrances of Isaiah and Jeremiah; and eventually, in 587 B.C., it was put to the torch by the Babylonians and the Temple razed to the ground. "We wept," wrote the Psalmist, "as we remembered Zion." Jerusalem—Zion—the City of David—continued to hold captive the hearts of its children even when they were in exile.

Those who returned from exile rebuilt the Temple, and ever-so-slowly the city revived. By the first century B.C. it was again an important and vibrant Jewish capital. Herod the Great made it a cosmopolis as well, face-lifting the Temple, adding palaces, fortresses, and Roman-style cultural institutions, and expanding the city area. That was the Jerusalem Jesus knew a generation later, a city thronged with people from many lands. Here he met his fate at the hands of the country's Roman masters. It was against those same Romans that the Jews revolted several times, the Great Revolt of A.D. 66–70 ending, again, in the destruction of both the Temple and of Jerusalem itself. It was redesigned by Emperor Hadrian in the second century A.D. as a pagan Roman city, Aelia Capitolina, an urban plan that shaped the Old City of today. Then, under the Christian Byzantines, Jerusalem regained something of its status, the repair and expansion of the city being accompanied by a wave of church building.

Except for a brief surge of attention under the Ummayads (late-7th and early-8th centuries A.D.), Jerusalem was merely a provincial town

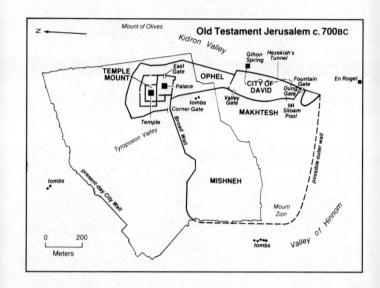

Old Testament Jerusalem c. 700 BC

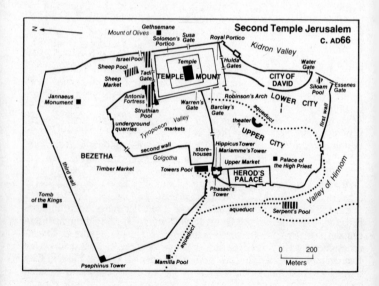

Second Temple Jerusalem c. AD 66

in the vast Muslim empires of the early Middle Ages. For almost all the 12th century, the Crusaders made it the capital of their Latin Kingdom, but soon it fell back into a languid provincialism under the Mamluks and Turks. Allenby's conquest of the Holy City in 1917 put it back on the map again, at least as far as the West was concerned.

For a city whose name traditionally means City of Peace, Jerusalem's history has often been written in blood. A rough calculation shows Jerusalem has endured well over 30 conquests.

West and East

The 1948 Arab–Israeli war left Jerusalem a divided city. A winding armistice line split the city in two: West Jerusalem (also called New Jerusalem, or Jewish Jerusalem) in the Israeli sector, and East Jerusalem (known as Old Jerusalem or Arab Jerusalem) in the Jordanian sector. Almost all the Holy City's religious sites, sacred to Christians, Jews, and Muslims alike, lay in East Jerusalem. Mount Zion was the only exception.

For 19 years, the only link between the two parts of the city was the Mandelbaum Gate, where non-Jewish tourists could make a one-time crossing (the Jordanian authorities did not permit re-entry into Israel, nor re-entry into Jordan, if the tourists made the crossing from there). Ironically, the Jordanians themselves triggered the city's reunification when they bombarded West Jerusalem on June 5, 1967. Two days later, East Jerusalem was in Israeli hands after some of the bitterest fighting of the Six Day War.

Yet despite its reunification in 1967, the differences between the two parts of the city persist. Even in hotels, the tourist will find the atmosphere subtly Jewish in West Jerusalem, Arab in East Jerusalem. Jews and Arabs mix freely during business hours and, for the most part, treat each other with utmost courtesy, but there is hardly any social contact between the two groups.

The terms East and West Jerusalem are as much political as geographic. Thus, no one would refer to the new Jewish neighborhoods built by the Israelis in formerly Jordanian-controlled areas as East Jerusalem. On the other hand, Mount Zion, which is south of the Old City, is often considered West Jerusalem because it was in Israeli hands before 1967.

WEST JERUSALEM

Except for the occasional walled monastery, nobody lived outside the Old City walls before 1860. In that year Sir Moses Montefiore, an English Jewish philanthropist, founded Mishkenot Sha'ananim, Dwellings of Tranquility, the first housing development to help relieve the congestion and poverty of the Jewish Quarter in the Old City. But as settling anywhere outside the security of the city walls—the gates were locked at night—was considered an insane invitation to bandits and thieves, initially he had few takers for his offer of free apartments. Eventually, however, the idea caught on, and by 1888 there were ten Jewish neighborhoods west and northwest of the Old City.

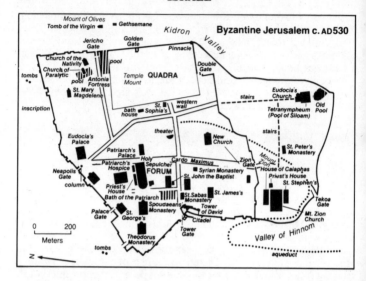

Looking west across the Hinnom Valley from Mount Zion, Montefiore's original long crenellated building is readily identifiable. Looming above it is his famous windmill, intended originally to serve the milling needs of the new communities. Its unfortunate location—not enough wind!—doomed it to become an historic landmark only. The windmill's interior is now an interesting small museum, but Montefiore's opulent carriage, used in 1894 and once on display nearby, was recently destroyed by fire. The old housing development is now a beautifully appointed guest house for visiting artists, writers, and musicians, and is run by the Jerusalem Foundation. Alongside is Yemin Moshe, a posh, red-roofed neighborhood including the homes and studios of many artists.

Going Downtown

A ten-minute walk up Jaffa Road from the Jaffa Gate, or 15 minutes by foot from Yemin Moshe and the King David Hotel, takes you to the heart of West Jerusalem. The downtown area is centered on a triangle made up of King George Street, Jaffa Road (the main thoroughfare), and Ben-Yehuda Street (now almost entirely a pedestrians-only area). At the meeting point of Jaffa Road and Ben-Yehuda Street is Zion Square. Ben-Yehuda Street's open-air mall (the *midrahov* in Hebrew) is a new development that was viewed with suspicion and anxiety by shop-owners in the area when first mooted. But their fears have proved groundless. It's become a magnet for Jerusalemites, and virtually throughout the year it's a great place to sit over coffee and a pastry and watch the passing parade.

Off Zion Square is the narrow Salomon Street, and off that a maze of alleyways with a collection of old houses and courtyards, a bric-a-brac shop, an artist's studio, and a restaurant or two. This is Nahalat Shiva, one of the earliest of the 19th-century neighborhoods. There are plans to renovate the quarter.

A half-kilometer up Jaffa Road is Mahane Yehuda (literally, Judah's Camp), another old neighborhood dating from 1888, which boasts this side of the city's food market. It is a colorful alley of superb fruit and vegetables, all at low prices. Interspersed with the tomato-green-pepper-cucumber stalls and the pear-apple-persimmon stalls, are fish stores, butchers' shops, cheeses-and-pickles stalls, felafel stands, and so on. The busiest days are Thursdays and Fridays when Jerusalem's householders stock up for the Sabbath when everything on this side of town is closed.

A Bastion of Zealotry

Recent years have seen a hardening of the lines dividing the devoutly religious from the more progressive and secular segments of the Jewish community in Israel. The ultra-orthodox have often been up in arms about one religious issue or another: autopsies; violation of the Sabbath religious laws prohibiting driving a car; and the claim that archeologists (in Jerusalem) and building contractors (in Tiberias) are excavating and desecrating ancient cemeteries. Nowhere are these issues hotter, or reactions fiercer, than in Mea She'arim.

The neighborhood was founded at a meeting of prospective settlers and supporters in November 1873, though the foundation stone was only laid the following year. The Torah (Five Books of Moses) is read in the synagogue over the course of a year, a successive portion each week. On the week of their historic decision the Torah contained the auspicious passage (Genesis 26:12): "And Isaac sowed in that land, and reaped in the same year a hundredfold. The Lord blessed him." The Biblical Hebrew phrase for "a hundredfold" is *mea she'arim*, and so the community was named.

Enter Mea She'arim and you enter a different world, the world of the Eastern European Jewish ghetto of the 18th and 19th centuries, a world that has long since disappeared elsewhere. Men in black broad-brimmed hats and long black coats hurry past purposefully—nobody strolls in Mea She'arim—their eyes intense and unseeing. Here and there a couple of men are deep in conversation, perhaps debating some fine point of Talmud, absently stroking their beards or twirling their long side-curls *(peyis)*. Some of the men may be wearing white stockings and black breeches gathered below the knee, a style preserved from 18th-century Poland and favored by some Hassidic sects. On the Sabbath and holidays, and the eves thereof, these same men will replace their black hats with *shtreimels*, flat, round fur hats. One explanation for this is that in Poland at one time the Jews were forced to wear a piece of animal fur as a badge of shame, but with characteristic ingenuity they turned the insult around by making the fur into a noble headgear.

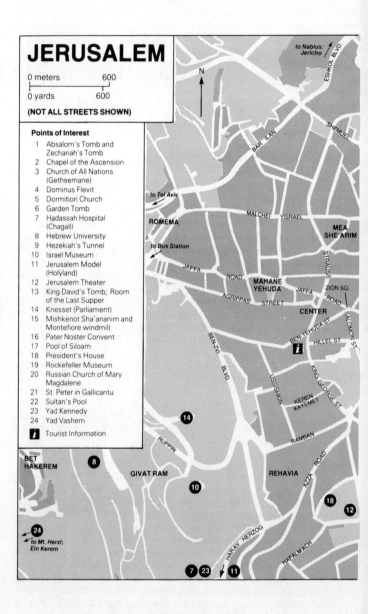

JERUSALEM

0 meters 600

0 yards 600

(NOT ALL STREETS SHOWN)

Points of Interest

1. Absalom's Tomb and Zechariah's Tomb
2. Chapel of the Ascension
3. Church of All Nations (Gethsemane)
4. Dominus Flevit
5. Dormition Church
6. Garden Tomb
7. Hadassah Hospital (Chagall)
8. Hebrew University
9. Hezekiah's Tunnel
10. Israel Museum
11. Jerusalem Model (Holyland)
12. Jerusalem Theater
13. King David's Tomb; Room of the Last Supper
14. Knesset (Parliament)
15. Mishkenot Sha'ananim and Montefiore windmill
16. Pater Noster Convent
17. Pool of Siloam
18. President's House
19. Rockefeller Museum
20. Russian Church of Mary Magdalene
21. St. Peter in Gallicantu
22. Sultan's Pool
23. Yad Kennedy
24. Yad Vashem

i Tourist Information

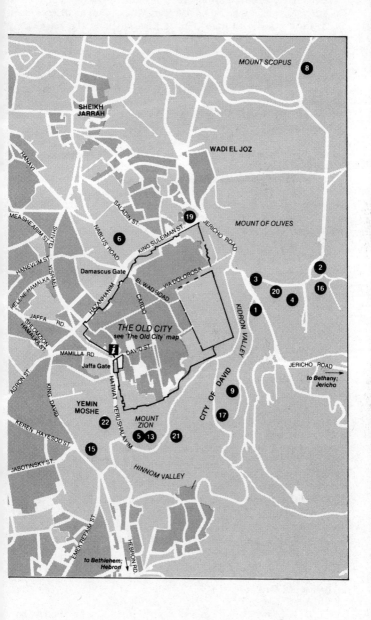

The women dress in puritanical manner: long sleeves, high collars, long dresses or skirts, and non-sheer stockings. Many married women shave their heads and wear a tight kerchief or a wig; once safely married, the thinking runs, they have no more use for a good head of hair which might only attract the glances of other men and inspire impure thoughts.

Very young children play here as very young children will, with laughter and tears and squealing. But they grow up quickly, absorbed at an early age into the sober, even somber, atmosphere, the boys into the world of scholarship, the girls (though they do go to school) into the responsibilities of the home.

The time to be in Mea She'-arim is on Friday when the whole community is preparing for *Shabbos,* the Sabbath. Men hurry home from the *mikveh,* the ritual bath, towels over their arms. Women shop from the market stalls. Kids stand in line at the bakery. (Incidentally, on Mea She'arim Street—the main vehicle thoroughfare—you will find one of Jerusalem's best bakeries.) To this day there is also a communal oven, dating from the pre-electricity era. Even now families without electric ovens will leave their dishes or bread at the communal oven to be baked, for a small fee.

As the Sabbath begins—a half-hour before sunset—the community, so to speak, gives a collective sigh, all work ceases, and for the next 25 hours (until nightfall on Saturday), total tranquility reigns. The roads are blocked to traffic, and any curious visitor toting a camera would be as welcome as the plague.

A stroll around the quarter, and its adjacent daughter communities, sometimes brings dividends. But a strong word of caution: Mea She' arim tolerates no exceptions to its strict dress codes and Sabbath observance. Posters stuck on many walls, and a banner across the main street, proclaim: "Jewish Daughter—The Torah obligates you to dress with modesty. We do not tolerate people passing through our streets immodestly dressed—Committee for Guarding Modesty." And this means behavior, too. It is considered unseemly to show affection in public, and a couple holding hands will draw opprobrium.

For years now a tiny but vociferous extremist group within the quarter, the Neturei Karta, an Aramaic term for the Guardians of the City, have daubed the quarter's walls with slogans (in English, for the benefit of the visitor) decrying Zionism and the State of Israel as anti-Jewish phenomena. Speaking Yiddish rather than the "holy" language of Hebrew, they see themselves living in the Holy City of Jerusalem and the *Land* of Israel, but a Jewish *state* that is not run in strict accordance with the prescriptions of the Torah is, to them, a contradiction in terms, and full political redemption should anyway await the coming of the Messiah.

The Israel Museum

Eclectic is a word that might well describe the Museum's collection, though this is not to say that it is merely fragmentary. Some of its exhibits are among the best of their kind in the world, and a visit could take you from ancient archeology or the Dead Sea Scrolls to a scientific exhibit, a heavily adorned Yemenite Jewish wedding dress, a painting by Picasso, a South Pacific mask, or a photographic series by Vishniac.

Opened in 1965 on a 22-acre plot on West Jerusalem's Givat Ram, the complex is divided into several different sections. The most striking edifice is a white, dome-like structure. This is the Shrine of the Book, which houses the famous Dead Sea Scrolls, perhaps the most spectacular find ever made in this region. The first of the Scrolls were discovered in 1947 in a cave near the Dead Sea by a Beduin boy looking for a stray goat. The subsequent tale of how the Scrolls eventually reached their resting place here is one of adventure and intrigue in the best Hollywood tradition. The shape of the dome-like building was inspired by that of the lids of the clay jars in which the Scrolls were first found.

The Scrolls were the work of a breakaway Jewish sect in the Second Temple period, generally identified as the Essenes. Their almost monastic community of Qumran (as it is known today) was wiped out by the Romans in A.D. 68, giving us a terminus date for the Scrolls. In fact, both paleographic and laboratory evidence indicate that they were written as early as 100 B.C.

In an outstanding state of preservation because of the intense dryness of the Dead Sea region, the Scrolls include the oldest manuscripts of the Hebrew Bible—the Old Testament—ever found, and their similarity to Hebrew texts in use today has confirmed the latter's authenticity. Many of the Scrolls are sectarian works of the Essenes, speaking of their way of life, their interpretations of the Bible and current events, and of their vision of an imminent "end of time" when they, the "Sons of Light," would defeat the "Sons of Darkness" and usher in a Messianic Age. Christian visitors are often intrigued by the suggestion that John the Baptist may have been a member of this strict ascetic community.

Part of the exhibit is devoted to later letters and documents (on parchment and papyrus), and to artifacts discovered in the '50s in other caves of the Judean Desert. The Bar-Kochba Revolt against the Romans was suppressed by the Emperor Hadrian in A.D. 135, and many Jews fleeing from the Roman legionaries sought refuge in these almost inaccessible caves in sheer desert canyons. They sometimes took their prize possessions with them—legal documents, personal effects, a glass bowl of stunning modernity—in the hope, the vain hope as it turned out, that they would survive to enjoy them again.

Just beyond the Shrine of the Book is the Billy Rose Sculpture Garden, designed by the Japanese landscape architect Isamu Noguchi. Rose, the great New York showman, was an art collector on a grand scale, and bequeathed his collection to the Israel Museum. Rodin, Henry Moore, and Daumier rub shoulders (so to speak) with lesser luminaries and more esoteric works, and the total effect, taking into account the magnificent view as well, is terrific.

The main buildings of the Museum, an interplay of white cubes by Israeli architects Mansfeld and Gad, contain all the other sections. As one progresses through the vast and fascinating Archeology exhibit from the Early Stone Age of, say, half-a-million years ago, to the Middle Ages just a few centuries back, one can marvel at the skill of ancient craftsmen: Prehistoric cult objects, Canaanite pottery, Philistine weapons, Israelite altars.

The art exhibit—once the independent Bezalel National Museum of Art—while modest in scope, contains many interesting pieces by Israeli artists, and Europeans such as Rembrandt, Picasso, Chagall, Soutine, and Miró. Features of this section include a faithfully restored 17th-century Venetian synagogue, a 19th-century German *sukkah* (a booth used for the Jewish Feast of Tabernacles), and period rooms from France and England. The Israel Museum's collection of Judaica (Jewish ceremonial art) is regarded as the finest in the world, though only part of its great collection is on public display. A new Ethnography Department exhibit shows family life in different Jewish ethnic traditions. The list of galleries is completed by those devoted to ancient coins, graphics, the excellent and active Youth Wing, and changing exhibits of art, photography, technology, and so on. A store and cafeteria serve the Museum.

Unrelated to the Museum, but standing among the olive groves in the valley below, is the massive fortress-like Monastery of the Cross, an incongruous curiosity amid the ultra-modern public buildings and condominiums. The monastery was founded by the Byzantines, but the present structure is medieval, and passed from Georgian to Greek Orthodox control in the 17th century. Tradition relates that here grew the tree from which the cross of Jesus was made. Only recently reopened to the public, the serene courtyards and stone-arched rooms of the monastery seem to block out the world beyond the walls. The church, the frescoes, the small museum, the view from the roof, and—yes—the charm of the English-speaking priest (at time of writing) all make a visit worthwhile.

"Masters of Their Own Fate": the Knesset

"Take two Israelis," the saying goes, "and you have three political parties!" To be sure, it often seems that way. Israel's parliamentary system of proportional representation may be particularly democratic —a party gaining just one per cent of the national vote is eligible for its first seat—but it produces a plethora of political groupings vying with each other every four years for the blessings of the electorate. Meanwhile, the ones already "blessed" debate, often tumultuously, the weighty affairs of state, and in their collective wisdom legislate the country's future.

The place where all this takes place is the Knesset, Israel's parliament, a modern, flat-roofed building across the way from the Israel Museum. Both its name and the number of its members (120) derive from *Haknesset Hagedola*, the Great Assembly of the Second Temple period. It moved to its present home in 1966.

On Monday and Thursday mornings free tours are available in most major languages, the highlights of which are the Session Hall, and Marc Chagall's three magnificent tapestries on the themes of Creation,

Exodus, and Jerusalem. (Bring your passport, and expect thorough security checks.) When the Knesset is in session, you may watch from the visitor's gallery. The sessions are, of course, conducted in Hebrew.

Outside the entrance of the Knesset is an eternal flame in honor of Israel's fallen soldiers in its various wars. Both the wrought-iron work enclosing the flame, and the outer gates of the Knesset complex were the work of the late Israeli artist David Polombo. Over the road from the main gates is a huge bronze *Menorah,* the seven-branched candelabra which is Israel's national symbol. A gift from the British Parliament in 1956, the Menorah displays events in Jewish history from Moses to the present day. The Hebrew inscription along the outer arms comes from the prophet Zechariah: "Not by might nor by power but by my Spirit says the Lord of Hosts."

Memorial to Six Million

The special Law of the Knesset which established the institution of Yad Vashem in 1953, gave it a mandate "to gather in to the homeland material regarding all those members of the Jewish people who laid down their lives, who fought and rebelled against the Nazi enemy and his collaborators, and to perpetuate their memory and that of the communities, organizations and institutions which were destroyed because they were Jewish."

Yad Vashem has done just that. Its Holocaust archives are the largest in the world (it was Yad Vashem that provided the evidence that convicted Adolf Eichmann in 1961). Through its museum and educational programs for youth, it tells the story of the annihilation of the Jews of Europe; by its very existence, it stands as an everlasting memorial (literally, *yad vashem* in the words of the prophet Isaiah) to those six million Jews massacred by the Nazis in World War II.

The Avenue of the Righteous leading from the parking lot to the museum is lined with carob trees, each marked with a plaque displaying the name and country of origin of a Gentile who risked (and sometimes lost) his or her life harboring Jews or aiding their escape.

The main museum displays archival photographs, mostly taken by the Nazis themselves, accompanied by full commentary in Hebrew and English. It begins (in the hall on the right) with Hitler's accession to power in 1933, and traces the events of the following 12 nightmare years. In the same building are the Hall of Names, which has thus far gathered biographical information on over three million victims of the Holocaust, and the Art Museum, a simultaneously wrenching and beautiful display of painting and sculpture by artists who perished (some works, incredibly, were done in, and then smuggled out of, the concentration camps themselves).

Leaving the museum on the upper level, one can cross the courtyard to the Hall of Remembrance, a heavy, brooding building of basalt and concrete, to pause a moment before leaving the site. Various impressive sculptures around the site await the unrushed visitor.

The experience of the Holocaust is so deeply seared into the national memory that understanding it goes a long way to understanding the

Jewish people themselves. It is not by chance that Yad Vashem is a mandatory stop on the itineraries of most State visitors.

A Scale Model of the City

Located adjacent to the Holyland Hotel West in the Bayit Vegan neighborhood, a huge model depicts Jerusalem as it was on the eve of the Great Revolt against the Romans in A.D. 66. Its scale of 1:50 means that two centimeters on the model represents one meter in reality, or roughly a quarter inch to the foot. Designed in the '50s by the prominent archeologist, the late Michael Avi-Yonah, it represents a city about twice the area of the Old City of today.

Many remains of the ancient city depicted here have been unearthed, and can be seen by the visitor in and around the Old City—the Western Wall of the Temple Mount, Josephus' "First Wall," the so-called David's Citadel area, and the Pools of Bethesda and Siloam, to name just a few. The focal point of the model is the Temple, as indeed it was of the city itself in its day. Reconstructed by Herod the Great where the Dome of the Rock now stands, it was a century in building, and soon gained a reputation as one of the wonders of the world. "He who has never seen Jerusalem in her glory," it was said in those days, "has never seen a beautiful city in his life." Recorded explanations in English are available at locations around the model.

The Western Edge

The beautifully landscaped memorial park of Mount Herzl is dedicated to Theodor Herzl, the founder of the modern Zionist Movement, whose tomb is at its summit. A biographical museum that includes a reconstruction of Herzl's study is on the site. Among other national leaders buried here are ex-prime ministers Golda Meir and Levi Eshkol. Israel's main military cemetery is adjacent.

Hadassah Hospital is a further ten minutes' drive at the end of the same road as Mount Herzl. This huge general hospital (and teaching hospital for the Hebrew University's medical and dental schools) was opened in 1962 to replace the original building on Mount Scopus, cut off by the armistice line of 1949. Hadassah, the American women's Zionist organization that built the place, commissioned artist Marc Chagall to design the windows for its synagogue. He was delighted to contribute, and refused any personal fee for the work. The results were stunning. The 12 stained-glass windows reflect in brilliant colors Jacob's blessings on his sons, and those of Moses on the tribes of Israel. They are well worth a visit (public tours in the mornings).

A left fork on the way to Hadassah takes you via Ora and Aminadav to Yad Kennedy, the Kennedy Memorial. Conceived in 1965 as a re-afforestation project in honor of the late American president, the memorial was dedicated a year later on the hill-top around which the forest was planted. Built with a series of concrete struts, each bearing the seal of an American state, the memorial from afar looks like the stump of a tree cut down in its prime. Inside is a bust of John F. Kennedy and a memorial flame.

In the valley between Mount Herzl and Hadassah Hospital lies Ein Kerem, a slow-moving, picturesque village of stone houses and a spring. Although now part of a much-expanded Jerusalem, the small, ancient village was remote from the city of its day. Tradition identifies it as the birth-place of John the Baptist, though its name is not mentioned in the New Testament. The large, orange-roofed Franciscan church dominating the village center is built over the supposed grotto of St. John's birth, apparently already enshrined by the Byzantines in the 5th century A.D. Its beautiful old paintings and glazed tiles are worth a visit. The path beyond the spring on the opposite side of the village climbs the hill, passes a Russian convent, and reaches the two-story Church of the Visitation (also Franciscan) where, it is said, Mary of Nazareth visited her cousin Elizabeth during the latter's pregnancy. Today, Ein Kerem's population is an odd mix of artists and ethnics.

THE OLD CITY

The focal point of a visit to Jerusalem is the Old City, the area of about one square kilometer (some 220 acres) within the 16th-century Turkish walls. You can find in the Old City both a cross-section of the country's history and a microcosm of Israel today. Within this bustling walled area can be seen Old Testament fortifications, Hasmonean towers, Herodian walls, Roman arches, Byzantine columns, Arab shrines, Crusader churches and Mamluk public buildings. In the Jewish Quarter the devout and the profane live side by side, and both a step from the Muslim Quarter. In the latter, the *muezzin*'s call to prayer mingles with the latest pop record from radios. Religious Jews from neighborhoods like Mea She'arim north of the Old City flow through the Damascus Gate and the Muslim Quarter on their way to the Western (Wailing) Wall. Arab women loaded with produce from the Old City markets cross the Western Wall plaza towards the Dung Gate and the village of Silwan beyond.

Eight gates breach the four-kms.-(two-and-a-half-mile) long wall encircling the Old City: on the west the Jaffa Gate; on the north the New, Damascus, and Herod Gates; on the east the Lions' (St. Stephen's) Gate and the blocked Golden Gate; and on the south the Dung and Zion Gates.

The ramparts along the city walls are open to the public. Not only does a stroll over the city walls give unparalleled views of the surroundings—West Jerusalem, East Jerusalem, and the Mount of Olives—but for the dedicated voyeur it offers a peek into the courtyards and alleys of the Old City, a fascinating mix of churches, children, and chickens. Access is possible at the Jaffa, Damascus, Lion's, and Zion Gates, and descent at any of these as well as at the New, Herod's, and Dung Gates. Only the wall along the Temple Mount area is not open, although at the Jaffa Gate the walk is interrupted by the gate itself.

Jaffa Gate and the Citadel

Like so many other gates of the period, the pedestrian part of the Jaffa Gate is angled so as to break the thrust of any attempted attack

on the city through it. An Arabic inscription outside the gate dedicates
it to Suleiman the Magnificent, who built it in the Year of the Hejira
945 (A.D. 1538). Its name indicates its westerly orientation, for from
here the road heads west from Jerusalem for Jaffa on the Mediterranean
(thus, too, Jaffa Road). In Arabic the gate is known as Bab el-Halil,
the Hebron Gate (literally The Beloved, referring to Abraham, the
Beloved of God, who is buried in Hebron), since the road to that
southern city also leaves from here.

The road through the gate is relatively new. In 1898 Kaiser Wilhelm
II of Germany visited Jerusalem, and the Turks breached the wall and
paved the road over the moat so that the German Emperor would not
have to dismount from his carriage. The British general, Allenby,
adopted a different approach when he entered the city as its conqueror
in 1917. He and his staff dismounted from their horses and entered the
Holy City on foot as pilgrims always have.

Inside the Jaffa Gate, on the left just beyond the Tourist Information
Office, is a small enclosure elevated above street level. Behind the iron
fence are a couple of cypress trees, a fig tree and two Muslim graves.
Tradition has it that these are the graves of the two architects of Sultan
Suleiman the Magnificent who rebuilt the walls of Jerusalem from
1538–42. The story of their death has several different versions. One
tells that Suleiman put them to death because they had neglected to
include Mount Zion, with the Tomb of King David venerated by
Muslims, within the city walls. Another version has it that Suleiman
was so pleased with what they had built that he executed them, so that
they would never be able to build anything more magnificent for anyone else.

The symbol of the Citadel is the so-called David's Tower (in reality
a 16th-century Turkish tower and minaret), best seen from the valley
outside and below the gate. More impressive is the Citadel's most
monumental structure, a massive 2,000-year-old square tower and the
largest of three built by Herod the Great, constructed with huge stones
similar to those of the Temple Mount. (The other two have not survived.) The courtyard of the Citadel has been excavated, and presents
a melange of archeological periods. A series of diagrams and photographs in the museum sorts out the more ancient walls and puts them
in context for you. For its modest entrance fee, the Citadel offers its
archeological excavations; a museum of finds from all periods made on
the site; a walk on the Citadel walls, including a grand view from the
top of the Herodian tower; the visual aids mentioned above; a wonderful exhibit of one-third-life-size dolls showing Jerusalem's different
ethnic and religious types; and, four times a day, a half-hour multi-
screen audio-visual presentation on Jerusalem. On summer evenings an
openair *son et lumière,* a sound and light show, takes place in the
courtyard (wear a coat).

Inside the Jaffa Gate, the pedestrian David Street plunges straight
ahead into the souk—the Arab bazaar—while the road veers right and
passes successively the Armenian Quarter, Zion Gate, the Jewish Quarter, and the Western Wall.

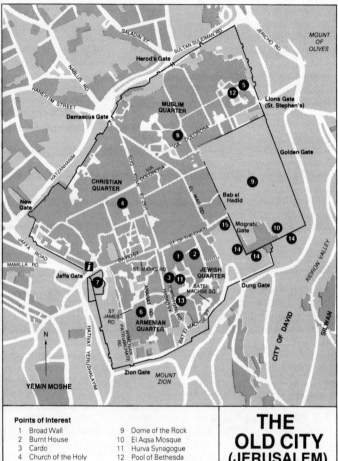

Points of Interest

1 Broad Wall
2 Burnt House
3 Cardo
4 Church of the Holy
  Sepulcher
5 Church of St. Anne
6 Church of St. James
7 Citadel and David's
  Tower
8 Convent of the Sisters
  of Zion

9 Dome of the Rock
10 El Aqsa Mosque
11 Hurva Synagogue
12 Pool of Bethesda
13 Sephardic Synagogues
14 Western and Southern
   Wall Excavations
15 Western (Wailing) Wall

i Tourist Information

THE OLD CITY (JERUSALEM)

(NOT ALL STREETS SHOWN)

0 meters	300
0 yards	300

—— City Wall

The Damascus Gate

As its name suggests, this is one of the northern gates, for from here the road (now called Nablus Road) once left Jerusalem towards Damascus. It is both the most beautiful and the busiest of the gates, being the chief link between the Old City and the Arab neighborhoods of East Jerusalem. A wide bridge approaches the gate. Below, and to the left, is one arch of the Roman gate built by the Emperor Hadrian in A.D. 135 as the entrance to his new city, Aelia Capitolina. It was his plan to raze Jerusalem and build a pagan city, complete with temples to Jupiter and Venus, that touched off the Jewish revolt under Bar Kochba in A.D. 132. Excavations just inside Hadrian's Gate have brought to light an almost entirely intact Roman tower which you can climb to join the Rampart Walk at the top. Just inside the arch segments of an open plaza have been discovered that correspond exactly to a 6th-century mosaic map of Jerusalem made in Madaba, today in Jordan. Originally a fine column with the Emperor's statue adorning it dominated the plaza, and additionally provided the point of reference for road distances throughout the country. The column has not survived (though a hologram shows what it looked like), but to this day the Arabic name of the gate is Bab el'Amud, the Gate of the Column.

The Jewish Quarter

The Jewish Quarter has changed enormously since the Six Day War in 1967, and provides a delightful smorgasbord of the unexpected. After its surrender to the Jordanian army by the Israelis in 1948 and subsequent evacuation, the Quarter was damaged substantially, and abandoned for a generation. With the re-unification of the city in 1967, the process of restoration began. With so many buildings no more than rubble, archeologists were provided with a unique opportunity to explore and excavate before the construction crews moved in. Half-a-dozen fascinating archeological sites are the result. Simultaneously, architects and builders set about restoring the surviving buildings, while putting up new buildings that, as far as possible, harmonized with the original architecture. Their efforts have been generally successful, and today the Jewish Quarter is the most attractive of the Old City's neighborhoods, a quarter of winding lanes, picturesque courtyards, and wide plazas, of the ancient and the new, of synagogues and condominiums, cafés and high-quality stores.

When the First Crusade reached Jerusalem in 1099, the main Jewish quarter was in the city's northeast quadrant, today the Muslim Quarter. The population of Jerusalem was almost annihilated by the Crusaders, and many of the Jews burned alive in their synagogue. When the Spanish rabbi Nachmanides, the "Ramban," arrived in Jerusalem in 1267, he found "only two Jews, brothers, dyers by trade." Together they re-established a congregation—apparently on Mount Zion—which moved to its present location—today's Jewish Quarter—around 1400. In 1492 the entire Jewish community of Spain was expelled. A generation later the Ottoman Turks conquered the Middle East and allowed these Sephardic (ex-Spanish) Jews to settle where they wished. Some put down roots in Jaffa, Hebron, Tiberias, and Safed. Many came to Jerusalem. The immigration of Ashkenazi Jews—from Central and Eastern Europe—also increased in the following centuries, so that by 1865, half the population of the Old City was Jewish. The resultant overcrowding and poverty of the Jewish Quarter by the 19th century was a major reason for the development of the first neighborhoods beyond the city walls.

Synagogues and Sages

One of the most attractive approaches to the Jewish Quarter is from the Armenian Quarter. On the road from the Jaffa Gate, and just before the entrance to the Armenian Compound and the Church of St. James (the latter well worth visiting), follow St. James Street to the left. Turn right at Ararat Street, and then left onto Hakinnor Street. Facing you at the bottom of this short street is a small, dark, wooden "house" built onto the second story of a new residential building. In 1643, one Baruch Mizrachi had a house here. In his will he instructed his heirs to preserve the dwelling so that when the Messiah came and the dead would be resurrected and follow him into the city, Mr. Mizrachi would have his lodgings immediately to hand. The will was lost, resurfacing only in 1905 when a local court verified its legality. Mizrachi's descendants divested themselves of the property. The building was later destroyed in the War of Independence. In 1977, when the reconstruction of the Quarter was well under way, and as part of the overall effort to reinforce the "historic nature" of the Quarter, Mizrachi's descendants were allowed to build the small wooden addition you see today. Baruch Mizrachi will have a roof over his head on that Great Day, but even to lie down he will have to take himself elsewhere.

How can services be conducted in four interconnecting synagogues simultaneously? We do not know, but that was the way things were for a few centuries in the Sephardic Synagogues on Misherot Hakehuna Street (next to the parking lot). The oldest of the complex—the Elijah the Prophet and Yohanan Ben Zakkai synagogues—are 400 years old, and date from the time when the Jewish community was evicted from its previous home, which was subsequently converted to a mosque. The synagogues were built below street level because of the Muslim injunction that no Jewish or Christian buildings should be higher than any Muslim ones in the area. Especially worth noting is the beautifully carved wooden ark containing the Torah scrolls in the Elijah synagogue. It is as old as the building itself, but came originally from an Italian synagogue destroyed in World War II.

In the heart of the Jewish Quarter is a plaza, and above it an obviously new, free-standing arch. It retraces the arched wall of the principal landmark of the Quarter until 1948—the Hurva Synagogue. Enter the ruined synagogue from Jewish Quarter Road. Around 1700, a large group of Ashkenazi Jews arrived in Jerusalem led by Rabbi Yehuda Hehassid, Judah the Pious. The old man died within a few days, depriving the group of both leadership and funds (his prestige was to have ensured the continued patronage of the "home community").

Nonetheless, they borrowed, and built a synagogue on this spot. In 1720, with the debt still outstanding, their creditors burnt it down. For over a century Ashkenazi Jews were *persona non grata* in Jerusalem, until the Turkish sultan annulled the old debt and gave them permission to return. A new and larger synagogue was built on the same site, known as the Hurva, or "Ruin," recalling its destroyed predecessor. Plans are afoot to rebuild the synagogue, though how is a matter of heated controversy.

Another attractive plaza in the Jewish Quarter is Batei Machse Square. Two long 19th-century buildings give the Square its name: Houses of Shelter. Near the roof of the old two-story building facing the square is the coat-of-arms of the Rothschild family. One solution to the difficult conditions of the Quarter in the 19th century was leaving to settle in new neighborhoods beyond the walls. Baron Edmond de Rothschild offered another: he built these rows of small apartments to offer rent-free to impoverished families for a three-year period. Today the building is the headquarters of "The Company for the Restoration and Development of the Jewish Quarter in the Old City of Jerusalem"(!). A self-guided tour is now possible through the intriguing maze of this area, an official booklet called *Quartertour* directing the visitor to sites marked with distinctive ceramic plaques.

Archeological Gems

The excavations conducted in the Jewish Quarter from 1969 to 1981 not only turned up wonderful treasures, but helped solve several conundrums that have absorbed archeologists and kept book publishers in business for a century. Four of these discoveries are of quite exceptional interest.

Taking them in no particular order, the first is the Cardo, dating from the late-Byzantine period. This was a wide, colonnaded street running north–south through the city, as shown in the 6th-century A.D. map found in Madaba, Jordan. Excavation of the Cardo on Jewish Quarter Road not only unearthed some of its 5 meter (16 ft.) -high columns and much of its pavement, but revealed its stunning dimensions—a street 22.5 meters (73 ft.) wide, the width of a modern eight-lane highway, running through the heart of the city. Six centuries later, the Crusaders adapted part of the Cardo (by now much narrower) as a sort of medieval shopping mall. Those same Crusader archways now grace the entrances to a series of fine modern stores which line the restored ancient street. Near the meeting point of the Cardo mall and the souk, a few small excavations reveal parts of Old Testament fortifications and the First Wall of the Second Temple period.

A few steps east of the Cardo, on Plugat Hakotel Street, is the second of those finds, perhaps the most historically significant of the area. This is the Broad Wall, affectionately nicknamed Avigad's Wall after the professor who headed the dig. For years "maximalists" and "minimalists" argued about the extent of Jerusalem's urban area in the Old Testament period. Here is the wall—7 meters (23 ft.) thick—built by King Hezekiah to defend the city in 701 B.C. End of controversy! Although the precise line of the wall to the west is uncertain, we are a long distance from the original City of David, and the indications are that in the last years of the Kingdom of Judah, Jerusalem's walls reached the Jaffa Gate and included today's Mount Zion and the Armenian and Jewish Quarters, in addition to the ancient City of David and Temple Mount.

"And on the 8th day of the month of Elul," wrote Josephus Flavius, "the sun rose over Jerusalem in flames." The date was September 20th, A.D. 70. The Temple had been destroyed by Titus' Roman legions a month before. The Upper City (today's Jewish Quarter) had fallen and the Great Revolt was at an end. Precisely 19 centuries later—in 1970—the Burnt House (on Tiferet Israel Street), originally the home of an aristocratic priestly family, and the third of our quartet of historical treasures, was exposed by the archeologist's spade. The evidence of destruction by burning was so vivid that visitors swore they could almost feel the heat and smell of the fire. The find, wrote archeologist Avigad, "was an emotional experience of great depth." Now open to the public, the Burnt House includes a display of the finds which aided the identification and dating of the site, photographs and diagrams, and an excellent 15-minute audio visual program.

To the right of the steps leading down to the Western (Wailing) Wall, an opening under a massive new building reveals the fourth of these marvelous finds. It is a basement area containing the remains of a large, palatial mansion of the Second Temple period, found complete with frescoes, mosaics, and fine glassware. (It has not yet been opened to the public.)

The Western (Wailing) Wall

No, it is not part of the Jewish Temple itself. But they are ancient, the huge stones of this wall, 2,000 years old in fact. At the end of the 1st century B.C., King Herod the Great rebuilt the Second Temple on a grand scale. In order to expand the plaza surrounding the Temple, he had massive retaining walls built on the slopes of Mount Moriah (on which the Temple stood), filled the inside with rubble, and thus created the vast platform known as the Temple Mount. Of these retaining walls, the Wailing Wall is simply the Western Wall of a sort of huge rectangular stone box.

After the destruction of the Second Temple by the Romans, the Temple area was put off-limits to Jews for generations. The memory of the precise location of the Temple was lost, so that even when access became possible, no Jew would venture into the area for fear of unwittingly trespassing on the sacred precincts. Eventually, Jews came to the one chunk of wall that was as close as they could get to the Sanctuary without actually entering the Temple Mount. There they mourned the destruction of the "House of God" (hence, the Wailing Wall), and prayed for its restoration. One may say, then, that The Wall, as it is simply known, is by way of being a holy place by proxy. It is not to the stones but *through* the stones that Jews pray.

Since it functions with all the regulations of an Orthodox synagogue, men and women worshippers at the Wall are segregated. Yet there is no one service at any time. Even on the Sabbath or on holidays different knots of worshippers will conduct their prayer service among themselves, quite independently of other small groups nearby. The Wall is accessible 24 hours a day, and in the quiet evening hours one can sometimes feel the deep emanations of the place, if only by association with the powerful hold the Western Wall has on the minds and hearts of the Jewish people—as a symbol of past glory and future redemption. But if you want to people-watch, come on Friday evening at sundown when the Sabbath begins, and *yeshiva* (seminary) students come dancing and singing down to the Wall, and the black-robed ultra-Orthodox are decked out in their special finery. (No cameras are permitted at this time.) Also interesting are Monday and Thursday mornings when Bar-Mitzvah services take place at the Wall.

Digging Around the Mount

Both the impressive scale and the hidden promise of the Temple Mount itself have attracted scientific investigation for more than a century. In 1867 a British Army engineer, Charles Warren, sunk shafts around the Temple Mount to check the depth of the Herodian foundations. Just inside today's men's side of the Wall, he went down about 18 meters (60 ft.) to bed-rock. In the same place, the so-called Wilson's Arch (above your head), which 2,000 years ago supported a bridge carrying a street and an aqueduct onto the Temple Mount, was found completely intact. In this area, too, were found the largest Herodian stones (unfortunately now closed off), 12.5 meters (41 ft.) long, 2 meters (6.5 ft.) high, 5 meters (16 ft.) thick, and weighing 400 tons apiece!

On the Western Wall continuation, near the southwestern corner of the Temple Mount, a massive piece of masonry angles out of the wall. This is the "spring" of Robinson's Arch, which had long been thought to have supported a bridge connecting the Upper City and the Temple Mount. Both the foundations of the arch and the steps leading up to it have shown that it never spanned the valley, however, but provided access to the Temple Mount from the Herodian street below. The paving stones of the ancient street have been uncovered as well, the very street Jesus knew.

Stand at this level and look up. The top of the wall (including its later renovations) is about 25 meters (80 ft.) above you. There is that much again below you down to bed-rock, and 2,000 years ago it would have soared above street level to twice its present height. The top cornerstone, toppled at the time of the Roman destruction of the Temple, was found on the pavement, bearing a Hebrew inscription indicating that on that lofty perch a priest would blow the *shofar* (the ram's horn) to announce the approach of the Sabbath.

Just north of Robinson's Arch, at ground level, is a Hebrew inscription in the wall, now covered by a sheet of glass. It is from Isaiah 66:14. "You shall see, and your heart shall rejoice; your bones shall flourish like the grass." One view is that this outburst of some Jewish pilgrim's hope of redemption dates to the reign of the Roman Emperor Julian "the Apostate" (A.D. 361-3) who encouraged the Jews to rebuild the Temple.

Accessible from the excavation area, but visible too from the road outside the city walls is the Southern Wall below the gray dome of the El Aqsa mosque. A wide staircase once led up to the Temple area through a "triple gate" and a "double gate," both bricked up, with only half of the latter now visible. Outside these gates, many *mikvehs* were found, ritual immersion baths for purification before entering the sacred area.

The Temple Mount

This vast open area of some 40 acres was possibly the largest religious enclosure of the entire ancient world. For centuries, as long as the Jewish Temple stood, it was the object of pilgrimage and devotion, and the symbol of national unity. Solomon's Temple, built around 950 B.C., was destroyed in 587 B.C. by the Babylonians. The Second Temple, built 50 years later by the returning Jewish exiles, was but a shadow of Solomon's. Herod the Great's expansion of the Temple plaza is still impressive today. Although one of the lowest parts of the Old City, the wide plaza, dotted with cypress trees and crowned by the spectacular golden Dome of the Rock, is easily the most visually dominating. Access to the Temple Mount (the Haram es-Sharif, the Noble Enclosure in Arabic) is now controlled by the Waqf, the Muslim Supreme Religious Council. While one may exit from most of the Temple Mount's nine gates, entrance to non-Muslims is permitted through only two—the Mograbi Gate near the Western Wall, and the Bab el Hadid, the Iron Gate.

Dome of the Rock and El Aqsa

More than one tradition considers the huge rock under the gold dome to be the center of the world. It is in fact the summit of Mount Moriah, and the identification of that name with the land of Moriah of Genesis 22 has led to the veneration of the place as the site of Abraham's near-sacrifice of his son Isaac. With King David's conquest of Jerusalem in 1000 B.C., however, we enter the realm of historical probability. Having carved out a great kingdom, David set about doing what any ruler needs to do—he took a census of the population. The Lord was angered—the nation of Israel was supposed to be uncounted and uncountable—and punishment in the form of a plague followed. But God spared Jerusalem itself at the last moment, as the Angel of Death stood with sword bared at the great rock, then north of the city limits. David bought the rock, used at the time as a grain-threshing floor, from its owner, one Araunah (Ornan) the Jebusite. He built an altar on it, and made a repentance offering to the Lord. In the next generation, David's son Solomon incorporated the rock in his magnificent Temple. But as what? The Altar? the Holy of Holies? No-one knows. The second Temple was later built on the identical site, but that, too, was destroyed without trace.

The rock had to be uncovered from beneath layers of debris by the conquering Arab caliph, Omar Ibn-Khatib, in A.D. 638. It is told that Omar asked his aide, the converted Jew Ka'ab al-Akhbar, where he should build his mosque. Ka'ab advised a spot north of the rock, hoping, the story suggests, that the Muslims praying south towards Mecca would thus include the Old Temple site in their obeisance. "You dog, Ka'ab," bellowed the Caliph, "in your heart you are still a Jew, for you want us to include the rock in our *kibla* [direction of prayer]." He thus deliberately built his mosque, apparently a temporary structure, south of the rock. A persistent tradition has attached Omar's name to the Dome of the Rock, the "Mosque of Omar," though it was in fact built 50 years later.

Jerusalem is not specifically mentioned in the Koran, the Muslim holy book, but the story of Mohammed's Night Ride is related thus: the Prophet Mohammed was woken one night by the Archangel Gabriel who bore him away on a fabulous winged horse to the *masjad el aqsa*, the "furthermost place (mosque)," from which they rose together to Heaven. There Mohammed met God face-to-face, received His commandments for the faithful, and returned home the same night. Jerusalem came to be identified with the "furthermost place," thus the "El Aqsa" Mosque, and the Rock as the very spot from which Mohammed rose to Heaven. His footprint can be seen on it to this day under the canister holding three hairs of his beard!

The splendid Dome of the Rock was completed in A.D. 691 by the Ummayad caliph, Abd el-Malik. An Arabic inscription in the building attesting to this fact was doctored some 140 years later by the new caliph of a rival dynasty who removed Abd el-Malik's name and inserted his own. Fortunately for history, the new man forgot to change the date of the building, allowing the forgery to be detected. There are no human or animal images to offend the iconoclastic Muslim faithful, and all motifs are either geometric, floral, or elaborate Arabic script, many quotations from the Koran. Under the Rock is a small cave which has attracted traditions associating it with Old Testament figures, including the prophets Elijah and Zechariah. A Muslim legend relates that as Mohammed rose to Heaven, the Rock tried to follow him and had already left the void (the cave) behind it when the Archangel Gabriel held it down. Another tradition calls this the Well of Souls, the entrance to the nether world, and the place where the Dead pray.

The octagonal building is essentially unchanged these 13 centuries. Many of the mosaics are apparently original, but the marble-work, superb examples of the stone-mason's art, is attributed to Saladin (12th century), and the exterior glazed tiles to Suleiman the Magnificent (16th century). The original dome, it is said, was made of real gold, which was later stripped and replaced by a 200-ton lead dome. Both the present 35-ton bronze-aluminum dome and the restoration of the exterior glazed tiles were part of the shrine's most recent renovation completed in 1963.

The El Aqsa Mosque, originally built about 20 years after the Dome of the Rock and capped by its large dark gray dome, stands at the southern end of the Temple Mount. Israel lies on a geological fault-line, and the earthquakes of centuries have wrought havoc on the Mosque. The Dome of the Rock, with its sturdy construction and built on solid rock, was able to withstand such shocks. Not so El Aqsa. Different stages of reconstruction are obvious within its cavernous interior, and the present building is the fourth on the site. Especially beautiful are the older stained-glass windows in the far southern wall near the *mih-rab* (the niche indicating the direction of prayer). The Mosque has known other dramas: in 1951, King Abdullah of Transjordan (King Hussein's grandfather) was assassinated here, and in 1969 a demented arsonist, attempting to destroy the building, set fire to a priceless medieval wooden *minbar,* or pulpit. Numerous Muslims come here to pray five times a day (at which time the Mosque and the Dome of the Rock are closed to tourists), but it is on Fridays and holidays that the crowds fill its vast hall. (Muslims pray at the Dome of the Rock, too, but individually rather than communally.) Near the El Aqsa Mosque is a museum containing artifacts and remnants of earlier buildings on the Temple Mount.

Between the two great buildings is a water fountain used by many Muslims to wash their feet before entering the mosques. Until recently small plaques on the surrounding grill recorded in Arabic and the original Hebrew (!) the passage in the Old Testament (Exodus 3) in which God confronts Moses at the Burning Bush: "Put off your shoes from your feet, for the place on which you are standing is holy ground." For this reason, anyone entering a mosque is required to leave their shoes outside (plus any bags and cameras, as well).

The Way of the Cross

The most convenient point of entry for anyone wanting to follow the Way of the Cross is the Lion's Gate (St. Stephen's Gate) in the Old City's eastern wall, but a bit of backtracking from the more easily accessible Damascus Gate will do as well. A little way inside the Lion's Gate on the right, a wooden door leads to a beautiful and tranquil garden courtyard. Here are two Christian sites: the Pools of Bethesda and the Church of St. Anne.

The King James version of John 5 speaks of Jesus curing a lame man by "a pool, which is called in the Hebrew tongue Bethesda" (that is, the Place of Mercy). The pools have been known for many centuries, witness the ruins of both Byzantine and Crusader churches built over them. More recently, they have been excavated to reveal the original structure complete with watertight plaster and steps, perhaps the very ones alluded to in the Gospel.

Adjacent to the pools is the beautiful and austere 12th-century Romanesque Crusader Church of St. Anne. According to tradition, the crypt below the church was the birthplace of Mary, whose mother Anne was. Although restored, the church is still the finest example of its type in Israel. Its most remarkable feature perhaps is its unusually reverberant acoustics. It is worth waiting for one of the frequent pilgrim groups which visit the church and almost invariably test the acoustics with some hymn-singing.

The Way of the Cross—the Via Dolorosa—begins another 300 meters or so further into the Old City. This is the route believed to have been taken by Jesus carrying the cross from the place of his trial to that of his execution and burial, and its 14 stations commemorate incidents along the way. Most of the way (stations I through VII) winds through the Muslim Quarter, the most densely populated of the Old City today. The Via Dolorosa tradition gelled in the 12th century, and while most of the stations represent actual Gospel accounts, some (III, IV, VI, VII, IX) are non-scriptural traditions. In paving the streets of the Old City in recent years, the Municipality of Jerusalem has indicated the Stations of the Cross by cobblestones on the street arranged in a semi-circle centered on the stations themselves. Pilgrims may join the Franciscan procession along the Via Dolorosa every Friday at 3, starting at Station I.

On the left, a ramp leads to a yellow metal door. Now a school, this was once the area of the Antonia Fortress and the possible location of Pontius Pilate's judgment hall: Station I—Jesus is tried and condemned. Across the road is the Monastery of the Flagellation (Station II) where Jesus was scourged and given the cross.

Just beyond this, an arch crosses the street. Ignore the newer structure on it; the arch is ancient. The 19th-century Convent of the Sisters of Zion on the right was built around the continuation of the arch in the belief that this had been the entrance to the Antonia, and thus maybe the place where Pilate presented Jesus with the words "Ecce homo!" (Behold the man!). But the Ecce Homo Arch was in fact one of Emperor Hadrian's triumphal arches built a century after Christ. The Convent is well worth a visit. In addition to the arch in its chapel, the lower level reveals a huge water cistern and a stone courtyard (*lithostrotos* in Greek) of the Roman period. On the latter, games were etched out by bored legionaries. One has been identified as the Game of the King, a cruel, annual event on the Roman calendar, the moves of which are tantalizingly reminiscent of the treatment of Jesus by the Roman soldiers.

The street continues to meet a wide thoroughfare, El-Wad Road. Turning left, you immediately find Station III where Jesus fell under the weight of the Cross for the first time. It is marked by a chapel built by Free Polish soldiers after World War II. A few meters further on is Station IV where Mary came out of the crowd to greet her son. At the next corner, a chapel reminds you that Simon of Cyrene was pulled out of the crowd by the Romans to help carry the cross; Station V. Here you turn right and begin climbing. Station VI, half-way up the street, recalls the tradition of a woman stepping up to Jesus and wiping His face, His image being preserved on the cloth. Her name has come down to us as Veronica, made up of the two words "vera icone," meaning true image. Facing you at the top of the hill is Station VII where Jesus fell under the cross for the second time. A step to the left and up a side-street finds "VIII" carved in stone: Jesus addressed the women of Jerusalem (Luke 23:28). Back to the main street (Suq Khan e-Zeit), turn south (left as you reach VII from VI). A hundred meters further on the right, opposite a confectionary shop, a ramp leads to a lane at the end of which is a pillar; Station IX, when Jesus fell for the third time. Stations X through XIV are all within the Church of the Holy Sepulcher. The picturesque route from Station IX is through the open gate to the Ethiopian monastery courtyard, down through the Ethiopian church and a backdoor to the Church of the Holy Sepulcher.

Calvary and the Holy Sepulcher

Most Christians venerate the site of the Holy Sepulcher as that of the death, burial, and resurrection of Christ, events that stand at the core of their faith. The present vast edifice was rebuilt by the Crusaders in the 12th century, and yet is only half the length of its Byzantine predecessors.

Note the fine stone-work above the entrance. Just inside on the right, steep steps lead up to Golgotha (from the Hebrew or Aramaic, via Greek), or Calvary (from the Latin): "the place of a skull." Here, in the Catholic chapel on the right are Stations X (Jesus is stripped of His garments), and XI (He is nailed to the Cross). The mosaics are especially interesting. The central candlelit Greek Orthodox chapel marks the place where Jesus died on the cross (Station XII). Under the altar is a bronze disc with a hole in it purporting to be the place where the cross stood. One can see here part of the actual rock of the hill. Between the two chapels the Franciscans indicate Station XIII where the body of Jesus was taken down.

Opposite the entrance to the church lies a slab, the Stone of Unction, where, it is said, the body of Jesus was cleansed and prepared for burial. The Gospels relate that His body was claimed by Joseph of Arimathea, who then buried Him in a yet unused rock-hewn tomb in a garden close at hand. The tomb (Station XIV) is now contained within a large and elaborate marble structure at the center of the rotunda. The great high dome which caps the rotunda is visible from many parts of the city, a landmark of the Christian Quarter.

At certain times of day, each denomination in turn exercises its right to follow the sequence of events from Calvary to the Tomb accompanied by chanting clergy with censers streaming pungent smoke. On the Greek Orthodox Easter the Church is jam-packed with candle-toting pilgrims tense with excitement. The Patriarch enters the Tomb, a flash of "holy fire" follows, within moments the church is a blaze of myriad candles, and the fire is quickly sent on its way to the Greek homeland.

A peculiarity of the Church of the Holy Sepulcher is that so many denominations have a presence in it. The Greek Orthodox are the major shareholders, if one may put it that way, controlling both Calvary and the Tomb. Most visible and influential after them are the Latins (Roman Catholics), while the Armenians and Copts have their sections, and the Ethiopians and Syrians have access rights.

Over the centuries the various denominations vied with each other, sometimes to the point of bloodshed, for control of the Christian Holy Places. The Crimean War, for example, broke out in 1854 against the background of just such a conflict of interests between France (Catholic) and Russia (Orthodox). In essence no major change in the balance of rights and privileges—the status quo—has been made since 1757, and each group jealously guards its claims. As recently as Christmas, 1984, Greek and Armenian clergy came to blows in Bethlehem's Church of the Nativity (where the status quo also applies) over whose right it was to clean a certain section of the church!

OUTSIDE THE WALLS—Mount Zion and the Valley of Hell

No natural valley separates the Old City from Mount Zion; it is simply the southerly continuation beyond the walls of the plateau on which the Armenian Quarter is built. Military logic should have dictated bringing Mount Zion into the Old City by building the walls on its steep slopes and using the deep Hinnom Valley as an excellent natural defense. The Jewish rulers of Jerusalem around 100 B.C. did exactly that, establishing a fortification line that would later withstand Roman onslaughts. Over two centuries later, when the Roman Emperor Hadrian plowed the ruins of Jerusalem and laid out a new pagan city—Aelia Capitolina—the security needs had changed considerably. The firm grip of the Pax Romana made enormous fortifications unnecessary, and anyway Hadrian preferred the classic square pattern of the "polis." Thus his city excluded Mount Zion, laying the groundplan for the Old City of today. (Though when, in the 5th century, the Byzantines rebuilt the walls, they again incorporated Mount Zion within the city, this time out of reverence for the Christian holy places on it.)

For 800 years Jewish pilgrims have lit memorial candles, muttered prayers, and read psalms at King David's Tomb on Mount Zion. The Bible tells that David was buried in the City of David, the ancient city of Jerusalem of 1000 B.C. Medieval men readily (but wrongly) identified this imposing hill as the site. Since the City of David was also the "Stronghold of Zion" (II Samuel 5), the hill got the name by which it is known today. The tradition is spurious, but so what? For at least eight centuries the site has been sanctified by the prayers and tears of the devout. The large stone cenotaph is draped with a velvet cloth inscribed with two Hebrew passages: "David King of Israel lives forever," and "If I forget thee O Jerusalem."

One story above the Tomb, but accessible only by detouring around the building, is the Cenacle, or Room of the Last Supper, the "Upper Room" of the Gospels. Here, it is believed, Jesus celebrated the Passover *seder* meal with his disciples, the consecrated bread and wine of the ceremony becoming the elements of the Christian Eucharist. The present room is Gothic, probably 12th-century Crusader, though some say a bit earlier. A Muslim prayer niche and Arabic inscriptions attest to its later use as a mosque, not as a result of Muslim identification with the Christian traditions, but with Nebi Daoud (the "prophet" David) supposedly buried one story below. Tradition has also attached to this room the gathering of the disciples on Pentecost (Acts 2).

Near the entrance to the Room of the Last Supper is an imposing round church with a conical roof and a high adjacent clock tower, Mount Zion's most identifiable landmark. This is the Benedictine Dormition Abbey, enshrining the tradition that here Mary "fell into eternal sleep." It was built at the beginning of this century in the hope that it would be only part of a much larger basilica complex that would include the Cenacle, but Muslim control of the site rendered any such plan still-born. Today organ, choral, and chamber concerts frequently attract Jerusalemites to the church.

Opposite the entrance to David's Tomb is the Chamber of the Holocaust, dedicated to the memory of entire communities wiped out by the Nazis.

Mount Zion's eastern slopes are dominated by a large, blue-domed church—St. Peter in Gallicantu, or St. Peter at Cockcrow, recalling the fulfillment of Jesus' prediction that when the cock crowed twice Peter would deny him for the third time. The Assumptionist Fathers identify this site as that of the house of the High Priest Caiaphas where Jesus was imprisoned overnight before being taken to Pilate for judgment. In fact, archeologists have established with certainty that Caiaphas' house was on the more prestigious crest of the hill, but the ancient remains under the church—what appears to be a rock-hewn prison cell, and a stepped street down the hill—are interesting and evocative.

The Hinnom Valley descends past the Jaffa Gate, sweeping around the base of Mount Zion to empty into the Kidron Valley on the east. In Biblical days, it was the border between the small tribe of Benjamin to the north, and the large one of Judah to the south. In the 7th century B.C., the cult of child-sacrifice to the god Moloch gained a foothold here. Some scholars think the sacrifice was merely symbolic, and no blood was actually shed. Be that as it may, the Hebrew name of the valley, Gei Ben Hinnom, in its contracted form Gehennom, or Gehenna, became a synonym for a hellish place of burning.

The City of David

Jerusalem was already 2,000 years old when King David conquered it and made it his capital in 1000 B.C. Until his son Solomon expanded the city northwards, it was confined to what is sometimes called the "southeastern hill," a tiny blade of land south of the Temple Mount, bounded by the deep Kidron Valley on the east and the shallow Cheese-makers' Valley (now an asphalt road) on the west.

To reach the City of David walk about 200 meters east of the Dung Gate towards Mount of Olives. Where the road turns left around the Old City walls, a paved path goes right to the famous "Area G" of the excavations. Clearly-marked parts of this dig include a large sloping wall, part of some massive royal edifice possibly from the days of David and Solomon, and partly restored town houses of the Old Testament period. Beyond Area G, steps take you down to Warren's Shaft.

Although there were local and regional strategic reasons for building Jerusalem where it was, the overriding one was water, specifically the Gihon spring at the foot of the hill in the Kidron Valley. The original Canaanite or later Jebusite inhabitants of the city sunk a shaft to the spring from within the city walls which would give them access to the water supply without venturing outside. It was up this vertical shaft that King David's men apparently penetrated and conquered Jerusalem (II Samuel 5). Some scholars claim that the shaft was built after David's time, despite the Biblical reference. The shaft was discovered by the English army engineer, Charles Warren, in 1867, and has been cleared and opened to the public. The ancient wall beneath which Warren's shaft runs was discovered a bit further down the slope by the

British archeologist, Kathleen Kenyon, in the '60s. There is controlled access to the spring from the courtyard at the bottom of the hill.

In 701 B.C., 20 years after the destruction of the northern Kingdom of Israel, Judah was invaded by the Assyrian king Sennacherib. Perhaps no Biblical event is as well-documented and supported by archeological evidence as this campaign. Having ravaged the countryside—the fall of Lachish is depicted on a palace wall-relief found in Nineveh—he prepared to assault the capital, Jerusalem. Hezekiah, King of Judah, prepared for the siege. He "built up the wall that was broken down" (II Chronicles 32), massive sections of which have been found in the Jewish Quarter—the Broad Wall (see above). But even more brilliantly, he built a tunnel through the rock under the city, diverting the water-supply to an inner-city reservoir, simultaneously guarding the city's water supply while depriving the enemy of his.

It was a work of genius. Teams dug the tunnel from both ends at once. After months of back-breaking toil, they met. How they did it is still not clearly understood, for the 533 meter (577 yd.) tunnel snakes its way unpredictably beneath the city. The Bible laconically states that "Hezekiah directed the waters down to the west side of the City of David." The diggers themselves were less restrained. In the rock wall of the tunnel they chiseled an inscription in the same ancient Hebrew: " . . . When the tunnel was driven through, the tunnelers hewed the rock, each man towards his fellow, pick-axe against pick-axe. And the water flowed from the spring toward the reservoir for 1,200 cubits." (The inscription was found in the last century, and is displayed in a Turkish museum, with a copy in the Archeology wing of the Israel Museum in Jerusalem.) Armed with a flashlight or candles (and matches to relight them!), the intrepid visitor can walk through the thigh-deep water of the tunnel from the spring to the pool at the far end—one-way traffic only! The chisel-marks and 2,700-year-old insulating plaster are very clear along the way, as are the zig-zags near the middle, where the teams began searching for each other by sound.

Hezekiah's Tunnel emerges in the Pool of Siloam at the southwestern point of the City of David. By Hezekiah's day, the city had expanded up Mount Zion to the west, and this valley—and thus the pool, of course—were within the city limits. In another era, Jesus restored the sight of a blind man by covering his eyes with clay and sending him to wash in the Pool of Siloam (John 9). No doubt the pool in the days of both Hezekiah and Jesus was larger and more impressive than it is today.

Mount of Olives and the Kidron Valley

If you want *the* panoramic view of the Old City, go to the top of the Mount of Olives, opposite the Intercontinental Hotel, in the morning. Of course, you'll have to run the gamut of the camel-drivers, and the postcard and olive-wood vendors, but there are quiet spots below the summit. Below you are the graves of the ancient and most sacred Jewish cemetery, a vast necropolis that spreads around the western side of the Mount of Olives. All await the Messiah, for Jewish tradition declares that on the day of his coming the dead will be resurrected and follow him into Jerusalem through the Gates of Mercy (the now-blocked Golden Gate). It is believed that this is the oldest cemetery in the world still in use. To be buried here is regarded as a privilege.

In the Kidron Valley itself, at the very foot of the Mount of Olives, stand two monumental structures: the conical-roofed Absalom's Tomb, and the pyramid-roofed Zechariah's Tomb, a single block of stone cut straight out of the mountainside. Neither has anything to do with the Old Testament figures after whom they are named. Instead, they are the elaborate tombs of anonymous but obviously substantial citizens of Jerusalem of the 2nd century B.C. Jewish pilgrims of the Middle Ages were oblivious to the Hellenistic influence in the architecture, but they knew their Bible: "Absalom in his lifetime had set up for himself the pillar which is in the King's Valley . . . and it is called Absalom's monument to this day" (II Samuel 18). "What else could this be?" said the pilgrims. Fathers were accustomed to bring their rebellious sons to the site to chastise them there, remembering Absalom's unsuccessful rebellion against his father David and its tragic end.

At the foot of the Mount of Olives, but further up the valley, is the Garden of Gethsemane, the Garden of the Oilpress. Here among the olive trees that gave their name to both the mountain and the garden, Jesus grieved and prayed, and was arrested by the Roman soldiers on the last night of his life. The olive trees in the beautiful garden are old enough to have witnessed those events. The Franciscan church, completed in 1924, is known as the Church of All Nations, each of the small domes of its ceiling carrying a mosaic dedication to a country which helped sponsor the church. It is built on the site of a 4th-century Byzantine sanctuary, and its modern mosaic floor imitates and continues the few surviving fragments of its ancient predecessor. The focal point of the church is the Rock of Agony, a natural part of the mountain, which tradition identifies as the place where Jesus sweated blood in his anguish.

Just above the Church of All Nations is the century-old Russian Church of Mary Magdalene, it, too, preserving the Gethsemane tradition. With its golden onion domes and old Muscovite style, it is, from the outside, arguably the most magnificent church in Jerusalem.

On the Mount of Olives itself, and on the main road running along its crest, is the small Chapel, or Dome, of the Ascension. It is built over a rock on which, since the Middle Ages, the footprint has been shown of Christ ascending to Heaven. Control of the site is in Muslim hands.

One-hundred meters down the road, a turquoise gate leads to the Pater Noster convent. The walls of the cloister are covered with ceramic plaques—more than 50—each containing the Lord's Prayer in a different language.

And one more church, Dominus Flevit, or "the Lord wept" (as he looked over Jerusalem), a small, modern building halfway down the mountain on the steep road from the cemetery to Gethsemane. A stunning view and some archeological remains make it worth a visit.

The Garden Tomb

One of the most intriguing examples of Biblical interpretation in Jerusalem was that put forward in 1883 by the British General Gordon, of Khartoum fame. Looking across the northern wall of the Old City, not far from the Damascus Gate, he was struck, as others had been before him, by the skull-like appearance of the rock-face opposite. His enthusiasm for identifying that hill as Calvary or Golgotha in preference to the traditional site of the Church of the Holy Sepulcher stimulated a fund-raising campaign which purchased the adjacent garden in 1894. Subsequent years of excavation revealed an ancient rock-hewn tomb, and evidence of an ancient "garden" (water cistern, wine-press, and so on)—in other words, all the physical elements of the story of the death, burial, and resurrection of Jesus.

Today the Garden is a beautifully-kept and tranquil haven in the hurly-burly of East Jerusalem. Its keepers do not insist dogmatically that this is the site of Jesus' death and burial, but the complementary finds are too strong to be dismissed out of hand.

The Garden Tomb is located in a lane off Nablus Road, just a few hundred meters north of the Damascus Gate, where the gracious staff are always ready to provide guidance to visitors to the site.

Other Sites

When the Tombs of the Kings were explored by the Frenchman de Saulcy in the 19th century, he accepted the local tradition that these were the tombs of the Kings of Judah. Not so, but royal tombs they indeed were. In the 1st century A.D., Queen Helene of Adiabene embraced Judaism—Adiabene was a small kingdom on the border of Persia—and came to live and die in Jerusalem, where she was buried. Located on Saladin Street where it meets Nablus Road, these catacombs are the finest example of their kind in Israel. The rock-hewn steps, the rain-water cisterns (for purification), and even the large courtyard were excavated out of solid rock. The entrance to the tomb is across a porch which once boasted two huge stone columns, and still has the frieze above it. You need a flashlight or candles (though the attendant is sometimes here to help). The mouth of the low entrance was once filled by a large stone, still to be seen, giving the visitor a clear understanding of the New Testament description of Jesus' burial in exactly the same era.

The view from Mount Scopus, as its name suggests, sweeps over all Jerusalem. In 1925, the Hebrew University opened its doors here, followed in 1934 by Hadassah Hospital. Both closed in 1948 when Mount Scopus—though it remained in Israeli territory—was cut off from West Jerusalem. (Both later relocated on the west side of town.) Since 1967 the two institutions have been reactivated, and a walk through the campus gives one a pleasing blend of wonderful views (west to the city, east to the desert), new landscaping, and architecture old and new. The World War I British and Allied Military Cemetery is also located here.

PRACTICAL INFORMATION FOR JERUSALEM

GETTING TO TOWN FROM THE AIRPORT. The cheapest way is by the regular Egged bus, # 945 or 947, on the Haifa–Jerusalem route; they run every 30–45 minutes. The journey takes 40 minutes, costs about $2, and terminates at the Central Bus Station at the entrance to Jerusalem. No buses run from late on Friday afternoon until Saturday night.

A sherut (shared taxi) is readily available at the airport, takes about seven passengers and leaves only when it is full. It will drop you at your front door in Jerusalem. You pay for your seat only, about $8, including the first large suitcase. A "special", i.e. a private cab or a sherut to yourself, will cost around $27. Add 25% after 9 P.M. and on the Sabbath.

TOURIST OFFICES. Israel Government Tourist Information Office, 24 King George St. (tel. 241281); also at the Jaffa Gate in the Old City (tel. 282295/6). Both open in summer, Sun. to Thurs. 8.30–6; winter, Sun. to Thurs. 8.30–5; closed Sat. and holidays, except the Jaffa Gate office which is open 10–1.

Christian Information Center, Jaffa Gate (tel. 287647). Open in winter, Mon. to Sat. 8.30–12.30, and 3–5.30; summer open until 6 P.M.; closed Sun.

There is a **Jewish Quarter Information Center** in the Cardo. The **Tourist Volunteer Service** staffs desks at many major hotels to help with directions and advice.

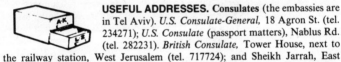

USEFUL ADDRESSES. Consulates (the embassies are in Tel Aviv). *U.S. Consulate-General,* 18 Agron St. (tel. 234271); *U.S. Consulate* (passport matters), Nablus Rd. (tel. 282231). *British Consulate,* Tower House, next to the railway station, West Jerusalem (tel. 717724); and Sheikh Jarrah, East Jerusalem (tel. 282481).

Travel Agents. *American Express,* 27 King George St. (tel. 222211). *ISSTA* (students only), 5 Elishar St. (tel. 231418). *Melia,* 33 King George St. (tel. 226381). *Peltours,* 2 Shlomzion Hamalka St. (tel. 234318), and the Hilton Hotel. *Promised Land,* 10 Hillel St. (tel. 233371). *Travex,* 8 Shamai St. (tel. 223211).

Driver-Guides. *Eshkolot Tours,* 36 Keren Hayesod St. (tel. 635555, 665555). *Yehuda Tours,* 19 Hutzot Hayotzer (tel. 280998, 280088).

Car Hire. *Avis,* 22 King David St. (tel. 249001/2/3). *Budget,* 14 King David St. (tel. 226143). *Hertz,* 18 King David St. (tel. 231351), 27 Saladin St. (tel. 283 415), and at the Ramada Renaissance and Sheraton Plaza Hotels. *National/Europcar,* 22 King David St., and at the Laromme and Hilton Hotels. All also have desks at the airport.

TELEPHONE CODES. The telephone code for Jerusalem is 02. To call any number in this chapter, unless otherwise specified, this prefix must be used. Within the city no prefix is required. Payphones take a token called an *assimon,* available at post offices, some vendors, and (generally) in hotels.

Useful Numbers. Police, 100. Ambulance, 101. Flight information (Ben-Gurion Airport) 03–971–2484.

HOTELS. Jerusalem is blessed with a multitude of hotels in all price categories. Peak seasons in both West
and East Jerusalem are generally April to May and late-
September through October, plus the weeks straddling
Easter and Christmas. Additionally, West Jerusalem hotels are always crowded
during Passover, in March or April. However, for the most part only the West
Jerusalem hotels have higher rates during the peak periods. All rates are subject
to a 15% service charge, but East Jerusalem hotels do not always add this on.

Generally, the standards in the West Jerusalem hotels are higher than in East
Jerusalem. All the Deluxe hotels have restaurants, central heating and aircondi-
tioning and rooms with bath. Rates include the sumptuous "Israeli breakfast."
Standards and facilities in Expensive hotels are almost as good.

All the West Jerusalem hotels have kosher restaurants—which in no way
detracts from the excellence or the variety of the food in most places.

Deluxe

Intercontinental Hotel, Mount of Olives, East Jerusalem (tel. 282551). 200
rooms with TV. Part of the international chain of this name. Located on the
summit of the Mount of Olives, and commanding a superb view of the Old City
(although not from its rooms). This is the least expensive Deluxe hotel in
Jerusalem. Facilities include **The Peacock Bar** and **The Bistro** restaurant, with
an excellent Saturday buffet lunch. Coffee shop, summer terrace, tennis court,
beauty parlour, shops, baby-sitting, but no pool. The hotel is remote for walking,
but has an hourly shuttle service and some buses. AE, DC, MC, V.

Jerusalem Hilton, Givat Ram, West Jerusalem (tel. 536151). 420 rooms, all
with great views. On a hill at Jerusalem's western entrance (from Tel Aviv), next
to Binyanei Ha'ooma (the National Convention Center). A prime convention
and businessman's hotel, but successfully pampers individuals and tour groups
as well. Facilities include the **Hamsa Grill** and the fine **Kerem** restaurant; coffee
shop, bar, health club/sauna, pool, tennis, mini-golf, travel agency, banks,
airline agencies, beauty parlour and other shops, and a disco every night except
Friday. Rooms have TV, plus in-house video. Shuttle service downtown and to
the Old City. AE, DC, MC, V.

King David, 23 King David St., West Jerusalem (tel. 221111). 258 rooms. In
an excellent location if you like walking, this is the city's venerable Deluxe hotel
(1930) and a national institution, with an atmosphere at once regal, Old World
and Eastern. A room facing the Old City walls and cocktails on the terrace
overlooking the beautiful gardens are recommended. Warm, intimate bar; the
La Regence restaurant; sauna, pool, tennis, bank, shops, beauty parlor, coffee
shop. AE, DC, MC, V.

King Solomon, 32 King David St., West Jerusalem (tel. 241433). 150 rooms,
the smallest of the Deluxe hotels. Good location with views of the Old City. Fine
Japanese restaurant and grill room, plus piano bar, pool, bank, shops, and
synagogue. Rooms have TV and in-house video. AE, DC, MC, V.

Laromme, 3 Jabotinsky St., West Jerusalem (tel. 697777). 312 rooms, most
with a view of the central courtyard or the adjoining Liberty Bell Garden. A
strikingly successful piece of architecture, out of the prevailing high-rise mold,
within walking distance of Jerusalem's theater and gallery district. Fine bar with
nightly dance music, except Friday, grill room, 24-hour coffee shop, heated
pool, TV, shops, aerobics and massages. AE, DC, MC, V.

Ramada Renaissance, 6 Wolfson St., West Jerusalem (tel. 528111). 389
rooms with TV. Brand new, located near Hebrew University's Givat Ram
campus. Beautifully appointed with lovely grounds, pool, tennis, health club,
indoor heated pool, sauna and Jacuzzi. Coffee shop, piano bar, beauty parlor,

synagogue, weekly folk-dancing, bingo on Friday, and barbecue twice a week in summer. Shuttle service downtown and to Old City. AE, DC, MC, V.

Sheraton Jerusalem Plaza, 47 King George St., West Jerusalem (tel. 228133). 414 rooms, with TV and in-house video which offers "What's On" information as well as the usual movies. Prides itself on guest activities and services, including free morning walking tours, and a day camp for kids in July and August, and Passover and Christmas weeks. Bar, coffee shop, health club/ sauna, pool, bank, shops, beauty parlour, synagogue. The French-style **Cow on the Roof** restaurant is arguably Jerusalem's finest. Good location. AE, DC, MC, V.

Expensive

American Colony Hotel, Nablus Rd., East Jerusalem (tel. 282421-3). 102 rooms, 91 with bath, 11 with shower only. Conveniently located for East Jerusalem and Old City sites. Much depends on the room you get; the better suites are in the Deluxe price range. A fine hotel in a marvelous 19th-century stone building, exuding a distinctly "old Jerusalem" ambience. Very good food, including pool terrace and courtyard meals and fine Saturday buffet. Bar, coffee shop, heated pool in winter, babysitting; TV on request. Partially airconditioned. AE, MC, V.

Central Hotel, 6 Pines St., West Jerusalem (tel. 223111). 77 rooms. Near city center; ultra-Orthodox Jewish. Package deals for Passover and Sukkot festival seasons. Coffee shop, babysitting. AE, DC, MC, V.

Eilon Tower Hotel, Migdal Ha'ir (City Center), 34 Ben Yehuda St., West Jerusalem (tel. 233281). 120 rooms. On upper floors of the City Center building in downtown Jerusalem; all rooms have a sweeping view—unfortunately there's a slow elevator. The **Skylight Restaurant** on top floor; coffee shop, bar, babysitting; TV on request. AE, DC, MC, V.

Holyland West, Harav Uziel St., Bayit Vegan, West Jerusalem (tel. 630261). 116 rooms. In slightly remote Bayit Vegan neighborhood, although on bus route. Offers a resort atmosphere, with airy views, lovely gardens, pool, tennis and fine outdoor terrace for lunch or tea, and bar. Hotel owns the adjacent model of ancient Jerusalem. Some rooms in the annex have kitchenettes. AE, MC, V.

Jerusalem Tower Hotel, 23 Hillel St., West Jerusalem (tel. 222161). 120 rooms. Downtown location; with bar, grill room, self-service restaurant; TV on request. AE, DC, MC, V.

Moriah Hotel, 39 Keren Hayesod St., West Jerusalem (tel. 232232). 301 rooms. Definitely top-of-the-line in this category. Centrally-located, with bar, coffee shop, rooftop pool and sun deck in season, bank, beauty parlor, shops, babysitting; TV on request. **Golda's Kitchen** is their moderately-priced restaurant featuring traditional Jewish cuisine. AE, DC, MC, V.

Sonesta Hotel, 2 Wolfson St., Givat Ram, West Jerusalem (tel. 528221). 172 rooms. Farther out, but on good bus routes. Bar, coffee shop, piano bar, babysitting; TV on request. AE, DC, MC, V.

Windmill Hotel, 3 Mendele St., West Jerusalem (tel. 663111). 133 rooms. Well-located (opposite the Moriah) and very good value; prides itself on providing service above its grading. Coffee shop, synagogue, babysitting; TV on request. AE, DC, MC, V.

Moderate

Capitol Hotel, 17 Saladin St., East Jerusalem (tel. 282561-2). 54 airconditioned rooms with bath. In the heart of East Jerusalem. Bar; TV on request.

Menora, 24 King David St., West Jerusalem (tel. 223311). 64 spacious rooms with bath, partially airconditioned, 16 of which can accommodate up to five people. Offers a very good deal, is excellently-located within an easy walk of downtown and the Old City, and has bar, coffee shop, synagogue, babysitting; TV on request. Sabbath-observing, AE, DC, MC, V.

Mount Scopus Hotel, at the top of Nablus Rd., Sheikh Jarrah, East Jerusalem (tel. 284891–2). 65 airconditioned rooms with bath. Located a bit far from the Old City, but good view. Bar, babysitting; TV on request. AE, DC, MC, V.

National Palace Hotel, 4 Al-Zahara St., East Jerusalem (tel. 282246–4). 108 rooms with bath. Partially airconditioned. Well-located, and something of a landmark. Justly renowned for its rooftop Middle Eastern restaurant. Bar, coffee shop, babysitting; TV on request. AE, DC, MC, V.

Ram Hotel, 234 Jaffa Rd., West Jerusalem (tel. 535231). 156 airconditioned rooms with bath. Conveniently-located by the Central Bus Station. Very fine hotel for price range. Bar, coffee shop and babysitting service. AE, DC, MC, V.

Talpiot Apartment Hotel, 9 Bet Ha'arava St., West Jerusalem (tel. 719131). 12 apartments. Fully furnished, serviced, two-room apartments with kitchen for up to five people at very reasonable rates. Located in the green and quiet Talpiot neighborhood, under 15 minutes by bus from downtown.

YMCA (West), 26 King David St., West Jerusalem (tel. 227111). 68 rooms, almost all with shower. Opposite the King David Hotel, and known locally as "Imka"; its bell tower is a city landmark. Coffee shop, heated pool, tennis court, babysitting service, and regular cultural programs, V.

Inexpensive

Alcazar Hotel, 6 Almuntab St., East Jerusalem (tel. 281111). 38 rooms with bath. Partially airconditioned. A bit out of the way, but in pleasant location, and well-run. Self-service restaurant, bar, coffee shop, kitchenettes; TV on request. DC, V.

Ambassador Hotel, Nablus Rd., Sheikh Jarrah, East Jerusalem (tel. 828211). 118 airconditioned rooms, most with bath. Not central, but one of the best in its class. Coffee shop, bar, shops, beauty parlor; TV on request.

Har Aviv, 16A Bet Hakerem St., West Jerusalem (tel. 521515). 14 rooms with baths. Pension-type hostelry in the Bet Hakerem quarter on the west side of town; recommended.

Palatin Hotel, 4 Agrippas St., West Jerusalem (tel. 231141). 28 heated rooms with shower. In relatively quiet street in heart of downtown area. AE, MC, V.

Pilgrim's Palace Hotel, King Suleiman St., East Jerusalem (tel. 284831). 95 airconditioned rooms, most with bath. Opposite the Old City walls near the Damascus Gate. Bar, coffee shop; TV on request.

Ron Hotel, 42A Jaffa Rd., West Jerusalem (tel. 223471). 22 heated rooms with shower only. Right on Zion Square. AE, DC, MC, V.

Shepherd Hotel, Mt. Scopus, East Jerusalem (tel. 828272). 52 rooms with baths. Partially airconditioned; bar.

Strand Hotel, 4 Ibn Jubeir St., East Jerusalem (tel. 280279). 55 rooms with baths. Partially airconditioned. Coffee shop, bar; TV on request.

 GUEST HOUSES. This unique arrangement of hotel/motel accommodations run by a kibbutz or moshav is familiar to many visitors to the Galilee. There are five such guest houses around Jerusalem itself. Standards are comfortably equal to or better than equivalent hotel grades, the food is generally good, and the atmosphere warm and relaxing. All are in the Judean Hills, with panoramic views and pine forests.

Kiryat Anavim (tel. 542691–8). 93 rooms, 52 with bath, 41 with showers only. About 15 minutes' drive from Jerusalem, one of the more veteran kibbutz settlements in the area. Partially airconditioned, with pool, bar and coffee shop.

Ma'ale Hahamisha (tel. 542591–7). 121 rooms, 94 with bath, 27 with shower only. About 20 minutes from Jerusalem. Pool, tennis, other sports facilities, bar and coffee shop.

Mitzpeh Rachel, Box 98, Jerusalem (tel. 715712). 90 airconditioned rooms with bath, some family rooms, some with kitchenette. Also 29 rooms, shower only, no airconditioning. At Kibbutz Ramat Rachel, on a hill with fabulous view of Bethlehem and Judean Hills, yet to all intents and purposes in Jerusalem itself. Great self-service cafeteria; large pool heated in winter; plus sauna, tennis, gymnasium, lawns, coffee shop.

Neve Ilan (tel. 541241). 80 airconditioned rooms. Best of the region's guests houses, about 15 minutes' drive from Jerusalem, easily reaching a standard above its official rating. Pool (heated in winter), tennis, coffee shop, bar. Very friendly and welcoming.

Shoresh (tel. 541171–4). 114 airconditioned rooms. Pool, tennis, bar, coffee shop. 25 minutes from Jerusalem.

Hospices. Casa Nova, Box 1312, Casa Nova Rd. (tel. 282791). In the Christian Quarter, just inside the New Gate.

Christ Church, Box 14037 (tel. 282082). Just inside the Jaffa Gate. Anglican.

Ecce Homo Convent, Box 19056, Second Station, Via Dolorosa (tel. 282445). Sisters of Zion, Catholic.

Franciscans of Mary, Box 19049, Nablus Rd. (tel. 282633). White Sisters, Catholic.

Greek Catholic Patriarchate, Box 14130, Jaffa Gate (tel. 282023).

Lutheran Hostel, Box 14051, St. Mark's Rd., near Jaffa Gate (tel. 282120).

Notre Dame of Jerusalem Center, Box 20531 (tel. 289723). Outside and opposite the New Gate. Catholic.

St. Andrew's Hospice, Box 14216 (tel. 717701). Near the railway station, West Jerusalem, but not far from the Old City, (Presbyterian). Somewhat more expensive than most others.

St. George's Hostel, Box 19018, Nablus Rd. (tel. 283302). Anglican.

Sisters of Zion, Box 17015, Ein Karem, West Jerusalem (tel. 419609). Catholic.

Youth Hostels. This list includes hostels affiliated to the Israel Youth Hostels Association (and thus to the international association) and Christian hospices. Stays in the former are open to non-members and there is no age limit, though you may not generally stay more than three days. Many of the Christian hospices offer dormitory accommodations only.

Bet Bernstein, 1 Keren Hayesod St., cnr. Agron St. (tel. 228286). 100 beds, family rooms available, heating. Excellent location, though noisy, five minutes' walk from downtown and ten minutes' from the Old City. Buses 4, 7, 9, 15, 19, 22.

Christ Church Hostel, Box 14037 (tel. 282082). Just inside the Jaffa Gate, Christian hospice.

Ecce Homo Convent, Box 19056, Second Station, Via Dolorosa (tel. 282445). Christian hospice; women only.

Ein Kerem, Box 17013, above the Spring in Ein Kerem (tel. 416282). 90 beds, heating. Remote but romantic location; good restaurants nearby. Bus 17.

Franciscans of Mary, Box 19049, Nablus Rd. (tel. 282633). Christian hospice; women only.

Lutheran Hostel, Box 14051, St. Mark's Rd., Old City (tel. 282120). Christian hospice, near the Jaffa Gate. Kitchen facilities available.

Louise Waterman-Wise, Box 16350, 8 Hapisga St., Bayit Vegan (tel. 423366, 420990). 310 beds, including new family rooms. Away from center, but on excellent bus routes—13, 17, 18, 20, 24, 26, 39, 40 to Mt. Herzl. Heating, members' kitchen, sports, library, music room, cultural activities.

Moreshet Yahadut, Box 7880, 2 Ararat St., Old City (tel. 288611). 70 beds. In a good Old City location on border of Jewish and Armenian Quarters.

Camping. Bet Zayit (tel. 537717). Good location on grounds of moshav in wooded hills about 5 km (3 miles) west of the city, with good facilities.

Ein Hemed (Aqua Bella) (tel. 542190). In idyllic situation in a national park with springs, lawns and Crusader ruins. Good facilities. About 10 km (6 miles) west of Jerusalem off the Tel Aviv highway.

Mevo Betar. Much further out, about 20 km (12½ miles) southwest of Jerusalem in the Judean Hills. Good and varied facilities.

Ramat Rachel (tel. 715712). Superb location on edge of town, with views, excellent cafeteria, coffee shop, store, pool and other sports facilities; good bus to the city.

 RESTAURANTS. In a nation where good home cooking is a source of pride, eating out is a concept that has caught on only gradually. As little as 15 years ago, visitors to Israel were wont to complain about the food. There is no longer any need to. Restaurants abound—fine restaurants where you pay something for the service and the silverware; homey restaurants where the brusqueness is part of the image but the food is good; and everything inbetween. Again, cosmopolitan Tel Aviv leads this gastronomic revolution, but Jerusalem has nothing to be ashamed of.

Take note that in Israel many a Middle Eastern restaurant is labelled "Oriental," a translation of the legitimate Hebrew term, but a bit confusing for the Westerner.

If you're more interested in cheaper, fast food, the downtown area is dotted with stands selling felafel (fried chickpea balls with salad in pita bread), *bourekas* and *shwarma,* as well as many small restaurants specializing in houmous, piquant soups and other Middle Eastern standards. The Mahane Yehuda area has these, plus a line of "steakiot" quick-grill places known for their mixed grill in pita at all hours of the day and night. For hamburgers, the best are **Burger Ranch,** on Shlomzion Hamalka St., and Luntz St., and **MacDavid's** near Zion Sq.

Reservations are recommended for Expensive and Moderate restaurants.

Expensive

Alla Gondola, 14 King George St. (tel. 225944). Italian, as the name implies, and expensive, but worth it.

Chez Simon, 15 Shamai St. (tel. 225602). Serving French food with a Moroccan touch, this restaurant is very strongly recommended; superb food, attentive service and a convivial atmosphere. AE.

The Cow on the Roof, Sheraton Jerusalem Plaza Hotel (tel. 228133). Top of the line and very expensive. The food is the ultimate in French nouvelle cuisine, the service is impeccable, and "kosher" simply means that certain dietary rules are observed. AE, DC, MC, V.

Elat Hayam, 3 Ben Sira St., off Hillel St. (tel. 246122). Serves seafood; intimate.

Katy's, 16 Rivlin St. (tel. 234621). French cuisine in an elegant, intimate atmosphere, with a well-stocked bar and mood music. AE.

Kerem, in the Hilton Hotel (tel. 536151), widely acclaimed authentic French cuisine, à la carte, plus changing gourmet set menu; French chef. AE, DC, MC, V.

Mishkenot Sha'ananim, in the Yemin Moshe Quarter (tel. 221042). French cuisine and magnificent view of the Old City—if you get the right table. Try their mixed hors d'oeuvres.

Teppenyaki, King Solomon Hotel (tel. 241433). The only Japanese restaurant in town, it has two tables d'hote in different sections. AE, DC, MC, V.

Moderate

Au Sahara, 17 Jaffa Rd. (tel. 233239). Moroccan food.

Derby, 2 Ben Yehuda St. (tel. 244454). Justly renowned for its excellent steaks. AE, DC, MC, V.

Feferberg's, 53 Jaffa Rd. (tel. 224841). Excellent and traditional Eastern European Jewish cooking.

Fink's, 2 Hahistadrut St. (tel. 234523). Tiny and satisfying, serving Continental food. Its bar and special atmosphere make it a popular hang-out for foreign correspondents.

Golda's, Moriah Hotel, 39 Keren Hayesod St. (tel. 232232). Eastern European Jewish cooking. AE, DC, MC, V.

Goulash Inn, Ein Kerem (tel. 419214). At the upper end of the Moderate category, serving fine Hungarian cuisine.

La Terrasse, Denmark Square, Bet Hakerem (tel. 527590). Specializes in fish and dairy dishes with a French touch, although the Italian influence is represented in the menu as well.

Maharajah, 11 Shlomzion Hamalka St. (tel. 243186). Good Indian food, convivial atmosphere; excellent value. AE, DC, MC, V.

Mandy Tachi, 3 Hyrcanos St. (tel. 248233). The most elaborate of the Chinese restaurants, serving very good food.

Marrakesh, 4 King David St. (tel. 221208). Moroccan dishes, good ambiance. AE, DC, MC, V.

Masswadeh, 8 Al-Masoudi St. (tel. 284048). Excellent Middle Eastern food. V.

Mei Nifto'ach, in Lifta, just down the hill from the Central Bus Station (tel. 521374). Serving good North African food in an old stone house with a courtyard, surrounded by greenery; a marvelous location. MC, V.

National Palace Hotel, 4 Al-Zahara St., East Jerusalem (tel. 282245). Middle Eastern food in a garden restaurant on the roof of the hotel. AE, DC, MC, V.

Norman's, 9 Yoel Salomon St., near Zion Square (tel. 227444). This is a place for a good old-fashioned steak or Texan-sized freshly ground hamburger. AE, V.

Petra, 11 El-Rashid St. (tel. 283655). One of the best Middle-Eastern restaurants in town; excellent value.

Philadelphia, Al-Zahara St., East Jerusalem (tel. 289770). Justly renowned for Middle Eastern cooking, it has its sworn partisans. The mind-boggling array of first-course salads (mezza) is a meal in itself, but save space!

Sea Dolphin, Al-Rashid St., East Jerusalem (tel. 282788). Still packing them in, Israelis and tourists alike. Not intimate, but it's lively and the food could tempt Neptune himself.

Shemesh, 21 Ben Yehuda St. (tel. 222418). Specializes in stuffed vegetables, and has a mixed European/Near Eastern character, and a "public figure" clientele.

Inexpensive

Chung Hwa, Zangwil St., next to the gas station, Kiryat Hayovel (tel. 422746). Excellent food and great value; Szechuan specialties.

Europa, 42 Jaffa Rd., at Zion Square (tel. 228953). Established restaurant serving traditional Eastern European Jewish cooking—good, cheap food.

Leah Rehavia, 15 Keren Kayemet St. (tel. 662166). Like the Europa—Jewish cooking; good value.

Mamma Mia, 18 Rabbi Akiva St., on Independence Park (tel. 248080). Vegetarian Italian restaurant; makes own pasta and has terrific lasagna and pizza. Terrace makes it a special lunch spot in fine weather.

Monitin, 220 Jaffa Rd., near Central Bus Station (tel. 536064). Fine North African cooking, excellent value.

Papi, 9 Ben Hillel St. Serves good Italian food, but for take out pizza has to compete with the many other pizzerias in the downtown area—**Richie's, Ami, Uri's, Rimini,** and more.

The Pie House, 5 Hyrcanos St. (tel. 242478). Makes its own wonderful pies (and other things), and enjoys unflagging popularity at all hours. The locals managed to guard the secret from the tourists for a few years, but you can't hide a light under a bushel forever.

Taj, 27 Jaffa Rd. (tel. 241515). Specializes in Persian dishes.

CAFES AND SNACKBARS. The pastries and cakes are great at **Duvdavan,** at the corner of Jaffa Rd. and King George St.; at **Ha'uga,** Hasoreg St., off Jaffa Rd.; at **Calderon,** on Hillel St., a few steps from the Jaffa Rd. corner; and at **Hane'eman** on Luntz St., where you can sit on the sidewalk. Especially good *dobosh* is to be had at **Max,** on Ben Yehuda St., below King George St. All of Ben Yehuda St., including the pedestrian *midrachov* and its side streets, is full of such places now. **Magdalena's** on Hamelech Shlomo combines coffee and homemade cakes with display of the owner's fine ceramic art-work.

Fine coffee shops that serve good light meals include **Cafe Camin,** in a terrific garden courtyard on Akiva St., off Hillel St.; **Bet Ticho,** on Rav Kook St. in an unequalled courtyard setting; **Hasha'on (The Clock)** at 7 Rivlin St.; **Atara** on Ben Yehuda St.; and **Hamifgash** on the third floor of the Hamashbir department store on King George St.

Also try the Middle Eastern vegetarian specialties at **Mifgash Bavli,** 54 Hanevi'im St. and at **Palmachi,** 13 Shamai St.; the natural food dishes at **Hameshek,** 14 Shlomzion Hamalka St.; the crepes at **Poire et Pomme,** Hama' alot St.; and the quiches of **Basograyim** on Emek Refaim St. in the German Colony.

HOW TO GET AROUND. By Bus. The bus service in West Jerusalem is comprehensive and cheap, about 30 cents to any destination in the city. Pay as you enter. Most people, including the drivers, speak some English and fellow passengers are generally helpful in telling you where to get off. Buses and bus stops are marked with the route numbers.

A new and vital addition is Route 99, the "Round-City Line," which has 32 stops throughout the city, including six points around the Old City, Mt. of Olives, Mt. Scopus and most West Jerusalem sites and major hotel areas. It leaves once an hour on the hour from opposite the Jaffa Gate, Sundays through Thursdays 9–5, Fridays and eves of holidays 9–2 (no service on Saturdays and holidays). A single unbroken journey of any length costs $1, a one-day ticket for unlimited travel costs $4, and a two-day ticket $5. Maps of the route are available at the Egged Central Bus Station and Tourist Information Offices.

By Taxi. Taxis can be hailed in the street, called for by phone, picked up outside the better hotels or at special ranks in the main centers. Fares are moderate. Drivers are obliged by law to operate their meters; however, some will want to bargain the fare—do so before you start, so a map and an idea of distances are useful. After 9 P.M. and on the Sabbath the rate is 25% higher.

All-Night Taxis. *Rehavia* (tel. 224444); *Palmach* (tel. 666662, 666617); *Nesher* (airport limousine only, tel. 223233, 231231).

On Foot. In the Old City you are obliged to walk, but it's an excellent way of seeing other parts of Jerusalem as well, especially the downtown areas and the old neighborhoods.

CITY TOURS. Walking Tours (all half-day or less). **Archeological Seminars** (tel. 273515). Five routes within the Old City, plus the City of David, each offered several times a week. Tours last approximately two hours, including a brief introductory seminar. Inexpensive and discounted 3-tour ticket.

Egged Tours (tel. 223454, 224198). Identical to United Tours, below.

Galilee Tours (tel. 246858). Tour of the Old City, four times a week, lasting three hours. Hotel pick-up and drop-off. Schedules and reservations at hotel or travel agent.

Jerusalem Municipality. Places of interest in the City. Leaves Sat. morning 10 A.M. from 34 Jaffa Rd. and is free of charge.

Sheraton Jerusalem Plaza Hotel (tel. 228133). Four different morning tours a week; no charge.

Society for the Protection of Nature, 13 Helene Hamalka St. (courtyard of the Ministry of Agriculture, downtown, tel. 222357, 244605). Offers several regular routes in the Old City and the City of David, as well as different off-the-beaten-track walks in both the Old and New Cities, and in summer a night ramble on the ramparts plus a bonfire. Tours last 2–5 hours. Schedules at the Society's offices.

United Tours (tel. 222187–9, 225013). Tours of the Old City six times a week. The synagogues tour on Friday mornings costs $9. All include hotel pick-up and drop-off. Schedules and reservations at hotel or travel agent.

Walking Tours Ltd. (tel. 522568). Four routes in the Old City, plus the City of David and Mt. of Olives, some offered several times a week. Tours lasting 3½ hours or two hours; family rates available, and if you take three tours you get the fourth free. Schedules at Tourist Information.

Bus Tours. Galilee Tours (tel. 246858). Covers Jerusalem West and East with three itineraries and seven departures a week. Tours last half a day and include hotel pick-up and drop-off. Schedules and reservations at hotel or travel agent.

United Tours (tel. 222187–9). Covers Jerusalem West and East. Offers one full-day and four half-day itineraries, including a Summer Night Tour; hotel pick-up and drop-off. Schedules and reservations are at hotels or travel agents. **Egged Tours** (tel. 223454) offer an identical program.

EXCURSIONS. A wide range of half-, one-, two-, three- and four-day tours from Jerusalem are on offer: to Beersheba, Masada, the Dead Sea and Jericho; to the Galilee and the Golan; to the coast (Tel Aviv, Caesarea etc.); and to the Negev, Eilat and Sinai. Prices vary according to distance and the sites included. For longer tours the price includes hotel accommodations with dinner and breakfast. In all cases brochures are available and reservations can be made at hotels and travel agents; the tour also includes hotel pick-up and drop-off.

Operators of these tours include: **Egged Tours** (tel. 223454); **Galilee Tours** (tel. 246858); **United Tours** (tel. 222187–9), including three in-depth tours with **Archeological Seminars,** and **Walking Tours Ltd.** (tel. 522568).

Desert Safaris. Not for everyone but, for those who don't mind roughing it, it can be the experience of a lifetime.

Metzoke Dragot (tel. 228114/5/6 or 057–84340). Perched on a cliff high above the Dead Sea is a "desert tour village" operated by the nearby Kibbutz Mitzpeh Shalem and specializing in the Judean desert. They have tours by foot and vehicle; rock climbing.

Ne'ot Hakikar, 36 Keren Hayesod St., opposite the Moriah Hotel (tel. 699385, 636494). Range of tours from one to seven days in the Judean, Negev or Sinai deserts.

HISTORIC BUILDINGS AND SITES. Jerusalem is immensely rich in historic buildings and sites of all types and periods. Most are described in detail in our main text. The following list is intended as a checklist and record of opening times.

Old City. **Armenian Cathedral of St. James,** Armenian Quarter. Open Mon. to Fri. 3–3.30 P.M., Sat. and Sun. 2.30–3.15 P.M.

Batei Mahse Square, Jewish Quarter. Rothschild building from the 19th century and ancient columns.

Broad Wall, Jewish Quarter. City wall from 8th century B.C.

Burnt House, Jewish Quarter. Destroyed with the Roman Conquest in A.D. 70. Open Sun. to Thurs. 8–4.30, Fri. 8–1; closed Sat. Audio-visual show 9.30 A.M., 11.30 A.M., 1.30 P.M., 3.30 P.M.

Cardo, Jewish Quarter. Ancient main street of Byzantine Jerusalem.

Chapel of the Flagellation, Second Station of the Cross. Roman striated pavement. Open 8–12, 1–5; in summer 2–6.

Church of the Holy Sepulcher, Christian Quarter. Traditional site of the crucifixion and burial of Jesus. Open 4.30 A.M.–7 P.M.; in summer until 8 P.M.

Church of St. Alexander, Christian Quarter. Russian. Second Temple Period walls and gate, Roman triumphal arch. Open Mon. to Sat. 9–1, 3–5; closed Sun.

Citadel and "David's Tower." Walls, towers and halls from second century B.C. through 17th century A.D. See *Museums* for details.

Damascus Gate. Excavations of an ancient Roman gate, tower and square. Open Sat. to Thurs. 9–5, Fri. 9–2.

Dome of the Rock and the El Aqsa Mosque. Most important Muslim shrines and site of the ancient Jewish temple. Open Sat. to Thurs. 8–11 A.M., 12.30–2.15 P.M. (all hours approximate); closed Fri.

Ecce Homo Convent, Via Dolorosa. Roman pavement with etched games, Roman triumphal arch, Second Temple Period cisterns. Open Mon. to Sat 8.30–12.30, 2–5; arch until 4 P.M.

Ethiopian Monastery. On the roof of the "extension" of the Church of the Holy Sepulcher, next to the Ninth Station of the Cross.

Hurva Synagogue, Jewish Quarter. Ruins of the 19th-century Synagogue.

Israelite Tower, Jewish Quarter. 100 meters north of Broad Wall. Dates from 8th century B.C., reused in 2nd century B.C. Open 8–5.

Nea Church, Jewish Quarter. Apse of huge Byzantine church built by Justinian in the 6th century A.D.

Ramparts Walk. On the city walls. Open Sat. to Thurs. 9–5, Fri. 9–2.

St. Anne's Church and Pools of Bethesda, near Lions' (St. Stephen's) Gate. A Crusader church and 2,000 year-old pools. Open Mon. to Sat. 8–12, 2.30–5; in summer until 6 P.M.; closed Sun.

Sephardic Synagogues, Jewish Quarter. Restored, from the 16th century. Open Sun. to Thurs. 8.30–4, Fri. until 1 P.M.; closed Sat. (except for services).

Western Wall and Excavations. The holiest Jewish site today, a remnant of the Temple Mount retaining wall. There are extensive excavations revealing several ancient periods. Open Sun. to Thurs. 8–4, Fri. 8–2; closed Sat. Local tour at 2 P.M.

Outside the Walls. Ammunition Hill, opposite Ramat Eshkol. A battle site in the Six Day War of 1967. Bus 9, 25, 28, 99.

David's Tomb, Mt. Zion. Open 8–5.

Cenacle, or Upper Room (Room of the Last Supper), Mt. Zion. Open 8.30–5.

Church of Mary Magdalene (Russian), Gethsemane. Open Tues. and Thurs. 9–12, 2–4.

Church of St. Peter in Gallicantu, Mt. Zion. Ancient remains of a prison and stepped street. Open 8–11, 2–5; closed Sun.

City of David, Warren's Shaft and Area G. Extraordinary finds of Old Testament Jerusalem. Open 9–5, Fri. 9–3.

Garden of Gethsemane (Church of All Nations). The place where Jesus was arrested by the Romans. Open 8–12, 2.30–5; in summer until 6 P.M.

Garden Tomb, Nablus Rd. Alternative (Protestant) site of the crucifixion and burial of Jesus. Open-air garden and antiquities. Open Mon. to Sat. 8–12, 2.30–5; closed Sun.

Hebrew University, Mt. Scopus. Founded in 1925, lately expanded and renovated. Bus 9, 28, 99.

Hezekiah's Tunnel and Pool of Siloam, City of David/Silwan. Old Testament Jerusalem, with an 8th-century B.C. water system and a Christian site. Open Sun. to Thurs. 8–5, Fri. 8–1; closed Sat.

Kidron Valley. Tombs of "Absalom", "Zechariah" *et al.*

Paternoster Convent, Mt. of Olives. The Lord's Prayer in different languages on ceramic tiles. Open 8.30–11.45 A.M., 3–4.30 P.M. Bus 42, 99.

Solomon's Quarries (Zedekiah's Cave), near the Damascus Gate. A deep quarry or cave under the city walls from the Second Temple Period. Legends relate it to King Solomon and Zedekiah. Open Sun. to Thurs. 8–4, Fri. 8–1; closed Sat.

Tomb of Mary, Gethsemane. Open 6.30–12, 2–5.

Tomb of the Kings, Saladin St. Jewish necropolis from the first century A.D. Open 8–12.30, 2–5; closed Sun.

World War I Military Cemetery, Mt. Scopus. War cemetery for the British and Allies. Bus 9, 28, 99.

West Jerusalem. Allenby Memorial, Kikar Ilit (Ilit Square), Romema, behind the Central Bus Station. Commemorates the British and Allied capture of Jerusalem from the Turks in December, 1917.

Jason's Tomb, 10 Alfasi St., Rehavia. A restored tomb from the 2nd century B.C. with ancient drawings. Open Mon. and Thurs. 10–1. Bus 9, 19, 22.

Knesset. Israeli Parliament building. Bus 9, 99.

Mishkenot Sha'ananim and Montefiore's Windmill, opposite Mt. Zion. The first neighborhood beyond the walls; sponsored by Sir Moses Montefiore.

Model of Ancient Jerusalem, Holyland Hotel, Bayit Vegan. A 1:50 scale model of Jerusalem about 20 centuries ago. Open 8–5. Bus 21, 99.

Monastery of the Cross, in the Valley of the Cross below the Israel Museum. This is said to be where the tree grew from which the cross of Jesus was made. Bus 9, 99. Open Mon. to Thurs., Sat. 9–4.30; Fri. 9–1.30; closed Sun.

Mt. Herzl. A memorial park with the tombs of Theodore Herzl, Golda Meir, Levi Eshkol and others. Open 8–5; in summer until 6 P.M. Bus 17, 18, 20, 21, 23, 27, 99.

Mt. Herzl Military Cemetery. A national cemetery for all wars. Buses as above.

President's House, Hanassi St. The official residence of Israel's Head of State. No visits. Bus 15, 99.

Ramat Rachel, on the edge of Jerusalem, overlooking the Jerusalem–Bethlehem road. A partially excavated tel, this was also a modern-day strong-point and battleground in the 1948 War of Independence.

Russian Compound, downtown area. A Russian church, a huge 2,000 year-old stone column, a British prison in the Mandate period.

 MUSEUMS. Opening times are subject to change and should be checked on the spot. Many museums give discounts to students with valid international student I.D.s, and to children.

Agriculture Museum, the Ministry of Agriculture compound, 13 Helene Hamalka St., in the downtown area. Displays old and ancient farming implements used in Israel. Open in summer, Sun. to Fri. 8–1; winter, Sun. to Thurs. 8–2, Fri. 8–1.

Ammunition Hill Memorial and Museum, opposite Ramat Eshkol. On the site of a major battle in the Six Day War of 1967. Dedicated to those who fell there, it traces the reunification of Jerusalem after 1967. The landscaped park is always open. The museum is open Sun. to Thurs. 9–5 (March to June), 9–7 (July and August), 9–4 (September to February); Fri. 9–11 A.M.; closed Sat. Bus 9, 25, 28, 99.

Armenian Art and History Museum, Armenian Quarter, Old City, between the Jaffa and Zion Gates. Displays Armenian arts and crafts, artefacts and manuscripts. Open Mon. and Wed. to Sat. 10–4.30; closed Tues. and Sun. Bus 1, 13, 19, 20, 23.

David's Citadel (City Museum). Archeological finds of all periods from the dig at this site, Jerusalem's history in diagrams, one-third-life-size dolls of ethnic and religious groups, observatory, detailed 19th-century model of city, audiovisuals. Open daily 8.30–4.30, Fri. till 2. Multi-screen audio-visual (in English) at 8.30, 10.30, 12.30, 2.30, 6. Fri. first three only, Sat. no screenings.

Hall of Heroism, within the former Jerusalem Central Prison in the Russian Compound, downtown area. An exhibit of Jewish Underground activities in the struggle for independence. Open Sun. to Thurs. 10–4, Fri. 10–1; closed Sat.

Herzl Museum, Mt. Herzl (Har Herzl). Biographical documents, memorabilia and the reconstructed study of Theodore Herzl, founder of the modern Zionist movement. The museum is within a magnificent park. Guided tours in the Museum are available on request. Open Sun., Mon., Tues. and Thurs. 9–5; Fri. and Sat. 9–1; closed Wed. Bus 6, 12, 13, 17, 18, 20, 23, 27, 99.

Greek Patriarchate Museum, Greek Patriarchate Rd. Christian Quarter of the Old City. Archeological finds and liturgical objects. Open Mon. to Sat. 9–1; closed Sun. Bus (via Jaffa Gate) 1, 13, 19, 20, 23, 99.

Islamic Art Museum, 2 Hapalmach St. A major collection of Islamic art and artefacts from all periods and regions. Open Sun., Mon., Tues., Thurs. 10–12, 3.30–6; Wed. 3.30–9 P.M.; Sat. 10.30–1; closed Fri. and holidays. Advance tickets for Sat. possible at Islamic Museum on Temple Mount (next to El Aksa Mosque). Bus 15, 99.

Israel Museum, Ruppin St. Contains the Shrine of the Book (Dead Sea Scrolls), archeological exhibits, Jewish ceremonial art, a sculpture garden, paintings, ethnography, a youth wing, temporary exhibits. Open Sun., Mon., Wed., Thurs. 10–5; Tues. 4–10 P.M. (Shrine of the Book, 10–9); Fri. and Sat. 10–2. Bus 9, 16, 24, 99.

Museum of Italian Jewish Art, 27 Hillel St., downtown area. Incorporates the interior of Italy's Canegliano Synagogue, plus religious objects. Open Sun. 10–1, Wed. 4–7 P.M.

Natural History Museum, 6 Mohliver St., off Emek Refaim. Displays indigenous birds, beasts and fish; human anatomy; working models—a good museum for children. Open Sun., Tues., Thurs. 10.30–1; Mon. and Wed. 4–6 P.M.; Sat. 10.30–1; closed Fri. Bus 4, 18.

Old Yishuv Court Museum, 6 Or Haim St., Jewish Quarter of the Old City. Through furnishings and artefacts it recaptures life in the Jewish Quarter in the 19th century, including two restored synagogues. Open Sun. to Thurs. 10–5.

Rockefeller Museum, opposite Herod's Gate, near the corner of Jericho Rd, East Jerusalem. Not only does it contain a vast and impressive collection of antiquities from archeological excavations in the region, but as an institution it is actually involved in exploration. Public lectures in English on related subjects. Open Sun. to Thurs. 10–5, Fri. and Sat. 10–2. Buy tickets for Sat. in advance. Bus 27, 43, 99.

Tourjeman Post Museum, 1 Hel Hahandassa St., near the Mandelbaum Gate. A former Israeli military outpost on the "green line"—the 1948–67 border through Jerusalem. Contains an exhibit of photographs on the creation and erasure of that border. There's a video presentation too. Open Sun. to Thurs. 9–3; closed Fri. and Sat. Bus 1, 2, 11, 12, 99.

Wolfson Museum, in "Hechal Shlomo", the seat of the Chief Rabbinate, 58 King George St., near the downtown area. A collection of unusual Jewish ceremonial art and artifacts. Tours daily. Open Sun. to Thurs. 9–1, Fri. till noon; closed Sat. Bus 4, 7, 8, 9, 10, 16, 17, 19.

Yad Vashem Holocaust Memorial and Museum, on the slopes of Mt. Herzl. The phenomenal tale of the destruction of the European Jewish community is told chronologically through photographs and explanations in English. Also a museum of art by victims and survivors. Open Sun. to Thurs. 9–4.30, Fri. 9–2; closed Sat. Bus 6, 12, 13, 17, 18, 20, 23, 27 to Mt. Herzl and walk, or bus 99 to the site itself.

 GALLERIES. Arta, 4 Rabbi Akiva St. (tel. 227829) and in the King David and Laromme hotels. The gallery is known for its works of Agam and of Judaica, but has its share of Chagall, Rubens and Castel as well.

The Artists' House, 12 Shmuel Hanagid St. (tel. 223653). Represents the works of the over 300 Jerusalem-based members of the Artists' Association. A bookshop and garden restaurant complete the complex.

Bet Ticho, Ticho House, Rav Kook St., just above and opposite Maskit. Traces the career of Anna Ticho; offers a tranquil haven from the city.

Herbert Bluhm, 5 Ma'alot Nahalot Shiva, off Salomon St., near Zion Square (tel. 858036, 634383). The painter exhibits his etchings and watercolors (many inspired by Jerusalem itself) in his studio, once a water cistern, in the old Nahalot Shiva Quarter.

Engel Galleries, Hutzot Hayotzer (tel. 289802); 13 Shlomzion Hamalka St (tel. 223523); and the Hilton Hotel. They have some marvelous Anna Ticho prints, and much else besides.

Ya'akov Heller, 22 King David St. (tel. 245320). The artist is by now world-renowned for his dynamic sculptures in silver, especially of Biblical scenes—one is in the White House.

Safrai, King David's Court, next to the hotel (tel. 221294) and in the King David and Plaza hotels. The gallery specializes in original graphics (Chagall, Mane Katz, Miro) and sculpture.

Wein, 18 Malki St., Yemin Moshe (tel. 242280). One of the capital's best known galleries, specializing in 19th and 20th century master prints, modern Israeli paintings and sculpture, and modern Jewish ceremonial objects.

The lobby of the **Jerusalem Theater** serves as a showcase for new talents in painting, photography, tapestry and so on. Good art is also to be found at **Hutzot Hayotzer** and the **Jerusalem House of Quality** (see Shopping) and at the **Israel Museum.**

PARKS AND GARDENS. Most neighborhoods have small parks and playgrounds, and there are several such green havens in or around the downtown area as well. Worth special mention are:

Independence Park between Hillel St., in the downtown area, and Agron St. It has lots of lawns and pine trees (not recommended for night-time strolling).

Ammunition Hill, opposite Ramot Eshkol. This is a landscaped memorial park, with a museum on the site. Bus 9, 21, 28, 99.

The Wohl Rose Garden, with hundreds of varieties, next to the Bank of Israel building and near the Knesset. Bus 9, 24, 28, 99.

Mt. Herzl, a beautifully laid out memorial park and picnic area with facilities. Bus 12, 18, 20, 21, 23, 27, 99.

Liberty Bell Garden, behind the Laromme Hotel. A bicentennial gift from America with a replica of Philadelphia's famous bell. Has a children's "Train Theater", which operates in season. Bus 4, 6, 7, 8, 15, 18.

The Biblical Zoo, Sanhedria. It has cages of animals mentioned in the Bible, all labeled with the appropriate quotation. Bus 1, 7, 15.

SHOPPING. A highlight of shopping in Jerusalem is likely to be combing the narrow alleys in the Old City—the **Souk**—especially in the region of David St., entered from the Jaffa Gate. It's fun and fascinating to shop in the bazaar here, but a word to the wise. Don't buy "antiques" without official authenticity guarantees—they'll likely be fakes. Stick to stores recommended by the Ministry of Tourism (a sign in the window) for these or for other costly items where quality isn't in question. For jewelry, for example, you're safer shopping in West Jerusalem. Comparison shopping is the rule in the bazaar, where there are no fixed prices, and quality fluctuates wildly. Haggling is accepted procedure, so don't let the first price put you off. At the same time, don't haggle unless you're serious about actually buying the item if the shopkeeper meets your price. Some of the shopkeepers have an aggressive approach, but there is no need to be intimidated.

The best Armenian pottery—plates, plaques, ashtrays, etc.—is probably to be found at **Jerusalem Pottery** next to the Sixth Station of the Via Dolorosa. Next door is the **Benevolent Arts**, a Christian "institution" store that makes the finest quality embroidered shirts, dresses, table-cloths, and so on. They will custom-make anything to your specifications. At both the above, prices are fixed. At the **Souk Aftimous**, a few steps away from the Church of the Holy Sepulcher, are shops literally overflowing with camel-skin items (especially bags), sheepskins and woven rugs. There are many good items here, but shoddy goods abound too.

More modern shops and better quality (and more expensive) merchandise are to be found in two new malls recently developed in the **Jewish Quarter** of the Old City—one on the Cardo, the other on the way to the Western Wall (next to the Burnt House). Both have an abundance of gifts, arts and crafts, souvenirs and books, while the Cardo area also offers leather fashions, furs and fine art.

Again, for a more modern environment, try the **Downtown** triangle of Ben Yehuda St., King George St., and Jaffa Road, with its side streets, as well as King David St. **Maskit** on Rav Kook St., just off Jaffa Rd, near Zion Square, has a wide range of high quality arts and crafts, jewelry, fashions and weaving, much inspired by native folklore. **Idit** on Ben Yehuda St., has fine jewelry. This is an area in which Israel particularly excels, both with traditional designs (some fabulous filigree work, for example) and very modern and classy creations. For original and elegant women's fashions, try **A.B.C.** on both King George St. and Helene Hamalka St. (behind the Russian compound).

Hutzot Hayotzer, just outside and below Jaffa Gate, was once designed as stables, used as a market, and today, after restoration, houses a whole community of superb craftspeople. Look for Daniel Elsberg's unusual creative jewelry, Uri Ramot's unique objets d'art combining ancient Roman glass with silver or gold, Zelig Segal's designs in silver and bronze, and the silver Judaica of Michael Ende or Ya'akov Greenvurcel.

Along similar lines is the **Jerusalem House of Quality** at 12 Hebron Rd. (behind St. Andrew's Church, and a couple of minutes' walk from the Railway Station in the direction of Mt. Zion). Many craftspeople have their workshops here, and there is a fine showroom displaying their high-quality work. Among the many unusual creations look for the painted wood pieces of Aviva Ha'ezrachy, the ceramics of Martha Sharbakowsky, Naomi Hind's knitwear and Rachel Pariser's filigree jewelry.

 MUSIC, MOVIES AND THEATERS. Information about music, movies and theaters is available at Tourist Information offices, posted on bill-boards around the city and at the venues themselves, and is listed in the Friday edition of the *Jerusalem Post,* the English-language daily. There are also various "What's On" type brochures available free at most hotels.

Information and tickets can be got at **Kahana,** 1 Dorot Rishonim St. (tel. 222831); **Klaim,** 8 Shamai St., upstairs (tel. 234061, 240896); **Ben-Naim,** 38 Jaffa Rd. (tel. 224008); and **Bnei Kadoori,** 204 Klal Building, Jaffa Rd. (tel. 233732, 241979).

Music. Classical music is Jerusalem's strong suit. The Israel Broadcasting Authority's Jerusalem Symphony Orchestra has regular concerts at the **Jerusalem Theater.** The Tel Aviv-based Israel Philharmonic Orchestra plays its subscription series at the large **Binyanei Ha'ooma.** Smaller ensembles often perform in the **Israel Museum**'s auditorium, or at the **Targ Center** in Ein Kerem. The **YMCA (West)** hosts a free Thursday afternoon concert (for live radio) and occasionally other events. Organ, vocal and choral recitals can often be found at the **Dormition Abbey** on Mt. Zion, and at the **Lutheran Church of the Redeemer** in the Old City.

In the summer several large-scale musical events take place in the huge open-air **Sultan's Pool** beneath the Old City walls. The star-studded "Israel Festival in Jerusalem" in the spring exultantly fills every venue in town, indoor and open-air alike, with a wonderful array of cultural fare. The "Liturgica" series in late December to early January features sacred music presented by local and guest choirs and artists.

Local popular performers appear regularly at several venues—watch the listings—and international performers also appear during the course of the year, particularly in spring and summer. Major pop, jazz, or folk artists would be likely to appear at Binyanei Ha'ooma or the Sultan's Pool.

Movies. Movie theaters in Israel are often not the well-upholstered, decorous experience some visitors know back home—though there are of course exceptions. Almost all the cinemas are in the downtown area, the only exceptions being **Binyanei Ha'ooma's** small auditorium (near the Central Bus Station), and **Semadar** (in the Germany Colony). The latter specializes in reruns, as does the **Israel Museum,** though with greater discrimination. Especially worth mentioning is the **Cinemateque** film club and archives, which has a weekly smorgasbord of older movies. Non-members may have difficulty getting into popular drawcards.

Theater. Theater is vigorous in Israel, though most productions are of course in Hebrew. Simultaneous translations (through headphones) are occasionally offered. A few small local groups working in English, as well as periodic guest artists or groups, make it worth watching the listings. Other theatrical forms like puppet theater and mime are also staged. In addition to the fine **Jerusalem Theater,** the **Khan Theater** is a picturesque and popular venue.

Dance, especially modern dance, is alive and well in Israel with some seven professional groups performing frequently in all parts of the country. Of these groups the **Israel Ballet** has a classical orientation, **Kol U'demama** combines both hearing and deaf dancers, and **Inbal** draws its choreographic inspiration from Israel's ethnic traditions. **Bat Sheva, Bat Dor,** the **Kibbutz Dance Group,** and the **Karmon Group** are known for their fine modern dance. Performances are usually at the Jerusalem Theater or at the **Gerard Behar Center.**

 BARS. For serious bars, try the **King David Hotel,** where you might find yourself drinking next to an international correspondent or peace negotiator, or the **Laromme Hotel,** which stays open later than most. Also popular are **Herod's** and **Goliath,** both piano bars favored by singles and both on King David St.

The younger set frequent the many little bars and pubs on Rivlin St. and nearby Nahlat Shiva St., especially **The Tavern, Champ's** and **Pini's Pub.**

For late-night music, check the **Khan Club,** opposite the Railway Station; and **Bet Ha'omanim** (Artists' House) on Shmuel Hanagid St., downtown.

 NIGHTLIFE. Jerusalem is justly renowned for many things. Its nightlife is not one. Apart from concerts, theater, movies and restaurants, most Jerusalemites tend to create their own entertainment themselves, or hang out (especially the younger set) at downtown cafes and pizzerias. But there are a few places to keep the night-owl occupied for a while. A few tourist-oriented "folklore" nightclubs offer a show of local singers and folkdancers, which costs about $13 with unlimited wine or fruit juice included (no other drinks available). The performers are usually pretty good, but the shows tend to follow a similar pattern wherever you go. Best known, perhaps, is the **Khan,** opposite the Railway Station. Once a Turkish caravansarai where every stone breathes atmosphere, it regularly features the veteran and polished Yaffa Yarkoni. Just down the road is **Jerusalem of Gold** in Abu Tor (walking distance away). A newcomer is the **Sabra Club,** located in Talpiot's industrial zone. A cheaper concert-type folklore performance is available several times a week at the **Y.M.C.A. West** on King David St., and at **I.C.C.Y.** on Emek Refaim St.

Two small clubs that often have good jazz, folk music, or other kinds of music are the **Pargod,** at 94 Bezalel St., and **Tzavta** on King George St. The **Zionist Confederation House** on Emile Botta St. (off King David St.) also hosts jazz evenings and other similar events. **Penny Lane,** 29 Hanevi'im St., near the Russian Compound, offers folk music or jazz along with its pies and salads. Watch the listings.

 SPORTS. Swimming. Public pools in Jerusalem are: Bet Taylor, Kiryat Hayovel, Bus 18; Ivy Judah Youth Center, Jerusalem Forest, Bus 33; Jerusalem Swimming Pool (the least expensive but the most crowded), Emek Refaim St., Bus 4, 18; YMCA (West), an indoor, year-round pool for hotel guests and members, King David St., Bus 6, 15, 16, 99; Mitzpeh Rahel, Ramat Rachel, Bus 7.

There are hotel pools at the King David, King David St., Bus 6, 15, 18, 99; the Holyland, Bayit Vegan, Bus 21, 99; the Diplomat, in Talpiot, Bus 8; the President, Ahad Haam St., Bus 4, 7, 8. Out of Jerusalem there are pools at Kibbutz Ma'ale Hahamisha, Moshav Bet Zayit, Moshav Neve Ilan, and Moshav Shoresh.

Tennis. Many swimming areas also have tennis courts: Bet Taylor (tel. 414362), Holyland Hotel (tel. 661101), Ramat Rachel (tel. 715711), Shoresh (tel. 538171), YMCA (West) (tel. 227111). Also at the Jerusalem Sports Club, 30 Hatzafira St., and the German Colony (tel. 632125), Bus 4, 18.

Details on all sports possibilities in Jerusalem are also available from the I.G.T.O.

 RELIGIOUS SERVICES. Jewish. The Western (Wailing) Wall has an immense pull for many worshippers, but every neighborhood is likely to have several synagogues, Ashkenazi and Sephardic alike. The two largest Ashkenazi ones are the magnificent new Great Synagogue on King George St. (opposite the Jerusalem Plaza Hotel), and the Yeshurun Synagogue on the same street a bit closer to downtown.

Catholic. Mass in English is celebrated daily at Notre Dame, opposite the New Gate; the Pontifical Institute, East Botta St., next to the King David Hotel; and at the Ratisbonne Institute, 26 Shmuel Hanagid St., downtown. Sunday mass is celebrated at these plus Gethsemane; Terra Sancta, on the corner of Keren Hayesod St.; and at St. Joseph French Hospital. For times of services contact the Christian Information Center inside the Jaffa Gate (tel. 287647).

Protestant. The following have weekly services: Garden Tomb (Evangelical, non-denominational); St. George's Cathedral, Nablus Rd. (Anglican); Christ Church, Jaffa Gate (Anglican); St. Andrew's Church, opposite the Railway Station (Presbyterian); Church of the Redeemer, the Christian Quarter of Old City (Lutheran); Baptist Tourist Chapel, 6 Rashid St.; and Jerusalem House, 35 Nablus Rd. (Baptist). The following also conduct services: Church of the Nazarene, 33 Nablus Rd; Pentecostal Church of God, Mt. of Olives; Seventh Day Adventists, 4 Lincoln St.; Church of Christ, Azahara St.; Christian Brethren Association, Smuts St. (tel. 631178). For Mormon services, tel. 815294. For further information contact the Christian Information Center, Jaffa Gate (tel. 287647). Evangelical interests are represented by the Christian Embassy (tel. 669823).

THE DEAD SEA

Including Jericho and the Jordan Rift

Stark desert landscapes, flowering oases, wandering nomads, and a taste of history—all await you just a short drive from the comfort of Jerusalem. And if you have time, you can float in the Dead Sea, reading your newspaper, just like the pictures on the tourist posters. The relatively quick descent from Jerusalem, about 750 meters (2,440 ft.) above sea level, to the Dead Sea, 400 meters (1,300 ft.) below sea level, makes for abrupt and sudden changes in climate. In the winter you can leave cold winds and rain in Jerusalem and eat lunch in the sun in Jericho under an orange tree half-an-hour later. In the summer, temperatures at the Dead Sea soar, but the very low humidity makes the area less uncomfortable than you might initially imagine, even though you should nonetheless take care to drink plenty of water.

This chapter describes the road from Jerusalem to the Dead Sea and the areas along the Dead Sea and the lower Jordan Valley. Geographically, it is part of one low-lying continuum—the Great Rift Valley—which in fact begins in the upper reaches of the Jordan river and continues southward to the Dead Sea, Eilat and thence all the way to Kenya and Tanzania in East Africa.

Our chapter begins by covering the route from Jerusalem to Masada, the most popular historic site in the country. A visit to Jericho and the road northward is described separately since many visitors include a tour of this area on their way northward, to Galilee.

A visit to the Dead Sea, including Masada, the mountaintop fortress where a group of Jewish fighters made a heroic stand against the Roman Empire, and the Ein Gedi Nature Reserve, where desert streams gush down the mountainside and ibex can be seen leaping from rock to rock, can be done in a day. By pushing hard, you might even be able to squeeze in the ancient town of Jericho, and Qumran where the Dead Sea Scrolls were found. On the other hand, to take advantage of the curative powers of the climate, mineral springs and mud baths, you can stay around the Dead Sea for days, even weeks. If you want to go out desert trekking, take note that some areas are closed military firing ranges and that even experienced hikers have been lost in what appears to be a small area.

Toward the Dead Sea

Leaving Jerusalem by way of the Mount of Olives, you find yourself on a steadily descending road (Route 1) which, to a considerable extent, follows the ancient caravan route from Jerusalem to Jericho and Amman across the Jordan river. This is the eastern side of the watershed formed by the Judean Mountains. Most of the rain clouds, which are blown from west to east, fail to cross it, and with the exception of the oases, the most notable of which are Jericho and Ein Gedi, the land becomes increasingly barren.

Just beyond Jerusalem is Bethany, a village whose Arab name, El Azariya, recalls that it is the town where Jesus raised Lazarus from the dead (John 11). The modern Roman Catholic church abuts the main road. An ancient grotto, traditional site of the miracle, was once accessible by a tunnel from where the church stands, but to reach it now climb the steep path to the right of the church.

Four or five kilometers further on, you'll see the modern apartment blocks of Ma'aleh Adumim to the right, perched a little incongruously in the barren wilderness above the road. Built on cheap public land with government assistance, it has attracted many young families from Jerusalem. Adding to the incongruity, yet simultaneously underlining the long human history of these parched hills, are the Beduin tents, with children tending herds of sheep and goats, scattered around this region. An additional picturesque touch is provided by the camels wandering around, apparently aimlessly, though all in fact have owners who are well aware of their movements.

Fifteen kms. (nine miles) out of Jerusalem is a rise characterized by an outcrop of red rock that gave the place its name. This is the ancient Ma'aleh Adumim, the Red Ascent. A border-marker between tribes in Biblical times (Joshua 15), it became the natural overnight pilgrim stop between Jerusalem and Jericho in the Byzantine and Crusader periods. On the right, a century-old Turkish building has become known as the "Inn of the Good Samaritan," recalling the inn in the New Testament parable (Luke 10).

Beyond the Inn, successive turns to the left put you on the old Jericho road with walking trails down to the canyon of Wadi Kelt

(Nahal Perat) with its springs (Ein Kelt), Herodian aqueducts and the spectacular St. George's Monastery. The present monastery, almost suspended from the sheer cliffs, was built by Greek Orthodox monks in the 19th century but remains of the 5th- and 6th-century Byzantine structures remain. It's a bit of a walk but well worth it. Modest attire is necessary for visitors, though even the view from the hillocks beside the old road is worthwhile.

Continuing down the old Jericho road brings you out above and south of Jericho at the recently-excavated remains of the 1st-century Hasmonean and Herodian royal palaces. From here you join Route 90—north into Jericho, south to the Dead Sea.

Back on Route 1, a stone marker by the side of the road informs you that you are at Sea Level. Soon, still far below you, you can see the Dead Sea shimmering in the distance. Just visible on the right side of the road is Nebi Musa, a shrine marking what Muslims believe to be the grave of Moses. According to the Jewish and Christian tradition as recorded in the Old Testament, Moses died in the Land of Moab, on the other side of the Jordan, and the site of his grave is not known. But the Arabs relate that Allah brought the bones of Moses from their secret grave to this site. In former years, the medieval mosque and complex of buildings for pilgrims were the object of a mass pilgrimage from Jerusalem in the spring, about the time of Passover and Easter. Occasionally, these processions would degenerate into attacks against Christians, and later they provided the impetus for riots against the Jews, especially in 1921 and 1929. The processions were then discontinued by Jordan's King Hussein, who feared they might turn into demonstrations against his regime.

The road now straightens out and crosses an arid plain. The road to Jericho, Route 90, branches off to the north. Continue directly eastwards. What appear to be large water tanks on your left are, in fact, experimental solar energy pools, which produce electric power, although not yet enough to make them economically viable. It is another attempt to garner some benefit from the sunshine, one of the country's few natural resources.

Near the shore of the Dead Sea, the road makes a sharp turn to go south along the seashore. Here a Beduin conveniently waits with his camel, ready to be photographed. Just further on is the newly-prepared Kalia beach with washing and changing facilities.

Qumran and Ein Gedi

Continuing southwards, a turn to the right will bring you to Qumran, and the ancient remains of the Jewish collective community of the Essenes. In the 2nd century B.C. this ultra-devout sect broke away from the Jewish religious mainstream and settled in this remote desert spot, far from the corruption of city life, in a virtually monastic community. Once known as Metzad Hassidim, the Fort of the Pious Ones, the site commands long views in all directions, giving warning of an approaching enemy. Such a warning may have prompted the hasty hiding in nearby caves of the community's archives—the Dead Sea Scrolls—just before Qumran succumbed to the Roman legions in A.D. 68.

The first of these scrolls were found in 1947 by a Beduin shepherd and the adventure and intrigue which surrounded them until their final collection in Jerusalem's Israel Museum is the stuff of which Hollywood thrillers are made. (For more on the startling insights into the Essene philosophy and way of life provided by the scrolls, see page 79). Perhaps the most interesting room found in Qumran by archeologists in the 1950s was the scriptorium, the very room in which the scrolls were written, complete with a smoothly-plastered writing desk and ceramic and bronze inkwells.

The site includes remains of the ancient fortifications, mikvehs or ritual immersion baths—some showing evidence of the earthquake of 31 B.C. which devastated the town—the ingenious flood-water catchment system, the meeting/eating hall, a potter's kiln and a view of Scroll Cave #4.

A couple of miles further south is Ein Fashcha, a nature reserve with natural springs which water a rich reed foliage and provide for a series of sweet water pools, ideal for bathing before and after a dip in the Dead Sea. Where the streams run into the sea, you can see tiny minnows swimming about just on the edge of the intensely saline waters, where no living thing can grow. The spot, a favorite for picnics by local residents, has a snack bar and changing facilities. Since the area is a nature reserve, it is illegal to pick any of the vegetation.

One of the few settlements along the way is Kibbutz Mitzpe Shalem, 17 kms. (11 miles) south of Ein Fashcha. One kilometer before the kibbutz, a good road climbs to the top of the cliffs for a breathtaking view of the Dead Sea and the adjacent awesome canyon of Nahal Dragot. Here, too, is Mitzpe Shalem's desert village, Mitzpe Dragot, which serves its desert tours and rock-climbing programs.

But the greenery of Mitzpe Shalem pales into insignificance when compared with that of Ein Gedi, a further 14 kms. (nine miles) south, a large oasis which the Bible mentions as the hiding place of David when he hid from the wrath of Saul. Kibbutz Ein Gedi, which is large and thriving, grows date palms, which you can see by the side of the road. Indeed, even in Roman times, the site was famed for its dates.

Next to the kibbutz is one of the country's best-known nature reserves, Nahal David, where you can follow a well-marked trail along cascading falls and through near-tropical foliage. A walk of about half-an-hour will bring you to a mountain pool large enough to swim in, while longer excursions can provide wilder terrain and more impressive views. Even the casual visitor can see ibex, or wild goats, and hyrax (a small furry animal). For bird-watchers, there is a lookout from which you may view species found only in this area. One of them is Tristram's Grackle, named after a 19th-century explorer. It is a black bird with deep orange patches on its wings. There are also a few leopards in the region, but it is virtually impossible for the casual visitor to catch sight of them. (They are no threat to humans but are a constant menace to the house pets of the kibbutz.) On a terrace above the springs are remains of a Chalcolithic-age temple of the 4th millenium B.C. There are also remains of an impressive synagogue from the Byzantine period, with a mosaic floor (currently removed for repair), depicting two peacocks and the words "Peace on Israel," as well as a curse on anyone who causes controversy between members of the community; who slanders a member of the community to the gentiles; who steals from his fellow; or who reveals the secrets of the community. The "secrets" are believed to refer to the cultivation of balsam, an aromatic substance used for cosmetic purposes, which was carried out here. The archeologists who excavated here found the synagogue cash box intact, with about 5,000 coins.

The kibbutz runs a guest house, and there is also a youth hostel nearby. On the other side of the highway is a small picnic and bathing area, as well as a service station and self-serve restaurant. A camping site alongside provides accommodations for those willing to rough it.

Further south is a large new spa facility, operated by Kibbutz Ein Gedi, with hot mineral baths and Dead Sea mud, which is said to relieve rheumatic aches and pains.

Masada

At first sight, the massive clifftop fortress of Masada, a further 18 kms. (11 miles) south, doesn't seem much different from the surrounding mountains. But for Israelis, its distinctive shape and extraordinary history make it a landmark of crucial significance, a veritable symbol of the State. "Masada will not fall again" is not just a slogan etched on the wall of the nearby youth hostel; it is part of the Israeli national experience, and the story of the valiant, if ultimately unsuccessful, defiance by a small group of Jewish rebels against the might of a vengeful Roman Empire is one Israelis love to retell.

You can reach the top of Masada by climbing the snake path, a circuitous route that involves about 45 minutes of hard walking. This was the route used by the rebels themselves, who, remarkably, managed to keep it secret from the Romans, and by Jewish youth groups in the years before the formation of the modern State, when a visit to Masada had some of the elements of a test of bravery. The last stretch had to be done with ropes, and tragic accidents were not unknown. Now even the snake path is safe, if tiring, but most visitors prefer to ascend by using the far more comfortable, if no less dramatic, cablecar. There is also an approach at the western end of the fortress, accessible by road from Arad, along the Roman attack ramp (of which more in a moment). Hardier souls still may like to pay homage to the tradition of climbing up the snake path before the dawn to see the sun rise over the Dead Sea.

Most of the building on top of Masada dates from the 1st century B.C., and is the work of Herod the Great. He constructed it as a sumptuous desert fortress to which he could retreat in case his disgruntled subjects revolted or if he was attacked by Cleopatra of Egypt. The buildings from this period are large and luxurious, with fine mosaics and even some remains of frescoes which have withstood the ravages of time. Large cisterns and storage rooms held supplies of food and water for a long siege.

It was to this desert refuge that a small group of Jewish fighters retreated to continue their struggle against the Romans, after the latter had destroyed Jerusalem in A.D. 70. In an account which scholars had

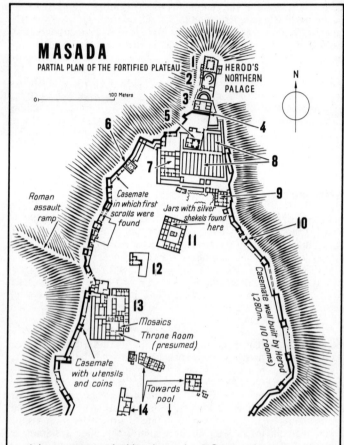

MASADA
PARTIAL PLAN OF THE FORTIFIED PLATEAU

HEROD'S NORTHERN PALACE

N

0 ⊢————⊣ 100 Meters

Roman assault ramp

Casemate in which first scrolls were found

Jars with silver shekels found here

Casemate wall built by Herod 1,280m. 110 rooms)

Mosaics
Throne Room (presumed)

Casemate with utensils and coins

Towards pool

1 Lower terrace—double columned room decorated with frescoes
2 Middle terrace—round pavilion
3 Upper terrace—living quarters
4 Inclined separating wall
5 Roman-style baths
6 Synagogue
7 Administration building
8 Storerooms
9 Villa
10 Snake – path gate (access from cable car)
11 Byzantine building on Herodian/Zealot remains
12 Byzantine chapel
13 Herod's Western Palace
14 Villas

long considered largely fictitious, the Jewish historian Josephus Flavius describes in great detail how the band of fighters, led by Elazar ben Yair, pitted themselves against the Roman general Silva, whose substantial and symmetrical military camp, built very much in the Roman tradition, is clearly visible from the top of the mountain.

Having long since realized that the fortress could not be taken by conventional means, Silva hit on a plan to storm it that, in its combination of imagination, ruthlessness, and thoroughness, speaks volumes for the Roman military genius. Using Jewish slaves, he took advantage of a natural spur of land abutting the fortress to build an immense earth ramp to the top of the mountain. Up this he marched his soldiers and set fire to the walls. Watching the flames on that day in the year A.D. 73 the Jewish rebels knew their time had come. A council was held and Elazar ordered his men to destroy all their possessions except the provisions of food, "so that the enemy will see that we voluntarily chose to die rather than submit to slavery."

Families kissed for the last time, "and everyone lay down in close embrace," according to Josephus. Ten men chosen by lot then set about the grim task of putting to death these voluntary martyrs "who bared their necks to the blades of the charitable executioners." When this had been done, one man of the ten was selected again by lot to end the lives of his nine companions, before taking his own.

In fact not all of the defenders were killed. Two women and five children, who had hidden away in a cistern, survived to tell the tale. The Romans duly attacked and took the fortress, meeting no resistance. When they reached the scene of desolation, they were so stricken that they spared the lives of the survivors.

For centuries, Masada lay desolate and unoccupied except for a few monks who came here in the 5th century and built a small chapel. The ruins of the fortress were gradually buried by debris. In the 19th century, explorers identified the site. But despite the continued interest of Jewish youth groups, Masada's secrets remained hidden, until the massive excavations carried out for 14 months in 1963–65 under the direction of Professor Yigael Yadin, with the help of hundreds of volunteers from around the world. Among the impressive structures uncovered and partially reconstructed are Herod's northern "hanging" palace, a luxurious set of rooms virtually chiselled out of the mountainside. Another palatial building has handsome mosaics, while a magnificent Roman-style bathhouse is also largely intact.

Less impressive physically, but perhaps more moving, are the remains of the Jewish rebels: little cell-like rooms, ritual baths, and, above all, a structure which the excavators believe to be a synagogue. If they are right, it is one of the oldest known synagogues yet found. It was here that the diggers found the remains of some of the defenders' sacred scrolls, including portions of Genesis, Deuteronomy, Psalms, and Ezekiel, as well as parts of the Apocrypha. Many Israeli army tank corps now hold their swearing-in ceremonies on top of Masada.

The Southern Dead Sea

From the top of Masada you also have a fine view of the Dead Sea, which has actually shrunk considerably over the past few decades as a result of water diversion projects by both Israel and Jordan. The Dead Sea is divided into two parts by a peninsula known as the Lashon, advancing toward the Israeli shore from the Jordanian side. As you can see as you drive along, the entire southern part of the Dead Sea, which is far shallower than the northern section, is now an artificial body of water, fed by a canal maintained by the Dead Sea Works. The shrinking of the Dead Sea is one of the main reasons for the now defunct Dead Sea–Mediterranean Canal project, which would have brought sea water from the Mediterranean to raise the level of the Dead Sea.

A short drive south will bring you to the Dead Sea hotel area. Some of the guests here are sufferers of psoriasis, a skin disorder which long-term sunbathing at the Dead Sea does much to alleviate. While unsure of the reason for this, doctors believe that the additional layers of atmosphere at this very low elevation, as well as the water vapor caused by the high rate of evaporation of the Dead Sea, act to filter out the harmful rays of the sun, while intensifying other, more beneficial rays. In any case, thousands of patients have discovered that the Dead Sea treatment is far more pleasant, and cheaper, than a hospital stay, as well as being more effective. Others come to seek relief from rheumatic pains or simply to rest and unwind in an atmosphere that seems naturally soothing. According to some experts, the high concentration of bromide in the water of the Dead Sea, and in the atmosphere as well, acts as a natural sedative.

Further south is the area traditionally associated with the Biblical Sodom. If you look at the rock salt formations rising above the road, you can easily find one which you might identify as Lot's wife. Here you will also find the Dead Sea Chemical Works, one of Israel's major industries, involved in extracting phosphates, bromides, and other chemicals from this extraordinary body of water. In a spot with no other sign of human activity, trucks shuttle in and out all day and huge conveyor belts carry chemicals far up the mountainside. At night the Works are brightly lit, providing a surrealistic vista. To extract the minerals, the water, which already has eight times the concentration of salts of ordinary sea water, is fed into ever shallower evaporation pans. A similar Jordanian plant is located on the other side, while in the distance one can see the stark hills of Moab rising sharply. At Neve Zohar, nearby, is a small museum of artifacts associated with the Dead Sea.

From here, you can continue southward to Eilat or turn to the west toward Arad and Beersheba (see *Negev* chapter). You can also retrace your route as far as the road to Jericho and visit this ancient site.

Jericho

Back at the junction of Route 1—the road from Jerusalem to the Dead Sea—and Route 90, head north up Route 90 to Jericho. A straight road leads into the town past a collection of mostly abandoned huts, a refugee camp, most of whose inhabitants fled to Jordan during the Six Day War. This desolate and depressing spot and the surrounding desert provide a sharp contrast to the greenery of Jericho's orchards and gardens. The town is especially attractive in winter when it remains balmy enough to sit in the sunshine and enjoy a cup of coffee or a meal at one of the garden cafés or restaurants. Indeed, before 1967, when the town lay in Jordanian-controlled territory, Jericho was a favored winter resort for residents of many of the surrounding Arab countries.

One of the signs leading to the town identifies it as "the world's oldest city." A visit to Tel e-Sultan, the site of ancient Jericho, tends to be confusing and gives no hint of Joshua and his trumpets. Parts of the tel are still unexplored, leaving work for future archeologists who may have more sophisticated technology. But even the casual visitor can discern a circular stone tower and staircase which the archeologists tell us is from the Neolithic period, around the 8th and 7th millenia B.C. But although the Biblical account of the fall of Jericho has made Jericho a favorite site for archeologists since the beginning of the century, they have found nothing resembling a Canaanite wall that might have crumbled as described in the Book of Joshua. Some scholars have surmised that this indicates that the Canaanites used an existing earlier wall. The best we can do is to stand on this ancient mound, formed by the building and debris of a hundred centuries, look out beyond the palm trees to the desert, and imagine that we are some of the residents of Jericho, gazing with fascinated horror at the ragged band of Israelites, circling the city for seven days and blowing their rams' horns.

Above you to the west is the flat-topped Mount of Temptation, "Qarantal" in Arabic, with a wall encircling its summit. The 19th-century Greek Orthodox monastery clinging to its sheer cliffs recalls Satan's mountain-top temptation of Christ by offering him the kingdoms of the world in exchange for his homage. Originally, however, there was a far older Byzantine chapel which was destroyed by the Persians in the 7th century A.D. Like other such monasteries in the Judean Desert, this had its roots in the 4th century, in the early Christian period, when hermits would go off to live by themselves in caves in the wilderness. At first they would gather for prayer on holidays and only later did they form communities. The revival of Greek Orthodox monastic life in the Holy Land in the 19th century came largely as a result of Czarist Russia, seeking to extend its power in the Middle East. Using their not inconsiderable influence over the Ottoman Empire, the Russians obtained permission to rebuild the site. Now most of the monks are from Greece, but like elsewhere in the world, there are fewer and fewer young men attracted to the monastic life.

Opposite the tel is the abundant Spring of Elisha, or Sultan's Spring, recalling the prophet's miraculous sweetening of the water (II Kings 2). Now topped by a pump-house, it is responsible for making Jericho such an eternally coveted oasis, the Biblical "City of Palms." An ancient mosaic synagogue floor was found by accident a bit to the north when builders were laying the foundations of a private house. The decorations are simple, with a *menorah,* a ram's horn, and objects identified with the Temple ritual, but the Hebrew inscription "Peace to Israel" is still apt. A long inscription in Aramaic at the foot of the mosaic calls for God's blessing on those who built the synagogue.

Another synagogue from a similar period was found at Na'aran, a short distance up the Ramallah road behind the ancient tel, by an equally serendipitous event: the explosion of a Turkish shell in World War I. Its mosaic floor illustrates the signs of the Zodiac, as at Bet Alfa and Hammat Tiberias, but has been removed for repair.

Continuing north, follow the signs to Hisham's Palace for a taste of the opulence once prevalent in Jericho. The enormous palace was built by the Umayyads in the 8th century as a winter resort for the caliphs who came down from Damascus to enjoy Jericho's mild weather. A brilliantly-colored mosaic illustrating the Tree of Life in the bathhouse of the palace is a must. But it is believed that an earthquake destroyed the palace before the caliphs were ever able to enjoy it.

About six kms. (four miles) east of Jericho is Allenby Bridge, one of the two crossing points over the Jordan. Despite the official state of war between Israel and Jordan, there is a lively flow of passengers and goods over the bridges. Much of the produce of the West Bank is sold in Arab countries, and many visitors from Arab states come on visits. You need a special permit to approach the bridge.

Also east of the town are a series of monasteries along the Jordan river, which once served many of the pilgrims who came to immerse themselves in the river and take small bottles of its water home with them. Because the monasteries are today in a security zone, they have been closed to the public, but lately the Greek Orthodox monastery has been opened once a year for their feast of Epiphany, which falls on January 18. An impressive procession down to the river is held. At the time of writing, plans were also afoot to open this monastery and the Roman Catholic monastery nearby throughout the year. (Another baptismal site is located on the Jordan near the Sea of Galilee; see the *Sea of Galilee* chapter).

Continuing northward from Jericho, Route 90 passes through the largely barren Jordan Rift. The Jordan River, twisting and turning as it meanders toward the Dead Sea, is out of sight to the east. To the west, on the hills overlooking the road, are a number of new Jewish settlements, their fields bordering the road itself. At one point, a stark memorial to Israeli soldiers killed in the area overlooks the road. Built by the Israeli sculptor, Yigal Tumarkin, it is constructed of parts of weapons and military vehicles. Route 90 continues on to Beit She'an, Tiberias, and the Jordan Valley (see the *Jezre'el Valley and Lower Galilee* chapter).

PRACTICAL INFORMATION FOR THE DEAD SEA

TOURIST OFFICES. The **Israel Government Tourist Office** in Jerusalem, 24 King George St. (tel. 02–241281), and Tel Aviv, 7 Mendele St. (tel. 03–223266), can both supply full information about the Dead Sea area. There is also an IGTO outpost at Allenby Bridge (tel. 02–922531), but this is only for visitors entering Israel from Jordan: you need a special permit to enter the area around Allenby Bridge.

Telephone Codes. We have given the telephone codes for all the areas in the lists that follow. These codes need only be used when calling from outside the dialling area concerned.

HOTELS AND RESTAURANTS. Apart from the Dead Sea Hotel area, where there is a large selection of accommodations, ranging from comfortable to deluxe, and a number of youth hostels, there are few places to stay in the area. Most visitors will probably stay in either Jerusalem or Tel Aviv and make day trips to this region. Restaurants are also few and far between, although all the larger hotels have them, and, aside from Jericho where the climate and atmosphere are the chief attractions, they are places to eat, rather than to dine.

DEAD SEA HOTEL AREA. Moriah (L), tel. 057–84221. 220 rooms. Full spa facilities, including hot sulphur pools, mud packs, underwater massage, inhalation. Has a heated indoor pool with Dead Sea water and an outdoor freshwater pool. AE, DC, MC, V. **Galei Zohar** (E), tel. 057–84311. 260 rooms. Has a dermatology clinic and rheumatic spa treatment; also excellent cuisine; pool. AE, DC, MC, V. **Lot** (E), tel. 057–84321. 200 rooms. A new hotel with a pool. AE, DC, MC, V. **Moriah Gardens** (E), tel. 057–84351. 184 rooms. Newly redecorated, with a pool; specializes in rest cures. AE, DC, MC, V. **Tsell Harim** (M), tel. 057–84121. New hotel with pool and private sunning balconies. AE, DC, MC, V.

DEAD SEA NORTHERN END. Restaurant. Lido Kalia (M). A simple cafe and restaurant on the shores of the Dead Sea. It serves coffee and light snacks and is open during the daylight hours only.

EIN GEDI. Kibbutz Ein Gedi Guest House (E), tel. 057–84757. 91 rooms. In a restful garden area on a bluff overlooking the Dead Sea, with a nearby spa.
Restaurants. Self-Service Restaurant (M), near the service station. Open for breakfast and lunch; airconditioned. **Spa Restaurant** (I). Very good fish and dairy; self-service.

JERICHO. Several garden cafes and restaurants are to be found along the main road northward. The best might be *Mount Temptation* (I—M), next to the ancient "tel." *El Gandool* (M) and *El Kayyam* (M) are also worth trying. Opening hours are irregular, but they are always open until the early hours of the evening.

Youth Hostels. Beit Sara, at Ein Gedi (tel. 057–84165). New and very comfortable with a pleasant dining room, a disco and rooms for families with showers. **Neve Zohar,** 20 kms. (12 miles) south of Masada (tel. 057–97847). Mainly for groups. **Taylor,** at Masada (tel. 057–84349).

Camping. Ein Gedi, tel. 057–84803. Large shaded camping area with washing and cooking facilities; bungalows and mobile homes for rent.

HOW TO GET AROUND. By Bus. There is a regular scheduled bus service from the Central Bus Station in West Jerusalem to Masada, Ein Gedi and the Dead Sea Hotel Area, as well as to Jericho and the Jordan Valley. Buses also leave the bus station in East Jerusalem regularly for Jericho. Always make sure you know when the last bus is scheduled to return. For information call **Egged,** tel. 02–248231.

By Car. This is probably about the best way of touring the area. Roads are good and well signposted. Service stations are fairly frequent, but it is a good idea to have at least half a tank of gas at all times. Remember to check the water in the radiator frequently.

Tours. Regular tours are available from Jerusalem and Tel Aviv to Masada, Ein Gedi and Jericho. Information is available and reservations can be made at your hotel or at **Egged Tours,** Central Bus Station, Jerusalem (tel. 02–551869), or 15 Frishman St., Tel Aviv (tel. 03–244177). **Galilee Tours,** 3 Ben Sira St., Jerusalem (tel. 02–246858) or 142 Hayarkon St., Tel Aviv (tel. 03–225817). **United Tours,** King David Hotel, Jerusalem (tel. 02–222187) or 113 Hayarkon St., Tel Aviv (tel. 03–298181).

Desert tours with open vehicles or on foot are available from **Metzoke Dragot,** Kibbutz Mitzpe Shalem (tel. 057–84340 or 03–246161), who have comfortable accommodations for participants at their desert village. **Neot Hakikar,** 36 Keren Hayesod St., Jerusalem (tel. 02–244177), or the **Society for the Protection of Nature in Israel,** 4 Hashefela St., Tel Aviv (tel. 03–375063).

MUSEUMS AND HISTORIC SITES. Historic sites and nature reserves are open daily and close half an hour before sunset. National Parks are indicated by N.P.

EIN FASHCHA. Nature Reserve, tel. 02–922494. Springs, sweet-water pools, Dead Sea bathing, picnic facilities.

EIN GEDI. Nature Reserve, tel. 057–84285. Desert springs, waterfalls, wild animals and archeological remains. Also a spa, tel. 057–97988, with sulphur pools.

JERICHO. Hisham's Palace, tel. 02–922522. The magnificent winter palace of the caliphs. N.P.

Tel e-Sultan. The site of ancient Jericho. N.P. **Synagogue** with mosaic floor, north of the tel. **Monastery of Temptation** (Qarantal), on mountain behind the tel.

MASADA. Tel. 057–90907. The **mountaintop desert fortress** of Herod and the site of an heroic Jewish revolt against the Romans. N.P.

NEVE ZOHAR. Museum of the Dead Sea. Artifacts and explanations about the Dead Sea.

QUMRAN. Tel. 02–922505. The site of the discovery of the **Dead Sea Scrolls** and the remains of an ancient monastic Jewish community. N.P.

THE WEST BANK

Judea and Samaria

The West Bank, which some Israelis prefer to call Judea and Samaria, is that part of the British Mandate of Palestine, west of the Jordan river, which was occupied by the Jordanian Arab Legion in the Israeli War of Independence in 1948 and annexed by Jordan the following year. In the Six Day War of 1967, this kidney-shaped area, which includes the hilly areas north and south of Jerusalem, was occupied by Israeli forces. It has remained under Israeli control ever since.

In many ways the West Bank has become a touchstone of the wider Arab–Israeli conflict, perhaps its most sensitive issue, capable of arousing deep and bitter passions. To the Arabs, Israel's occupation is seen as a particular injustice, reducing them to little more than second-class citizens in a state they want no part of. Moreover, Israel, they argue, has no legitimate claim to a region which has long had a predominantly Arab population and which was in any case awarded to the still-born Palestinian state under the U.N. Partition Plan of 1947.

A good many Israelis, on the other hand, claim with equal force that the West Bank is an integral part of the State of Israel, even if it has not been formally annexed by the modern State. Not only was it the historic heartland of ancient Israel, but its military and strategic significance have become central to the continued defence of Israel and the security of her borders. To a considerable extent this view has predomi-

131

nated within Israel, sparking off a massive building program of new Jewish settlements and towns in the West Bank, intended to consolidate and perpetuate the Jewish presence. The vigor and determination with which this program has been embraced by the more nationalist and extreme elements of Israeli society have been matched only by the bitterness of certain Arab communities on the West Bank, determined to halt it.

At the same time, a substantial proportion of Israeli opinion views the future of the West Bank with a good deal less certainty, believing that permanent Israeli occupation will lead either to the denial of citizenship to a large segment of the population or to the possibility of an Arab majority within a generation or two.

Thus far, the nearest both parties have come to a settlement remains the Camp David Agreement, under which Israel is to grant a measure of autonomy to the Arabs of the West Bank. Exactly what form this should take has proved a sizeable stumbling block and is the subject of continued negotiations.

West Bank Background

But whatever the political difficulties, for the visitor this is an area rich in history. This is largely because the hilly areas were the main areas settled by the ancient Israelites. (Jericho and the Jordan Rift, which are also part of the political entity of the West Bank, are covered in our *Dead Sea* chapter). As such, many sites in this area are also associated with the life of Jesus. Thus, for the pilgrim or just the curious—Jew, Christian or Muslim—there is much to see.

This chapter describes the two main thoroughfares in the West Bank, extending north and south from Jerusalem. Broadly speaking, the region south of Jerusalem is known as Judea, the area of the Kingdom of Judah, and includes Bethlehem, a town of significance in both the Old and the New Testaments, and Hebron, a city sacred to both Jew and Muslim as the burial place of their mutual ancestor, Abraham. Just a short distance north of Jerusalem is Samaria, where the breakaway Kingdom of Israel held sway until its inhabitants, the Ten Lost Tribes, were exiled by the Assyrians. Nablus, the Biblical Shechem, is the largest and most important city here and is still the principal center of the Samaritans, who trace their descent from the Ten Lost Tribes.

SOUTH FROM JERUSALEM

Few people realize that Bethlehem is just a few minutes, about seven kms. (four miles), from Jerusalem. There are regular bus services from East and West Jerusalem and sherut taxis from East Jerusalem. Heading south out of Jerusalem on the Hebron Road, you see above you on your left Kibbutz Ramat Rachel, the last Jewish outpost on the border with Jordan before the Six Day War. The kibbutz was the scene of bitter fighting during the War of Independence in 1948, when its inhabitants faced the combined might of the Jordanian and Egyptian armies and the local Arab forces. All the buildings except one were reduced to rubble; this shell-scarred structure has been left as a memorial. Like many such strategic positions, the kibbutz also marks the site of an ancient fortress, dating from the Judean monarchy and discovered during excavations in the '50s. The excavations have since been renewed. While they continue the antiquities are closed to the public.

A short distance down the road, facing the kibbutz, is the Greek Orthodox Monastery of Mar Elias. Built in the 17th century over Byzantine and Crusader ruins, it served as a frontline position for the Arab forces in 1948. It was subsequently used as a Jordanian army post until 1967, following which it was restored and reoccupied by Greek Orthodox monks.

Just beyond it, near the sign pointing to the new Jerusalem suburb of Gilo, is the Ecumenical Institute of Tantur, a center of advanced theological study for Christians of all denominations, dedicated to furthering Christian unity. Christian scholars representing the Catholic, Protestant and Orthodox branches of Christianity come from all over the world to study on their own and participate in lectures and seminars, which are often presented by local Jewish and Muslim experts in their fields. For many, Tantur represents an island of peace and understanding in an area all too often torn by hatred and strife.

Bethlehem

As you enter Bethlehem you pass by Rachel's Tomb, on your right, located in a small domed building built in 1841 by the British-Jewish philanthropist, Sir Moses Montefiore. According to the Bible, Rachel, the wife of the patriarch Jacob, was buried here after she died while giving birth to Benjamin. The large velvet-draped tomb-marker inside attracts Jewish pilgrims, especially women who come to pray for a child (Rachel was for long barren). Since Rachel's Tomb is also venerated by Islam, a Muslim cemetery has grown up alongside.

Bethlehem, which means House of Bread in Hebrew, is mentioned in the Book of Ruth as the place where Ruth and Boaz fell in love. It was also the birthplace of King David, Ruth's great-grandson. For Christians, of course, it is holy as the birthplace of the Christ child and a place of pilgrimage for Christians from all over the world, especially at Christmas.

Just beyond Rachel's Tomb, there is a fork in the road. The right-hand route heads down to Hebron; that on the left leads directly to Manger Square and the Church of the Nativity, which marks the spot where Jesus was born.

The Church of the Nativity

Although originally built in the 4th century A.D. by Helena, mother of the Emperor Constantine, the present, almost fortress-like Church of the Nativity is the result of a 6th-century rebuilding by Justinian, and Crusader repairs 600 years after that. In the facade of the church is Justinian's square doorway and the Crusader's arched one—both blocked up—and the present-day low entrance, originally designed to protect the beleaguered Christian community against hostile neighbors.

The two rows of columns inside the rather austere church are from the 6th century, making this the oldest standing church in Israel. It survived the Persian invasion of A.D. 614, some say because a contemporary painting of the Nativity story depicted the Wise Men of the East in Persian attire, and the invaders were impressed enough to spare it. Wooden trapdoors in the floor reveal remains of the mosaic floor of the original 4th-century church.

High up on the walls are additional mosaics from the 12th century. The wooden ceiling is made of stout English oak, the gift of Edward IV. But the vast quantities of lead which he also donated to cover the roof were melted down by the Turks to use as ammunition in their wars against the Venetians.

Underneath the main altar is a grotto, reached by stairways on either side. On the floor under the altar a silver star marks the birthplace of Christ. Next to it is the Chapel of the Manger, where Mary placed the new-born babe. The grotto, like the main body of the church itself, is under the jurisdiction of the Greek Orthodox Church, although other denominations, the Armenians and Roman Catholics in particular, share some rights to it. The main Roman Catholic church, St. Catherine's, is actually next door, though linked to the main church by a door on the left as you face the altar. It is in St. Catherine's that the traditional Christmas midnight mass is celebrated on the night of December 24. St. Catherine's is also the site of several additional grottoes: one containing the Chapel of St. Joseph, where an angel appeared to Joseph and commanded him to flee to Egypt; and another containing the Chapel of the Innocents, recalling the deaths of the babies killed by Herod the Great. There is also the Chapel of St. Jerome where that early Bishop of Bethlehem translated the Old Testament into Latin (the "Vulgate").

For many Christians seeking a quiet place of prayer and meditation in this, one of the holiest sites of Christianity, the Church of the Nativity, with its monks selling candles and groups of tourists charging through, can come as a rude shock. Their dismay is heightened when they learn that the church is also the scene of violent infighting between members of the various sects responsible for its upkeep, each battling for what they see as their legitimate rights to the church. Even a disagreement over the right to stand on a certain step or wash a particular part of a particular pillar can lead to quite violent brawls, with inflamed monks cracking chairs over their rivals' heads and generally behaving in anything but a Christian manner. However, other Christian visitors manage to view such incidents with understanding, if not with equanimity. For them it is enough that Christians have held the site holy and have continued to pray here since the early days of Christianity. For those seeking a quieter place, perhaps the best spot is the small cloister just outside St. Catherine's.

Manger Square

Manger Square, just outside the Basilica, is never a quiet place, but it comes into its own at Christmas. In addition to the Western Christmas on the night of December 24, the Greek Orthodox, who follow a different calendar, observe their Christmas on January 7, while the Armenians celebrate it on January 19. Each celebration is marked by a colorful procession in which the patriarch of the respective sect arrives from Jerusalem, accompanied by dignitaries, Boy Scouts playing bagpipes, mounted policemen and a police band. On the Western Christmas these festivities continue into the evening with choirs from all over the world singing in Manger Square, and the mass itself shown on a giant television screen in the square for those unable to get into the church.

All around the Basilica are chapels and cloisters belonging to the various Christian denominations, with other churches further afield. One of the favorites is the Milk Grotto on Milk Grotto Street, south of Manger Square. Here, according to tradition, the Virgin spilled a few drops of her milk, turning the entire cave, or grotto, to a chalky white stone. Little packets of the powdered white stone, which may be obtained here, are said to increase the milk flow of nursing mothers. Near the Milk Grotto, look toward the east for a splendid landscape, with the Field of Ruth and the Judean Desert unfurling toward the Dead Sea. Along this street and in the square are shops which specialize in carved olive wood and objects made with mother of pearl, a craft which has existed for centuries in Bethlehem.

Also in Manger Square are the new Government Tourist Office and a mosque built during the Jordanian period. Behind them is a bustling market, held in the morning. This is a good place to note the traditional dress of many of the women from the nearby villages. It is believed that the design of some of the old habits of European nuns was based on the dress of Christian women from the Bethlehem area.

Finally, also near Manger Square are King David's Wells, three large wells where David is said to have "longed to drink" when Bethlehem was held by the Philistines.

Herodion and Mar Saba

To reach these intriguing sites, take Route 356 out of Bethlehem, which leads off to the left just before Manger Square. You descend to the Arab Christian town of Beit Sahour, and the Shepherd's Fields, traditionally the place where the shepherds saw the angels announcing the birth of the Christ child. Different denominations control different sites in the area, but the Catholic one, with its cave, antiquities, views and small church, is the most interesting.

Route 356 bears off to the right and then suddenly you top a ridge and the distinctive shape of Herodion looms in front of you—an almost perfect flat-topped cone. King Herod built it in the first century B.C. as one of a series of desert palace-fortresses, among them Masada. Like Masada, Herodion was a stronghold of the Zealots in the Great Jewish

Revolt against the Romans between A.D. 66 and 73, and one of the last to fall. The Bar Kochba fighters in the next century used it again in the Second Revolt.

The fortress was one of Herod's most magnificent monuments. Built at a height of 758 meters (2,464 ft.) above sea level, it commands a sweeping view of the Judean Desert and the Dead Sea on the one hand, and the mountain range from the Hebron Hills to the ridges of Jerusalem, on the other. Herod's architects shaved off the apex of the mountain and built up the rest to make it perfectly symmetrical, with defensive walls over 23 meters (70 ft.) high and towers over 33 meters (100 ft.) from the floor of the fortress. After Herod's death a mausoleum was built here, relates the Jewish historian Josephus Flavius, writing almost a century after the event, but Herod's tomb at Herodion has not yet been found.

From Beit Sahour, Route 398 strikes off to the left. Some distance later a side road to the right—partly unpaved—winds down towards the gorge of the Kidron Valley. Here, certainly off the beaten track, you will find the Monastery of Mar Saba, founded by St. Saba of Cappadocia in the 5th century. Sacked repeatedly, it was subsequently entirely rebuilt by the Imperial Russian government in 1840. Somewhat gruesomely, the skulls of monks killed in attacks on the monastery are kept here in a special chapel. The bones of St. Saba were taken by the Crusaders to Venice and only returned recently, following the visit of Pope Paul VI to the Holy Land in the '60s, who arranged for their return as a gesture of good will toward the Greek Orthodox Church.

At one time there were said to be 5,000 monks here, but few young men today seek the monastic way of life, with the result that their numbers have dwindled to no more than a handful. A road was paved to the monastery a few years ago, bringing it closer to the temptations of civilization. Men are permitted to enter the monastery, but women—and even female animals—are strictly forbidden. There is, however, a special tower to the south of the building from which women may look down into the monastery.

To the west of Bethlehem is the Arab town of Beit Jalla, set among olive groves and vineyards. There is also the Cremisan Monastery beyond the town, whose monks preside over a fine vineyard. They have come up with a number of creditable wines, which you can sample and buy. Near the monastery, on the crest of Mount Gilo, is a small pine forest, planted by Russians who were building a church here before the Russian Revolution put a halt to their activities. It is now the site of a Nature Protection Society field school.

Toward Hebron

From Bethlehem, Route 60, the Hebron Road, continues to wind south. A few miles beyond Bethlehem on the left are three giant cisterns known as Solomon's Pools. Despite their name, the pools are Herodian/Roman in origin (though repaired by the Turks), and were built in various stages some 2,000 years ago as key elements in two stunning water-engineering projects: the Aroub/Lower Aqueduct, 61 kms. (40 miles) of gravitational flow to Jerusalem's Temple Mount; and the later Biyar/Upper Aqueduct, a shorter, partly-siphon system via Bethlehem to the Jaffa Gate.

Further south, to the right, you'll catch sight of the Etzion Bloc. This group of Jewish farming settlements was destroyed by the Arab armies in the 1948 war and most of the inhabitants killed. For almost 20 years afterwards, some of the buildings were used as a Jordanian army outpost. Following the Six Day War they were resettled as farming communities; some of the new settlers are the children, evacuated when the fighting started, of those killed in 1948. One of the settlements, Kfar Etzion, has built a new youth hostel near the old Jordanian barracks. A museum in Kibbutz Kfar Etzion charts the history of Jewish settlement here and recounts the valor of the fallen defenders.

Hebron

High up in the Judean mountains, Hebron, 12 kms. (seven miles) from Kfar Etzion, is 926 meters (3,050 ft.) above sea level. Venerated by Jews and Muslims alike as the burial place of the Patriarchs, it has been the scene of repeated strife between the two communities, principally on this account.

It was by Hebron in the Plain of Mamre that Abraham pitched his tents. As is not unusual in the Holy Land, there are two rival sites, each claiming to possess the Oak of Mamre, or Abraham's Oak, although both trees are relative youngsters, no more than a couple of hundred years old.

But the real focus of interest here is the Cave of Machpela, which Abraham bought as a burial site for his wife, Sarah. Abraham, too, was buried here, according to the Bible, as were the patriarchs Isaac and Jacob and their wives, Rebecca and Leah. The monumental structure over the tombs was built by Herod; the similarity between the great stones used here and those in the Western Wall in Jerusalem, also built by Herod, is striking. After the Arab conquest of the Holy Land in A.D. 638, a mosque was added to the structure and, in the 12th century, non-Muslims were forbidden to enter, a prohibition that remained in effect until 1967. Today the building, with its lavish Muslim decorations, rich green and gold cloths over the cenotaphs and 700-year-old stained glass windows, is open to everyone. The tombs themselves are said to be far below, in a grotto directly beneath the monuments. There is also a niche which Muslims claim is the tomb of Joseph, although Jews believe he was buried in Nablus. Across from the Cave of Machpela is a hill known as Tel Rumeida, the site of Biblical Hebron. It has achieved some notoriety in recent years following attempts by some Israelis to settle here.

Through the centuries, Jews have only been allowed to stand and pray at the seventh step leading up to the tomb. Nonetheless, the city always had a small Jewish community, and Jews also continued to visit Hebron on pilgrimages. However, the Jewish community in Hebron was forced to abandon the city in 1929, following Arab rioting which resulted in the deaths of some 60 Jews, the remainder being evacuated by British troops. Today the Arab residents of Hebron number among the most fanatically religious of the West Bank; the city doesn't even boast a movie theater. After the Six Day War, a number of Jews demanded that they be able to return to Hebron, and were eventually given permission to establish the new, largely Orthodox, suburb of Kiryat Arba, one of the Biblical names for Hebron. More recently, a number of small groups of extreme nationalist Jews have insisted on living in the city itself, in property owned by Jews who left in 1929. The market of Hebron with its narrow alleyways has a certain attraction, but most visitors are deterred by the ever-present threat of politically motivated violence, by both Arabs and Jews.

There is no such deterrent, however, on the outskirts of Hebron, where there are several glass-blowing shops and visitors can see crude, but attractive, glass objects being made over open fires with techniques which are centuries old. For those willing to risk the possibility of breakage, these handsome glass objects make especially nice gifts to bring home.

The road from Hebron twists and turns southwards past picturesque Arab villages toward Beersheba, the terrain ever more arid and barren. A sign along the way will direct you to the 4th century A.D. synagogue of Eshtemoa, with its mosaics and fine carved stonework. This was the first such synagogue discovered south of Jerusalem, proving that Jewish life continued in this area even after the ill-fated revolt against the Romans. Soon after crossing the 1967 border, you will arrive at the Beersheba–Arad highway, Route 31. This area is covered in our *Negev* chapter.

NORTH FROM JERUSALEM

As countless travelers before you have done, you may start your journey north from the Old City in Jerusalem from the Damascus Gate, going up the Nablus Road, Route 60. As Jerusalem proper thins out into suburbs, a tall minaret on a high rise can be seen on the left. This is Nebi Samwil, said to be the tomb of the prophet Samuel. It was from here that the Crusaders had their first view of Jerusalem; appropriately they named the hill Mons Gaudii, the Mount of Joy. It was in fact the Crusaders who identified the spot with Samuel, and they built a church here, which later became a mosque as well as a place of pilgrimage for Jews. The road also passes Jerusalem's Atarot Airport from which there are flights to Eilat.

The town of Ramallah, 13 kms. (eight miles) north of Jerusalem, through which the road then passes, is one of the most beautiful in the West Bank, with well-kept gardens and attractive homes. The cool breezes made it a favorite summer resort in the Arab world. Many of the local residents have now gone to America, but return often, giving the town a prosperous holiday atmosphere, especially in the summer. Ramallah, which is Christian, has a Muslim town, El-Bireh, adjacent to it, and virtually indistinguishable from it.

Just north of Ramallah are the Arab village of Beitin and the Jewish settlement of Bet El, both reminders of the Biblical Bethel, where Jacob dreamed he saw a ladder going up to heaven. The site has been extensively excavated, but there are few remains to interest the casual visitor. There is rather more to see farther north, at recently excavated Shiloh, the main Israelite shrine during the period of the Biblical Judges.

The road winding through the rolling, lush landscape and pastoral hills of Samaria crosses a gorge known as Wadi el-Haramiye, the Pass of the Thieves. The Arab village of Sinjal a bit further on, takes its name from the Crusader name for the place, St. Giles. All around you can see ruins from the Crusader period.

Nablus

Nablus, the largest city in the area, 46 kms. (29 miles) from Jerusalem, with a population of over 50,000, is a thriving industrial and trade center. It is known as the site of the Biblical Shechem, although the exact site of the Biblical city is at Balata, a little to the east of the modern city. It was here that Abraham entered the Promised Land and offered his first sacrifice to God. Not far from the ancient site you may see Jacob's Well, inside a Greek Orthodox monastery. Nearby is a small domed building marking Joseph's Tomb, said to house the bones brought by the children of Israel from Egypt. Towering over the site is Mount Gerizim, which Moses referred to as a place of blessing.

The mountain was, and still is, the center for the Samaritans, a people most often remembered from a few parables in the New Testament. In fact, their history goes back to the time of the Second Temple when, as descendants of the remnants of the northern kingdom, and other, non-Jewish, peoples, the Samaritans offered to participate in the building of the new temple, only to be rebuffed by the Jews who had returned from the Babylonian exile.

Ascribing to Mount Gerizim many of the attributes which the Jews ascribe to Jerusalem, the Samaritans then built a temple there. In the Roman period they numbered hundreds of thousands, but they were largely wiped out as a result of war and persecution. Ironically, the Byzantines used the New Testament parables concerning the Samaritans to declare them a Christian schismatic sect and massacre them. Now they number only about 600 and are sometimes called the smallest nation in the world. About half live in Nablus and closely resemble their Arab neighbors, while the other half live in Holon, near Tel Aviv, and are typical Israelis, who serve in the Israeli army.

Now that they are few in number, their schism with the Jews is almost healed. In fact it was only a decision on the part of the Samaritan elders earlier in this century to allow their young men to take Jewish women as brides that probably saved them from extinction. In their synagogue, in ancient Hebrew script, is the parchment scroll containing their version of the Pentateuch, or Five Books of Moses, which together with the Book of Joshua is the only part of the Bible they accept as holy writ. Their elders claim that the scroll goes back to the time of Moses.

Perhaps the most striking thing about the Samaritans is their observance of the Passover sacrifice on Mount Gerizim in the ancient manner, slaughtering a lamb, roasting it and eating it hurriedly at midnight, as enjoined in the Book of Exodus. The ceremony, held on the ruins of their ancient temple, begins at sunset with the chanting of prayers led by their high priest, the oldest descendant of the tribe of Levi among them. All the men are dressed in white, even small babies. When the first sheep is slaughtered a cheer goes up and the men dab their foreheads with its blood. The animals are then lowered into round pits in which fires have been raging since early in the day. At midnight they eat the meat with their unleavened bread which, like the Jewish matza, though the latter is more like a cracker, resembles a very thin Arab pitta. The houses on the mountaintop are used by the Samaritans only for the three Biblical pilgrimage festivals, but there have long been plans for them to move there permanently and thus solve the chronic housing shortage which they face in Nablus.

The Ten Lost Tribes

About 11 kms. (eight miles) northwest of Nablus on Route 60 is the site of Biblical Samaria, usually known by its Roman name, Sebastia. It was here that Omri, and his son Ahab, the husband of Jezebel, set up the capital of the northern Kingdom of Israel which had broken away from Judah after the death of Solomon. The kingdom was to last until 722 B.C., when it was destroyed by the Assyrians. They exiled its inhabitants, who thereafter became known as the Ten Lost Tribes. Some remains from the ancient Israelite kingdom have been uncovered, but far more impressive are those from the Herodian and Roman periods, when Sebastia was a flourishing city, with its amphitheater, acropolis and columned streets.

In the adjacent village of Sebastiya is a mosque, once a Crusader church, under which is said to be the burial place of John the Baptist. From here you can continue northward to Afula and Galilee, westward to Netanya or eastward to the Jordan Rift.

PRACTICAL INFORMATION FOR

THE WEST BANK

TOURIST INFORMATION. Information on travel and tourism in the West Bank may be obtained from the **Israel Government Tourist Offices** in Jerusalem, 24 King George St. (tel. 02–241281), or Tel Aviv, 7 Mendele St. (tel. 03–223266). There is also a joint government-municipal Tourist Information Office in the Bethelehem Municipality Building on Manger Square.

TELEPHONE CODES. We have given the telephone codes for all the areas in the lists that follow. These codes need only be used when calling from outside the dialing area concerned.

HOTELS AND RESTAURANTS. Accommodations are limited in the West Bank, and often even the restaurants are not what they should be. Bethlehem, which has a steady stream of tourists, has a few modest hotels, which are of course booked well in advance for the Christmas season, and a number of restaurants offering simple, but satisfactory meals. Most tourists visiting the West Bank will be staying in Jerusalem or Tel Aviv and making relatively short day trips.

BETHLEHEM. Bethlehem Star (I), Al Baten St. (tel. 02–743249). 54 rooms, all with shower or bath. Coffee shop, roof garden. AE, DC, MC, V. **Handel** (I), El Dahisha St. (tel. 02–742494). 40 rooms, all with shower or bath. Coffee shop, garden.
   Restaurant. El Andalus Restaurant (M), Manger Square. Indoor dining room and sidewalk tables; meals and light snacks. **Vienna Restaurant** (M), Milk Grotto St. (tel. 02–742783). European and Middle Eastern dishes.

ETZION BLOC. Elazar Restaurant (M), Moshav Elazar (tel. 02–931191). Meals and snacks. American settlers run it; there's also a shop for needle-point patterns on Israeli and Jewish themes. Closed Friday afternoon and Saturday.

HEBRON. Eshkolot Hebron (I), Kiryat Arba (tel. 02–961819). 45 rooms. Orthodox Jewish atmosphere.
   Restaurant. Machpela Restaurant (I), near Machpela Cave. Operated by Kiryat Arba settlers. Closed Friday afternoon and Saturday.

NABLUS. Jacob's Well Restaurant, across from Jacob's Well. Middle Eastern food.

RAMALLAH. Naoum (M), Mughtaribeen Sq. Beautiful garden setting; try their enormous selection of meze or appetizer salads. **Grand Hotel** (I). Coffee served in a large park under towering pine trees.

Youth Hostel. Kfar Etzion, tel. 02–931533. 150 beds.

 HOW TO GET AROUND. By Bus and Sherut. Buses leave regularly for Bethlehem, the Etzion Bloc and Hebron from the Central Bus Station in West Jerusalem and to all towns and villages in the West Bank from the East Jerusalem Bus Station. Sherut taxis also ply the main roads and may be hailed from the Jaffa Gate and Hebron Road in Jerusalem, if you're heading southward to Bethlehem and Hebron, and from the Damascus Gate and Nablus Road if you're heading northward to Ramallah and Nablus.

By Car. Roads in the area are satisfactory, if sometimes a bit narrow. There are road signs on the major roads and the local inhabitants are usually helpful and friendly if you ask them for directions. Service stations are fairly frequent, even if they sometimes look a bit dirty.

Tours. There are regular daily tours from Jerusalem to Bethlehem and regularly scheduled, if less frequent, tours to Hebron. Tours may be booked at your hotel or any travel agent.

MUSEUMS AND HISTORIC SITES. Historic sites and nature reserves are open daily and close half-an-hour before sunset. Some opening hours are not always reliable, so check on the spot.

BETHLEHEM. Church of the Nativity, Manger Square. Open daily in daylight hours.

David's Wells. Large cisterns and the remains of a Byzantine church and tombs.

Herodion, east of Beit Sahur. Herod's desert fortress and palace. Open daily 8–5; in winter until 4 P.M. National Park.

Milk Grotto, Milk Grotto St. Open daily 8–12, 4–6.

Mar Saba Monastery, east of Beit Sahur. Open daily except Sunday. Ring the bell to enter; women not allowed.

Rachel's Tomb, on the main highway. Open Sun. to Thurs. 8–6, Fri. 8–1.

ETZION BLOC. Museum at Kfar Etzion. Display of the history of Jewish settlement and a memorial to the defenders of this settlement in the War of Independence. Open Sun. to Thurs. 8.30–4, Fri. 8.30–2.

HEBRON. Alonei Mamre, at the northern entry to the city. An ancient walled area said to be where Abraham built an altar.

Eshtemoa Synagogue, on the highway south from Hebron. Dates from the 4th century A.D.

Machpela Cave. The tombs of the patriarchs. Open Sun. to Thurs. 7.30–11.30, 1–2.30, 4–5; Sat. 1–2.30, 4–5.

NABLUS. Jacob's Well, in the Greek Orthodox Monastery, near the entrance to the city. Open 7–12, 3–6.

Joseph's Tomb, near the entrance to the city. Closed Fri. afternoons and Sat.

Mount Gerizim, south of Nablus. The remains of a Samaritan temple and a modern Samaritan synagogue.

Sebastia, north of Nablus. Site of the Biblical, Herodian and Roman city; impressive remains. Open daily 8–5; in winter until 4 P.M. National Park.

JERUSALEM CORRIDOR, SHEFELAH AND PHILISTINE COUNTRY

A Land of Little Gems

The distance between Tel Aviv and Jerusalem is only 60 kms. (38 miles), and it takes less than an hour by car or bus. There are, however, numerous sights along the way, as well as side trips for excursions of a few hours between the two cities.

The centerpiece of this chapter deals with this Jerusalem Corridor, the area between Tel Aviv and Jerusalem. Indeed, a glance at any map of Israel before 1967 makes very clear just why it is called the Jerusalem Corridor, for until the Six Day War it formed the *only* link between the modern city of Tel Aviv on the coast and Jerusalem, the historical, religious, and psychological capital. Held initially by the Jews in 1948, it was quickly overrun by the Arabs, determined to prise loose the tenuous Israeli hold on Jerusalem and snuff out the ebbing Jewish resistance there. Though the Arabs succeeded eventually in bringing about the fall of Old Jerusalem—and of course the Old City remained in Arab hands until 1967—the Jews nonetheless regained most of the

143

corridor itself before the end of the War of Independence. Its key strategic value was vividly reflected in the fierceness and bitterness of much of the fighting here.

In addition, we cover the foothills of the Judean mountains; the plains that lie to the west of them, the Shefelah in Hebrew; and the Gaza Strip, the coastal strip to the south of Tel Aviv and Ashkelon.

Geographically, the area is immensely varied, far more so than its small scale suggests. Historically, too, the area covered in this chapter has had a varied past. The hill country was the stronghold of the ancient Israelites, while their traditional enemies, the Philistines, lived on the plains and near the sea. Unsurprisingly, the foothills, where Samson is said to have lived, saw many confrontations between the two, including the showdown between David and Goliath. The coastal area, too, saw more than its fair share of violence, providing as it did a natural highway for invaders from both north and south. The Egyptians had outposts here, as did the Phoenicians and later the Greeks. It is no accident that the Maccabees, the heroes of the Chanukah saga, who led the Jews against the Hellenized Syrians of Antiochus Epiphanes, came from the little village of Modiin in these foothills. Later the Crusaders were to settle along the coast, though they also made inroads into the hilly areas. Much later, it was up along the coast that Napoleon marched with his army. General Allenby also came northward along the coast with the British army during World War I.

Although the area is settled with towns, villages, and kibbutzim, there is little in the way of accommodations and most visitors will prefer to see it by making side trips from either Tel Aviv or Jerusalem. For any tour in this area, you could leave your hotel in the morning and still get home well in time for your evening meal.

Along the Jerusalem Corridor

Leaving Tel Aviv along the main road (Route 1), you soon find yourself driving through an area with orange groves on either side. In the early spring, when the trees are in flower, their aroma fills the air. These are the Jaffa oranges for which the country is justly famous. On your right as you drive towards Jerusalem, you will notice a solid wall of high shrubbery. This marks the edge of Kfar Habad, a village inhabited by members of an ultra-Orthodox Hassidic sect, the Habad Hassidim, whose leader, the Lubavitcher Rebbe, lives in the U.S. Unlike some other ultra-Orthodox groups, they have a vast public-relations network through which they try to influence other Jews to become more observant, trying to achieve their goals through persuasion rather than force. They have grown the shrubbery to cut off their view of the highway so that they will not have to see their fellow Jews transgressing by driving on the Sabbath.

A sign marks the turnoff to Ben Gurion Airport, the country's only major international airport, although charter flights from abroad land regularly in Eilat, and a few flights land in Jerusalem. Just beyond the airport are Israel Aircraft Industries, one of the country's largest industrial employers. They deal mainly in the overhauling and repair of aircraft, but are also involved in the manufacture of military aircraft nd electronic systems, and civilian planes like the Westwind, a small rivate jet, which has done well on the world market.

The town of Lod, or Lydda, to the south of the airport, is best known s one of the possible birthplaces of St. George, the dragon slayer. Although the patron saint of Great Britain, he was decanonized a few ears ago by the Catholic Church. But he is still venerated by the Greek Orthodox and they have a church here which marks the site of his omb. This church, which was built recently on the ruins of earlier Byzantine and Crusader churches, is adjacent to the local mosque, which also occupies part of these remains. In the '20s and '30s during he British Mandate, Lod also became an important rail junction on the Damascus–Cairo railway. Having then already become a significant ransport center, it was decided, logically enough, that Lod should be he site of the country's airport. During the War of Independence in 1948, most of the Arab residents fled and the town was settled with ewish immigrants, but the changing population has not interfered with he regular Tuesday morning market, to which farmers and Beduins ome from all over the area.

To the south of Lod is Ramle, founded in A.D. 716 by the Caliph Suleiman. It is, in fact, the only town in the country which was established by Arabs, although it was also occupied by the Crusaders, who erroneously associated it with the site of Arimathea. Near the market s the Great Mosque, originally the Cathedral of St. John; indeed, its Romanesque columns make its Christian origin clear. An underwater storage vault, built for Haroun el-Rashid, bears the unlikely name of St. Helena's Cistern. Its vaults were once used as a lunatic asylum, and ater as a center for whirling dervishes, a Muslim mystical sect. The municipality sometimes organizes boat rides in the cisterns. Once a major intersection of the road to the north, the Via Maris, and that to Jerusalem, Ramle also boasts a monastery where Napoleon stayed on his campaign through the country. On the outskirts of the town is the so-called White Tower, a square, six-story structure built in the 14th century as the minaret of a large mosque, the latter long since destroyed. The tower commands a fine view of the coastal plain to the west; it is said that Napoleon commanded his troops there.

A short distance northeast of Ramle is the War Cemetery, where the fallen of both World Wars are buried. The total number is 1,595, covering some 22 nationalities. This is the largest of the War Cemeteries in Israel, though there are 12 others, the second largest being that at Khayat Beach near Haifa.

Back on Route 1 past the Ramle turnoff, the highway begins its climb up to Jerusalem. However, an exit sign posted "Ben Shemen and Jerusalem (North)" takes you on an interesting detour down Route 443, a two-lane highway that twists and turns through Arab villages and past Jewish settlements. At the beginning of Route 443 is Neot Kedumim, a vast botanical garden devoted to growing every plant mentioned in the Bible and the Talmud. Various paths and groves have been laid out according to subject. Thus there is a walk devoted to the books of Judges and Kings, and a valley of the Song of Songs. Those familiar with the Bible in the standard English translations will often be surprised to find that many of the plants mentioned are not what

they seem. There are sections with plants from the hilly areas, from th
deserts, and from the valleys. Staff members can conduct tours fo
groups, and there are self-guided tours for individuals.

A short distance further down Route 443 are the graves of th
Maccabees; large, rock tombs, now mostly empty, on a stony outcro
near the ancient village of Modiin. It is from these tombs that ever
year a Chanukah torch is lit and carried on foot to Jerusalem an
elsewhere to mark the beginning of the holiday. The irony of thi
decidedly Hellenistic event—reminiscent of the opening of the Olympi
Games, for example—being used to mark a holiday celebrating th
victory of the Jews over the forces of Hellenism, has been remarked o
by more than one commentator.

Continuing along Route 1 to Jerusalem, at Latrun, near the exits fo
Ramallah and Ashkelon on Route 3, is the Ayalon Valley, a vita
strategic point and the scene of many battles throughout the ages. I
was here that Joshua commanded the sun to stand still, while othe
armies that have marched through here include those of the Macca
bees, the Romans, the Arabs, the Crusaders, and the British in Worl
War I. Latrun was also the site of some of the fiercest fighting fo
control of the Jerusalem road during the War of Independence. Indeed
hundreds of Jews, many of them survivors of Concentration Camp
who had, quite literally, been marched or driven from the boats tha
brought them to Israel direct to the battlefield, lost their lives here. Th
Israelis were unable to win complete control of the road and from 194
to 1967 the highway to Jerusalem made a wide detour to avoid passin
under the guns of the Arab Legion here. The present route was onl
reopened following the Six Day War. From the highway, you can se
a tank on a concrete platform to your right, a memorial to the armore
brigade which fought here.

The tank and other memories of war provide a sharp contrast to th
peace and tranquility of the nearby Latrun Monastery, located abov
the road to the right. It is hard to believe that this monastery, whic
seems as old as time itself, was only built in 1927, though the ruins o
a 12th-century Crusader fortress are nearby. Stop and sample th
home-made wines; you can buy these and other products made in th
monastery. The monks are Trappists—they take a vow of silence—bu
the monk who sells the wine has a special dispensation to speak an
is happy to talk to visitors and show them around if there are not to
many buyers. The side-road which passes the monastery also leads t
Neve Shalom, a settlement established by Jews and Arabs intent or
proving that they can bring about greater understanding and brother
hood between the two peoples by living together in harmony. Th
settlement is still struggling and its members have yet to come to term
with some problems, such as how to educate their children when the
get beyond kindergarten level, but it is growing slowly and becomin
more established.

Across the road are the ruins of one of the two sites which vie fo
the title of Emmaus, the town mentioned in the New Testament as tha
where Jesus revealed himself after the Resurrection. There are ruin
here of a Byzantine and Crusader church. Above them is the French
Archeological Institute, while just beyond is Canada Park, a large are

with trees, lawns, sports fields, and children's play areas, as well as facilities for picnics. Interspersed between all this are ancient wine presses and millstones, and a spring with water, an unusual sign in this all too dry country. The park is usually jammed for three days a week, with Muslims coming on Friday, Jews on Saturday, and Christians on Sunday; the rest of the week it is almost deserted.

Back on the highway, the beginning of the Judean hills is marked by a ruined khan, or inn, at the pass known as Sha'ar Hagai. Here the Turks also had a toll station where they took a tax from every traveler.

Though hilly and winding, the road here is considerably wider and straighter than during the War of Independence. Indeed, this stretch, too, was the site of further bitter fighting in 1948 when convoys of trucks and buses, carrying vital provisions to Jerusalem and protected only by inadequate homemade armor plating, were regularly ambushed by the Arabs. The burnt-out remains of some of these vehicles have been left by the road in many places, eloquently silent memorials to those who died.

About eight kilometers (five miles) beyond the gas station of Sha'ar Hagai, a turn to the left leads to the two veteran kibbutzim of Ma'aleh Hahamishah and Kiryat Anaivim, the younger moshav of Neve Ilan, and the Arab village of Abu Ghosh, all located to the north of Route 1. Both the two kibbutzim and the moshav have guest houses which also offer meals and snacks to passing visitors. Also near here is Yad Hashmonah, a kibbutz set up by Finnish Christians, supporters of Israel. Most members come for a few years and then return to Finland.

Abu Ghosh, said to be Biblical Kiryat Ye'arim where the Ark of the Covenant remained for some years after its recovery from the Philistines, boasts a 20th-century hilltop church, Our Lady of the Ark of the Covenant, with a gigantic statue of the Virgin dominating the landscape. Far more beautiful, however, is the Crusader church in the ravine below it, lovingly restored by the Benedictines, who hold it in trust for the French government. There is also a restaurant and coffeeshop in Abu Ghosh where you can sit on the terrace and sip your Turkish coffee and hear tales about the days when the road to Jerusalem ran through here and the villagers took a "tax" from every traveler, and of the War of Independence, when the residents of this village backed the Jews rather than the Arabs and even aided the Jewish underground, the Irgun.

At the point where the road from Abu Ghosh again meets the road to Jerusalem is Aqua Bella, an area with a spring and the remains of a convent from the Crusader period, which has been turned into a beautiful park. A camping site is open here in the summer. A steep hill leads up to the Kastel, whose name derives from the Latin, Castellum, once the site of a Crusader fortress and another scene of fierce fighting during the War of Independence. From here you can catch your first glimpses of the western outskirts of Jerusalem.

Sorek and Bet Guvrin

Leave the main highway at Sha'ar Hagai, about two-thirds of the way from Tel Aviv to Jerusalem, turning southward onto Route 38 toward Bet Shemesh. This pleasant, winding, tree-lined road was for many years part of the main highway to Jerusalem. The agricultural villages along the way were settled by immigrants who came in the early '50s. On your left is the Forest of Martyrs: six million trees planted here commemorate victims of Nazi fury. Route 395, off to your left, climbs several kilometers to the Scroll of Fire memorial, an eight-and-a-half meter (20 ft.) bronze monument on a hilltop with an impressive view of the coastal plain. It is in the form of an open scroll, commemorating the destruction of the European Jewish community and the rebirth of the State of Israel. The road continues up to enter Jerusalem through Ein Kerem.

Back on Route 38, you soon come to Bet Shemesh, a development town established in 1950. Through Bet Shemesh occasional signs direct you to a new road which climbs into the mountains to the Sorek (Stalactite) Cave, also known as the Avshalom Reserve. This is a small but remarkable limestone cavern containing a veritable treasurehouse of stalactites and stalagmites. Indeed, it is claimed that the cave has examples of every type of stalactite and stalagmite known. It was discovered by accident in 1967 as a result of a routine blast in the neighboring quarry. The cave has been intelligently and dramatically adapted for visitors, and a visit here is a delight. A short film, in both English and Hebrew, explaining how it was formed and discovered is shown before visits. The cave can also be reached on Route 386 leaving Jerusalem through Ein Kerem.

About eight kms. (five miles) south of Bet Shemesh on Route 38 you enter the Ela Valley, scene of David's confrontation with Goliath. The small brook crossed by the road is likely the very one from which David selected his sling-stones (I Sam 17). Route 375 strikes off to the east here, reaching Jerusalem through Ein Kerem via Bar Giora (with access en route to the Sorek Cave), or Solomon's Pools and Bethlehem. Just south of the valley, on a terrace to the right, is a row of milestones, one with an extensive Latin and Greek inscription, part of an ancient Roman road from Ashkelon to Jerusalem. At Kibbutz Bet Guvrin the road veers west, joining Route 35.

Near the kibbutz are the visible remains of the 12th-century Crusader town of Bethgibelin, and earlier Roman and Byzantine structures. Take the first turning to the left. A short way in the road forks, the right branch leading to the flat-topped tel of ancient Maresha, and nearby numerous caves carved out of the soft chalk as tombs, oil-presses, water cisterns, grain stores, and the like. It is best to explore with a guide if you want to be sure of finding the more interesting caves and avoid hidden danger-spots. The left fork reaches the famous Bell Caves, a series of interconnected caverns used in the Hellenistic, Roman and Byzantine periods as an ecologically perfect quarry for extracting lime for cement. Crosses high on the cavern walls are witness to the use of the caves by early Christian refugees from Roman persecution. From the parking area, walk as if continuing the road, bear right through a shallow cave, and take the left path. Don't leave valuables in your car.

Just six kms. (four miles) west of Bet Guvrin on Route 35 a turn to the left takes you past the huge tel of Lachish, the most prominent Biblical city in the region, currently being excavated. You pass the modern village of Lachish heading towards that of Amaziah. Several kilometers on, a smaller road to the right takes you to the Shefelah's newest tourist site, the Bar Kochba caves of Amaziah. At time of writing the turning is somewhat poorly marked with a red sign.

A video presentation at the site prefaces a guided tour of an underground labyrinth carved out of the native chalk by Bar Kochba's warriors in the Second Jewish revolt against Rome (A.D. 132–135). Hidden water cisterns, immersion baths, unique oil stores and subterranean dwellings bear witness to the determination and endurance of the Jewish rebels against whose modest numbers Emperor Hadrian was forced to commit eight of his top legions. The site is newly opened and strongly recommended.

Ashkelon and Gaza

Back on Route 35, continuing westward to Ashkelon, you pass Kiryat Gat, established in 1954 as the urban hub of a new agricultural development area for immigrants. It is hard to believe that just a few decades ago this thriving community with homes, schools, factories and warehouses, was a virtual wasteland.

Ashkelon would be well worth a visit for its white sandy beach alone, but the town also happens to have a rich and fascinating past. There are no signs, however, of the Philistines who ruled here during Biblical times, nor of the shallots and scallions, both of whose names derived from the name of the town during the period when the Crusaders ran a flourishing onion export trade from here.

North of the beach is the national park, with picnicking and camping areas, interspersed with the remains of monumental marble statues from the Roman period. The whole area is enclosed by the ramp of the 3,500-year-old Hyksos city-wall, with massive chunks of 12th-century A.D. Crusader fortifications clawing skywards from its crest. Further north near the beach is a Roman tomb, complete with frescos and a mosaic floor, and the remains of a Byzantine church. Unfortunately, the town has acquired a reputation for vandalism, and visitors should not leave anything of value unattended in cars, on the beach, or in the national park. At the entrance to Ashkelon, vendors from nearby Gaza sell baskets and furniture made from plaited cane.

South of the town on Route 4 is Kibbutz Yad Mordechai, named after Mordechai Anilewicz, leader of the Jewish Warsaw Ghetto uprising against the Nazis in World War II. The kibbutz suffered the brunt of the invading Egyptian army during the War of Independence in 1948, and was captured and destroyed by the Egyptians before the Israelis retook it. A dramatic re-enactment of the battle has been set up, complete with weapons from the period and explanations in a number of languages. Nearby is a museum devoted to the heroism of the Ghetto fighters and to the lost world of Eastern European Jewry, destroyed by the Nazis.

Just a short drive south of Ashkelon is the Gaza Strip, home to about 500,000 local residents and Palestinian refugees. The area, which was held by the Egyptians after 1948, was conquered by Israel during the 1956 Suez campaign and then returned to Egypt, only to be occupied again during the Six Day War. The Peace Treaty of 1979, which provided for the return of Sinai to Egypt, left Gaza in Israeli hands, although it stipulated that the Gaza Strip should be awarded "autonomy," a term which has been accorded vastly differing interpretations. At present, tens of thousands of Gazans commute daily across the old border to work in Israel. Despite its rich history, which began with Gaza as a Philistine town and continued with it as an important center on the road to and from Egypt—the Via Maris—there is little for the visitor to see. Moreover the threat of unrest makes visits inadvisable. At the southern tip of the Gaza Strip is Rafah, a town which was divided as a result of the terms of the Peace Treaty. Here is the major border crossing into Egypt.

Heading north from Ashkelon along Route 4 is Ashdod, a sea port which was dredged out of the sands in 1957. Freighters and passenger liners alike use the port, which has become busier as a result of the opening of the Suez Canal to Israeli shipping following the Israeli–Egyptian Peace Treaty. But though pleasantly laid out, the town has little to offer visitors other than a beautiful beach.

Continuing north from Ashdod along Route 4 to Tel Aviv, you can turn off at Rishon Lezion for a view of one of the main centers of Israel's wine industry. Founded in 1882 by Russian immigrants, it soon came under the patronage of Baron Edmund de Rothschild of France, who provided the financial backing and the first vines for the wine cooperative which still flourishes here. There are guided tours of the cellars, with their enormous oak barrels. Afterwards the wine is available for tasting.

Just a short drive southeast of Rishon Lezion is Rehovot, home of Chaim Weizmann, Israel's first president, and the Weizmann Institute. You may visit his home and nearby grave in a quiet setting at the end of a majestic avenue of swaying cyprus trees. Tours of the Institute, Israel's principal center for post-graduate research in the pure sciences, are also available.

From here it is but a short drive north to Tel Aviv.

All Aboard

For a very different view of this area, some visitors, especially those with small children, might like to take the train between Jerusalem and the coast. It's hardly the last word in comfort, and it takes longer than any other form of transport save walking, but the line continues to be popular. With its very low fares, the train seems to attract the most colorful part of the population. Beduins with long, flowing robes squat on the seats. Their wives wear embroidered gowns and gold jewelry, with an occasional ring in their nose. Ultra-Orthodox Jews, with long, black coats and sidelocks, gather at one end of the train to recite their daily prayers.

The line was completed in 1892 by the Turks. Then the journey from Jaffa to Jerusalem took some four hours. Now it takes about half that, but is still twice as long as by road.

Leaving Jerusalem, with its picturesque station, the train begins winding its way around the hills through the Arab village of Beit

Safafa, which was divided until 1967, the railway line marking the border. The wadi, or river bed, through which the train passes, is known in Hebrew as Emek Refaim, the Valley of Ghosts. But in broad daylight it is anything but spooky, with its trees and lush greenery. Soon you pass the Arab village of Batir, site of Betar, the last stronghold in the second Jewish revolt against the Romans. Unlike Masada, it has not been excavated. All around you see little gardens and fruit trees. As you pass through the valley below the settlements of Bar Giora and Nes Harim, you can see the tomb of an Arab sheikh, a small domed structure, standing all alone by itself on a hillside.

From Bet Shemesh, the route becomes straighter, going through the plains. Now is the time to try the dining car, where you can get coffee, cold drinks, sandwiches, and, if the chef-waiter has time, an omelet. It's all very informal, and of course it's the only railway dining car in the world that keeps kosher, observing the Jewish dietary laws.

The station at Lod proves something of a surprise. After rolling along on a single track and passing stations that look like farmhouses, here are several platforms, all dating from the '20s and '30s and World War II when it was a major junction along the Damascus–Cairo line. And it was from here that the British soldiers would return to the front lines in North Africa, after resting in Palestine.

PRACTICAL INFORMATION FOR THE

JERUSALEM CORRIDOR, SHEFELAH AND

PHILISTINE COUNTRY

TOURIST OFFICES. Israel Government Tourist Office, Ashkelon, Afridar Center (tel. 051–23807). In addition, the IGTO in Jerusalem, 24 King George St. (tel. 02–241281) and in Tel Aviv, 7 Mendele St. (tel. 03–223266) can provide information on the areas described in this chapter.

Telephone Codes. We have given telephone codes for all the areas in the lists that follow. These codes need only be used when calling from outside the dialling area concerned.

HOTELS AND RESTAURANTS. Much of the area covered in this chapter has no hotels, as visitors prefer to stay in either Jerusalem or Tel Aviv, making side trips to the region. But, suitable accommodations might be found in a number of kibbutz and moshav guest houses just outside Jerusalem; for details, see *Practical Information* for Jerusalem. Restaurants are for the most part simple with relatively limited menus.

ABU GHOSH. Restaurant. Caravan Inn Restaurant (M), main road (tel. 02–542744). Pleasant view, Arab cuisine.

ASHKELON. Dagon Hotel (E), 2 Moshe Dorot St. (tel. 051–36111). 38 rooms with bath, 14 with shower only. Easy walk from beach, pleasant lawns and informal atmosphere. Partly air-conditioned. Pool. AE, DC, MC, V. **Shulamit Gardens Hotel** (M), 11 Hatayassim St. (tel. 051–36222). 108 rooms with bath. Modern, near beach, airconditioned; coffee shop, bar, sauna, tennis. AE, DC, MC, V. **Samson's Gardens Hotel** (I), 38 Hatamar St. (tel. 051–36641). 22 rooms, 5 with bath, rest with shower.

Restaurants. Rico Restaurant (M), Afridar Center (tel. 051–24592). Pleasant rustic atmosphere. **Heh Daroma Restaurant** (I), Moshav Mavkiim, south of Ashkelon (tel. 051–29511).

MOTZA. Restaurant. Motza Inn Restaurant (M), main highway (tel. 02–531713). Pleasant rustic atmosphere, Moroccan cuisine. AE, DC, MC, V.

REHOVOT. Restaurant. Inn of the Sixth Happiness Restaurant (M), 53 Herzl St. (tel. 054–57128). Yemenite cooking.

RISHON LEZION. Restaurant. Gan Dror Restaurant (I), 12 Tarmav St. (tel. 03–942416). Middle-Eastern food.

Holiday Village. Club Ashkelon (M), Afridar Beach, Ashkelon (tel. 051–36733). 196 units. Open in summer only. Has full sports activities, including tennis, windsurfing and horseback riding. AE, DC, MC, V.

Youth Hostels. Bar Giora, Judean Hills (tel. 02–911073). Mainly for groups. **Haezrahi,** Kiryat Anavim (tel. 02–539770). Convenient for Jerusalem.

Camping. Aqua Bella, tel. 02–527300. Open summer only. **Ashkelon National Park,** tel. 051–25228.

 HOW TO GET AROUND. By Bus. The express service between Tel Aviv and Jerusalem is frequent, but tourists wishing to get off anywhere along the way must take one of the local buses, which leave about once every hour. Services are also frequent between Tel Aviv and Ashkelon, Ashdod, Rehovot and Rishon Lezion.

Services to other destinations, however, are sporadic and tourists would be well-advised to enquire in advance about when the next bus, or returning bus, is expected.

By Train. For information concerning schedules in Jerusalem call 02–717764, and in Tel Aviv, tel. 03–254271.

By Car. This is generally the best form of transport, especially if you want to see out-of-the-way places. Except for the main highways between Tel Aviv and Jerusalem, and from Tel Aviv south to Ashdod, the roads are two lanes wide only. Take care and watch out for other drivers less cautious than yourself, especially on blind curves.

Tours. Regular tours leave from Jerusalem to the Sorek Stalactite Cave, and from Tel Aviv to Rishon Lezion and Rehovot. For information contact **Egged Tours,** 15 Frishman St., Tel Aviv (tel. 03–244177), or at the Jerusalem Central

Bus Station (tel. 02–551870). Alternatively, try **United Tours,** 113 Hayarkon St., Tel Aviv (tel. 03–298181) or King David Hotel, Jerusalem (tel. 02–222187).

 MUSEUMS AND HISTORIC SITES. This region of Israel is significantly less rich in places to visit than many other areas of the country. Nonetheless, among the highlights are:

AMAZIAH. Ancient **labyrinth** designed as a refuge; video presentation, horse-riding. Open Sat. to Thurs. 9–4, Fri. 9–1. Sat. is crowded and reservations are necessary (tel. 051–880267).

AQUA BELLA. Tel. 02–527300. Remains of a **Crusader convent;** picnic area. Open daily during daylight hours.

ASHKELON. National Park, open daily during daylight hours. Roman sarcophagi; next to Public Library.

BET GUVRIN. Cave complexes and archeological remains.

NEOT KEDUMIM. Botanical Gardens, tel. 08–233840. Garden open Sun. to Thurs. 8–5, Fri. 8–12. Groups should call in advance.

REHOVOT. Weizmann Home, tel. 08–83328. Tours every half hour, Sun. to Thurs. 10–3.30. Groups should call in advance.
Weizmann Institute. Guided tours for visitors Sun. to Thurs. 8–3.30, Fri. 8–1. Film at 11 A.M. and 3.15 P.M.; on Fri. at 11 only.

SOREK. Stalactite Cave, tel. 02–911117. Open Sat. to Thurs. 8.30–3.45, Fri. to 12.45. Film, in Hebrew and English, shown regularly.

YAD MORDECHAI. Kibbutz with a reconstruction of a battle site from the 1948 War of Independence and a museum, tel. 051–20528. Charts the Warsaw Ghetto and the lost world of East European Jewry. Open Sat. to Thurs. 8 A.M. to dusk, Fri. to 5 P.M.

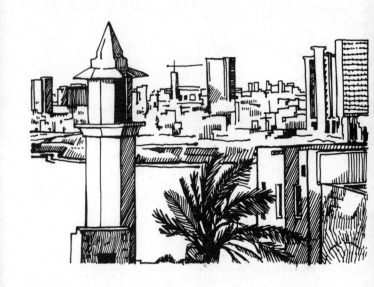

TEL AVIV

Shopkeepers and Sophisticates

Bold and brash, crass and cultivated, Israel's busiest city evokes feelings of both scorn and envy on the part of the rest of the country. At worst it seems a poor imitation of New York or Miami. At best it boasts a vitality that has attracted about a quarter of the country's population, and an even greater share of its cultural and commercial life. At first glance, it seems the archetypal concrete jungle, albeit with a Mediterranean flavor, a hodge-podge of ugly square buildings, many apparently decomposing in the sea air. It is only with time that the visitor can feel something of the spirit of the city, the charm of its quaint corners, and the vigor of its people.

Tel Aviv Orientation

For many, the first view of the city, and one of the finest, is from the air, as your plane passes directly overhead on its way to Ben Gurion Airport. To the south are the domes and minarets of Jaffa, the ancient city that the founders of Tel Aviv left in 1909 when they set out to establish a new Jewish city on the sand dunes to the north. (Though these early pioneers may have turned their backs on Jaffa, today people from the entire greater Tel Aviv area flock there for entertainment and relaxation.) Running north along the sea is a new pedestrian walk that

154

has done much to restore the role of social center to the seafront which it held in the '20s and '30s. Indeed, according to those who were around in those days, every evening the entire population would go down to the beachfront, especially in the summer, to catch the cool sea breeze. It was there that gossip was exchanged, matches were made, business was conducted. For many years the beachfront fell into disrepute, with much of it a hangout for unwholesome types. Today, with a new face, it is attracting the crowds again.

Parallel to the sea are the thoroughfares of Hayarkon, Ben Yehuda, Dizengoff, and Ibn Gvirol streets. It is along Hayarkon Street that the overwhelming bulk of the city's hotels are located, either directly opposite the beach, or no more than a few minutes away. Even from the air, you can see the towering hotels, a sight which does not please some critics, who would have preferred greater public access to the waterfront. But for tourists, the situation is ideal, with hotels in the very heart of the city. More than one hotel has taken full advantage of this location by providing dining rooms, coffeeshops, lounges, and terraces with a sea view.

Allenby Street in the south and Arlosoroff Street in the north, provide outlets eastward. The former, one of the first streets built in Tel Aviv, has become decidedly congested these days, and is now somewhat down at heel. The latter ends near Kikar Hamedina, a huge traffic circle that has made a name for itself as the city's most expensive shopping area. Between these two major east–west roads are a jumble of little streets guaranteed to confuse the newcomer. No street seems to go more than a few blocks without turning and twisting or coming to an abrupt halt.

To the north, the Yarkon River, once the northern border of the city, is now the center of a recreational area that marks the beginning of suburbia. It is a river only by local standards; visitors from Europe or America would probably call it a stream. In addition, much of the water that once ran through it has been pumped off to serve the country's vital need for water. And, adding insult to injury, the river has long suffered by receiving sewage from a large part of the country. Efforts to revive it are moving slowly. Meanwhile, the worst of the sewage has been siphoned off a few miles from the sea, and the river here in Tel Aviv is actually filled with sea water.

Both north of the Yarkon River and stretching to the east and the south of Tel Aviv proper are small towns, all fiercely independent, even though they are really part of the urban sprawl. Indeed, it is estimated that close to one million people live in the greater Tel Aviv area. Many of the surrounding towns, once rural settlements, are now dormitory suburbs whose residents work in the city, clogging the roads morning and evening.

Like many large cities, Tel Aviv seems to suffer from a lack of planning. In this case, the haphazard development was often caused by the uncertain finances of the city fathers who could only buy limited parcels of land at a time. Thus Allenby Street, for example, makes a sharp turn at one point, marking the place where the road originally dwindled off into the sand dunes, only to be continued a few years later when the developers were able to buy another parcel of land from the

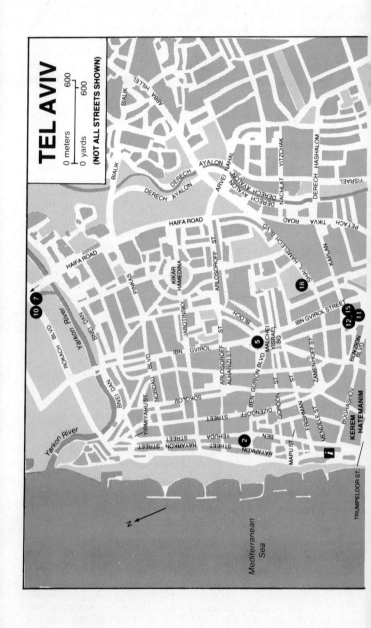

TEL AVIV

0 meters 600
0 yards 600

(NOT ALL STREETS SHOWN)

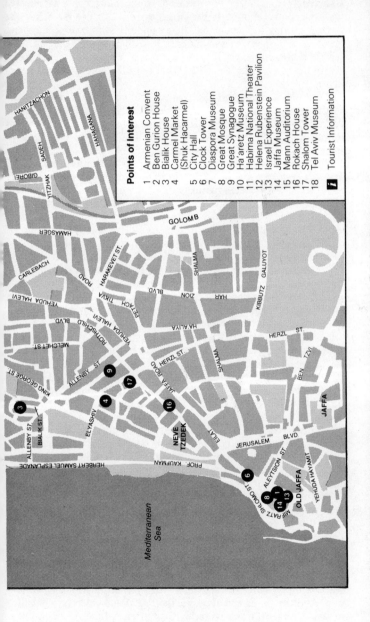

Points of Interest

1 Armenian Convent
2 Ben Gurion House
3 Bialik House
4 Carmel Market
   (Shuk Hacarmel)
5 City Hall
6 Clock Tower
7 Diaspora Museum
8 Great Mosque
9 Great Synagogue
10 Ha'aretz Museum
11 Habima National Theater
12 Helena Rubenstein Pavilion
13 Israel Experience
14 Jaffa Museum
15 Mann Auditorium
16 Rokach House
17 Shalom Tower
18 Tel Aviv Museum

𝒊 Tourist Information

absentee Arab landlords who owned it. Another factor that has affected the growth of Tel Aviv is the presence of water not far below the surface, making it difficult to build an underground transport system. Nor can we forget the surrounding townships, whose officials fight fiercely to preserve every iota of their power, even when they agree in theory that there must be some sort of overall planning for the entire area.

Generally, development has been from south to north, and the best neighborhoods seem to be moving steadily in that direction. In south Tel Aviv, on the other hand, neighborhoods that were once residential are now filled with offices. Many of the city's wealthier citizens have moved out to the suburbs, compounding the problems of the city, but the flight to the suburbs, while a factor, is far slower and less critical than the similar trend in many North American cities. And just as elsewhere in the world, in recent years areas which seemed to have long since lost their shine have been rediscovered, first by artists and bohemians, who found them picturesque, and later by others who realized their value. The first to undergo this process was Old Jaffa, which was transformed almost overnight from a slum into an artists' quarter, complete with galleries, cafés, and smart shops. At the time it was said that few real artists could afford to buy an apartment or studio in the renovated area, but the project seems to have left its imprint on adjoining areas as well. Now artists, or simply people who enjoy living in picturesque neighborhoods, dwell in other parts of Jaffa and in the nearby Neve Zedek area, once also written off as a slum.

It is not surprising that many Tel Avivians seek the old and the picturesque, when you stop to consider that 80 years ago the entire area was just sand dunes, and this in a country where anything less than 1,000 years old is considered relatively wet behind the ears. The newness of the city is compounded by the fact that here in particular it is the real estate developer who seems to wield the ultimate power. When a building gets too old, it is torn down to make room for something bigger and newer. Many of the original buildings of the city have fallen victim to developers' bulldozers. This in turn gives rise to a reaction, with the nature-lovers fighting to preserve every hovel on the grounds that it is linked with the history of the city. For the visitor, as often as not confused by the Stone Age, the Bronze Age, and the Iron Age, it is probably something of a relief to be somewhere where nothing goes back further than the Concrete Age.

But it is all this newness that gives the city its vitality. The shows are better here, as is the food, and people are better dressed. Tel Aviv is *the* place in Israel to find entertainment; anything from symphony orchestras and theater (with English translation) to the best in restaurants and belly dancing. For shopping, too, this city is in a class of its own, whether you're looking for a suede jacket or an ancient brass lamp. And the shops and theaters, the restaurants and concert halls, are filled with local residents rather than tourists. Indeed, in a country which seems to be in the throes of economic difficulties, one wonders how they can afford it all.

A Glance At History

It all started, of course, with Jaffa, which claims to be the oldest port in the world, and is said to have been founded by Japhet, the son of Noah. Early Egyptian records show that it was conquered by Thutmose III in 1468 B.C. (he was heading north into Canaan to quell a revolt of his subject peoples in the Jezre'el Valley). Similarly, archeological excavations in old Jaffa have uncovered the name of Ramses II, from 1270 B.C. From the Egyptians it then passed into the hands of the Philistines. (Local wags, who like to poke fun at the reputed crass materialism of Tel Avivians, joke that it was Zionism which restored the Philistines to the coastal plain.) Later, conquered by King David, it was at Jaffa that the cedar trees used in the building of Solomon's original Temple in Jerusalem (around 950 B.C.) were unloaded.

Following the Babylonian exile in the 6th century B.C., Jaffa came under the control of the Phoenicians and then the Greeks. It was these Hellenistic residents of the city who loaded the small Jewish community in boats and sank them during the Maccabean revolt in 165 B.C. In revenge, the Maccabees burned the city and its inhabitants. Largely abandoned in the Middle Ages, the city regained its importance as a port in the 19th century. Napoleon stopped here on his campaign through the country and, according to some sources, ordered 4,000 wounded soldiers to facilitate his withdrawal.

At the end of the 19th century, it was to Jaffa that the early Jewish pioneers, and other western travelers, came when they arrived in the country. Because of the treacherous rocks, their ships would anchor off the coast and passengers and freight alike would be loaded into small boats or lighters. Diaries from the period tell of passengers being literally thrown from one Arab porter in the ship to another in the lighter while the porters would laugh at the visitor's discomfort. But the visitors kept coming, and most of them stayed. Soon Jaffa could boast churches, mosques, and synagogues, and colonies of Americans, Germans, and Russians. At the same time, because it was the gateway to Jerusalem, Christians of many denominations built churches and institutions here.

Then in 1909, a group of Jews from Jaffa decided that they wanted to leave the narrow crowded streets of the town. They bought a stretch of worthless sand dunes north of Jaffa and called it Ahuzat Bayit—which, in due time, was to become Tel Aviv, said to be a poetic translation of Theodor Herzl's book, *Altneuland* ("Old–New Land"). In World War I, many residents of Tel Aviv were deported by the Turks, who later evacuated the entire town. Arab riots in 1921 in Jaffa spurred Tel Aviv's growth, and it became a separate municipality under its first major, Meir Dizengoff. More riots in 1929 caused additional Jews to leave Jaffa for the safety of Tel Aviv.

Also contributing to the growth of the city were the many immigrants from Poland who came in the '20s. It was they who established Tel Aviv's reputation as a city of small shopkeepers. But it was the influx of German Jews fleeing Nazism in the '30s that left an indelible print on the city, adding not only to the cultural scene, but also establishing Tel Aviv's reputation as a city of sidewalk cafés.

In retrospect, the early accomplishments of Tel Aviv seem meager. The country's first modern Hebrew high school, the Gymnasia Herzlia, built in 1910, has since been replaced by the Shalom Tower building. A port in north Tel Aviv, built to make the Jewish city independent of the port in Arab Jaffa, has since closed down, to become a center of entertainment. The Great Synagogue, completed in 1926, now sits rather unhappily in a scruffy commercial area; a new facade has done little to improve its appearance.

But the city has continued to grow and flourish, as have its cultural institutions. The Habima Hebrew theater company, founded in Moscow, arrived for a visit in 1928 and decided to stay. Now, as the Habima National Theater, it must compete with several other repertory companies. The Palestine Philharmonic Orchestra, founded in 1937 by violinist Bronislaw Huberman to provide employment for Jewish musicians ousted from Hitler's Germany, is now the world-famous Israel Philharmonic and has a secure home in the elegant Mann Auditorium. The Tel Aviv Museum, once housed in the former home of Tel Aviv-founder Meir Dizengoff, now has a new home of its own, where displays of the best of local art can be seen.

It was in the old Tel Aviv Museum that David Ben Gurion, Israel's first prime minister, read out the new Jewish state's Declaration of Independence in May 1948. In those days Tel Avivians were not shy about singing and dancing in the streets, and they celebrated the event with their fullest enthusiasm. For a short period Tel Aviv was actually the capital of the state. The Knesset, Israel's parliament, met in a building at the foot of Allenby Street, near the seashore, which was to become the Israel National Opera (now defunct). Meanwhile, some Arab residents of Jaffa fled and their homes were occupied by immigrants, largely from Turkey, Greece, and Bulgaria.

In 1950, Jaffa and Tel Aviv were combined into one city.

People in Motion

The city has much to see: museums, such as the new Diaspora Museum; historical sites, especially Old Jaffa; theaters; concert halls, parks, markets; and even, in the midst of the urban sprawl, some fine architecture. But its major resource remains its people, and people-watching remains a very popular Tel Aviv pastime. True, the old-time residents of Tel Aviv will tell you that they never go walking. It is all those people from the suburbs, they will say, who have nothing better to do with their time. Still, whoever it is out there, they provide a fine show. Dressed to the hilt, flamboyant in their movements and expressions, they seem to have no inhibitions about bringing their personal lives into the streets. Romances are made and broken in full view of the public, and if you are sitting alone, don't be surprised if someone comes along and asks if they can sit down next to you. If you're not interested, just say no—no one will be offended. For a grandstand seat, choose one of the cafés along Dizengoff street or nearby Ibn Gvirol street, or better still, the newly-constructed promenade along the entire length of the seafront. Here the municipality has thoughtfully provided chairs for people-watching (and the Tel Avivians have surprised themselves by not making off with them at the earliest opportunity). But don't let the sea keep you away from some of the city's fine, old tree-lined streets, such as Rothschild, Ben Zion, or Ben Gurion Boulevard, where life seems to move at a slower pace. It is on these streets that it is hard to imagine you are not somewhere in Central Europe.

Jaffa

But the serious sightseers inevitably start with Old Jaffa, whose towers and minarets seem to act like a magnet, drawing the visitor. One can spend hours just wandering through the little streets and alleyways or sitting on the grassy bluff overlooking the old port and enjoying the view of Tel Aviv to the north. According to Greek legend, it was to one of the rocks that the god of the seas, Poseidon, chained the hapless Andromeda, who was to have been eaten by a sea monster. Instead, she was rescued by Perseus, who married her. According to the Bible, it was from Jaffa that Jonah set sail, before his fateful encounter with the whale. And it was in Jaffa that St. Peter raised Tabitha from the dead.

Starting your visit from the clock tower, built by the Turks in 1906, you are at the hub of things in Jaffa's central square. To your right, up the hill, is Old Jaffa. Just behind you is the road which circles around to the port. And on your left is the flea market, for seeking out bargains. Along the street, straight ahead of you, are several bakeries where you can buy varieties of Middle Eastern pizza, dough baked with salty cheese, an egg, spinach, or mushrooms.

By making your way up the hill, you will come upon the restored area, in the center of which is a large excavated plot. Here you can see parts of a six-meter (20-ft.) thick wall, built by the Hyksos rulers of Egypt in the 13th century B.C., and part of the city gate, bearing the name of Ramses II (also 13th century B.C.). Remains include a Canaanite city; a Jewish city built at the time of Ezra and Nehemiah; a 3rd-century B.C. wall; a statue of Aphrodite; Hasmonean ruins; and traces of Roman occupation.

The square is dominated by the 19th-century Roman Catholic church and monastery of St. Peter, while down the hill is Jaffa's main mosque. Though the mosque is often closed, you can admire the ornate fountain alongside it. Across the street from the mosque, in the midst of a pleasant park, is the Jaffa Museum, where many of the finds that were unearthed in the excavation site at the top of the hill or elsewhere during the restoration project are on view. It is housed in what was once the Turkish governor's house. Adjoining it is the old Turkish bathhouse, or *hamam,* now a nightclub. All around here is the Jaffa artists' quarter, with its winding streets, little balconies, and arched doorways and windows. Even if you're not particularly interested in art, it is worth going into some of the studios and galleries just to see the interiors of the buildings. It is in this maze of streets that you will find the Armenian Convent that served as a hospital for Napoleon's troops. Above the artists' quarter is another park and a natural amphitheater where performances are held almost daily throughout the summer. If you bought one of the Middle Eastern pizzas at the bakeries mentioned above, this is the perfect place to enjoy your picnic lunch.

But not everyone is enamored with Old Jaffa. There are those who feel that it is too shiny and too new-looking, too spruced up; in short, too touristy. For those who yearn for a more natural ambiance, the Ajami quarter, just a few blocks south of the renovated area, will do the trick. It is a jumble of tumbledown buildings, beautifully-kept homes, chic boutiques, galleries, and workingmen's cafés. Dividing the two is the Israel Experience, a multi-media, multi-visual presentation with adjoining shops, restaurants, and attractions for children.

For an equally authentic experience, visit the flea market. Its little stalls are to the right and left of Olei Zion Street, close to the Clock Tower. Everything except food is on sale. Housewives coming here are usually after old or new household furnishings, and mix with tourists in streets of shops and through a couple of narrow, covered passageways going from one street to another. At night, iron curtains seal them off, locking up all the shops at once. This is the Kingdom of junk, of old stuff, where scrap-iron and discarded furniture hold sway. It's also the lair of zealous artisans who work in full view of the public, naively letting the passers-by watch them conscientiously at work reproducing some antique object that will be hawked as having been "discovered at the site of an excavation and spirited away at incalculable risk from the long arm of the museums." Right across the street, in the window of an antique shop, you will find another finished replica of the same object, properly worm-eaten and with an impeccable patina showing under the careful coating of dried mud.

Neve Tzedek and the Carmel Market

Moving northward from Jaffa, you pass the Neve Tzedek quarter, a Jewish neighborhood which actually predates Tel Aviv. Its small homes are rendered almost invisible by the towering buildings along the sea. Once slated for demolition, it has been saved from the bulldozers and now serves as another center for artistic endeavors, with galleries and studios. A former school building houses an experimental theater and the Inbal dance troupe, which has made a special contribution to the country's cultural life by introducing the unique dances of the Yemenite Jewish community to Israel.

A special treat in the Neve Tzedek quarter is the Rokach House, built by the founder of the neighborhood, Shimon Rokach, and lovingly restored by his sculptress granddaughter, Lea Majaro-Mintz. Where the original plans or structure existed, she followed them, but where, for example, a ceiling had fallen in and completely disintegrated, she used her own imagination. The house itself is filled with her works, which consist mainly of far from idealized and often humorous ceramic studies of women. She freely admits that her sculpture is highly introspective. The house also serves as an informal coffeeshop, and makes a pleasant rest-stop for the sightseer.

In the little streets north of Neve Tzedek, dozens of clothing designers have their workshops. For many of the city's women, this is the place to go when they shop for clothes, and it is often possible to find great bargains.

Rising above the area is the Shalom Tower, Israel's tallest building, constructed in 1957. It also houses the country's first department store. From the roof, there is a fine view of the whole of Tel Aviv. Here, too, you can visit the country's only wax museum. On one wall of the building is a ceramic mural representing the Gymnasia Herzlia, the country's first Hebrew high school, which moved northward to make room for the skyscraper.

Continuing north, we come to the Carmel Market (Shuk Hacarmel), the city's largest open-air market, where tomatoes and cucumbers vie for space with clothing and chickens. The vendors seem to have an unlimited store of good humor, and compete with each other in shouting out catchy slogans to attract buyers. They also seem to have infinite patience in arranging their wares to display every apple and peach to its best advantage. Like Tel Aviv itself, the Carmel Market is a melange of East and West, Ali Baba and the *Shtetl,* with a bit of the Lower East Side or Petticoat Lane thrown in for good measure. To stock up for a picnic lunch, it can't be beat, but even if you just want a bit of fruit for the room it's worth visiting. Just remember to bring your own shopping bag. Nearby is Kerem Hatemanim, one of Tel Aviv's Yemenite quarters. This is the home of some of the city's best restaurants. Additionally, not that there is any connection, many of the country's best known singers have been born here.

Not far from the market, on the other side of Allenby Street, is Bialik Street, where much of Tel Aviv history seems encapsulated in just a few blocks. At one end is Tel Aviv's first city hall, now a museum devoted to local history. On the facade is a mural symbolizing early Tel Aviv. Just down the block is the home of Reuvin Rubin, a painter whose work was largely devoted to the changing face of the city over the decades. The house is now a museum with constantly-changing exhibitions based upon the painter's own collection. Finally, there is the house of Chaim Nachman Bialik, often described as the Hebrew national poet. His house, too, is now a museum, devoted to his life and times.

The City Center

Another fascinating area in the city is the block—up by Rothschild Boulevard and Hakiriya Street in the center of the city—that seems to house about half of all of Tel Aviv's cultural life, principally in the shape of both the Mann Auditorium and the Habima Theater. In between are pools, a coffeeshop, and aged sycamore trees that have been pruned to within an inch of their lives to provide shade for an ingenious multi-level patio. The Mann Auditorium, which can seat 3,000 people, is the country's largest and best equipped concert hall. It is here that the Israel Philharmonic Orchestra plays to full houses. Habima, the country's oldest and best established theater company, was long heir to the old Russian tradition of histrionics, and was considered by many to be old-fashioned and stodgy, but it changed all that by setting up avant garde, experimental groups.

Occupying a third corner of the block is the Helena Rubenstein Pavilion, a branch of the Tel Aviv Museum, which provides space for visiting exhibitions. And just in case you were wondering, it was indeed built with funds donated by Helena Rubenstein, who made her fortune by telling women how to be beautiful.

A walk of about 15 minutes down Ibn Gvirol Street and onto Sha'ul Hamelech Boulevard will bring you to the other, and main, section of the Tel Aviv Museum, which has the country's most extensive collection of local painting and sculpture. This building, and others nearby, such as Asia House and the IBM Building, form an island of imaginative architecture among the concrete boxes. To get to the bustling downtown area and all those cafés, retrace your steps and continue past the Dizengoff Center and Dizengoff Circle, once an idyllic traffic circle and now a space-age traffic island where the pedestrians walk overtop the cars. It is newly crowned by a multi-media sculpture which combines a fountain, a jet of flame, color, movement and music.

The Ha'aretz and Diaspora Museums

Much farther to the north, across the Yarkon River and the large park along its banks, is the Ha'aretz Museum, really a collection of small museums in one complex. Separate pavilions are provided for numismatics (coins), ancient ceramics, science and technology, and a planetarium. But if you have only a little time, the two gems of this museum are the glass collection, reminding us that it was in this part of the world that glass production began, and the ethnography section, with a fine collection of Jewish folk art from Eastern Europe. The ethnography museum was the focus of dramatic interest a few years ago when practically the entire collection, much of it consisting of silver objects, was stolen. Happily, almost all of it was found a year later, bricked up behind a false wall in a Tel Aviv apartment.

Close to the Ha'aretz Museum is the highlight of Tel Aviv sightseeing: the Diaspora Museum, on the campus of Tel Aviv University. It gives a dramatic and imaginative picture of Jewish life throughout the world for the last 2,500 years. The visitor is assailed by a myriad modern museum techniques, including dioramas, audio-visual displays, models, and a computer programed to give information on Jewish communities and families from around the world. All this represents something of a revolution in thinking in Israel, where for many years it was argued that the Jewish experience outside of the Land of Israel was of little value.

If all this sightseeing has tired you, why not spend a few hours in the sun at Herzlia, a suburb just north of Tel Aviv, with some of the finest beaches in the country. The section near the beach is Herzlia Pituach, where most of the country's diplomats and a good part of its millionaires make their homes.

PRACTICAL INFORMATION FOR TEL AVIV

GETTING TO TOWN FROM THE AIRPORT. United Tours (tel. 03–242124) runs a bus service from the airport every hour on the hour, from 5 A.M. to midnight, to the air terminal on Harakevet St. and the hotel area on Hayarkon St., stopping at all the hotels. Egged, the national bus cooperative, has buses which are cheaper, but often fairly crowded. They stop at the airport throughout the day, from 5.30 A.M. to 11 P.M., going to the Tel Aviv Central Bus Station.

Sherut (shared) taxis and private taxis are also available at the airport. They are more expensive, but their fares are regulated by the government and a sign listing the official rates is posted at the exit from the air terminal.

TOURIST OFFICES. Israel Government Tourist Office, 7 Mendele St. (tel. 223266). Located in the heart of the hotel area. The clerks here, who usually speak several languages between them, can find you a hotel room if necessary, provide free maps and brochures on sites throughout the country and tell you about special events.

In the large hotels you will find a member of the **Tourist Volunteer Service,** usually retired people who give their time to make the visitor's stay more pleasant. Naturally they will help anyone and not just guests in that particular hotel; they can often provide excellent recommendations and are usually quite helpful in times of difficulty. For current information about upcoming events, a free magazine, *What's On,* is available in hotel lobbies.

USEFUL ADDRESSES. Embassies. *British Embassy,* 192 Hayarkon St. (tel. 249171). *Canadian Embassy,* 220 Hayarkon St. (tel. 228122). *U.S. Embassy,* 71 Hayarkon St. (tel. 654338).

Travel Agents. *Egged Tours,* 15 Frishman St. (tel. 242271). *Meditrad* (American Express Representatives), 16 Ben Yehuda St. (tel. 294654). *Travex,* 99 Hayarkon St. (tel. 223017).

Car Hire. *Avis,* 75 Hayarkon St. (tel. 651093). *Budget,* 74 Derech Petach Tikva (tel. 336126). *Gan-Car,* 100 Hayarkon St. (tel. 225772). *Hertz,* 81 Hayarkon St. (tel. 656248). *Thrifty,* 126 Atarim Sq. (tel. 283281).

TELEPHONE CODES. The telephone code for Tel Aviv is 03. To call any number in this chapter, unless otherwise specified, this prefix must be used. Within the city, no prefix is required.

HOTELS. Hotels in Tel Aviv range from the luxurious to the plain and modest side-street hotel. The great mass of hotels, large and small, are located near the beach along Hayarkon St. or in the immediate vicinity. There is much to be said for staying in this area; it's right in the heart of things and especially convenient if you want to take a dip in the sea before or after a day of touring.

Another prime location is the beach of Herzliya, a little north of Tel Aviv proper, where the hotels tend to be all-round resorts, with lots of sports facilities and activities to keep you busy all day if you like. Naturally, however, the best bargains are to be found away from these two areas; for those with cars it might even be more convenient to stay away from the main hotel area where congestion is chronic and parking is at a premium. Visitors without reservations can find help in securing accommodations from the IGTO in Tel Aviv or at Ben Gurion Airport.

There are some hotels which are not recommended by IGTO and while these can be very cheap, they are often not as clean as they should be.

Because the season is year-round, there is little variation in rates.

Deluxe

Accadia, Herzliya (tel. 052–556677). 192 rooms. Located on the beach with a large heated swimming pool, tennis and sauna. AE, DC, MC, V.

Carlton, Hayarkon St. (tel. 291291). 282 rooms. Ultramodern, overlooking the Tel Aviv Marina. AE, DC, MC, V.

Dan, 99 Hayarkon St. (tel. 241111). The oldest of Tel Aviv's deluxe hotels, with a spacious lobby, enclosed pool and Jacuzzi in winter. AE, DC, MC, V.

Daniel, Herzliya (tel. 052–544444). 350 rooms. Newest and snazziest of the hotels in the area. Has a complete spa and health club, two pools, seven restaurants, beach. AE, DC, MC, V.

Hilton, Independence Park (on Hayarkon Street), (tel. 244222). 609 rooms. Elegant, international-style hotel. Has a special V.I.P. section with large luxurious suites. A popular meeting place for businessmen. AE, DC, MC, V.

Sharon, Herzliya (tel. 052–78777). 200 rooms. An old-world spacious resort hotel. AE, DC, MC, V.

Sheraton, 115 Hayarkon St. (tel. 286222). 360 rooms. Newly redecorated rooms and lobby, with friendly service. Separate V.I.P. floors with a businessmen's lounge. AE, DC, MC, V.

Expensive

Basel, 156 Hayarkon St. (tel. 244161). 138 rooms. In an excellent location, it has a solid reputation as a good, unpretentious hotel. AE, DC, MC, V.

Grand Beach, 250 Hayarkon St. (tel. 241252). 208 rooms. Has a rooftop pool. AE, DC, MC, V.

Moriah Plaza, 155 Hayarkon St. (tel. 299555). 348 rooms. In essence a comfortable deluxe hotel with all facilities. Deluxe prices only April–May. AE, DC, MC, V.

Ramada Continental, 121 Hayarkon St. (tel. 296444). 340 rooms. Part of the "deluxe hotel strip", though a bit below its neighbors. Deluxe prices April-May. AE, DC, MC, V.

Ramat Aviv, 151 Haifa Rd. (tel. 413181). 118 rooms. Located near the Ha'aretz and Diaspora museums, it has a parklike atmosphere. AE, DC, MC, V.

Sinai, 11 Trumpeldor St. (tel. 652621). 250 rooms. Modern and pleasant. AE, DC, MC, V.

Moderate

Adiv, 2 Mendele St. (tel. 229141). 68 rooms. AE, MC, V.

City, 9 Mapu St. (tel. 246253). 96 rooms. AE, DC, MC, V.

Habakuk, 7 Habakuk St. (tel. 440011). 18 suites. An apartment hotel with moderate rates for two-room suites. AE, DC, MC, V.

Mandarin, North Tel Aviv (tel. 428161). 225 rooms. A little out of town on the beach, this is a new hotel with luxury facilities at bargain rates. AE, DC, MC, V.

Tadmor, 38 Basel St., Herzliya (tel. 052–78321). A hotel training school, run by the Tourism Ministry and an exceptionally good buy. AE, DC, MC, V.

Inexpensive

Dizengoff Square, 2 Zamenhoff St. (tel. 296181). 54 rooms, all with bath or shower. Boasts an Indian restaurant. AE, DC, MC, V.

Florida, 164 Hayarkon St. (tel. 242184). 52 rooms, all with bath.

Kfar Hamaccabia, Ramat Gan (tel. 715715). 138 rooms. A holiday village with full sports facilities. AE, DC, MC, V.

Maxim, 86 Hayarkon St. (tel. 653721). 60 rooms, all with bath or shower. AE, DC, MC, V.

Moss, 6 Nes Ziona St. (tel. 651655). 70 rooms, all with bath. AE, DC, MC, V.

Ora, 35 Ben Yehuda St. (tel. 650941). 54 rooms, all with bath or shower. AE, DC, MC, V.

Youth Hostels. Tel Aviv, 32 Bene Dan St. (tel. 455042). 250 beds. Airconditioned, with kitchen.

Yad Lebanim, Yahalom St., Petah Tikva (tel. 922666). 200 beds.

Guest House. Shefayim, Kibbutz Shefayim (tel. 052–70171). 110 rooms. Sports facilities. AE, MC, V.

RESTAURANTS. Tel Aviv is unquestionably home not only to the largest concentration of restaurants in Israel, but to the best as well. As is only to be expected in a city that prides itself on sophistication and highliving, you can eat as well here as in practically any other city in the world. Restaurants come in all price categories and cover an enormous range of types, from the humblest Middle Eastern cafe to the most chic haute cuisine. Prices in the better restaurants are predictably high, but if you don't mind aiming a little lower, you will find quality and low prices co-existing very happily.

Expensive

Alhambra, 30 Jerusalem Blvd., Jaffa (tel. 834453). Considered by many to be the best restaurant in the country, despite its location in a rather seedy part of Jaffa. Mediterranean cuisine with a South of France flavor. AE, DC, MC, V.

Le Beaujolais, 33 Yirmiyahu St. (tel. 449722). Elegant and intimate. Try the home-made goose-liver paté. AE, DC, MC, V.

Casba, 32 Yirmiyahu St. (tel. 442617). The favorite of many Tel Avivians. Roast duck is a specialty. AE, DC, V.

Dan Grill, Dan Hotel (tel. 241111). Excellent buffet lunch daily. AE, DC, MC, V.

Henry VII, De Shalit St., Herzliya (tel. 052–78586). With a friendly atmosphere, this is a neighborhood hangout for diplomats. AE, DC, V.

King Solomon, Hilton Hotel (tel. 244222). For very elegant dining. Creative chefs. AE, DC, MC, V.

Russalka, 88 Herbert Samuel Esplanade (tel. 653530). Russian cuisine and entertainment. AE, DC.

Moderate

Arnold (Balkan Corner), Rakah Blvd. (tel. 417440). An unlikely restaurant in an unlikely location, this constitutes a genuine culinary adventure. Claims to cook eggplant in a hundred different ways. V.

Baiuca, Yehuda Hayamit, Jaffa (tel. 827289). A family-run restaurant with Brazilian cuisine.

Keton, 145 Dizengoff St. (tel. 233679). The place to go for Eastern European Jewish specialties.

Ma Jardin, 186 Ben Yehuda St. (tel. 231792). Romanian grilled steaks. AE, DC, MC, V.

Nektar, 209 Bene Ephraim (tel. 478022). A supper club in a suburban shopping center; its owners entertain and the guests join in the singing.

The (Red) Chinese Restaurant, 326 Dizengoff St. (tel. 448408). Despite the name, it features Thai specialties. AE, DC, MC, V.

The Second Floor, 87 Ben Yehuda (tel. 220234). Fish and dairy, with considerable flair. AE, DC, MC, V.

Shaul's Inn, 11 Elyashiv (tel. 653303). Excellent Middle Eastern cooking in the heart of the Yemenite quarter. AE, DC, MC, V.

Yin Yang, 64 Rothschild Blvd. (tel. 621833). Authentic Chinese cooking. The specialty is smoked duck. AE, DC, V.

Inexpensive

Avazi, 5 Yordei Hasira (tel. 379918). Serves grilled meat of all kinds, including goose liver.

Banana, 334 Dizengoff St. (tel. 457491). Vegetarian and natural foods.

Bonanza, 17 Trumpeldor St. (tel. 285803). Good food in a pub atmosphere. AE, DC, MC, V.

L'Entrecote, 195 Ben Yehuda St. (tel. 230726). Good steaks, salad, dessert and wine.

Goulash Corner, 108 Hayarkon St. (tel. 236859). Hearty food.

Little Tel Aviv, 300 Hayarkon St. (tel. 450109). AE, DC, MC, V.

Me and Me, 49 Bograshov St. (tel. 287382). Middle Eastern food. AE, DC, MC, V.

Shely, Dizengoff Center (tel. 290369). Good soups and salads. MC, V.

Tayelet, 80 Herbert Samuel Esplanade (tel. 656992). You can dine outdoors overlooking the sea. AE, DC, MC, V.

 CAFES AND SNACKBARS. Virtually all Tel Aviv cafes serve light meals, but no one will bother you if you order a cup of coffee or a bottle of beer and while away an hour or two talking, reading, writing letters or just watching. Don't be surprised if the people at the table next to yours start a conversation with you. They're just as curious about you as you are about them.

Apropos, 4 Tarsat Blvd. A trendy cafe in the Mann Auditorium complex, worth visiting if only to read the menu.

Balloon, 78 Herbert Samuel Esplanade. Ice cream creations; on the beach.

Cherry, 166 Dizengoff St. Young crowd, health food.

Frack, 131 Dizengoff St. A grandstand seat for the pedestrian parade.

Kapulsky, 166 Dizengoff St. If you're into rich cream cakes, this is the place to go.

Kassit, 117 Dizengoff St. A hangout for Tel Aviv bohemians in the good old days, it still attracts a few of the arty crowd.

Mersand, 70 Ben Yehuda St. Home-made cakes, self-service. A favorite of the elderly set.

Piltz, 81 Hayarkon St. A resurrected '30s social meeting place in a prime location overlooking the beach. Dancing with an orchestra.

HOW TO GET AROUND. By Bus. Public buses run often to all of the major tourist and business destinations, except on the Sabbath. A set fare (no transfers) is collected either by the driver in front or by a ticket collector in back. Just watch to see where everybody else gets on.

A special bus run by United Tours links Hayarkon St. along the Tel Aviv beach with the Herzliya hotel area. The company also plans to run a special circular tourist bus (number 99) from Old Jaffa to the Diaspora Museum, stopping at all the tourist sites on the way. Look for notices in hotel lobbies.

By Taxi. Taxis are reasonable, but drivers sometimes "forget" to use their meters. Taxis may be found outside all the major hotels and most drivers know English. Sherut, or shared, taxis run along route #4 from the Central Bus Station to near the hotel district.

 CITY TOURS AND EXCURSIONS. Tours ranging in length from half-a-day to a week leave practically daily from Tel Aviv for all parts of the country. Inquire at **Egged Tours,** 15 Frishman St. (tel. 244177), **Galilee Tours,** 142 Hayarkon St. (tel. 225817), **United Tours,** 113 Hayarkon St. (tel. 754–3333), or any hotel or travel agency.

A free guided walking tour of Old Jaffa leaves every Wednesday at 9.30 from the clocktower. Several organizations offer tours of their institutions, among them: **Amit** (tel. 220187); **Na'amat** (tel. 210791); **Soldiers' Welfare Association** (tel. 262291); **Tour Ve'aleh** (tel. 258311); **WIZO** (tel. 232939); and the **Women's League for Israel** (tel. 283194).

 HISTORIC BUILDINGS AND SITES. Bar Ilan University, Bnei Brak. The country's only university which combines secular studies with an Orthodox Jewish outlook.

City Hall, Malchei Yisrael Square. The newly built municipal building fronts a massive square which is the country's most popular site for political demonstrations.

Russian Monastery, Tel Kabir, Jaffa. According to the Russian tradition, this is the site of the raising of Tabitha from the dead by St. Peter. It incorporates part of an ancient Jewish cemetery.

Shalom Tower, 1 Herzl St. Has a rooftop view and a wax museum.

Tel Aviv University, Ramat Aviv. See the newly built campus of the city's largest institution of higher learning.

 MUSEUMS. Artists' House, 9 Alharizi St. Israeli sculpture and painting. Open Sun. to Thurs. 10–1, 4–7, Fri. and Sat. 10–1.

Ben Gurion House, 17 Ben Gurion Blvd. Home of Israel's first Prime Minister. Open Sun. to Thurs. 8–2, Mon. and Thurs. also 5–7; Fri. 8–1; closed Sat.

Bible House, 16 Rothschild Blvd. Books, manuscripts and paintings relating to the Bible in the home of Tel Aviv's founder and first mayor, Meir Dizengoff. There's also an Israel Independence exhibit in the hall where the State of Israel was proclaimed. Open Sun. to Fri. 9–1; closed Sat.

Diaspora Museum, Tel Aviv University, Ramat Aviv. An extensive exhibit of 2,500 years of Jewish life outside Israel. Open Sun. to Thurs. 10–5, Wed. until 7, Sat. 10–2. No children under 6.

Ha'aretz Museum, Museum Center, Ramat Aviv. Has separate sections covering glass, coins, ceramics, the alphabet, science and technology, ethnography and folklore, and archeology. Open Sun. to Fri. 9–1, Tues. also 4–7, Sat. 10–1.

Hagana Museum, 23 Rothschild Blvd. Exhibits on Israel's War of Independence. Open Sun. to Thurs. 9–3, Fri. 9–12.30; closed Sat.

Helena Rubenstein Pavilion, 6 Tarsat Blvd. Visiting exhibits. Open Sun. to Thurs. 10–2 and 5–9, Sat. 11–2 and 7–10; closed Fri.

Independence Hall, where the State of Israel was proclaimed. Within Bible House (see above).

Jaffa Museum, 10 Mifratz Shlomo St., Jaffa. Archeological finds from ancient Jaffa. Open Sun. to Fri. 9–1; closed Sat.

Lasky Planetarium, Museum Center, Ramat Aviv. For times of English presentations, tel. 415244.

Rubin House, 14 Bialik St. The home of one of Israel's leading painters, with a rotating exhibit of his work. Open Sun., Mon., Wed., Thurs. 10–2; Tues. 10–1, 4–8; Sat. 11–2; closed Fri.

Tel Aviv History Museum, 27 Bialik St. Documents and photographs relating to the founding and history of Tel Aviv. Open Sun. to Fri. 9–1, except Tues. 4–7 only; closed Sat.

Tel Aviv Museum, Shaul Hamelech Blvd. Israeli and foreign painting and sculpture. Open Sun. to Thurs. 10–10, Sat. 10–1, 7–11.

Theater Museum, 3 Melchet St. Exhibits on the history of Yiddish and Hebrew theater. Open Sun. to Thurs. 9–1; closed Fri. and Sat.

PARKS AND GARDENS. Tel Aviv's largest park, the **Yarkon Park,** is at the northern end of the city along the Yarkon River. It offers acres of trees, lawns and children's play areas, as well as boats for hire and boat rides in larger boats. On Saturdays in good weather, it's crowded with picnicking families enjoying themselves. One section of the park, near Rokach Blvd., contains a tropical garden, open 10–4.

Other notable parks in Tel Aviv are **Independence Park,** which overlooks the sea alongside the Hilton Hotel, and **Meir Park** on Ben Zion Ave., one of the city's oldest. The **Tel Aviv Zoo** was recently transferred to the **Safari Park** in Ramat Gan, which includes a large conventional zoo area and a smaller section where visitors can drive among lions, hippos, giraffes, etc.

SHOPPING. The city's two large department stores are the **Shalom** in the Shalom Tower and **Hamashbir** in Dizengoff Center. Both have a large selection of clothing, books, souvenirs and even religious objects. The prices may be a little higher than elsewhere, but you also have the assurance that you're not being taken for a ride.

For those who want to get right into the swing of things, try going to the little boutiques all round the Shalom Tower, particularly for women's clothing. Each of these little shops is a factory where the clothing is designed and made up, often in fairly limited numbers. At least some of it will find its way to very elegant shops in Paris, London and New York. A more basic bargain hunting ground for clothing, offering items at rock-bottom prices, may be found at the **Polish Market** at Piccioto and Yehuda Halevi St., near the **Carmel Market.** The latter is itself loaded with stands, especially those selling children's items. A T-shirt or sweat shirt with a slogan in Hebrew may be just the solution to the problem of what to bring the kids back home.

Another bargain item, but one which you will never see in an open market, is furs. It's not exactly something you'd expect in a country with a climate like Israel's, but many of the furriers came to Israel from far colder climes. Allenby Rd. and Ben Yehuda St. have several fine furriers and tax exemptions for tourists make their wares a good buy.

For artwork, Gordon St. is almost solid with galleries for the first few blocks from the sea. The selection is eclectic, to say the least, with galleries showing very serious works alongside others exhibiting pure kitsch. Here your taste will have to be the final arbiter. The other center for art and fine crafts is of course Old Jaffa, where visitors are welcome to come and browse in many of the artists' studios. Among the chief attractions are small statuettes in silver or less precious metals, often on Biblical themes.

Return travelers to Israel often make straight for a shop called **Maskit,** with branches on Ben Yehuda St. and in Old Jaffa, which specializes in folk crafts. The selection of fabrics, ceramics, metal work, jewelry and fashions is enormous. And speaking of jewelry, one cannot forget the many fine jewelers throughout the city, in particular in the large hotels.

Another area in which Israel has become well known in the last few years is leather wear. Recently designers have become more daring, mixing leather with cloth fabrics to create striking new forms. Shops specializing in these items are found in Old Jaffa, on Dizengoff St. and in many of the large hotels.

If you're an antique hunter, your first stop will no doubt be the **Jaffa fleamarket,** where there is always the chance that a real treasure may be hidden in among the junk. You'll find copper and brassware and an occasional piece of good inlaid mother-of-pearl work. The fancier antique shops in Jaffa are located up the hill in Old Jaffa, but an area that many tourists seem to overlook when it comes to antiques is Ben Yehuda St. with its many shops solidly stocked with family heirlooms from Eastern and Central Europe. This is an especially lucrative area for the collector of Judaica.

 MUSIC, MOVIES AND THEATERS. Music. Concerts of the Israel Philharmonic are usually sold out, but often a good number of tickets are returned, which may be had at the box office of the **Mann Auditorium.** The concierge of your hotel can often help you here. For other concerts there are several ticket agencies throughout the city.

Movies. All films are shown in their original language with subtitles. There are usually two evening shows at 7 and 9 P.M. See the Friday edition of *The Jerusalem Post* for a complete listing of Tel Aviv movie theaters.

Theater. Both the **Habima** and **Cameri** theaters often have simultaneous translations for their plays, read by professional actors and broadcast to earphones rented for the performance.

 NIGHTLIFE. Tel Aviv is by far the country's liveliest city for nightlife. All along the beachside hotel strip, the top hotels have bars with music, discos and night clubs. For many Tel Avivians, a night out almost automatically means a visit to "Little Tel Aviv," the area in the far north of the city near the old port, in the vicinity of the intersections of Ben Yehuda and Dizengoff Sts. with Yirmiyahu and Yordei Hasira Sts. Dozens of restaurants, bars and cafes line the streets, catering to virtually every pocket book. The other area for a night out is Old Jaffa, where more night clubs with shows are to be found.

However, here too the streets are jammed with people nightly, some of whom may only splurge on a cup of coffee. Some clubs and discos to try:

The Bell, at the north end of Ben Yehuda St. Good for jazz.

The Cave, Kedumim Sq., Old Jaffa. One of the better spots for a geared-to-tourists show of Israeli folklore.

Le Club, corner of Ben Yehuda and Yirmiyahu St. A members' club which admits tourists. Run by Rafi Shauly, the ex-husband of Mandy Rice-Davies of Profumo scandal fame, it is the hangout for Tel Aviv's successful swinging set. A favorite place to go after you've done the rounds of all the night clubs.

Habima Cellar, underneath the Habima Theater. An informal atmosphere for the young in spirit.

Omar Khayam, Kedumim Sq., Old Jaffa. The grandfather of Israeli night-clubs is still going strong with Israeli-flavored international-style entertainment.

Penguin, 43 Yehuda Halevi St. A very young crowd, keeping very late hours. Israeli rock music.

Sky, Tel Aviv Marina. Young, but subdued patrons.

The Slick, London Mini-stores Complex, Ibn Gvirol St., in the basement. Young and old gather here nightly to join in singing old Israeli favorites. If you don't know the words you can just hum along.

 SPORTS. Swimming and water sports. Virtually all the large hotels have pools and there is a large municipal pool at Gordon St. on the beach. The center for surfing and windsurfing is near the Dolphinarium, opposite the Astoria Hotel. Equipment is available for rent. A water slide operates on the beach in Herzliya.

Boating. There are boats for rent on the Yarkon River at the northern end of Ibn Gvirol St. Sail boats are available at the Tel Aviv Marina near Atarim Square.

Tennis. Courts can be found at the Hilton, Country Club and Herzliya hotels. There are also several courts on Rokach Blvd., including those of Maccabi, Hapoel and the Israel Tennis Center. Tourists are welcome at the last mentioned and your hotel can book a court for you.

Squash. Herzlia Squash Club, Shivat Hakochavim Blvd., Herzlia (tel. 052–557877). Has eight courts, showers and refreshments.

Jogging. This is a popular sport on the beach, especially in the early morning hours.

Calisthenics. Several groups gather to work out on the beach at about 5 A.M. The most popular seems to be that held at the so-called Sheraton Beach (actually opposite the Palace Hotel, which was once the Tel Aviv Sheraton).

 RELIGIOUS SERVICES. Jewish. Many of the large hotels have their own religious services, especially on the major Jewish holidays. Unless otherwise indicated, the synagogues listed below are Orthodox. Friday evening services are held at sundown; times are listed weekly in the Friday edition of *The Jerusalem Post.* **Bilu Synagogue,** 122 Rothschild Blvd., Fri. evening service with children's choir; **The Great Synagogue,** 110 Allenby St., Sat. 8 A.M.; **Ihud**

Shivat Zion, 86 Ben Yehuda St., Sat. 8 A.M.; **Ohel Moed** (Sephardic), 5 Shadal St., Sat. 7.30 A.M.; **Sinai Congregation** (Conservative), 10 Kaplan St., Sat. 9 A.M.; **Kedem Synagogue** (Progressive), Sat. 9.30 A.M.

Christian. Immanuel (Lutheran and Anglican), 15 Beer Hoffman St., Jaffa, English service, Sun. 10 A.M.; **St. Anthony** (Roman Catholic), 51 Yefet St., Jaffa, English mass, Sun. 10 A.M.

UP THE COAST TO HAIFA AND
MOUNT CARMEL

Gateway to Galilee

Not only the scenery changes once you put some distance between yourself and Tel Aviv. Passing Netanya, and heading north along the coast for Haifa and Mount Carmel, or inland to the Jezre'el Valley and the Galilee, you are almost there: this is the gateway to Hatzafon—the North.

Indeed, the region covered in this chapter was, to some extent still is, a sort of transition zone between the center of the country and the North. The wide Sharon Plain that runs along the Mediterranean as far as Hadera and Caesarea has historically most often been linked to mountainous Samaria to the east, the heartland of the ancient Kingdom of Israel. But Mount Carmel, with its narrow coastal strip, is already a different area, it feels different, and its through-roads beckon north.

You have the choice of two main roads heading north: the fast, multi-lane highway, Route 2, which takes you from Tel Aviv to Haifa in a little over an hour; or the so-called old road a little inland, Route 4.

The Sharon Plain

As late as the 19th century, travelers still wrote about the forests of the Sharon Plain. Indeed, its very name—from the ancient Accadian, a-Sharnu—means forest. Its forests have entirely disappeared today, however. The armies that stomped along the international highways that crossed the region used its trees for camp-fires and siege-machines; nomads burned them down to create open areas for grazing their flocks; and local peasants cut down inessential, that is non-producing, trees to avoid an Ottoman tree tax. And in World War I, the Turks struck the final blow by cutting down what was left of them to make sleepers for their railway lines.

There are still many sand-dunes along this part of the coast. Elsewhere the soil is better, but only modern farming techniques and new crops have been able to bring the area to life. Independent small farmers grow oranges, flowers, grapes, and vegetables; only occasionally will you see the cotton fields, fish-ponds, or banana plantations of the communal kibbutzim.

Orde Wingate—The Friend

Eleven kms. (seven miles) north of Herzlia on the main highway, eight kms. (five miles) before you get to Netanya, is the Wingate Institute. Easily distinguishable by its inverted, cone-shaped water tower, this is a university-level college of physical education, sports instruction, and physiotherapy. Its excellent training facilities and hostelry makes it the preferred place not only for Israeli sports teams preparing for international competitions, but for European teams seeking warmer climes for winter training.

Orde Wingate was a British army officer stationed in Palestine in the '30s. A devout Christian, he was also a staunch supporter of the Jewish national cause. At the same Spring of Harod in the Jezre'el Valley where Gideon had mustered his commandos, Wingate secretly trained Jews in his highly-effective anti-terror tactics, creating the Special Night Squads. In order not to compromise his official position, the Jews never used his name in public. He was simply referred to as *Hyadid*, the Friend. Since Wingate's ideas did not reflect British policy in Palestine, his superiors eventually succeeded in having him transferred out, his passport endorsed, "not to enter Palestine." In World War II he rose to the rank of Major-general, and met his death in a plane crash in Burma in 1944.

Wingate persistently championed the cause of physical education for the young. When the Institute was established in 1955 it was clear to all that there was only one man after whom it could be named.

Netanya

There are many ways of writing its name, but however you spell it, Netanya remains a delightful resort city of manageable size with pleasant parks and no less than 11.5 kms. (seven miles) of fine bathing beaches. Founded in 1929 as a village of citrus farmers, it had grown to a town of 9,000 inhabitants by 1948, and passed the 100,000 mark just 30 years later. By that time it had long since outgrown its citrus groves—though it still serves as a major packing center—and had developed the industrial and tourism infrastructure that gives work to most of its 130,000 citizens today.

The city was named in honor of the Jewish philanthropist, Nathan Straus, owner of Macy's department store in New York at the turn of the century, some-time New York park commissioner and later health commissioner, and initiator of several emergency board-and-lodging programs for the destitute. It is estimated that he gave some two-thirds of his fortune to various projects in this country, mostly in the fields of health and child welfare.

Among Netanya's most important enterprises is diamond-cutting and polishing, an industry brought to Israel during and after World War II by Jewish diamond-cutters from Belgium and Holland. Today Israel is the world's largest exporter of cut and polished diamonds, and Netanya one of its major centers. Several factories in town offer an audio-visual presentation on the history of diamonds, a tour of the plant, and, of course, an opportunity to buy their jewelry.

Hadera—The Green One

The old road—Route 4—takes you through Hadera, the most important town in the vicinity. It has come a long way since its tortuous beginnings in 1890 when a 7,500-acre tract of mostly swampland was bought by Jewish settlement organizations. The unbounded enthusiasm of the young settlers blinded them to the real meaning of the Arabic word *Hadra*—the Green One. What seemed pleasant, grassy turf became a breeding ground for the malaria mosquitos after the rains. One after another the settlers succumbed to the dread fever. But they managed to hold out until the marshes had been drained and fortune began to smile on them at last. The pioneering history of Hadera has now been reconstructed in the old Turkish *khan,* the decrepit caravanserai that once served as the settlers' first makeshift home; look for it alongside the central synagogue.

Now a town of about 40,000 inhabitants, Hadera's central location has made it a major service center for the surrounding villages, and, as important, a processing center for their produce. In the right seasons you can see bales of ginned cotton or crates of oranges prepared for shipment. In the summer, the heady fragrance of orange groves assails your nostrils even before you reach the town.

By-passing Hadera, Wadi Ara (Route 65), the old Via Maris, heads northeast to Afula and the Galilee, and the Haifa-bound railway stops here. Outside town, on the old road to Haifa, a small building with a dome that looks more like a half-watermelon than anything else remembers Absalom Feinberg, a son of Hadera and a member of NILI, the Jewish World War I spy ring, of which more below.

On the coast, two 250-meter-high (812-ft.) smoke-stacks mark Israel's newest power-station, and its only coal-burning one, built despite

the protests of Hadera's residents. The coal is unloaded on special
wharfs at sea and brought to the storage areas on conveyer belts.

Caesarea—the Maritime Metropolis

A few kilometers north of Hadera on the coast is Caesarea, which
owes its fame to Herod the Great. If there was one trait that could be
said to be most characteristic of Herod, apart that is from his paranoia
and cruelty, it was his love of grandeur. Indeed his building projects
throughout Israel, as well as overseas, reflected his determination to
enhance his prestige and carve a niche for himself in the history of
civilization. Caesarea—named in honor of Herod's Roman patron
Augustus Caesar who, around 30 B.C., had confirmed Herod's position
as King of the Jews and expanded his territory—was just one among
this cruel despot's many ambitious projects.

Herod transformed an old and crumbling Phoenician town of the 3rd
century B.C.—Strato's Tower—into a magnificent coastal city, "larger
than Piraeus" according to Josephus Flavius. The city was built in a
mere 12 years, complete with fine man-made port, theater, amphitheater, hippodrome, water system, palaces, and temples. Only Jerusalem
was more splendid.

When Herod died in 4 B.C., his kingdom was divided among his
surviving sons. Archelaus, the oldest, got Judea and Samaria, including
Jerusalem. But he was the wrong man for the job, and 10 years later
the Romans exiled him to Gaul. In his place came the first in a long
series of Roman governors, the Procurators. With Jerusalem an all-
Jewish city, they set up their seat of administration in the mixed but
predominantly Hellenistic city of Caesarea. It was here that Simon
Peter converted the Roman centurion Cornelius, the first gentile to
profess faith in Jesus as the Christ, the Annointed One. During his
two-year imprisonment here, Paul defended himself before the Roman
governor Festus, and Agrippa II. The sparks that set off the huge
conflagration of the Great Revolt of A.D. 66 were struck in Caesarea,
when Hellenists and Jews clashed over a provocative pagan ceremony
near the synagogue entrance on the Jewish Sabbath, and the Roman
authorities spurned Jewish appeals for justice. After Jerusalem was
destroyed in A.D. 70, Titus celebrated his triumph in Caesarea, the
immolation of 2,500 Jews in the arena being one of the main events.
It was again in this seat of Roman authority that Rabbi Akiva, the
spiritual mentor of the Bar Kochba Revolt in the 2nd century A.D., was
tortured to death. Jerusalem was eclipsed, and Caesarea's preeminence
was assured, a status it retained until Constantine Christianized the
Empire in A.D. 325.

The Roman Theater

What city in the Roman period with cosmopolitan pretensions
would not have had a theater? Not only did Herod make sure that
Caesarea was thus equipped, but his theaters here and elsewhere in
Israel were the first of their kind in the ancient Near/Middle East.
Although smaller than the better-preserved Roman theater of Bet She-

'an (see the *Jezre'el Valley and Lower Galilee* chapter), Caesarea's
theater has become by far the most famous in the country. Its reputation has been enhanced in recent years by performances—ranging from
rock to opera—given in the spring and summer.

The Roman Theater is the first part of Caesarea you reach coming
off the fast highway, Route 2. A mounted plaque greets you in the open
area just inside the gate. This is a replica of an inscription found here
during the excavations of 1959–63 (the original is in the Israel Museum
in Jerusalem). Although partly destroyed, you can clearly read "TIBE-
RIVM" (a reference to the Emperor Tiberius), and, on the second line
" . . . TIVS PILATUS"—Pontius Pilate, governor of Judea at the time
of Jesus. What makes this find extraordinary is that although Pontius
Pilate is well-documented in contemporary sources (including the New
Testament) as one of the most vicious Roman governors ever to set foot
in Israel, this is the only archeological evidence of him.

As you enter the theater through one of the *vomitoria*—an unfortunate term that simply means a vaulted passageway—you find yourself
on the aisle half-way up the *cavea*, the auditorium. Most of the seats
are modern, but a few are original, as are the foundations of the
structure. Today the theater can seat upwards of 2,500 people, but
probably had twice that capacity in ancient times when the uppermost
part of the *cavea* was intact. A recessed box was reserved for the guest
of honor—the king or governor—and the semi-circular orchestra in
front of the stage for the V.I.P. seating (on chairs, as today). Much later
the orchestra was converted to a pool for water performances. The
scaena, the wall at the back of the stage, has three doorways. Just as
there are conventions in opera today (heroes are generally tenors,
villains basses), so in the Roman world the color of an actor's toga
underlined the character he played, as did the doorway through which
he made his entrance: main characters through the central entrance,
secondary ones by the side. The stage itself is refurbished. In later
centuries a semi-circular, arena-like area was added behind the stage,
possibly for blood-sports.

You have a superb view of the Mediterranean as you loll in your seat
waiting for the play to begin. The view and cool sea breezes were no
doubt major considerations in building the theater here. The ancient
granite columns lying around the site in heaps were quarried in Aswan
(Upper Egypt) and sent down the Nile for Herod's original project
2,000 years ago. In the 18th century, the best were filched by the Turks
to build a *khan*, or inn, in Acre (see the *Acre and Western Galilee*
chapter). The large outer wall between the theater and the sea is Byzantine, part of the abortive attempt to convert the theater into a fortress
against the Arab invasion of A.D. 638.

The Crusader Town and the Holy Grail

Ancient Caesarea's most important facility—indeed its *raison d'être*
—was its port. When the city was revived by the Crusaders in the 12th
century, they centered their fortified town on the all-important harbor.
Medieval Caesarea covered an area of just 35 acres, about one-sixth the
size of the original Roman city.

The Crusader walls are visible from the theater and only a short distance away. Through the upper entrance, you cross the moat and pass through the angled gate-house. The fortifications are typically medieval—the sloping "glacis" against the outer wall, the postern gate, the vertical embrasures (shooting niches). The threshold of the gate is made of Roman or Byzantine marble reworked by the Crusaders. You can clearly see the hinge-sockets and the place where a cross-beam secured the doors. Between two parallel arches, an iron portcullis, a heavy latticed gate, could be dropped as an extra defense. The outer-left and inner-right angles of the gate-house are worn smooth, no doubt by the armored hips of mounted knights.

Inside the walls are many good examples of Crusader architecture, particularly the finely-carved apses of the large, unfinished church. The Crusaders began their church on a prominent rise, not realizing that below it were the ancient warehouses of King Herod's port. As the church grew and became heavier, it collapsed into the warehouses, and was never rebuilt.

Down the main street are the remains of Herod's 2,000-year-old temple, dedicated to Augustus Caesar. Herod, himself from an Idumean family that had converted to Judaism, was in no way a devout man. He built the Temple of God in Jerusalem as a sop to his Jewish subjects, and more to his own glory than to the glory of God. Like the man who buys life insurance in several different companies in case one should fold, Herod simultaneously built a temple in Caesarea dedicated to his patron Augustus, and another in Sebastia dedicated to Jupiter.

The port is today a pleasant little beach complete with changing facilities, while the buildings of the 19th-century Muslim village house restaurants and gift shops.

Herod's original quays and breakwaters were traced by underwater archeologists in 1960, and more thoroughly by a recent joint Israeli/American expedition. Their barnacled finds tell of the commercial importance of this great Mediterranean port.

Fallen chunks of Crusader masonry lie upended in the water, the Roman columns which they reused protruding for all the world like a battery of cannon. When the Crusaders captured Caesarea in 1101, they immediately embarked on an orgy of slaughter and pillage. Carried away as booty by the Genoese, whose fleet assisted the conquest, was a large goblet declared to be the Holy Grail, the very vessel used by Jesus at the Last Supper. Visitors to Genoa can still see this relic today.

Most of the Crusader fortifications were rebuilt on a grand scale by King Louis IX of France—St. Louis—who after his release from Egyptian captivity in 1251, spent a year at Caesarea, helping the "sacred" task of rebuilding, literally with his own hands. When the town fell to the Mamluk Baybars in 1265, the Sultan assisted in the dismantling of town defenses with *his* own hands. "What a king has built," he is quoted as saying, "a king will destroy." This treatment was meted out to most Crusader fortresses along the coast by the Mamluks who feared a renewed Crusade might gain a foothold there.

Losing Your Head

Just over the road from the upper entrance to the Crusader city, among a grove of feathery tamarisk trees, is a Byzantine street. When Constantine accepted Christianity for the Roman Empire (around A.D. 325) and moved his capital from Rome to Byzantium, the events were accompanied by a wave of zealous building in Israel. By virtue of its central role in the Christian story, Jerusalem immediately regained its one-time preeminence. Caesarea continued to be important, however, and this marble-paved street was adorned with two old *heathen* imperial statues—both of them now headless.

No one knows which emperors are represented by these massive white marble and red porphyry statues (of the 2nd and 3rd centuries A.D. respectively), but there are convincing explanations as to how they came to lose their heads. They may have fallen victim to Iconoclasts—zealous Jews, early Muslims, or Christian sects in the Byzantine or Early Arab periods offended by the graven images the Bible prohibits and who had no compunction in decapitating statues and gouging mosaics. Alternatively, they may have been disposed of after a coup, the new ruler substituting his own likeness for the destroyed heads. Why waste an expensive statue, especially if it was muscular, well-proportioned, and larger than life?

A short distance inland along the road, there is a stone gate on the right with a cross preserved on it. Behind it is a large, oval enclosure, now a banana field, with embankments around it. Originally this was a hippodrome, a chariot-race stadium seating 20,000 spectators, and a venue for athletic competitions like Herod's five-yearly Caesar's Games.

The next turn-off to the right takes you to the only golf course in Israel, a picturesque and highly-rated 18 holes. Visitors are welcomed. Next door is the deluxe Dan Caesarea hotel. Turn left at the same intersection and drive through modern Caesarea, an affluent suburban community, to the famous aqueduct.

Lacking any natural water-source, Herod's town-planners built this marvelous aqueduct to bring water to Caesarea from springs at the foot of Mount Carmel 13 kms. (eight miles) away. Later, Roman legions doubled its capacity by duplicating the chain of arches and the water-channel they supported. A long and impressive section of the aqueduct has survived. If you walk a good way along the aqueduct on its sea side, you can find marble plaques in several places dedicated to the auxiliaries (support troops) of the different legions that worked here. The third one is blank. It is thought to have once been dedicated to the 22nd legion that was annihilated by Bar Kochba's rebel forces in the 2nd century A.D., and forever disgraced. The plaque would then have been defaced.

The Rothschild Connection

Baron Edmond de Rothschild, head of the French branch of this illustrious and wealthy family, involved himself directly and intimately with the lives of his fellow-Jews in 19th-century Palestine, laying the foundation for many modern villages and towns along the coastal plain and in parts of the Upper Galilee. This paternalistic system was not without its problems, however: in the Baron's absence, his administrators often became petty tyrants ruling his "colonies" as they saw fit, sometimes reducing the already economically dependent settlers virtually to the level of serfdom.

But no one doubted the sincerity of the Baron himself. The tomb of *Hanadiv Hayadu'a,* the Well-known Benefactor, as Rothschild was widely known, is set amid strikingly lovely grounds at Ramat Hanadiv on the Carmel range between two of the villages he helped found, Binyamina (from his Hebrew name, Benjamin), and Zichron Ya'akov (from the Hebrew for James, the Baron's father).

Like other pioneering settlements of the late-19th century, Zichron Ya'akov saw its full share of hardship and suffering in its early days. In this case the difficulties were great even before the settlers reached their rocky new home. They were not allowed to land at Haifa, and only after an extended odyssey, touching the ports of Jaffa, Port Said, and Haifa again, did the group reorganize and set out for their village site. Roads in the area were non-existent, and the settlers had to bring building timber on their shoulders from Haifa some 30 kms. (19 miles) away. With the help of the Rothschilds, the settlement was eventually able to get on its feet. By 1886, the famous Carmel winery began operating, and viniculture has remained one of the village's most important mainstays.

The NILI

Palestine suffered greatly under Turkish rule at the beginning of the century. After the outbreak of World War I, the country fared even worse, the Turks ravaging Palestine to support their war effort. The country was stripped of its produce, men were forcibly conscripted, whole communities were uprooted and exiled. The "official" reaction in the Jewish community was to keep a low profile and avoid confrontation with the rapacious Turks; but to a group of young Jews from Zichron Ya'akov and Hadera this was not enough. It was clear to them that in addition to fears for the future raised by the Turkish massacre of the Armenians, any hope of fulfilment of Jewish national aspirations lay not with the corrupt and backward Ottoman Empire, but with a take-over of Palestine by the British, then in Egypt. Thus was the NILI spy ring formed.

The group took its name from an acronym of the Hebrew Biblical phrase "The Eternal One of Israel will not prove false" (I Samuel 15). Its leaders included the scientist Aaron Aaronson, his sister Sarah, and his assistant at the Atlit Experimental Station, Absalom Feinberg. The group was able to gather a great deal of valuable intelligence material through Aaron's mobility as head of the official locust-control unit, and the vivacious Sarah's popularity at parties for high-ranking Turks. Nevertheless the British were slow to take advantage of NILI, and it was only in 1917 that regular contact was established with British ships anchored off-shore.

The end of the tale is hardly less dramatic than the rest of it. Absalom Feinberg set off to cross the Sinai desert to re-establish contact with the British. He was killed in an ambush near Rafah in the Gaza Strip and no trace of him was found. In 1967, Israelis entering the Gaza Strip were shown a palm tree under which, locals said, "a Jew had been buried." Absalom's remains were recovered from the hasty grave into which he'd been laid 50 years earlier, the palm tree itself growing from the dates he had in his pockets. Sarah Aaronson was captured by the Turks in her home when they uncovered the spy ring. She was tortured for four days until, given permission to wash up alone, she took a revolver from a hidden cupboard and shot herself. Other leaders of the organization were caught by the Turks and executed. Aaron Aaronson died in an air crash over the English Channel in 1919. Rebecca Aaronson lived to a ripe old age, never married, and died just a few years ago. A museum near the Aaronson home in Zichron Ya'akov recounts the episode of the NILI.

Dor and the Carmel Caves

Two kms. (one-and-a-half miles) north of the intersection between Route 2 and Route 70, the latter slicing east through the Carmel Hills to the Jezre'el Valley, a turn-off to the left takes you to Kibbutz Nachsholim. This is old Tantura, ancient Dor, with a fine beach and holiday cottages. On a spit of land is the tel of ancient Dor, a city founded in the Late Canaanite period, about 35 centuries ago. Its small bay made it the best harbor between Jaffa and Acre, and thus a target for many imperial ambitions from the ancient Egyptians and the "Sea Peoples" through Solomon and on down. It was a flourishing trade center under the Persians and the Greeks, and by the 3rd century B.C. was a Phoenician colony, along with Strato's Tower (Caesarea) further south. Dor was famous for producing a dye known as the purple of Tyre, derived by processing an extract from a locally abundant shellfish, murex. Recent excavations and the ancient quarried port make the tel an interesting place for the nimble to scramble about.

Back on the old road—Route 4—and heading north, you pass the Carmel Caves on your right. The caves were discovered in the '30s when mounds of sand at their mouths were being removed for the building of Haifa port. Archeological excavation brought to light abundant and important evidence of prehistoric cultures. Eleven kms. (seven miles) beyond the Nachsholim intersection you turn to the right, to Ein Hod.

Ein Hod—Artists' Village

In 1950 the Dadaist painter Marcel Janco was sent by the Israeli Government to explore the mountains and make recommendations for the creation of a National Park. He happened on an abandoned Arab village, now Ein Hod. Said Janco: "The beauty of the place was staggering. I had been told this village was to be demolished. But as I gazed at the panorama of mountains and sea, and studied the unusual stone buildings, the feeling grew—this should not be harmed." Thus the idea of creating an artists' village here was born. There were no roads, no water, and no electricity, and weeds and scorpions ruled the village, but 20 others joined Janco and set to work to make the neglected place habitable again.

Today over 60 families live in Ein Hod—painters, sculptors, and craftsmen in a semi-cooperative society that runs an art school and workshops, a showcase-gallery of local work, and a beautiful, brand-new gallery dedicated to Ein Hod's founding father, Marcel Janco. An open-air amphitheater attracts top-class musicians and entertainers from afar, while a popular-priced restaurant lets you soak in the ambience from its shaded patio.

Looking from Ein Hod to the sea, a soaring, ruined wall is clearly visible on the shore. This is but one surviving part of the mighty Chastiau Pelerin, the Pilgrim's Castle, built by the Crusader Knights Templar with the help of European pilgrims in 1218. It successfully resisted two Muslim sieges—in 1220 and 1265—and was finally abandoned only in 1291 when every other Crusader town and fortress in the Holy Land had already fallen to the Mamluks. The Crusader ruins are presently closed to the public.

You are 16 kms. (10 miles) from Haifa. If you have the extra time and fancy a beautiful approach to the city, take the Bet Oren turnoff (two kms./one-and-a-half miles beyond Ein Hod on Route 4), a winding climb through absorbing mountain scenery that comes out on the top of Mount Carmel.

HAIFA

Etched into the mountainside, spreading up and across the wooded slopes of Mount Carmel, and finally spilling down to the fine sandy Mediterranean beaches, Haifa's combination of mountain and sea is unrivaled in Israel. It is best appreciated from the top of the Carmel itself with the broad bay sweeping north to Acre, seen in clear detail on the opposite side. On a good day the white chalk cliffs of Rosh Hanikra even further north beckon to you.

The city is built on three levels, reflecting to some extent its development. The Downtown area includes the Old City, the Port, and the main trade district. Midtown, and especially Hadar Hacarmel—Splendor of the Carmel, simply known as Hadar—is a veteran residential area, and the busiest shopping area. The Uptown area, the summit of Mount Carmel itself, contains the city's youngest and poshest neighborhoods.

As is to be expected when you live in a beautiful city, Haifa's citizens are matter-of-factly chauvinistic about their home-town . . . and not without justification. In addition to its natural situation, Haifa is probably the country's greenest and cleanest city. Some of the natural greenery of the Mount Carmel ranges has been preserved within the city itself, and this has been enhanced by the parks and gardens planted by its diligent citizens.

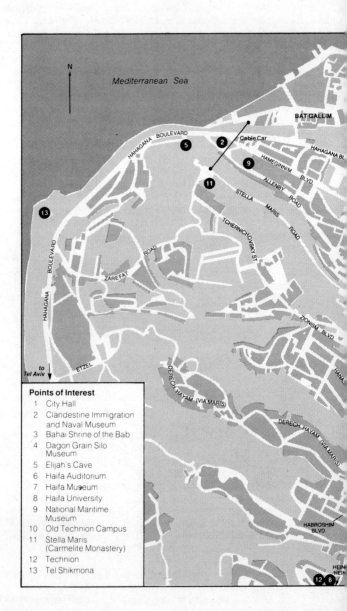

Points of Interest

1 City Hall
2 Clandestine Immigration
   and Naval Museum
3 Bahai Shrine of the Bab
4 Dagon Grain Silo
   Museum
5 Elijah's Cave
6 Haifa Auditorium
7 Haifa Museum
8 Haifa University
9 National Maritime
   Museum
10 Old Technion Campus
11 Stella Maris
   (Carmelite Monastery)
12 Technion
13 Tel Shikmona

HAIFA

0 miles 1

0 kilometers 1

(NOT ALL STREETS SHOWN)

Mediterranean Sea

HELHAYAM

ion

JAFFA ROAD

TEL AVIV

HAMEGINNIM BLVD

JAFFA RD

④ PLUMER SQ

ALLENBY

BEN-GURION BLVD

HA'AZMA'UT

HABANKIM ST

ROAD

GERMAN COLONY

HAGEFEN ST

PARIS SQUARE

HAPALYAM BLVD

OLD CITY

HERZLIA ST

SHABBETAI LEVI ST

⑦

HANEVI'IM ST

HA'NEVI'IM ST

Memorial Park

③

ahai Gardens

HERZLIA

ACHAD HA'AM ST

① WADI SALIB

BAERWALD ST

⑩

HERZL

HANASSI BLVD

ELIYAHU

GOLOMB

BALFOUR ST

MORDAU ST

HADAR HACARMEL

ARLOSOROFF

HATIVAT GOLANI ROAD

Gan Ha'em

HERZL ST

YEFE NOF

ARLOSOROFF

⑥

HANYIM ST

MEGIDDO ST

WEDGEWOOD

KISCH

HA'ASIF

LEON BLUM

RUPPIN

to Acre;
Nazareth

The Carmel Panorama

From the several vantage points along Panorama Road (right below the Dan Carmel Hotel), you can discern something of the layout of the city, and even the history of its development. Many old buildings, primarily from the Turkish period, show the original site of the Old City, at the foot of the hill somewhat to the right of the port. In 1868, a Christian German society called the Templars (not to be confused with the medieval order of that name), acquired land outside the town and built a "colony," with wide, well-laid-out streets, gardens, and attractive, red-roofed houses. With characteristic diligence and technical sophistication, these settlers introduced modern enterprises into Haifa. As long as German influence in the Ottoman Empire persisted, they prospered, and eventually expanded onto the top of Mount Carmel as well. Still called the German Colony today, this attractive area lines Sederot Ben Gurion (Ben-Gurion Boulevard) from the port to the foot of the mountain. The Bahai Gardens crowned by the Shrine of the Bab are directly in line with the top of the boulevard.

The year 1905 was a turning-point in the city's development. A new railway line was being built from Constantinople via Damascus and down to the Muslim holy cities of Mecca and Medina (in modern Saudi Arabia). A spur of this so-called Hijaz Railway was also built between Damascus and Haifa. Both the actual construction of the line and the benefits it brought when completed provided a tremendous boost to Haifa. Patterned on the successful Tel Aviv experiment, new Jewish neighborhoods began developing, like Herzlia in the Midtown area, established in 1912.

There was a hiatus in development, however, caused by the near-starvation conditions prevailing in Haifa during World War I. But following the British conquest of 1918, development was renewed with vigor. Midtown Hadar Hacarmel was founded in 1920, Ahuza on the summit in 1921, Neve Sha'anan on the southeastern slopes below the Technion in 1922, and Bat Gallim on the sea west of today's port in 1923. These were boom years: the railway line from Kantara in Egypt to Haifa was completed; major industries were built; the modern, deep-water port was opened in 1931; and the oil refinery (together with a pipeline from Iraq) in 1939.

Haifa Works

Jerusalem studies, Tel Aviv dances, Haifa works! This epigram sounds better in Hebrew, the language it was written in and in which it rhymes. It also has some truth to it. Because of its holiness, Jerusalem has always attracted venerable spiritual institutions and centers of learning. Tel Aviv is certainly Israel's most vibrant cosmopolitan center. Haifa, on the other hand, with its port and heavy industrial area, has long been identified as a blue-collar city. Although it now shares the maritime traffic with the newer deep-water port at Ashdod in the south, Haifa has been the country's major gateway for trade and cruise-ships for over half a century. Similarly, Israel's largest concentration of heavy industries lies to the east of the city on the wide Zebulun Plain, named after the ancient Israelite tribe that was allocated this area but never apparently possessed it. Included here is one of the country's five power stations and Israel's oil refinery. Just beyond the industrial area is a series of small towns known as Hakrayot, the Townships.

A tribute to Haifa's reputation as a workers' city is the fact that it was here that the Histadrut—Israel's huge and powerful General Labor Federation—was founded in 1920. And Haifa is the only Jewish city in Israel which, through workers' pressure, has a bus-service on the Sabbath.

Haifa has come of age, however, and its image is not so exclusively industrial as it once was. This city of almost 300,000 inhabitants has two fine universities: the world-famous Technion, of which more below, and Haifa University. Good music, theater, night spots, and restaurants are plentiful.

A Backtrack into Antiquity

As you enter Haifa from the south, exactly at the point where the mountain descends steeply to within a stone's throw of the sea and next to the modern Oceanographic Research Institute, there is a tiny tel. The little mound, the result of ancient towns built in successive periods on the same site, was Shikmona. It owes its location not to any advantage of the coast—on the contrary, there is no safe anchorage here—but to the strategic nature of the narrow pass. This highway running up the coast continued from Shikmona to Acre, Achziv, and on to the Phoenician centers of Tyre and Sidon.

But Haifa itself is not found in Biblical sources. Vespasian, in the 1st century A.D., established a way-station here between Caesarea and Acre. In the following century, Hadrian linked it by roads to the Galilee. The disciple and aide of the great Rabbi Yehuda Hanassi around the year A.D. 200, was one Yose of Haifa. At the same period, the city became famous for its imperial purple dyes which were extracted, as elsewhere on the coast, from a shellfish found here. Jewish settlement was to be found, too, at the mouth of the Kishon River, and on the top of Mount Carmel itself.

The Byzantine period ushered in a time of persecution of the Jewish community by the Christian rulers, and a massacre in A.D. 628 followed the expulsion of the Persian invaders from the area. Under the Arabs in the later 7th and 8th centuries, the lot of Haifa's community improved significantly, and a port and shipyards aided its economic situation. The Crusaders captured Haifa in 1099, and, as was their wont, butchered the Jewish population for its refusal to convert. The Carmelite Order was established in Haifa in 1156 around the belief that here Elijah the Prophet hid from King Ahab. Like much of the Crusader Kingdom, Haifa was lost and regained by the Crusaders, only to be destroyed by the Mamluk sultan Baybars in 1265, and abandoned completely with the final Crusader evacuation of 1291.

For several centuries Haifa lay neglected until its brief revival as a small Ottoman port in the 16th century. For a while it served as a base for Maltese pirates, becoming known as Little Malta. Its true revival began with the ascendency of Daher el-Omar, the Bedouin sheikh who wrested independence from the Turks and controlled much of the Galilee in the mid-18th century. Its port now began to compete with that of Acre across the bay, for while its harbor was not as good as Acre's, Mount Carmel offered a natural barrier against the strong southwesterly winds, and therefore a comfortable anchorage.

When Napoleon's Eastern Campaign failed at the gates of Acre in 1799, his possession of Haifa was critical to his safe retreat. He left his wounded soldiers at the hospital of the Carmelites at Stella Maris on the Carmel. The local Muslims bided their time in apparent quiescence, but as soon as Napoleon was out of sight, they fell on the French soldiers and butchered them.

Against All Odds

The development of Haifa in the '20s and '30s under British rule has already been discussed. From 1939, however, Haifa was witness to a series of tragic events. In May of that year, with a European war looming again, the British Government published a White Paper, or policy statement, restricting Jewish immigration to Palestine and prohibiting Jews from buying land there. It was a policy designed to appease Arab circles and keep the oil-rich Arab countries in the Allied camp. The Jewish community was appalled: not only did the White Paper renege absolutely on the terms of the Mandate for Palestine granted to Great Britain by the League of Nations, it sounded the death knell for masses of Jews trapped in Hitler's Europe. The clandestine Jewish para-military organizations translated their opposition into physical defiance. The effort to bring in refugee-packed ships was stepped up.

The little boats and over-crowded tramp-steamers that managed to elude the vigilant British warships and spotter planes stopped at secret beaches along the coast at night to put ashore their human cargoes. But those ships that were captured by the British were towed into Haifa, where over the following years a series of alternately ecstatic scenes— from those permitted to land—and pathetic scenes—of those turned back—were played out. The heart-rending tragedy of those deported at the very moment when their cherished goal of "coming home" was within reach, deeply affected the people of Haifa. On occasion the tragic victims actually set foot on the hallowed ground before they were returned to Europe, shipped to Mauritius prisons, or, after the War, to Cyprus.

The most celebrated incident was that of the *Exodus* in 1947, whose 4,530 passengers were forcibly transferred back to Germany itself. But there were other equally tragic incidents. In 1940, for example, the *Patria,* packed with 1,900 refugees bound for Mauritius, blew up in Haifa Harbor in mysterious circumstances with the loss of over 250 lives. A more notorious incident was the *Struma* affair. In December 1941, this leaky, 180-ton tub carried 769 Jewish refugees from the Black Sea coast of Romania but was forced to anchor in Istanbul for repairs. Unable to land, unable to continue, unwilling to return, the boat wallowed in Istanbul harbor for two months, finally sinking a few miles offshore. There was one survivor. One of the successful blockade-runners was an old American tank-landing craft renamed *Af-al-pi-chen* ("Nevertheless"), which has been lifted out of the water and serves as the centerpiece of the moving Clandestine Immigration and Maritime Museum, its interior reconstructed to tell the story of its sad but heroic last days at sea.

Boats from the Beginning

If you still have your sea legs, pull off to one side, hoist yourself up a few decks, and visit the National Maritime Museum on Allenby Road right next door. This unusual museum was conceived and pushed to completion against all sorts of obstacles by Aryeh Ben-Eli, genial ex-Israel Naval officer. The background story is interesting. Ben-Eli's hobby was ship models, and he began by exhibiting his personal collection under the sponsorship of the municipality. The displays now trace the development of navigation in the Middle East from prehistoric times, and include tiny carved figures manning the decks of miniature vessels. Some of the items are originals; others are copies of models from various periods of history. The models of Egyptian funeral barges from 4,000 years ago are particularly interesting.

Elijah and the Star of the Sea

Across Allenby Road from the National Maritime Museum, a flight of steps in the cliff-face takes you up to Elijah's Cave. An early Byzantine tradition of about the 4th century A.D. identified it as the cave in which Elijah found refuge from the wrath of King Ahab. Jews and Muslims embraced the tradition as well. Recent cleaning of the cave has revealed inscriptions made by pilgrims of all faiths, although symbols like the seven-branched *Menorah* indicate that Jewish veneration of the site predominated at an early stage, as it does today.

At the top of the hill, at the very extremity of the Carmel cape, stands the Carmelite monastery of Stella Maris, the Star of the Sea. Apart from the interesting features of the Carmelite church (rebuilt in 1831) and the Fathers' archeological exhibit, the cave over which the church is built is also associated with the Prophet Elijah, and, indeed, with his disciple and heir Elisha as well.

Elijah may have ascended to heaven in a fiery chariot, but we must be content with a short ride in a brand-new cable-car. It runs from Stella Maris Gallim, with its beaches, promenade and a variety of restaurants.

Bahai and the Oneness of Mankind

The most spectacular building in Haifa is without question the Bahai Shrine of the Bab. It is situated half-way up Mount Carmel, at the head of a long avenue of trees surrounded by the manicured Persian Gardens. The Bab—literally, the Gate—was the "Forerunner" in the Bahai faith. Like John the Baptist in Christianity, the Bab was considered a prophet in his own right, but foretold the imminent coming of one greater than himself. He was martyred for his teachings in his native Persia in 1850, and his remains reburied here in 1909. In 1953 the present magnificent marble-and-gold edifice was dedicated.

In 1863, one Mirza Husayn Ali, exiled from Persia for his espousing of the Bab's teachings, declared himself to be the Baha'ullah—the Glory of God—and the long-awaited Promised One of all religions. His teachings, pronouncements, and prescriptions form the basis of Bahai belief and practice. Five years later, Baha'ullah was exiled by the Turks to Acre, across the bay from Haifa. Here he spent his last 24 years, half of them as a prisoner in the city, half in Bahji, the fine house and gardens just north of Acre, where he died and was buried. His tomb is Bahai's holiest shrine.

"Ye are the fruits of one tree and the leaves of one branch," declared Baha'ullah, asserting the essential unity of mankind. Bahais believe that throughout history great prophets have appeared to reveal divine truths in a manner appropriate to the time. Among these have been Moses, Zoroaster, Buddha, Jesus, Mohammed, and, most recently, Baha'ullah. Each phase, they teach, represents a progression in the march towards spiritual perfection. In a world in which major religions have often clashed in the absolute certainty that each alone holds the key to ultimate truth, the Bahai faith asserts that the purpose of religion "is to safeguard the interests and promote the unity of the human race, and to foster the spirit of love and fellowship amongst men." A utopian goal, perhaps, in an era where the future sometimes appears darkened by a mushroom-shaped cloud; but these high ideals have nevertheless won the hearts of several million adherents world-wide.

Haifa is the world center for the Bahais. Above the Shrine of the Bab and across Zionism Avenue (of which more in a moment) is the green-roofed Archives building; still further up the slope is the newest edifice —a large, white-domed, neo-classical building. This is the seat of the Universal House of Justice, the supreme administrative body of the Faith. These latter two buildings are closed to the general public. Visitors to the Shrine will find a handful of superb photographic possibilities, including an unimpeded view down an avenue of trees which directly lines up with Ben-Gurion Boulevard, and the red-roofed, 19th-century houses of the German Templars. While the Shrine itself is only open in the mornings, the Gardens, with their view of the Shrine's exterior, are accessible all day. You are asked to leave both cameras and shoes outside the Shrine. The Bahai are at pains to point out that all artefacts and sculptures both within the Shrine and in the Gardens— urns, peacocks, etc.—are ornamental and have no symbolic significance.

What's in a Name

The main road that climbs past the Bahai Shrine to the top of Mount Carmel is known today as Sederot Hatziyonut, Zionism Boulevard. It follows the route laid down by the Templars in the 19th century to connect their old colony at the foot of the mountain with a new one at its summit. How its name came about has a history to it.

Following the historic U.N. vote on November 29, 1947 to partition Palestine into two states, one Jewish, the other Arab, Jews throughout Israel spontaneously named streets and squares in honor of that august international body or after the date of the partition vote. That the plan was unworkable, and was in any case rejected out of hand by the Arabs, who immediately declared war on the fledgling Jewish state, was of no consequence.

Then for almost three decades, citizens of Haifa drove down Sederot Ha'oum, U.N. Boulevard, past the splendid Bahai Shrine, on their way from their homes on the Carmel to their places of work in Hadar or Downtown. On November 10, 1975, the same U.N. General Assembly, now vastly expanded and its rival political groupings more clearly defined, took another decision. Led by the Arabs, the Communist bloc and many Third World nations (and opposed almost without exception by the Western democracies), the U.N. in its dubious collective wisdom, passed a motion equating Zionism with racism. Again quite spontaneously the same Jewish towns that had hailed the U.N. in 1947 now renamed their streets. In Haifa, U.N. Boulevard became Zionism Boulevard!

Some Haifa Cityscapes

Unless you're embarking on a ship, taking a train to Tel Aviv or Jerusalem (a slow but lovely trip), visiting the Grain Museum at Bet Dagon (the great, grey grain elevator in the Port), or going to an airline office, there is no good reason to invest too much time in the Downtown area. To the west (towards Tel Aviv), the Bat Gallim neighborhood near the Central Bus Station contains the famous Rambam Hospital and Technion's towering new Medical School and Research Center, but is best known for its fine beaches and fish restaurants. Eastwards, on your way to Acre or Nazareth, you pass through the unwalled Old City; run-down but interesting if you have an eye for architecture.

Take the bus up to Hadar, Haifa's Midtown, and the difference in atmosphere is palpable. A veteran residential area, this is also where Haifa shops. The axis of Herzlia–Hanevi'im–Herzl streets is lined with stores and eateries, and thronged with people day and night. The best felafel, *shwarma,* or *bourekas* are to be found here. In addition, many of the city's movie theaters are here, as are the City Hall, the Haifa Museum, and the palatial old Technion Campus on the corner of Balfour and Hanevi'im streets. It was built before World War I and was at the time the largest building in the northern part of the country. With its greenery and fine views of Gan Hazikaron (Memorial Park) opposite, City Hall is an excellent place for you to take your lunch of felafel and orange juice. Hanevi'im itself has been turned into a *midrachov*—a pedestrian mall—imitating the urban fashion in other cities.

Find one of the frequent buses again, and you're on your way ever upwards, to Merkaz Hacarmel, the center of the lovely green residential district on the top of Mount Carmel. The views from up here are breathtaking. We have already mentioned Panorama Road, but the Dan Carmel and Nof Hotels offer you that same sight from your private balcony. Haifa is a city of museums, and several of them are up on the Carmel, as the locals call the area. The Haifa Auditorium periodically hosts the Israel Philharmonic Orchestra and other major cultural attractions, and the sidewalk cafes lend a Continental touch to the atmosphere.

Following the main street in a more-or-less southerly direction takes you along the spine of Mount Carmel, through some of Haifa's most pleasant quarters, offering sweeping views over the Mediterranean on both sides. At Kikar Samuel, Samuel Square, the multi-laned Derech Pica, Pica Road, goes off to the left taking you to the Technion, Haifa's venerable technological university. Watch for the turn-offs to the right!

The Technion was founded in 1912, but did not open for 12 years, partly because of the deprivations of World War 1, partly because of a heated internal debate as to the language of instruction: the native German of many of the scientists, or the language spoken by Elijah 29 centuries earlier and recently revived. The Hebrew-speakers prevailed. A new video-equipped visitors' center showcases the impressive scope and sophistication of the Institute's faculties and departments.

Waiting for Rommel

In 1942, a plan was prepared to turn Mount Carmel into a latter-day Masada, a mountain fortress into which the Jews of Palestine would be crammed, and defend to the death if the German Army broke through the British lines in North Africa's Western Desert. The contingency was not at all far-fetched. By June of that year, Tobruk had fallen to Rommel's Afrika Korps, and the Allies were on the defensive. A British evacuation of Egypt and Palestine seemed imminent.

With the outbreak of World War II, the Yishuv, the Palestinian Jewish community, had responded to the Allied cause with great enthusiasm and alacrity. Resistance to the British, fanned by the discriminatory 1939 White Paper was, for the moment, forgotten. Following calls by the Jewish leadership in Palestine for volunteers to join the British armed forces, 136,000 enrolled in the first five days. By 1943, 63 per cent of the Jewish labor force in Palestine was occupied in direct defence-related work. While Haj Amin Husseini, the Grand Mufti of Jerusalem and the most influential Arab leader in Palestine, was being received by Mussolini and Hitler, the Jews closed ranks with the British against the Nazi menace. The Jewish leader Chaim Weizmann (later Israel's first president), diplomatically referring to the confrontation between the British Mandatory authorities and their Jewish subjects as "differences," assured His Majesty's Government that "we would like these differences to give way before the great and pressing necessities of the time."

But both sides were aware that the alliance was temporary. Thus, the British nodded with approval at the Jewish resolve to stand fast against a German advance—but refused to give them arms with which to defend themselves. "It is sad to recall," wrote an Israeli journalist recently, "that at the very moment they were contemplating their own flight, the British feared that, if the Jews survived, they might not return the arms."

In the event, the Carmel Plan was never needed—General Montgomery's El Alamein offensive in November 1942 forced Rommel to retreat—but in the Dania quarter of Haifa, near the Haifa University, lines of rusty iron rails driven into the ground as tank barriers bear mute witness to a Masada that might have been.

Along the Spine of Mount Carmel

Guarding the exit from Haifa, as it were, is the tall, modern building of Haifa University. Founded under the auspices of the Hebrew University of Jerusalem, Haifa University became an independent institution in 1972. Rather than compete with the older and prestigious Technion down the hill, the University has concentrated its energies in the fields of humanities, social sciences, and education.

Not far beyond Haifa University's skyscraper, you meet the true Mount Carmel—the natural forests and gorges that characterize the area. Many picnic spots and lovely walking trails await the visitor. A spectacular descent to the northern routes is via Nesher, the turn-off (to the left) clearly marked near the high communications-relay antenna. The road is full of hair-pin bends and not recommended for the faint-hearted. Two kms. (one-and-a-half miles) beyond the Nesher road is the Bet Oren road (to the right) which descends through superb mountain scenery to join Route 4, the old Tel Aviv–Haifa highway.

Druze Villages

Continuing along the spine of the Carmel range, you reach the two largest Druze villages in Israel—Isfiya and Daliyat el Carmel, with populations of about 5,500 and 7,500 respectively. The Druze are an Arabic-speaking people with a secret religion, the result of a break with Islam 1,000 years ago. They are fiercely proud of their separate identity and are not to be confused with their Arab neighbors. The young in T-shirts, jeans, and sneakers are indistinguishable from their contemporaries elsewhere; but the older generation are easily identified as Druze. For the men a bushy walrus-moustache is a mandatory source of masculine pride. The traditional among them wear black, baggy trousers with a copious fold in the nether regions, though nowadays this is more often only seen in more remote rural communities. The head-gear is a pure white scarf, tied differently and minus the black cord usually worn by Muslims. A few old men will wear a red-topped turban. These are the religious leaders, some of the approximately six per cent of the community initiated into the secrets of the Druze religion. The women have a penchant for brightly-colored dresses, and gracefully drape veils over their heads without covering their faces. In fact, the traditional status of Druze women is significantly better than that of their Muslim counterparts.

In Daliyat el Carmel you'll find several shops catering to local and tourist trade. Israelis go out of their way to shop here for furniture, rugs, basketware, native fur throws, and hand-stitched or woven wall-hangings. No prices are fixed, and the atmosphere is more congenial than in Jerusalem's Old City. You can also find good felafel, Turkish coffee, and ice-cream.

The villages reflect a curious blend of the traditional and the modern. In communities so close to a large city, the 20th century has irrevocably swept them along with it. You see it in the dress, the architecture, the choice of work. Fewer and fewer till the soil, and more and more work in commerce or industry, commuting to the city.

Elijah vs. the Priests of Baal

Just beyond Daliyat el Carmel, a narrow paved road branches off to the left. The unofficial local dump soon gives way to wooded picnic spots and the Carmelite Monastery of Mukhraka, traditional site of Elijah's confrontation with the priests of Baal (I Kings 18).

The times were evil; the people of Israel had been seduced by the pagan cults introduced by King Ahab's wife, the Phoenician princess Jezebel. "How long will you go limping between two opinions?" Elijah stormed at them. "If the Lord is God, follow him; but if Ba'al, then follow him." The rules of the contest were drawn. Elijah and the priests of Ba'al would each erect an altar, cut up an ox on it, and appeal to his god: "and the God who answers by fire, he is God." All day long the priests of Ba'al went through their rituals, "but there was no voice; no one answered, no one heeded." Come evening and Elijah built his altar of 12 stones for the 12 tribes of Israel, saturated the wood and the sacrifice with water, and called on the name of the Lord. "Then the fire of the Lord fell, and consumed the burnt offering, and the wood, and the stones, and the dust, and licked up the water that was in the trench. And when all the people saw it, they fell on their faces; and they said 'The Lord, He is God; the Lord He is God.'" On Elijah's orders, the hapless priests of Ba'al were taken down to the Brook of Kishon and executed.

A fierce statue of Elijah watches all visitors to the site. The chapel with its altar of 12 stones is interesting, but what you've come for is the view from the roof. To the west, over the Carmel hills, lies the Mediterranean; to the east, in the palm of your hand, so it seems, the Jezre'el Valley with the impressive tel of Yokne'am at your feet, the hills of Nazareth, Moreh and Gilboa, and on a clear afternoon, the mountains of Gilead beyond the Jordan.

Back on the road, traveling away from Haifa, you immediately begin descending until you join the Zichron Ya'akov–Yokne'am road (Route 70); right to Tel Aviv, left to the North.

PRACTICAL INFORMATION FOR THE COAST

 TELEPHONE CODES. We have given telephone codes for the towns and areas in the lists that follow. These codes need only be used when calling from outside the area concerned.

HOTELS AND RESTAURANTS. Both Haifa and Netanya have large numbers of hotels; these are given in the separate listings that follow our Practical Information for the rest of the area. However, outside these two cities, places to stay, and eat, are limited.

CAESAREA. Dan Caesarea (L), (tel. 06–362266). 110 rooms, all with bath and airconditioning. Beautifully appointed deluxe hotel in own grounds with pool, tennis, golf, health club, sauna. Good restaurant, self-service restaurant, coffeeshop and bar. AE, DC, MC, V.

Restaurants. There are several quite decent little restaurants here where you can sit over a meal and watch the waves ripple up to the beach. The **Citadel** makes a great fresh water trout in butter and garlic if you come when they're not too busy. The **Crusader** Inn does a good calamari. There's also a self-service restaurant at the gas station as you come off the main highway (Rte. 2).

EIN HOD. Restaurant. The rustic restaurant at this artist's village will serve you on the shaded terrace in good weather.

HADERA. There are several unprepossessing eateries on and off the main road through the town. Many serve the commercial and truck traffic and tend to specialize in local dishes like houmous, tehina and shishkebab. On the town's main intersection, where the road to the north runs through, is **Mifgash Hamallard,** where they serve grilled mallard—a sort of cross between a wild and a domestic duck—on a skewer.

ZICHRON YA'AKOV. Bet Maimon (M), 4 Tzahal St. (tel. 06–390212). 24 rooms. Rates rise during high season.

Youth Hostels. Emek Hefer, at Kfar Vitkin, about 6 kms. (4 miles) north of Netanya on Rte. 2, the Tel Aviv–Haifa road (tel. 053–96032). **Young Judea,** at Ramat Yochanan, 3 kms. (2 miles) from Kiryat Ata just north of Haifa (tel. 04–442976). 130 beds, sports facilities, family rooms available, members' kitchen.

Guest Houses. Bet Oren (M), on Mt. Carmel, turnoff from top of Carmel between Haifa and Druze villages; or from Rte. 4, 2 kms. north of Ein Hod intersection (tel. 04–222111/2). 67 rooms, half with bath, half with shower, partially airconditioned. Wooded location; pool, bar, coffeeshop, synagogue. MC, V. **Nir Etzion** (M), above Ein Hod, on the slopes of Mt. Carmel, turnoff 12 kms. (7 miles) north of the Zichron Ya'akov junction on Rte. 4; Hof Carmel Mobile Post (tel. 04–942541/3). 74 rooms, 43 with bath, rest with shower, all airconditioned. Beautiful situation, bar, coffeeshop, synagogue. **Shefayim** (M), near beach, about 6 kms. (4 miles) north of Herzlia off Tel Aviv–Haifa Highway, Rte. 2 (tel. 052–70171/2). 110 rooms, 50 with bath, 60 with shower, all airconditioned. Pool, sports facilities, tennis. Bar, coffeeshop, synagogue. AE, DC, MC, V.

Holiday Villages. Kayit Veshayit (M), at Caesarea as you enter from Rte. 2 (tel. 06–362927/8). 53 rooms on the beach. Part of Kibbutz Sedot Yam. **Nahsholim** (M), at Hof Dor (Dor Beach), turn-off from Rte. 4 2 kms. (1½ miles) north of Zichron Ya'akov Junction; Mobile Post Hof Hacarmel (tel. 063–99533). 55 rooms with shower, partially airconditioned. Right on the beach, with kitchenettes, self-serve cafeteria, tennis courts.

Camping. Beitan Aharon, 3 kms. (2 miles) north of Netanya (tel. 053–22186). **Dor,** next to Kibbutz Nahsholim, turnoff from Rte. 4, the "old" road, 2 kms. north of Zichron Ya'akov Junction (tel. 06–399018). Right on the beach. **Neve Yam,** 13 kms. (8 miles) south of Haifa on either Rte. 2 or Rte. 4, turnoff to Atlit and follow road to its end (tel. 04–942240).

HOW TO GET AROUND. Sherut, or shared taxis, run between Tel Aviv, Netanya, and Haifa. Trains, though infrequent, follow an interesting route between Tel Aviv and Haifa. The Egged bus service is comprehensive and frequent between the major cities, less so to more remote locations.

MUSEUMS AND HISTORIC SITES. CAESAREA. Site of ancient Roman, Byzantine, and Crusader cities, a Roman theater, and an aqueduct. Open 8–4 winter months, 8–5 summer; Fri. closed one hour earlier.

(N.P.)

MUKHRAKA. On Mt. Carmel, just after Daliyat el Carmel as you come from Haifa. Site of Elijah's confrontation with the priests of Baal. Spectacular view. Open daily 8–11.45, 2–5; closed Fri.

RAMAT HANADIV. On Mt. Carmel, just south of Zichron Ya'akov. Rothschild's tomb. Open 9–6 summer months, 9–4 winter.

SPORTS. Israel's only 18-hole **golf** course at Caesarea (tel. 06–361174). Visitors welcome. **Swimming** in the Mediterranean from south to north: Herzlia, Shefayim, Netanya South, Netanya, Netanya North, Michmoret, Givat Olga, Sedot Yam, Nahsholim, Neve Yam, Haifa.

PRACTICAL INFORMATION FOR HAIFA

GETTING TO TOWN FROM THE AIRPORT. The scheduled Egged bus routes 945 and 947 link Jerusalem and Haifa via Ben-Gurion International Airport. From the airport to Haifa takes a bit over an hour-and-a-half. A *sherut,* or shared taxi, is sometimes also available. For early departures, a special crack-of-dawn bus runs from Haifa to the airport (tel. 384667 or 670170 for details).

TOURIST INFORMATION. Government Tourist Information Office, 18 Herzl St., Hadar (tel. 666521/3); and at Shed no. 12 (Port), only on arrival of ships (tel. 663988). **Haifa Tourism Development Association,** 10 Achad Ha'am St. (tel. 671645). **Municipal Information Offices,** Central Bus Station (downtown), 2 Sederot Hahagana (tel. 512208); 23 Hanevi'im St., Hadar (tel. 663056); 119 Sederot Hanassi, Central Carmel (tel. 383683). Recording of *What's On in Haifa* (tel. 640840).

Telephone Code. The area code for Haifa is (04).

HOTELS. Hotels in Haifa are to be found either on the Carmel (top of the mountain), or in Hadar (the older and bustling midtown area). There are no increases during high season, though prices *drop* by 10% during the low season.

Deluxe

Dan Carmel, 87 Sederot Hanassi (tel. 386211). 220 rooms with bath. An "all-frills" hotel located on the Carmel, with a spectacular view of the bay. Half the rooms face onto the bay (always preferred), the rest look onto the pleasing trees-and-sea landscape of Mt. Carmel. Fine French à la carte restaurant in addition to its other dining rooms. Great bar, piano bar, coffeeshop. Pool in lovely grounds, health club, sauna—the works. AE, DC, MC, V.

Expensive

Dan Panorama, 107 Sederot Hanassi (tel. 352222). 270 rooms with bath in very modern tower in central Carmel. Business-like atmosphere. Good location. Pool, babysitting. AE, DC, MC, V.

Nof Hotel, 101 Sederot Hanassi (tel. 388731). 100 rooms with bath, all with bay view. On the Carmel next-door to the Dan. Friendly and efficient service. AE, DC, MC, V.

Shulamit, 15 Kiryat Sefer St. (tel. 242811). 70 rooms with bath. On the Carmel, but not nearly as centrally-located as the Nof or the Dan; quiet neighborhood. An older property, it has its regulars who return year after year. AE, DC, MC, V.

Moderate

Carmelia, 35 Herzlia St., Hadar (tel. 521278/9). 50 rooms, some with bath, most with shower only, all airconditioned. In the heart of the midtown area. Has some inexpensive rooms. AE, DC, MC, V.

Dvir, 124 Panorama Rd. (tel. 389131). 39 rooms, most with bath, all airconditioned. Excellently located on the Carmel. A front room is preferred; avoid the annex. AE, DC, MC, V.

Marom, 51 Hapalmach St. (tel. 254355). 29 rooms, 19 with bath, 10 with shower, partially airconditioned. In the remote Romema neighborhood on Mt. Carmel.

Vered Hacarmel, 1 Heinrich Heine Sq. (tel. 389236). 22 rooms, most with shower only, all airconditioned. Well-located in a green side-street within walking distance of central Carmel.

Ya'arot Hacarmel, on Mt. Carmel outside Haifa (tel. 229144/9). 103 rooms, almost all with bath, partially airconditioned. Resort-style hotel with nightly entertainment. Can be expensive.

Zion Hotel, 5 Baerwald St. (tel. 664311/5). 94 rooms, almost all with bath, airconditioned. Centrally-located in midtown Hadar; pleasant hotel with a reputation for decent food. AE, DC, MC, V.

Inexpensive

Beth-Shalom Carmel, 110 Hanassi St. (tel. 337481). 31 rooms with bath. A Protestant guest house; minimum 3-night stay.

Nesher, 53 Herzl St. (tel. 640644). 15 rooms, most with shower, partially airconditioned. In the Hadar section.

Talpiot, 61 Herzl St. (tel. 673753/4). 24 rooms, most with shower, partially airconditioned. In midtown Hadar.

Hospices. **Carmelite Pilgrim's Hospice** (Catholic), Stella Maris, on the Carmel, P.O. Box 9047 (tel. 523460).

German Hospice (Catholic), 105 Jaffa Rd. (tel. 523705). Downtown location.

International Tourist Hostel, 40 Hagefen St. (tel. 521110). In midtown Hadar.

St. Maximos Hospice, 3 Megiddo St. (tel. 81274). On the Carmel.

Youth Hostel. **Carmel Hostel,** just outside town off the "old" road to Tel Aviv, behind the World War I military cemetery; Hof Hacarmel Mobile Post (tel. 531944). 436 beds, sports facilities, airconditioning, family rooms available, members' kitchen. Bus 43 from Haifa.

RESTAURANTS. Haifa has several first-class restaurants with prices here generally less costly than in other Israeli cities. The **Banker's Tavern,** 2 Habankim St. (tel. 528439), takes top honors for posh meals and delicacies, but also has a business lunch menu with special prices from 12–6 P.M. plus a well-tended bar and good service.

The **Balfour Cellar,** Balfour St., features Jewish and international cuisine; the **Dan Carmel Hotel** offers French specialties, and the garden-restaurant **Gan Rimon,** 10 Sederot Habroshim (also on the Carmel), tel. 381392, features European dishes (lunch only).

For Chinese treats, the **Pagoda,** at 1 Bat Galim Ave., is often rated Israel's best Chinese restaurant, despite its quite moderate prices for its special Central Chinese dishes; Shanghai cooking is the specialty at **Chin Lung,** 126 Hanassi (tel. 381308). Good Chinese food also at **Man Jai,** 17 Ben-Gurion Ave.

In the (M) range there is quite a choice. The **Gan Airmon,** 16 Hanevi'im St., next to the cinema, has perhaps the widest range of Oriental, European and dairy cuisine in town; the **Mataamim,** 24 Herzl St. (tel. 665 172) is good for meat and dairy lunches; the **Quick Bar,** 15 Nordau St., is really quick, with good Viennese fare. **La Boheme,** 139 Hanassi Blvd., has French and other international food, as well as an inexpensive tourist menu.

The following are definitely worth trying: On Mt. Carmel: **Panorama 120,** at 120 Panorama Rd. Middle-Eastern, amazing selection of salads; **La Trattoria,** 119 Sederot Hanassi, European cuisine. In Hadar: **MiVaMi,** 17 Sederot Ben-Gurion, European cuisine. Downtown: **Misha,** 48 Jaffa Rd., Romanian grill. Bat Gallim: **Dolphin,** 13 Sederot Bat Gallim.

Good pub food at **Hagan** in Gan Ha'em. An excellent French-style restaurant is **Mirabelle** at 35 Tchernichovsky St., Stella Maris (tel. 3307990).

Up in the Merkaz section, two good European-style restaurants specialize in things like Swedish plates, goulash, schnitzel and kebab; the **Carmel** opposite the Israel Discount Bank and **Cafe Pe'er,** Hanassi and Mahanyim Sts., an outdoor cafe, whose indoor walls are papered with magazine advertisements that show people eating. A good Oriental restaurant up here is the **Finjan,** 4 Mahanayim St., and a new favorite is **Fandu Club,** near Haifa Univ., a restaurant-cum-piano bar at 56 Antwerpen St.

Stella Maris, a cafe-restaurant on Tchernikovsky St., has home-style meals, great cakes and sweets, fabulous views. **London's Pride,** 84 Ha'atzmaut, is a club that welcomes tourists from noon to wee hours. **Ron,** 139 Hanassi, serves exclusive European and Oriental dishes; also has a piano bar.

In Bat Gallim, **Misadag,** 29 Margolin St. (tel. 524441), offers fish specialties, as does **Neptune,** 19 Margolin Street. The **Rimini** (3 addresses: 20 Havevim, 119 Sd. Hanassi, Romema's Derech Ruppin) serves good Italian food. **Pininat HaMizrach,** 35 Sd. Ben-Gurion, dishes out good Oriental fare, as does **Amron** and **Benny Ori** (Hadar), 23 Halutz St. Oriental and seafood specialties are found at **Zvi,** 3 Hameginim.

Cafés. Café-sitting is as popular in Haifa as it is all over Israel. Haifa's favorite cafes are the **Atara,** Balfour St., the **Paris,** on a broad terrace overlooking the main intersection, and the **Strauss,** across the street, corner of Herzl and Balfour Sts. The **Ritz,** 5 Haim St., is favored by artists and intellectuals.

Pubs. **Ahuza,** 6 Pica Rd., in the neighborhood of the same name caters to a younger crowd. **Hagan,** in Gan Ha'am, is a pub restaurant. **Ha'okaf** (the Saddle), 56 Antwerpen St., is an intimate pub all the way across Mt. Carmel in the Dania Quarter. **London Bridge** is at Stella Maris. **The Pub,** 125 Sederot Hanassi, is in central Carmel. **Savta,** in Gan Ha'em, has an intimate and unique atmosphere, serves fondues.

HOW TO GET AROUND. Haifa can be a difficult city to walk around because of Mt. Carmel's steep slopes, but a good bus service covers the city, on Saturdays as well. Taxi services within the city: Carmel (tel. 382727); Carmelit (tel. 664640); Hamonitex (tel. 664343); Merkaz Mitzpa (tel. 662525); and Neve (tel. 222222).

Most interurban travel is by bus from the Central Bus Station downtown. Sherut, shared taxis, link Haifa with Jerusalem—*Aviv,* 10 Nordau St., Hadar (tel. 666333); Tel Aviv—*Aviv,* (see above) *Amal* next to Central Bus Station (tel. 522828), *Arie,* 9 Baerwald St. (tel. 673666); Acre/Nahariya—*Kavei Hagalil,* 16 Hanevi'im St., Hadar, and Kikar Plumer, downtown (tel. 673666). Infrequent, relatively slow, but pleasant rail services reach Nahariya, Tel Aviv, and Jerusalem.

For car hire contact: *Budget* (tel. 538558), *Avis* (tel. 674688), *Hertz* (tel. 665425), *Europcar* (tel. 529504), *InterRent* (tel. 644069).

Tours. Before you make final plans, we suggest you visit or write the Haifa Tourism Development Association, 10 Achad Ha'am St. (tel. 04–671645/7). They give away *Haifa At Your Fingertips,* an easy-to-use pamphlet full of all sorts of useful tourist information. Also ask for the *Discover Haifa By Yourself* brochure. And, of course, G.T.I.O. is also on hand with maps, advice, latest details on Haifa walking tours, special tours of the environs, etc. A free walking tour departs every Saturday at 10 A.M. from Panorama Rd. (Yefe Nof), at the corner of Shaar Halevanon St.

EXCURSIONS. A wide range of ½-day and full-day excursions are available from Haifa, including a city tour; Caesarea and Tel Aviv; Acre and Rosh Hanikra; the Druze villages and Megiddo; the Upper Galilee and Golan; and Nazareth and Sea of Galilee region. Some tours terminate in Tel Aviv, making them a productive and interesting way of traveling south. Contact *United Tours,* 5 Nordau St. (tel. 665656), or *Egged Tours* in Hadar (tel. 643131). Alternatively, your hotel will be pleased to book for you.

HISTORIC BUILDINGS AND SITES. Bahai Shrine, Zionism Blvd. Tomb of the Bab. Open daily 9–noon; gardens until 5. (Modest dress.)

    Cable car from Stella Maris atop Mt. Carmel to Bat Gallim on the coast. Open Sun. to Thurs. 9 A.M.–11 P.M.; Fri 9–4; Sat. 6–11 P.M.

Stella Maris (Carmelite Monastery). Open daily 8–1.30, 3–6. (Modest dress).

Elijah's Cave, above Allenby Rd. Open Sun to Thurs. 8–4; Fri. 8–12; Closed Sat. (Modest dress).

Technion, Institute of Technology. New Visitors' Center (tel. 292111). Open Sun. to Thurs. 8–2; Fri. 8–12. Closed Sat.

MUSEUMS. Clandestine Immigration and Naval Museum, 204 Allenby Rd. Open Sun, Tues. 9–4; Mon., Wed., Thurs. 9–3; Fri. 9–1. Closed Sat.

Dagon Grain Silo Museum, Kikar Plumer (Plumer Sq.). Ancient cultivation, collection and storage. Guided tour only at 10.30, Sun. to Fri. Closed Sat.

Edible Oil Museum, dealing with the long history of the subject in this country. At Shemen Oil Factory, Haifa Bay (tel. 670491). Open Sun. to Thurs. 9–12. Closed Fri. and Sat.

Haifa Museum, 26 Shabbetai Levi St. Ancient and modern art, music, and ethnology. Open Sat. to Thurs. 10–1; Tues., Thurs., Sat. also 6–9 P.M. Closed Fri.

Mane Katz Museum, 89 Panorama Rd. (Yefe Nof). Collection by the artist, on the Carmel. Open Sun. to Thurs. 10–1, 4–6; Sat. 10–1. Closed Fri. Winter hours subject to change (tel. 383482).

Museum of Archeology, University of Haifa. Open Sat. to Thurs. 10–1; plus Tues. 4–6. Closed Fri.

Museum of Japanese Art, 89 Sederot Hanassi. On the Carmel. Open Sun. to Thurs. 10–5; Sat. 10–2. Closed Fri.

Museum of Prehistory, Gan Ha'em. Collection from the region, located on the Carmel. Open Sun. to Thurs. 8–2; Sat. 10–2 (in July and Aug. 10–6). Closed Fri.

Natural History Museum, 124 Hatishbi St. within Haifa Zoo. Open Sun. to Thurs. 8–4 (in July and Aug. 8–6); Fri. 8–1; Sat. 9–4 (in July and Aug. 9–6).

National Maritime Museum, 198 Allenby St. Open Sun. to Thurs. 10–4; Sat. 10–1. Closed Fri.

Railway Museum, Old East Train Station, opposite 40 Hativat Golani Rd. Open Sun. to Thurs. 10–1. Closed Fri., Sat.

Technoda (National Museum of Science and Technology). In old Technion Building, between Balfour and Shmaryahu Levin Sts., Hadar. A new "please touch" working-model state-of-the-art complex. Open. Mon., Wed., Thurs. 9–5; Tues. 9–7; Fri. 9–1; Sat. 10–2. Closed Sun.

ART GALLERIES. Artists' House, tel. 522355; **Bet Abba Khoushy,** tel. 227850; **Goldman's,** tel. 380480; **Horovitz,** tel. 673939; **Rothschild Gallery,** tel. 383424.

PARKS AND GARDENS. Allenby Garden, Panorama Rd. (Yefe Nof). In Central Carmel. **Gan Ha'em,** on the Carmel; includes zoo. **Gan Hazikaron** (Memorial Garden), in Hadar opposite City Hall. **Sculpture Garden,** Zionism Blvd., above Bahai Shrine.

SHOPPING. The major shopping area is around the City Hall, particularly along Herzl St., Balfour, and Nordau. Also, the Central Carmel Center which is expensive and new. There are a number of diamond and jewelry dealers here; the city is famous for them. The leading hotels also have good shopping arcades, particularly the Dan Carmel. The local branch of Israel's major department store chain, **Hamashbir Lazarchan,** has just about everything. Along Jaffa Rd. are shops selling pottery, copper, and other souvenirs at prices much less than in the fancier places.

MUSIC AND THEATERS. Haifa Auditorium, 138 Sederot Hanassi on the Carmel, hosts the Israel Philharmonic Orchestra when it comes to town, though Haifa does have its own small orchestra. **Haifa Municipal Theater** is one of the country's best, though most productions are in Hebrew; tel. 670956/7/8 for details.

Listings, postings, and a 24-hour *What's On* service (tel. 640840) will tell you what's happening. Folklore performances are frequent, and an annual festival takes place here.

NIGHTLIFE. For a city of its size, Haifa has a lot happening in the evenings. In the Old City area downtown, known as Wadi Salib, is the delightful **Al Pasha,** Hammam el-Pasha St. (tel. 671309). A varied snack lightmeal menu, live music, a folksy atmosphere where people are not beyond getting up on the rustic wooden tables and dancing. Closed Sun. **London Pride,** 85 Ha'atzma'ut Rd. in the downtown area, is a bar and disco.

In Hadar, try the **Silverline Club,** at the corner of Nordau and Balfour Sts. A disco with live entertainment.

On Mt. Carmel is **Hamo'adon** (The Club), 130 Hatishbi St. (tel. 389560). Private club in the European style, with entertainers and dancing/disco. Closed Sun. The **Denia Club,** 56 Antwerpen St. (tel. 256662), is of similar style. Closed Sun. and Mon. The **120 Club** on Panorama Rd, and the **Vogue** on Sederot Hanassi, attract the younger set; both closed Sun. Likewise the **Fever** disco in Central Carmel

Students are welcome at Technion's **Club 2:2** (tel. 234148), and Haifa University's **Assam Club** (tel. 240519).

SPORTS. Swimming pools at Galei Hadar, 9 Hapoel St. (tel. 667854) and Maccabi, Bikkurim St. (tel. 380100), the latter heated in winter. The Dado, Carmel, and Bat Galim municipal beaches have lifeguards on duty May through October. The private Hashaket Beach is open year round. **Tennis** at Israel Tennis Center, Kfar Zamir (tel. 522721); Maccabi, Bikkurim St. (tel. 386028), and Carmelia (Migrash Hako'ach), 32 Zionism Blvd. **Windsurfing** Center, tel. 521136. **Diving** is also available; tel. 512418 for details.

RELIGIOUS SERVICES. Catholic: Mass at St. Joseph's, 80 Sederot Hameginim; in Latin, Sun. 10 A.M. Also at Stella Maris the Carmelite Monastery; in Arabic and English Sun. 7 A.M.

Jewish: Many Orthodox synagogues. The Central Synagogue is at 60 Herzl St. in Hadar. The Moriah Conservative Synagogue, 7 Harav St., has services Fri. 5.30 P.M. and Sat. 9 A.M. The Progressive (Reform) Congregation, 142 Sederot Hanassi, has services Fri. 5.30 P.M. and Sat. 9 A.M.

Protestant: St. Luke's (Church of England), 4 St. Luke's St. (tel. 522713). Holy Communion Sun. at 10 A.M. at the Lutheran Community Center, 43 Meir St. (tel. 515019).

PRACTICAL INFORMATION FOR NETANYA

TOURIST INFORMATION. Government Tourist Information Office, Kikar Ha'atzma'ut (tel. 27286).

Telephone Code. Netanya's area code is (053). No area code is necessary when calling within this dialing area.

Useful Telephone Numbers. Egged Central Bus Station tel. 37052. **Car Hire:** Hertz (tel. 28890); Avis (tel. 31619); Budget (tel. 30618).

 HOTELS. The unusually large number of hotels for a town of this size is explained by the fact that Netanya is as popular a resort for vacationing Israelis as it is for foreign tourists. High season, when rates soar, is usually held to August, and, for some, the more important Jewish holidays. There is often a corresponding drop in rates during the low season.

Deluxe

Dan Netanya, Nice Blvd. (tel. 30044). 129 rooms with bath, airconditioning. The only top-drawer hotel in town. On the beach, it also has a heated pool, sauna, tennis courts. AE, DC, MC, V.

Expensive

There are no hotels in this category, but most of the Moderate hotels we list leap into it during high season—Blue Bay, Bet Ami, Galil, Grand Yahalom, King Solomon, Park, and Residence.

Moderate

Bet Ami, 41 Shlomo Hamelach St. (tel. 91222). 85 rooms with bath. Beach, pool. Bar, coffeeshop, piano bar, synagogue, T.V. on request. AE, V.

Blue Bay, 37 Hamelachim St. (tel. 37131). 225 rooms, most with bath. Some garden rooms available. Beach, pool, tennis. Bar, coffeeshop, piano bar, nightclub, beauty parlor. AE, DC, MC, V.

Galil, Nice Blvd. (tel. 92096). 84 rooms with bath. Pool, sports facilities, bar, nightclub.

Gali-Zans, 6 Melachim St. (tel. 39241/2). 65 rooms with bath. Beach, heated pool, health club, bar. Sabbath-observing.

Goldar, 1 Ussishkin St. (tel. 38188). 150 rooms with bath. Pool, bar, coffeeshop. AE, MC, V.

Grand Yahalom, 15 Gad Makhnes St. (tel. 35345). 48 rooms with bath. Heated pool, bar, piano bar, nightclub.

King Solomon, 18 Hama'aplim St. (tel. 38444). 99 rooms with bath. Pool, health club, sauna. AE, DC, MC, V.

Metropol Grand, 17 Gad Makhnes St. (tel. 38038). 64 rooms, most with bath. Pool, bar, coffeeshop, piano bar, T.V. on request. AE, DC, MC.

Park, 7 King David St. (tel. 33347). 90 rooms with bath. Pool, bar. AE, DC, MC, V.

Residence, 18 Gad Makhnes St. (tel. 33777). 96 rooms, most with bath. Bar. AE, V.

Inexpensive

Atzmau'th, 2 Ussishkin St. (tel. 22562). 20 rooms with shower, partially airconditioned. Bar, coffeeshop.

Daphna, 24 Rishon Le'Zion St. (tel. 23655). 17 rooms with shower. One of the cheapest in this category.

Galei Hasharon, 42 Ussishkin St. (tel. 25125). 24 rooms with shower and airconditioning. Bar. At the lower end of the category.

Ginot-Yam, 9 King David St. (tel. 41007). 35 rooms, most with shower, all airconditioned. Bar, piano bar, coffeeshop.

Hof, 9 Ha'atzma'ut Sq. (tel. 31304). 30 rooms, most with bath, all airconditioned. Grill room, bar, coffeeshop. MC.

Margoa, 9 Gad Makhnes St. (tel. 34434/5). 34 rooms, most with shower, all airconditioned. Bar, coffeeshop. AE, V.

Maxim, 8 King David St. (tel. 39341). 90 rooms with bath, airconditioned. Pool, tennis, bar, coffeeshop, piano bar, nightclub, color T.V. AE, DC, MC, V.

Metropol, 18 Rishon Le'Zion St. (tel. 38038). 27 rooms, most with shower, partially airconditioned. Pool, bar, coffeeshop. AE, MC.

Mitzpe-Yam, 4 Karlebach St. (tel. 23730). 28 rooms with shower, partially airconditioned. Bar. Extra-inexpensive.

Reuben, 25 Ussishkin St. (tel. 23107). 27 rooms, most with shower, all airconditioned.

Sironit, 19 Gad Makhnes St. (tel. 40688). 62 rooms, 24 with bath, rest with shower, all airconditioned. Bar, coffeeshop.

Topaz, 25 King David St. (tel. 36052). 64 rooms with bath, airconditioned. AE, DC, MC, V.

Yahalom, 11 Gad Makhnes St. (tel. 35345). 48 rooms, half with bath, half shower, all airconditioned. Heated pool, bar, beauty parlor.

RESTAURANTS. The center of town is packed with interesting pavement cafés. The **Restaurant Renaissance** is on Ha'atzma'ut Sq. (tel. 28653), its streetside cafe serving light food, while the back restaurant is quite posh. Nearby is the new **Taipei** (tel. 28145), a Chinese restaurant with service both inside and out. Pricey. Try **Capris,** 27 Herzl St., for cakes, toasts, and light meals. **Chez Raphael,** 2 King David St., has excellent Moroccan food. **Lucullus,** in Ha'atzma'ut Sq., has wonderful seafood in an exclusive setting.

MUSEUMS. Attractively-bedecked horses pull carriages around town for an unusual form of sightseeing. The Promenade along the Mediterranean beaches is a pleasant place to stroll. The downtown Kikar Ha'atzma'ut—Independence Sq.—is closed off to traffic on the weekend and becomes a giant pedestrian plaza.

Cultural Center for the Blind, Central Library, 4 Hahistadrut St. (tel. 25321). Braille and "talking" books. Sun. to Thurs. 8–2; closed Fri. and Sat.

Museum of Jewish Legion, Moshav Avihail just north of Netanya (tel. 22212). Story of this famous unit in the British Army in W.W.I. The moshav was founded in the '30s by veterans of the Legion. Take the local bus from the Central Bus Station. Open Sun. to Thurs. 8–2, Fri. 8–1; closed Sat.

Netanya Diamond Center, 90 Herzl St. (tel. 34624). A free audio-visual presentation on the industry, plus a tour of the cutting/polishing plant. Fine showroom of the finished product (no free samples). Open Sun. to Thurs. 8–7, Fri. 8–2; closed Sat.

NIGHTLIFE. The Aristo, 3 Rehov Tel Chai, is a recent club and highly recommended. There are two discos: the **Don Camillo,** 2 Smilansky St., and the **To Hell,** 1 Smilansky St. A disco just for students and teenagers is the **Bar-Orion,** 31 Herzl St., a nice place with no hard drinks, record music.

SPORTS. Swimming at many of the excellent beaches in this lovely resort town. Pools are offered at many of the hotels. **Tennis** at the Maccabi club, tel. 24627. Finally, there is **golfing** at Caesarea, only 15 minutes away.

ACRE AND THE WESTERN GALILEE

Crusaders and Castles

Though smaller than any other area covered in this book, Acre and the Western Galilee are none the less interesting for that. Quite the contrary, the short distances make it easy to establish yourself in, say, Nahariya or one of the kibbutz guest houses, and range out from there. And there is much to see: great natural beauty, walking trails, fine beaches, many picnic spots. You will repeatedly meet the Crusaders here—we are close to their most continuous base at Tyre (today in Lebanon), and their reconquest of the coast in 1191 began from the north. But many of the memories here are of more recent history. Israel's birth in 1948 was not painless, and Acre and the Western Galilee fill several pages in any account of it.

Northwards out of Haifa, the coastal road, Route 4, breaks off to the left at the intersection still known from its Mandate days as the Check-post. For a while you pass through Israel's largest heavy industrial area, and several of Haifa's daughter towns, known collectively as Hakrayot, the Townships. One of the best views of Acre is across its small bay before you actually reach the town.

205

Acre—A Port for All Reasons

"In the land of the blind," the saying goes, "the one-eyed man is king." The coast of Israel is not blessed with an abundance of harbors and inlets, and in the absence of better defense against storm and sea, ports like Ashkelon, Jaffa, and Dor grew to greater significance than their natural advantages deserved. Acre—Akko in both the Bible and modern Hebrew—was different. It had a well-protected harbor, a well-watered and fertile hinterland, and a strategic position on the coastal road linking Egypt and Phoenicia (Lebanon). In addition, it served as the natural Mediterranean outlet for trade not only from the Galilee, but even from Syria and Mesopotamia beyond. All these factors made it a prize worth fighting for. In its heyday only Alexandria and Constantinople exceeded its volume of commerce, and it overshadowed even Tyre as the principal port of the eastern Mediterranean.

The ancient Akko mentioned in 4,000-year-old writings is buried beneath the large tel just east of the modern town. Its priority then was to straddle the coastal highway, and its port was at the mouth of the Na'aman River. Although assigned by Joshua to the territory of the tribe of Asher, the Asherites were not able to drive out the Canaanite inhabitants (Judges 1). By David's day, however, it had become part of the Israelite kingdom. For long periods it was a Phoenician city, but when the Hellenistic king Ptolemy II of Egypt gained control of the country in the 2nd century B.C., he renamed it Ptolemais, the name it retained through the Roman and Byzantine periods. The Arab conquest of the 7th century A.D. revived the Biblical name, however, and when the Crusaders took Akko in 1104, they found a large and thriving commercial town. The city became known as St. Jean d'Acre by the French knights, and Acre it has remained to Westerners to this day.

The Cross and the Crescent

Throughout the 12th century, Acre served its historic destiny as the best harbor in the land, and the second capital of the Latin Kingdom of Jerusalem. But though it was a great and well-built city, eye-witness accounts of the period attest to its unsavory character and unsanitary conditions. Thus a Muslim traveler in 1185: "Unbelief and unpiousness there burn fiercely, and pigs and crosses abound. It stinks and is filthy, being full of refuse and excrement. The Franks [Europeans] ravished it from Muslim hands . . . and the eyes of Islam were swollen with weeping for it; it was one of its griefs. Mosques became churches and Minarets bell-towers . . . "

After the disastrous defeat of the Crusader armies at the Horns of Hattin in 1187, Acre surrendered to the victorious Saladin without a fight. But within two years, king Guy de Lusignan and his knights were back, and began a two-year siege which has been described as "one of the most fascinating dramas in the history of war." The besieging Crusaders bottled up Acre, but were soon themselves besieged by a Muslim army arrayed behind them. Each side inflicted damage and casualties on the other, but neither had a decisive enough advantage to carry the day. Only after two years of this stalemate was the balance finally tipped—in favor of the Crusaders—by the arrival of two armies led by Philip II Augustus of France and Richard the Lionheart of England. Acre fell to the Crusaders again.

They regained much of the coastal plain, too, these Knights of the Cross, and later most of the Galilee; but Jerusalem, the revered and Holy City, eluded them. In the 13th century Acre became the effective capital of the much-shrunken Latin Kingdom. Since the Kingdom's early days the brunt of the defense of the realm had been borne by the "fighting monks," the Hospitallers and Templars, each of whom had a quarter in Acre. Other areas of the city were ceded to the mercantile communes of Venice, Genoa, Pisa, and Marseilles, whose powerful navies had helped in the conquest of Muslim coastal towns. Relations between the factions were always tense, often bloodstained. The Bishop of Acre, one James of Vitry, related: "Acre is a monster of nine heads, each of which is fighting the other. Nightly men are murdered within the city, men are strangled, women poison their husbands, drug-vendors and whores are prepared to pay high rents for rooms, so that even priests lease houses to them."

The end, when it came, was brutal and swift. The Mamluks took Acre on 18th May, 1291, massacring every last Crusader left alive. The city was systematically destroyed, and remained in its devastation for centuries.

The Bedouin sheikh Daher el-Omar asserted his independence from his weak Turkish overlords in the early-18th century, extending his control over most of the Galilee. In 1749 he moved his capital from Tiberias to Acre, perhaps because the former was uncomfortably close to Syria from where he expected reprisals. He rebuilt the walls of Acre, but his major project was a new and powerful fortress, complete with watch-tower, constructed over the remains of the fortified Hospitaller Quarter. In order to make the fortress virtually impregnable, Daher el-Omar filled the Crusader halls below with rubble, creating a high and solid foundation for the new citadel above.

In 1775 Daher el-Omar was assassinated by one Ahmed el-Jazzar, "the Butcher," the Albanian-born governor of the Sidon district, who made Acre his capital and extended his semi-autonomous rule over much of Israel. His cruelty was legendary. He had workers buried alive, murdered his wives with his bare hands, and mutilated anyone of whom he disapproved. The beautiful, large mosque, the famous bathhouse (now the Municipal Museum), and the massive city walls were built during his rule.

In 1799 Napoleon, fresh from his victory in Egypt, appeared at the gates of Acre. His heavy artillery, sent by sea, had been sunk by the British fleet. Nonetheless, with his light cannon mounted on the ancient tel (known locally as Napoleon's Hill), he breached the city walls. But unable to press home his attack, he eventually withdrew to France, his eastern campaign in shambles.

The Mosque of the Butcher

The best way to enter Acre's Old City is along Weizmann Street, off the main thoroughfare. A parking-lot is on your right, while a bank, a pharmacy, and, inside the entrance to the Crusader city, a post office are all nearby.

Just around the corner is the Mosque of Ahmed el-Jazzar, "the Butcher," Pasha of Acre, built over Crusader remains, possibly those of the Cathedral of St. Croce. The courtyard is an island of palm-fronded tranquility in the raucous ebb and flow of Old Acre. Each column or cistern has a story to tell, and it's worth accepting the offer of the local custodian to take you around. The mosque is a vast, high-ceilinged building with an austere interior and carpeted floors.

You enter respectfully . . . oblivious to everything around him, a solitary Arab is absorbed in his prayers . . . a single hair from the beard of the Prophet Mohammed is said to be enshrined here. You should dress modestly, but need not remove your shoes for there is a sort of visitors' vestibule at the entrance to the Mosque.

Crusaders Underground

The entrance to the old Crusader Hospitallers' Quarter is opposite the el-Jazzar Mosque. From the Quarter's courtyard you can see the Citadel of Daher el-Omar built above the Crusader buildings. During the British Mandate, the Citadel became a high-security prison whose inmates included members of clandestine Jewish organizations caught training with arms, running the British blockade with refugees from Hitler's Europe, or in action against the British. In 1947 a dramatic escape from the prison captured headlines around the world, and provided Leon Uris' *Exodus* with one of its most dramatic moments.

The Knights' Halls are now used for chamber concerts in the summer. In the ceiling of the middle of the three halls is a small patch of concrete plugging the secret tunnel of an abortive escape attempt from the cell above in 1946. Through the Hospitaller store-rooms, the arrows lead you down a few steps to the most impressive hall in the complex, and perhaps in all the monumental Crusader buildings in Israel. This is the Crypt of St. John, probably the Hospitaller refectory, maybe the very hall in which Louis IX of France—St. Louis—convened the knights of the realm in 1250. The stone reliefs of the *fleur-de-lys,* the emblem of the French royal house, certainly argue for the ceremonial function of the great hall. It takes six adults, arms outstretched, to surround each of the giant columns supporting the roof. It is said that this is one of the oldest Gothic buildings in the world.

When the halls were excavated in the '50s and '60s, an oddity came to light: the top layers of rubble removed by the archeologists contained Israelite (Old Testament) pottery, below that were Roman potsherds, and deeper still Crusader pieces. Topsy-turvy stratification! What had happened here? When Daher el-Omar's builders packed the old Crusader buildings with debris to create a solid foundation for his citadel, they first used rubble close at hand (Crusader), then further afield (Roman), and finally chipped away at the old tel itself (Israelite)!

If you're severely claustrophobic, return the way you came. If not, go down and through the medieval secret tunnel to emerge across the street at the Posta, the hospital and hospice of the Knights of St. John.

A Photographic Phantasmagoria

The exit takes you onto a narrow street. Turn right to the Municipal Museum, housed in el-Jazzar's old Turkish bath-house, where a fascinating and eclectic collection of ancient archeology, illustrated snippets of old history, and slightly more recent folklore relate something of Acre's colorful, even gaudy, past. Known as Hammam el-Basha, the Pasha's Hot-baths also featured in the novel and motion-picture *Exodus*.

Head left, and a few minutes' walk brings you to the souk. Unlike Jerusalem's Arab bazaar where you can hardly see the tomatoes for the trinkets, the souk here is geared to local consumption. That doesn't mean that the tourist is not tempted by the small cafés, the little restaurants with shishkebab roasting on open grills outside, or pastry-shops with baklava swimming in cloying sweet syrup; but the souvenir shops are located where the large tour groups go, and this is not their regular beat.

A turn to the left through an arbor where the Arab men gather to play cards and drink coffee, and you reach the marvelously picturesque harbor. Distinctly identifiable Crusader buildings with their square pillars and arches still serve as dwellings or restaurants these 700 years later; while out in the bay is an isolated tower, once the end of the fortified arm of the Crusader port. It is known as the Tower of the Flies, taken from the name of the ancient Canaanite god Beelzebub—Ba'al Zevuv, Lord of the Flies. Today this is a fishing harbor and a small marina. Several waterside restaurants prepare fish straight out of the Mediterranean, along with the inevitable houmus, tehine, and green olives.

You can reach the harbor by car along a narrow road from the el-Jazzar Mosque: ask the locals for directions. But if you're on foot, retrace your steps via the cobble-stone courtyard and enter a large gate beneath a high square tower. This is Khan el-Umdan, the Inn of the Pillars, which during Acre's renaissance in the 18th century, served some of the vast numbers of merchants and travelers that passed through the city. The gate would once have been closed at night. The pillars which give the Khan its name are made of pink or gray granite, and were filched by the Turks from Roman Caesarea. During the summer, the Khan hosts various cultural and entertainment events as part of the city's Nights of Acre series.

Out the other side and to the left and you find yourself at the sea walls: some remains are Crusader, the powerful existing ones from the end of the 18th century. A delightful stroll along the new promenade on the walls themselves, and you find yourself at the lighthouse on the edge of the cape on which the Old City is built. Several copper-workers are located here, shaping the plates and plaques for which the town is famous.

Follow the sea walls along the main street. Some way down is a white-washed building with turquoise shutters. This is the house where Baha'ullah, the Prophet of the Bahai faith, lived out 12 years of exile in the 19th century. He is buried in a beautifully landscaped park on the edge of town, just off the Nahariya road.

The Citadel of Acre

Just before you leave the Old City walls, a gate to the right takes you to the Museum of Heroism, housed in several wings of the old British Prison, originally Daher el-Omar's Citadel. On the way in you pass the outside wall of the Citadel; the difference between the large Crusader building stones and the smaller Turkish ones above them is easy to spot. From the moat you can see cannonballs embedded in the walls. They date from the British bombardment of Acre in 1840, an attempt to dislodge the rebel administration of Ibrahim Pasha. An airconditioning vent tells you you're on the opposite side of the wall from the Knights' Halls!

Access to the Museum was once, disconcertingly, through a low-security mental asylum. This has been transferred elsewhere, and efforts are now being made to refurbish the somewhat neglected museum itself. Despite its state of neglect, the Museum's impact is electrifying. The original cells and their meagre contents tell of day-to-day life in the prison; and through photographs, documents, and press clippings, the history of Jewish resistance in the '30s and '40s to British rule in Palestine is reconstructed. One room graphically follows the story of the "great escape" from the prison. Near the exit are the condemned cells and the gallows. A short and easy street takes you back to the parking-lot where you first came in.

Apart from its historical sites, mostly accessible by car, Old Acre is a city to meander through. In many ways the city has preserved its special personality, and, despite its often run down and less-than-sanitary appearance, remains romantic and alluring, vigorous though captive within its ancient ramparts, and steeped in the waters of the Mediterranean.

Josephus' Footsteps and New Pioneers

With your back to Acre and the sea, drive east on Route 85, the main road to Safed, the Sea of Galilee, and the Upper Galilee. If that is your destination you will pass the town of Karmi'el, 21 kms. (12.5 miles) out of Acre. Founded as a new development town in 1964, it has a reputation for an exceptionally good quality of life and environment.

But for the purposes of this trip, turn right (south) at the Ahihud intersection eight kms. (five miles) out of Acre onto Route 70. Three kms. (two miles) down the road, turn left onto Route 805. You are in the western Lower Galilee, an area in which Arab villages predominate. In recent years a fair number of new Jewish settlements, mostly moshavim, have been built in the area. Because of the scarcity of available farm-land, these communities have developed new sources of income, from computer-programming and high-technology electronics to manufactured gemstones and vacation facilities.

Nine kms. (five-and-a-half miles) from our last turn-off, turn right up a good road towards Yodefat. Before reaching the village, a road to the right heads for the new settlement of Manof. This is one of the *mitzpim,* or look-outs, the name given to many of the new settlements as a result of their hill-top locations. The settlement operates a number of comfortable holiday cottages and a small factory which cuts and mounts zircon jewelry.

Back on up to Yodefat: there was a town here in Old Testament times, but the place is best remembered for Josephus' Last Stand. Joseph the son of Mattatiah was the man's real Hebrew name, and at the beginning of the Great Revolt of the Jews against the Romans in A.D. 66, he was sent to organize resistance in the Galilee. Among the towns he fortified was Yodefat. The Romans began their reconquest of the country in this area. After 47 days of siege Yodefat fell, and its population was butchered. Joseph and 40 companions escaped to a cave where they made a suicide pact (shades of Masada still to come). As lots were drawn, the wily Joseph succeeded in being one of the last two left alive, and persuaded his companion that perhaps the pact was not such a great idea after all. They surrendered to the Romans, who spared their lives. Joseph then became a favorite of General (later Emperor) Vespasian, changed his name to Josephus Flavius, and accompanied the Roman campaign, faithfully recording it for posterity in *The Jewish War.* While Josephus' historical writings are inestimably valuable, his personal conduct is, to put it mildly, a source of controversy and ambivalence among contemporary scholars.

Modern Yodefat was founded as a moshav by a group of ex-classmates from a Haifa high school who were inspired by a teacher, one Dr. Shechter, to establish their own community where they would strive to create an unusual and high standard of living. Until it was joined recently by settlements like Manof, Yodefat lived for years in a sort of splendid isolation. There is a look-out tower at Yodefat, and the fine view of the Bet Netofa Valley to the south alone can justify the trip.

Between Acre and Nahariya

Only 10 kms. (six miles), but no less than eight farming villages, separate these two coastal towns. About halfway between them on your right is a multi-tier, arched aqueduct built in 1815 to bring water from the Kabri springs to Acre. Other aqueducts in the area date from the slightly earlier era of el-Jazzar.

Right next to the aqueduct is the large, square museum building of Kibbutz Lochamei Hageta'ot, the Ghetto Fighters. The kibbutz was founded in 1949 by survivors of the Polish and Lithuanian Jewish ghettoes, and veterans of the ghetto uprisings against the Nazis. The Museum and Research Center was established in 1951 to pay tribute to their compatriots, and to perpetuate the memory of those tragic events. Unlike the Museum of Yad Vashem in Jerusalem which relates the Holocaust story chronologically, Lochamei Hagetta'ot has halls devoted to different themes—the Nazi concentration and death camps; the ghettoes and the deportations; Jewish involvement in the partisan movements of Europe; the Warsaw Ghetto Uprising; and "Vilna—the 'Jerusalem of Lithuania' ".

Situated right on the Mediterranean shore, Shavei Zion, a mile or so north, was founded in 1938 by Jewish immigrants from a single village in Germany's Black Forest. It functions as a moshav shitufi, a form of settlement combining the collective economic organization of a kibbutz with the more individualistic family life of a moshav. In 1955, a Byzantine church with a fine mosaic floor was uncovered on the site.

Immediately opposite Shavei Zion, a turn-off to the right leads through avocado orchards and past greenhouses to the unusual village of Nes Ammim. It is an ecumenical, devoutly-Christian community drawn mainly from Holland, Germany, Switzerland, and the United States. The community's express purpose is to revolutionize both the form and substance of the somewhat bloodstained Jewish–Christian relationship of the last 1,900 years. Referring to St. Paul's Epistle to the Romans, the Nes Ammim movement believes that missionary activity among Jews is unscriptural, and that as Christian guests among a Jewish majority for the first time in two millennia, they are in a position to give positive and concrete expression to this belief, to "do" rather than just "declare." The idea of such a community was mooted in 1960 by a Dutch mission doctor whose 10 years of working in Tiberias had brought him to a "re-orientation in his vision of Judaism and Israel." The deep and still-fresh trauma of the Holocaust, and the proximity of a kibbutz founded by Holocaust survivors (Lochamei Hagetta'ot) did not make Israelis at either official or grass-roots level immediately receptive to the idea of a Christian community in their midst. But the sincerity of the Nes Ammim movement's declared policy of "lived solidarity" with and in Israel was undeniable. The green light was eventually given, and in 1964 the first settlers arrived. Taking their name from Isaiah 11:10, Nes Ammim—an Ensign of the Peoples —has pioneered export-quality rose-cultivation in the area, and, despite its relatively small permanent population, has put itself on the local map as an economically stable settlement and a positive presence in the region.

A Honeymoon Hideway

Nahariya was founded in 1934 by German Jews who had come to eke out a living from the soil. More familiar with soirees and seminars than poultry and plows, they sweated on their little farms by day and read their agricultural manuals by night. Their meagre and hard-earned returns on such exhausting labor were hardly enough to keep body and soul together. For new means of livelihood, Nahariya's residents turned to its great natural resource—its location on one of the country's best beaches. Families began taking in paying guests for the holiday season, and Nahariya as a resort was born. The town has grown, of course—there are over 30,000 citizens now—but it retains the old world charm that drew honeymooning couples to it in the '40s. Its strawberries and cream were legendary among British soldiers on leave in World War II, and its warm hospitality made it a favorite rest-and-recreation stop.

Many of the veteran German-speaking settlers never adapted to a Hebrew culture. Oldtimers still relate with relish the tale of Nahariya's prompt reaction to the British Peel Commission back in 1937 which had devised a partition plan for Palestine in which the future Jewish State would exclude Nahariya. The town's staunch residents immediately telegraphed Jewish statesman Chaim Weizmann: "Whatever happens, Nahariya will remain German!" Similarly, the story is told of a veteran restaurateur whose establishment was popular with British soldiers in the War years. One soldier, to show off the smattering of Hebrew he'd picked up, complimented Max on the food: "Me'od tov. Yesh yotair?" ("Very good. Is there more?") Max stared uncomprehendingly. The soldier repeated it. Max turned to his wife and said "Ich werde nie Englisch verstehen!" ("I'll never understand English!")

In the '40s, the beach and relative remoteness of Nahariya made it a preferred landing spot for several of the small, overcrowded ships with their cargo of desperate Jewish refugees, playing maritime hide-and-seek with British destroyers. Just north of the town, a monument on the beach, made up of the hull-plates of just such a ship, recalls that dramatic chapter in the pre-State history of Israel.

A site near the shore, found and excavated in 1947, seems to indicate that Nahariya's connection with newly-weds is not a modern phenomenon. It was a Canaanite or Phoenician temple of the 18th–17th centuries B.C., dedicated to the sea goddess, Astarte, who, among the other tasks in her crowded portfolio, was concerned with love and fertility. Some claim a now-submarine spring cures barrenness even today.

The small Ga'aton stream runs through the town's main street under the shade of huge eucalyptus trees. Colorful horse-drawn carriages take visitors on a leisurely ride through the town. Fine, safe beaches, an Olympic-size swimming pool, a Lido, and a sailing/windsurfing center are all here for the vacationer seeking activity or indolence. At night the main street takes on a distinctly Continental atmosphere with its crowds of strollers and sidewalk cafés, and pizza and apple-strudel hold their own against the felafel and bourekas.

Yehi'am—the Convoy and the Castle

From Nahariya, Route 85 strikes directly east towards the Upper Galilee via Ma'alot and Sasa (see *The Upper Galilee and Golan* chapter). Four kms. (two-and-a-half miles) from Nahariya is the Kabri intersection. Turn right (south) and half-a-mile further on, a sign-posted side-road to the left takes you to the memorial to the Yehi'am Convoy. In the bitter fighting of the early stages of the War of Independence in 1948, many Jewish towns and settlements were isolated and besieged. Among these were Yad Mordechai in the south, the Etzion Bloc in Judea—and, indeed, Jerusalem itself—and, in the western Galilee, Nahariya and Kibbutz Yehi'am. At the end of March 1948, a convoy of home-designed armored trucks set out from Haifa to bring supplies and reinforcements to Yehi'am. The element of surprise brought the convoy as far as Nahariya without incident, but at a loop in the narrow, east-bound road (as it was then), the convoy was ambushed and wiped out after a 10-hour battle. The route and details of the battle are inscribed at the memorial site.

To get to Yehi'am itself, return to the Kabri intersection and continue east. Just three kms. (two miles) further, the road to Yehi'am breaks off to your right. Kibbutz Yehi'am is built next to a great medieval castle, and it is this we have come to see. This was the Crusader Castle Judin, apparently built by the Templars in the late-12th century, and transferred to the Order of Teutonic Knights in the early-13th. It was destroyed in 1265 by the Crusaders' nemesis, the Mamluk sultan Baybars, but even its ruins were impressive enough to be incorporated into the Bedouin sheikh Daher el-Omar's palatial citadel 500 years later. It has been partially restored and the site landscaped by the National Parks Authority.

Achziv, Not A Town, But . . .

Well, it was a town once, and an important one at that. Like Acre it was a Canaanite city in the days of Joshua, assigned to the tribe of Asher but only captured by the Israelites centuries later. Because of its location on the coastal road—about five kms. (three miles) north of modern Nahariya—it came under Phoenician control about 3,000 years ago. Today it is a cluster of resort-oriented sites.

Club Mediterranée's huts sprawl over a prime piece of sandy beachfront. Adjoining the club is a public beach, built to satisfy the local citizens who protested the Club's acquisition of such choice sea frontage. The tel of ancient Achziv just to the north of it has been turned into a national park with extra-safe lagoon swimming. Few of its ancient buildings remain, and the interesting old structures seen today are relatively recent. The site is presided over by a somewhat graceless old house on a hill inhabited by a middle-aged latter-day Bohemian type who for years resisted Government pressure to dislodge him from this valuable and beautiful spot, and, tongue-in-cheek, eventually declared himself the independent Achzivland. Across the highway is the access road to Kibbutz Gesher Haziv with a fine guest house; its membership includes many former Americans.

A stone's-throw north, and the road crosses the sometimes dry riverbed of the Keziv Stream, taking its name from the ancient city and passing it on to the modern kibbutz. Just east of the road is the old railway bridge in use until the '40s. On a clear night in June, 1946, the Haganah simultaneously blew up 11 bridges linking Palestine with neighboring Arab countries. The team attacking the Achziv bridges was spotted by British sentries before they could reach their target. A chance bullet hit the explosives which one of the men carried on his back. The resulting explosion did in fact blow up the bridge, but 14 men were killed. A memorial marks the spot.

The Achziv complex is completed by a campground, a good youth hostel, a hamburger joint, and a field study center of the Nature Preservation Society, all a bit up the road. In addition to its exploration of the mountains and valleys of the Western Galilee, the field study center has a special interest in shore-line marine life, and a day with its guides poking around Mediterranean rock-pools is an unforgettable, off-the-beaten-track experience.

Montfort—the Mountain of Strength

Just north of Achziv, and eight kms. (five miles) out of Nahariya, a highway breaks off to the right to the little town of Shlomi, and beyond that into the rugged mountains of the Upper Galilee to meet the Ma'alot road at Sasa near Mount Meron. About 11 kms. (seven miles) from the intersection, and just beyond Kibbutz Eilon, a side road on the right is marked as the J.N.F. Goren Forest. A few minutes' drive on a hard dirt road brings you to a picnic spot and a view that is at one and the same time powerful, evocative, and supremely tranquil. You are upstream on Nahal Keziv, the same Keziv Stream spanned by the bridges at Achziv (see above). And before you is Montfort.

The prospect is magnificent. The slopes of Nahal Keziv are steep and densely wooded, and the stark ruins of one of Israel's finest medieval fortresses seem to claw skyward from a narrow spur of hill 180 meters (585 ft.) above the bed of the bubbling stream. What is particularly interesting about the fortress is why it should be here in the first place. It has no port like Caesarea, commands no heights like Safed, controls no highway like Ma'ale Adummim, and guards no border like Belvoir. In the 12th century it was a small fort, nothing more, to protect and administer the domains of the lords of the manor at Mi'ilya not far away. Lost to the Muslims in 1187, it was regained in 1192, and in 1228 sold to the Order of the Teutonic Knights of St. Mary. They expanded the fortress on a grand scale, translated its French name to Starkenberg, and withdrew their headquarters to it from the city of Acre. Here they kept their archives and their treasure until their capitulation to the Mamluk sultan Baybars in 1271. They were allowed to leave in peace, taking their possessions with them. The archives have survived in their entirety, a treasure trove for scholars.

A reasonably good path leads down to the gorge, and the approach to the fortress itself is from its south side, on your right as you look at it from here. It's a stiff climb back up. The castle is also accessible through the Arab village of Mi'ilya, 16 kms. (10 miles) east of Nahariya on Route 89. Most visitors will find it sufficient to contemplate the quiet beauty of the view over a picnic lunch.

The Sea Grottoes of Rosh Hanikra

You have been following Route 4 all the way up the coast: Rosh Hanikra is the end of the road. Just beyond the Frontier Ahead sign is Lebanon. Here the high mountain ridge descends to the sea, but finding no pass through or around it, the way even in ancient times had to climb over the chalk cliffs as it headed north to the Land of the Phoenicians. The ascent was known as the Ladder of Tyre, after the first major Phoenician city beyond the ridge. Its Hebrew source, Sulam Tzor, is the official name of the modern regional council.

Even before you get in line for the short cable-car ride to the grottoes, take a moment to look at the fine view back down the coast. Note the three levels of coastline reflecting the changing conditions over the last several million years—the present shoreline, the fields of Kibbutz Rosh Hanikra above and behind it, and the kibbutz itself on another terrace above and behind that. Still clearly visible is the route of the railway line, now mostly a dirt road, built through the hillside in 1943 by New Zealand army engineers to extend the Cairo–Tel Aviv–Haifa line to Beirut. You will see its two tunnels at the mouth of the grottoes below.

Many visitors find the grottoes here no less fascinating than the better-known ones at Capri. Over eons of time, the waves have pounded away at the white chalk cliffs, reaming out the vertical cracks in the cliff face to form these natural wonders. Man-made corridors lead from one section to another, offering many spots to lean on the railings and be mesmerized by the heave and crash of the waves. The grottoes are accessible in almost any weather; in fact, the rougher the sea, the better the show.

Powerful local swimmers sometimes like to swim around the bluff and into the grottoes, but the currents are tricky, the tide-pull onto the rocks is strong, and straying over the invisible border at sea is not appreciated by the guards on either side of it.

PRACTICAL INFORMATION FOR
THE WESTERN GALILEE

TELEPHONE CODES. This whole region is within the Haifa dialing area. The area code (04) need not be used if calling from within the district.

GUEST HOUSES. Bet Hava (M), at Shavei Zion, 7 kms. (4½ miles) north of Acre (tel. 922391/2). 85 rooms, all with airconditioning, 57 with bath, 28 with shower. Beach, pool, sports facilities, tennis. Bar, coffee-shop. **Gesher Haziv** (M), a kibbutz 5 kms. (3 miles) north of Nahariya (tel. 825715). 48 rooms, all with airconditioning and bath. Bar, pool, sauna, wind-surfing club. Evening lectures. AE, DC, MC, V. **Nes Ammim** (M), turn-off to Reg-ba, 7 kms. (4½ miles) north of Acre (tel. 922566). 48 rooms with bath and airconditioning. Pool, bar, self-serve restaurant. Lectures.

Youth Hostel. Yad LeYad, near Achziv (tel. 921343). 260 beds. Well-run, family rooms available, members' kitchen. Hamburger/beer joint next door.

Camping. Achziv Camping Site, Mobile Post (tel. 921792). 100 yards from the beach with very good facilities. Open Apr. through Dec. **Kabri,** 5 kms. (3 miles) inland, Mobile Post Oshrat (tel. 921476). Transportation to beach. Open Apr. through Dec. **Liman,** near the Youth Hostel (tel. 926206). Fine location.

HOW TO GET AROUND. Egged buses operate out of Acre and Nahariya, and access to sites on main highways is reasonably easy. However, buses on the secondary roads are far less frequent, so check schedules. Sherut (shared taxis) ply between Nahariya, Acre, and Haifa. A slower but cheaper and more pleasant way to go is by train; Nahariya–Acre–Haifa–Tel Aviv or Jerusalem (or vice versa, of course).

HISTORIC SITES AND MUSEUMS. Achziv, about 4 kms. (2½ miles) north of Nahariya. Ancient **tel,** now landscaped, with beach. (N.P.)

LOCHAMEI HAGETA'OT. 5 kms. (3 miles) north of Acre. **Museum** with theme areas related to the Holocaust.

MONTFORT. Crusader fortress. To Mi'ilya by car on Rte. 89, 16 kms. (10 miles) east of Nahariya and then hike; or by car to an overlook via Rte. 899 at intersection 8 kms. (5 miles) north of Nahariya, and off to Goren Forest about 12 kms. (7½ miles) east.

ROSH HANIKRA. At the border, 11 kms. (7 miles) north of Nahariya. Spectacular sea **grottoes** reached by cable-car. Open 8.30–5.30.

PRACTICAL INFORMATION FOR ACRE

TOURIST INFORMATION. Government Tourist Information Office, Municipality Building (tel. 910251). **Municipal Tourist Information Office,** at entrance to Subterranean Crusader City (tel. 910251).

HOTELS. Argaman Motel (M), on seashore at entrance to Acre (tel. 916691). 75 rooms with bath and airconditioning. Beach, bar, piano bar, grill room, self-serve restaurant.

Youth Hostel. Box 1090, Acre (tel. 911982). 120 beds, family rooms available, members' kitchen. In a converted palatial Turkish mansion next to the sea walls, in the heart of the old city. Single women are advised to treat the local young men with friendly caution.

RESTAURANTS. Locals prefer the **Monte Carlo** next to el-Jazzar Mosque, with Continental and local dishes. **Achim Ouda** in the souk, but also accessible from Khan el-Faranj, specializes in Middle-Eastern salads and grilled shishkebab. Right on the harbor is **Abu Cristo** with fish and other seafood, and the smaller **Ptolemais** with a similar selection. **Migdalor** at the lighthouse serves fish and light meals. **Zor** on the sea just outside the old city walls features European food.

New Acre's main thoroughfare, Ben Ami St., has the usual range of inexpensive eateries including local food, pizza, and cafés. Just off Ben Ami St. is a whole line of felafel stands, where you can heap the salads of your choice on the chickpea balls in your pita bread.

 HISTORIC SITES AND MUSEUMS. Bahai Gardens, north of Acre. Open Sun., Mon., Fri., Sat. 9–12.

Crusader Subterranean City, opposite el-Jazzar Mosque. Hospitaller Quarter, Knights' Hall, and St. John's Crypt. Open Sat. to Thurs. 9–4.45, Fri. 9–12.45.

Khan el Umdan. Beautiful 18th-century Turkish caravansarai. Venue for some summer events.

Municipal Museum, housed in the old Turkish bath. Archeology, ethnography, history. Can be visited on the same ticket as Crusader City. Open Sat. to Thurs. 9–4.45, Fri. 9–12.45.

Museum of Heroism, Hahagana St. just inside the city walls. Located in 18th-century Citadel/20th-century prison. A record of the Jewish resistance movement in the '40s and the mass escape from prison in 1947. Open Sat. to Thurs. 9–5 (winter 9–4), Fri. 9–12.30.

Sea Walls, built in the late-18th and early-19th centuries. Promenade on walls.

 ENTERTAINMENT. Summer series "Nights of Acre" with variety of offerings in different venues. Watch for listings. Bar/nightclub **Le Coq d'Or** inside Old City.

RELIGIOUS SERVICES. Church of St. John the Baptist, near the lighthouse. Catholic mass in English, Sun. 10 A.M.

PRACTICAL INFORMATION FOR NAHARIYA

 TOURIST INFORMATION. Municipal and Government Tourist Information Office, Egged Building, Sederot Ga'aton (tel. 922126).

 HOTELS. Carlton (M–E), 23 Sederot Ga'aton (tel. 922211/6). 198 rooms with bath and airconditioning. Nahariya's premier hotel, with bar, piano bar, nightclub, heated pool, tennis. AE, MC, V.

Astar (M), 27 Sederot Ga'aton (tel. 923431). 26 rooms with bath and airconditioning. Coffeeshop, T.V. on request.

Frank (M), 4 Ha'aliya St. (tel. 920278/9). 50 airconditioned rooms, 18 with bath, 32 with shower only. Bar, T.V. on request. AE, V.

Pallas Athene (M), 28 Hama'apilim St. (tel. 922381/2). 53 rooms with bath and airconditioning. Fine views overlooking the Mediterranean. Bar, piano bar, nightclub, health club, sauna. V.

Erna House (I), 29 Jabotinsky St. (tel. 920170). 11 rooms with shower and airconditioning. The least expensive on our list.

Kalman (I), 27 Jabotinsky St. (tel. 920355). 12 rooms, 4 with bath, all with airconditioning. Bar, coffeeshop, self-serve restaurant. Family-run.

Karl Laufen (I), 31 Hameyasdim St. (tel. 920130). 28 rooms with shower only. Partly airconditioned.

Panorama (I), 6 Hama'apilim St. (tel. 920555). 25 rooms, half with bath, half shower only; all airconditioned. Nice view of the Mediterranean.

Rosenblatt (I), 59 Weizmann St. (tel. 923469). 35 rooms, most with shower only, all airconditioned. v.

 RESTAURANTS. Sederot Ga'aton, the main street, is lined with restaurants and coffeeshops, many of them with an open sidewalk section. Some, like the **Penguin**, have dancing. In warm weather the townspeople take to the streets, and the sidewalks are as thronged as at any time in the day. Two Chinese restaurants, and the French-style **Café de la Paix**. **El Gaucho** specializes in good grills, and **Donau** has an interesting Romanian menu.

 HISTORICAL SITES AND MUSEUM. Remains of an ancient **Canaanite temple** are located along the shore. The **Municipal Museum** is housed in the Municipality Building.

 ENTERTAINMENT. Children's Amusement Park with special boat ride lies near the beach at the end of the Ga'aton Stream running through the town. Nightlife includes the disco at the Carlton Hotel.

 SPORTS. There is a good beach and a public **swimming** pool on Hama'aplim St. Water sports center for **sailing**, etc. Recall Riding Academy (tel. 920534) near the Police Station, does **horseback** tours of the area. **Hiking** every Saturday with local nature lovers' club; contact Mr. Zeiger (tel. 920246), or Mr. Dayan (tel. 921923).

THE JEZRE'EL VALLEY AND
THE LOWER GALILEE

Crossroads of the North

Lush might well be the first word that comes to mind to describe the valleys of the Jezre'el and the Jordan, but they were not always so. The early pioneers in the teens and '20s of this century found swamps riddled with malaria, fields neglected for generations, and rocks that had to be removed by hand before any plowing could be done. Indeed, it was only because nobody else wanted the land that they could buy it at all. The co-operative village of Merhavia, next to Afula, for example, was founded in 1911 under such conditions, and was forced to build its cemetery before its first house was completed. Today, the Jezre'el Valley—in Hebrew simply Ha'emek, the Valley—is generally regarded as the most fertile in Israel.

The Jezre'el Valley forms more or less an equilateral triangle in shape, each side about 40 kms. (25 miles) long, fixed by its points of Jenin at the entrance to Samaria in the south, Mount Tabor in the northeast, and Bet She'arim and the passage to Haifa Bay in the northwest. From Afula, a narrow extension, the Harod Valley, links it with the Bet She'an Valley, part of the Jordan Rift, to the east. South of Bet She'an the land rapidly deteriorates to semi-desert, but to the north it continues as the Upper Jordan Valley, green and eye-pleasing, for some 25 kms. (16 miles) to the Sea of Galilee.

In antiquity, as today, major arterial roads crossed these valleys. The famous Via Maris linking Egypt and Mesopotamia separated into three branches as it left the Mediterranean coastal plain and penetrated inland. Each of the three followed a natural pass, and at the mouth of each pass, where it joined the Jezre'el Valley, a city stood sentinel. The most important of these roads was the central one, and Megiddo was built to guard its mouth. Further north, Yokne'am effectively commanded another pass, while to the south Ta'anach monitored traffic along the Dothan Valley. The latter is familiar to many as the route of the Egypt-bound Ishmaelite caravan to which Joseph was sold by his brothers (Genesis 37).

One of the finest descriptions of these three branches, and incidentally one of the earliest written accounts of a battle, was found on an Egyptian *stele,* an inscribed stone slab, from the reign of Pharaoh Thutmose III. It relates how in 1468 B.C. the cities of Canaan (Israel) rose against Pharaoh Thutmose III, their Egyptian overlord. Thutmose marched into Canaan to quell the revolt. Faced with the choice of which of the three roads into the Jezre'el Valley to take, Thutmose chose the central, against the advice of his generals, emerging through a narrow defile at Megiddo. Here he surprised the Canaanite armies and crushed them.

This scenario has been repeated numerous times throughout history. In 609 B.C. King Josiah of Judah was killed here trying to stop the northerly advance of an Egyptian army. The Romans kept a legion to guard the pass. And in 1919 General Allenby's brilliant outmaneuvering of the Turks and Germans in the Jezre'el Valley secured the Galilee, and thus the whole country, winning Allenby the title Viscount Allenby of Megiddo.

Megiddo: A Tale of 25 Cities

It is known that there was a prehistoric settlement at Megiddo, but the city came into its own in the great "urbanization movement" of the Early Bronze Age (Early Canaanite Period) about 5,000 years ago. An altar and outlines of temples from this period can be seen on the site. The Late Canaanite gate of Megiddo has been uncovered too, possibly the very one shut in anticipation of Thutmose III's attack in the 15th century B.C. But the Biblical echoes of Megiddo are the ones that most visitors listen for. All in all, in several different archeological excavations, 25 levels of settlement, one upon the other, have been unearthed here, revealing 35 centuries of history.

The buildings at the foot of Megiddo, once used as the headquarters of the University of Chicago's archeological expedition (1925–39), house a small museum. The artifacts on display are few, but there are some interesting visual aids worth your time—a map, some schematic and chronological diagrams of the tel (the mound of Megiddo), and a model of the whole tel showing an artist's reconstruction of some of its structures.

Like Hatzor to the north and Gezer to the south, Megiddo is identified as one of King Solomon's "chariot cities," a regional administrative and military center. The ramp leading to the excavations at Megiddo deposits you immediately opposite Solomon's gate, almost identical in design and dimensions to those found at Hatzor and Gezer. For a long time the chariot stables too were related to the time of Solomon, but Solomon's city wall was later found below this level, forcing a revision of the dating. Apparently they were built by Ahab, King of Israel, who we know to have had a substantial chariot army in the 9th century B.C.

The most impressive and exciting part of one's visit here is the water system. Originally the people of Megiddo had to venture outside their city walls to reach the spring at the bottom of the mound. In the 9th century B.C. they replaced this vulnerable system by a piece of master engineering: they dug a vertical shaft from within the city to the level of the spring, and joined it to the spring itself by a horizontal tunnel. With access from within the city secured, they blocked the outer entrance to the spring, thereby both protecting their own water supply while depriving the enemy of his. The evidence of building—chisel-marks and so on, and many of the original rock-hewn steps—is clearly visible in the water system. It's 170 steps down the shaft, and 83 up the other side, bringing you out a 10-minute walk away from the parking-lot where you entered the site.

There is a fine view from two look-out points on Megiddo over the valley that has so often rung to the clash of arms. The very sound of the city's name, one fancies, was a clarion-call to war: "Har Megiddo" (Mount Megiddo), of which St. John made one thundering word, Armageddon—the ultimate battlefield.

The Spring of Harod

The town of Afula, 10 kms. (six miles) northeast of Megiddo, has a reputation for the best *garinim* (roasted sunflower seeds) in Israel. But if those are not on your shopping list, you can bypass the town via the Ta'anach settlements and Kibbutz Yizre'el (site of Ahab's winter capital and Jezebel's death) to the Harod Valley.

On the right (south) is Mount Gilboa, a spur of the greater Samaria range further south. On your left is the high, pointed Hill of Moreh. From the Afula–Bet She'an road, a turn-off to the right to the village of Gidona takes you to the beautiful park of Ma'ayan Harod. Here you will find the Spring of Harod, where Gideon gathered the Israelites for battle, "and the camp of Midian was north of them, by the Hill of Moreh, in the valley" (Judges 7). In order to avoid a battle in which the Israelites could claim that their own strength had given them victory, God separated the army at the spring into those that lapped water with their tongues "as a dog laps," and those that knelt down to drink. The "lappers," a mere 300 in all, were selected for the battle. Their tactics were psychological in the main. Equipped with rams' horns, and clay jars with flaming torches hidden in them, the Israelites stealthily surrounded the Midianite camp. Woken by the nightmarish din of 300 horn-blasts, 300 crashing jars, 300 shouts, and the sudden appearance of 300 blazing torches, the Midianites were panicked into flight, Gideon's men on their heels, and the battle was won.

Some 24 centuries later, in A.D. 1260, a very different battle was fought here. The Mongols from the Asian steppes had penetrated this far south, and threatened to overrun the region. At this very spring (Ain Jaloud in Arabic) they were stopped by the powerful Mamluk army of Egypt. It is told that the Mongols, having learned to respect Mamluk strength, later embraced Islam as "the religion of the strong."

In the late-'30s this same isolated grove and the wooded hillside above it were the training grounds of Orde Wingate's Special Night Squads, anti-terror units whose members were drawn from the ranks of the Haganah, the clandestine Jewish army. This experience in unorthodox commando tactics was to prove invaluable in the War of Independence a decade later when many S.N.S. veterans had risen to command positions in the fledgling Israeli Defense Forces. Today, Ma'ayan Harod is a superb park of lawns and immense eucalyptus trees, and a swimming pool fed by the spring.

On the opposite side of the main road and a kilometer or so towards Bet She'an is Kibbutz Ein Harod, or rather two kibbutzim of the same name. Established in 1921, and on its present site since 1927, the kibbutz was rent asunder in 1953 by the passionate debate that swept socialist circles in the country at that time. The issue was one of ideological orientation, and so fiercely was it felt that the communal dining hall was partitioned between the two factions until one had formally seceded and established itself as an independent community next door. The experience was repeated elsewhere in the country, but since those heady days the two movements have moved from a *modus vivendi* to active co-operation in many areas, and subsequently to a remerger. Ein Harod (Me'uchad) has Bet Sturman, a fine museum of the Natural and Human History of the area, as well as an art museum functioning as a showcase for kibbutz artists.

Bet Alfa and Sachne

Three kms. (two miles) beyond the Ein Harod gas station towards Bet She'an, a secondary road (Route 669) turns off to the right (at the white-washed prison complex). The first settlement you reach is Kibbutz Heftziba, on the grounds of which was found the mosaic floor of the Bet Alfa synagogue. Do not be confused—*Kibbutz* Bet Alfa is the next village along. There is a sign on the main road pointing to the site; turn left immediately you enter the main gate.

The mosaics were unearthed in 1928 in a remarkable bit of serendipity. Members of Kibbutz Heftziba were digging an irrigation trench when their tools hit the stone floor. It was immediately excavated to reveal the best-preserved mosaic of its period found in Israel. An Aramaic inscription in the mosaic dedicates it in the reign of Justinian, that is to say the second quarter of the 6th century A.D. A Greek inscription alongside credits the workmanship to one Marianos and his son, Aninas. The whole structure is oriented towards Jerusalem, in accordance with Jewish tradition. There are technically more sophisticated mosaics in Israel, but the charm and loveliness of the floor of Bet Alfa lies as much as anything in its touching simplicity.

The main part is divided lengthwise into three panels. The upper one declares in no uncertain terms what the building was. It contains all the quintessentially Jewish symbols in use at the time: the Ark flanked by the seven-branched *Menorah,* the *shofar* (ram's horn), lion, incense shovel, and *lulav* and *etrog* (palm-branch and citron) used on the Feast of Tabernacles (Sukkot). The middle panel is at once the most interesting and surprising: the Hellenistic wheel of the Zodiac, complete with human figures, all labeled in Hebrew, and, in the center, the sun-god Helios driving his chariot. And this in a synagogue! Yet scholars do not seriously believe that the mosaic represents a divergent, non-orthodox Jewish movement of the time, though obviously there was greater laxity in interpreting the commandment not to make "any graven image." What is likely is that it was simply a conventional way of representing the orderly annual cycle—the four seasons are also depicted by human figures at each corner—without attempting any representation of God Himself. The third panel relates the drama of Abraham's near-sacrifice of his son Isaac (Genesis 22).

We are at the foot of Mount Gilboa, the mountain cursed by David ("let there be no rain or dew on you"), for here King Saul and his sons, including Jonathan, were killed fighting the Philistines. "On the morrow, when the Philistines came to strip the slain, they found Saul and his three sons fallen on Mount Gilboa. And they cut off his head, and stripped off his armor, and sent messengers throughout the land of the Philistines, to carry the good news to their idols and to the people. They put his armor in the temple of Ashtaroth, and they fastened his body to the wall of Beth-shan." (I Samuel 31:8–10). These Philistines were a long way from their home on the country's southern coastal plain, deep into Israelite territory, an indication of how weak King Saul had become. The Bible relates that after their defeat, the Israelites "forsook their cities and fled; and the Philistines came and dwelt in them." And lo and behold the excavation of the tel of Bet She'an brought to light Philistine anthropoid clay coffins (now on display at the Israel Museum, Jerusalem).

Just east of Bet Alfa, an avenue of palm trees leads to Sachne, a beautiful landscape of natural pools and greenery. The springs here have a year-round temperature of about 28° C (82.4° F), making them popular even on a fine winter day. In Hebrew, the site is known as Gan Hashlosha, the Garden of the Three, in memory of three Jewish pioneers (including Sturman of Ein Harod) who were killed by an Arab landmine in 1938. Changing facilities and a restaurant are provided.

Bet She'an and the Valley of the Jordan

The plain in which Bet She'an is situated is the wide meeting point of two valleys—the Jezre'el/Harod and the Jordan—and thus of two ancient routes of travel. This was the key to the strategic location of the ancient city, whose tel dominates the northern part of today's small town. A University of Pennsylvania expedition began excavating the tel in 1921, and unearthed abundant evidence of Bet She'an's role as an

Egyptian provincial capital in the Late Bronze and Early Iron Ages, 14th–12th centuries B.C. Bet She'an declined in the late Old Testament period, and was revived only in the 3rd century B.C. as the Hellenistic city of Scythopolis. Under the Romans it became, for a while, the capital of the Decapolis, a league of 10 Hellenistic cities in the region.

The most magnificent surviving structure of Bet She'an is its Roman theater, built around A.D. 200. Although the upper tiers of the theater have not survived, the archeologists who excavated the site estimate its one-time capacity at 8,000 people. Built in an attractive combination of black basalt and white limestone, the theater was primarily used for dramatic productions. Sporting events would more likely have taken place in the amphitheater discovered close by. The theater was entered through vaulted passages called *vomitoria*. Near the vomitoria are stone basins, built as part of the whole structure, with apertures between them and the seating area. It has been suggested that the summer breezes wafting over a water-filled basin would create a cool draft through the aperture and provide airconditioning for the audience. Behind the wide stone stage was a richly decorated structure, the *scaena*, with doorways through which the actors made their entrances. Some of the original stone-work and statuary were found among the debris on the site.

If you have the time and like an off-the-beaten-track experience, stop in at the Bet She'an Museum. It's not even signposted, but you should have no difficulty finding it. It is in an old building, at various times a Byzantine church, medieval mosque, and a Turkish inn, on the right just a few hundred meters north of the Central Bus Station on the Tiberias road. Here you can get the key to the nearby 6th-century Byzantine Monastery of Lady Marie to see its beautiful mosaics. But Bet She'an's history buff is Aryeh, the "curator" of this little museum, who for about $1.50 per person will take you in your car on the "official" half-hour tour of Bet She'an's undeveloped sites that even the tour guides do not know.

South of Bet She'an are a group of kibbutzim founded in the late-'30s as tower-and-stockade settlements, prefabricated wooden structures that went up literally overnight to establish a security belt in this border region. One of them, Tirat Zvi, has another claim to fame: it registered the highest temperature ever recorded in Israel. In June 1941 the thermometer read 54°C (129.2°F) in the shade.

Belvoir—Star of the Winds

There is no shortage of impressive Crusader buildings in Israel. Despite their small permanent numbers in the Holy Land, the Crusaders built a great deal and on a grand scale. Belvoir, meaning Beautiful View, was not the largest fortress in the realm, but for spectacular location and massive fortifications, it had few rivals. (Turn left off Route 90 13 kms. (eight miles) north of Bet She'an. The road from Kibbutz Ein Harod via Moledet is passable but very bad in places.)

The medieval history of Belvoir is short. The Hospitallers (Knights of St. John) acquired the site in 1168 and completed the fortress five years later. In 1187, the Crusader armies were crushed by Saladin at the Horns of Hattin not far from the Sea of Galilee, bringing to an end the Latin Kingdom of Jerusalem that had been brought into being by the First Crusade in 1099. The Crusaders were swept out of the country. Soon Tyre, today in southern Lebanon, was the only city remaining to the Crusaders, and Belvoir their only fortress. For one-and-a-half years the Muslims tried unsuccessfully to breach its defences. The knights for their part were not inactive, and from time to time sallied forth to attack the besiegers. Although Saladin succeeded eventually in undermining the outer eastern tower, the defenders retreated to an inner, equally impregnable part of the fortress. But though the Muslims could make little headway, with the rest of their kingdom gone the Christians saw no point in further resistance. They surrendered, and Saladin, in recognition of their bravery, allowed them safe passage to Tyre, their banners unfurled and held high. Around 1220, in the face of rumors that the Crusaders were coming again, Belvoir was dismantled by the Sultan of Damascus to prevent it falling into Crusader hands again.

From the parking lot, do not enter the fortress by the western bridge. Walk down its right side until you reach the panoramic view which alone justifies the trip. It is best in the afternoon. You are 550 meters (1,788 ft.) above the Jordan Valley floor. Crossing the dry moat and following the lines of the fortifications, you cannot but marvel at the strength of the place and appreciate how it resisted all assaults.

Three kms. (two miles) north of the Belvoir turn-off on the Jordan Valley road (Route 90) is Kibbutz Gesher. In May 1948 an invading Iraqi army crossed the Jordan opposite Gesher and attacked it.They failed to capture the settlement, and their advance on Belvoir was repulsed. A tiny old French-made cannon mounted by the Israelis at Belvoir managed to hit an Iraqi vehicle, and the unexpected intervention of "heavy" artillery convinced the Iraqis that the victorious road to Haifa was not paved with roses, and they retreated back across the river.

Twelve kms. (seven-and-a-half miles) north of Gesher and you reach the Sea of Galilee at the Tzemach Junction.

THE GALILEE HILL COUNTRY

Historically, you will find two major themes in the hill country of the Galilee. One is of the activities of Jesus, and in this context we shall visit Nazareth, Cana, Mount Tabor, and Nain (it is often to this land of hills and valleys that the Bible refers when it speaks of the Galilee). The other is the theme of Jewish life in the 2nd and 3rd centuries A.D., when, after the suppression of the Bar Kochba Revolt in A.D. 135, the center of the community and the seat of the Sanhedrin moved successively to Usha, Shefar'am, Bet She'arim, and Tzippori, before finally settling in Tiberias in the 4th century.

We keep coming back to the destruction of the Second Temple in A.D. 70 as a turning-point in Jewish history. It was not merely the destruction of *a* building, but of *the* building, the House of the Lord, of the entire ritual structure erected around it, and thus, too, of the fabric of day-to-day Jewish religious life. In addition, the wholesale killing that characterized the five-year Jewish War against the Romans, the Great Revolt, was followed by a further orgy of bloodshed once the revolt had been suppressed, and the exile and/or enslavement of substantial numbers of the populace. The extent and depth of this national-religious trauma cannot be exaggerated. It was only the inspired spiritual leadership of Rabbi Yohanan Ben-Zakkai and his colleagues, who fled the doomed city of Jerusalem for Yavne during the siege of the capital, that enabled anything to be salvaged from the wreckage. Among other things, their solution to the problem of the destroyed Temple and the now-ended sacrifices was to introduce a prayer service in which certain prayers and prayer times symbolized certain sacrifices that were now impossible. Many of these prayers are part of the Jewish liturgy to this day.

Whatever destruction Titus had left unfinished in A.D. 70, Hadrian completed in A.D. 135 with the end of the second revolt, the Bar Kochba revolt. Jerusalem was rebuilt as a pagan city, off-limits to the Jews, and for the next 500 years, until the Muslim conquest of Israel, the Galilee was to become the fulchrum of Jewish life and the center of its spiritual authority.

Yehuda Hanassi and the Mishna

A giant of a personality on the Jewish scene—or so he appears 1,800 years later—was Rabbi Yehuda Hanassi. Around the year A.D. 200 he took up residence in Bet She'arim, and almost at once the town became a magnet for pilgrims and petitioners. After his death, its attraction if anything increased, for it was deemed a special privilege and a good augury to be buried in the company of Rabenu Hakadosh, the Holy Teacher—for when the Messiah came, surely the Rabbi would be one of the first to be resurrected and follow him to Jerusalem?

The title of Nassi (literally, Prince or President) was at this time accorded to the head of the Jewish community in the country, responsible both for its internal workings and its relations with the Roman authorities. Some incumbents were men of great learning and spiritual authority, others were practical men and articulate diplomats who could liaise with the Romans on their terms. No-one combined both characteristics more brilliantly than Rabbi Yehuda Hanassi. Respected by the Romans, he was revered by the Jews.

Yehuda Hanassi's enduring achievement was the compilation of the *Mishna*, that at last committed to writing the Oral Tradition passed down by word of mouth for generations. If we may think of the Torah, the Law of Moses, the 613 do's and don'ts of the Bible, as the "Constitution" of ancient Israel, the Mishna (and the Gemara which followed it, together forming the Talmud) could be considered the "Supreme Court precedents." Rabbis would consider real-life situations in light of the Torah and give their legal opinions. The degree to which a particular opinion was considered authoritative depended on the prestige of the rabbi that had expressed it.

Bet She'arim—A Palatial City of the Dead

The site of Bet She'arim was excavated over some 13 years by Benjamin Mazar in the '30s and Nachman Avigad in the '50s. Bet She'arim is in a hilly area on the very edge of the Jezre'el Valley at its northwestern end near the narrow pass connecting it with the Haifa coastal plain. Access to the site is through the suburban community of Kiryat Tivon, about 21 kms. (13 miles) from Haifa on Route 75, or from the Yokne'am–Alonim bypass Route 722. The city flourished from the end of the 2nd century A.D. to A.D. 352 when it was destroyed by Gallus in the suppression of the Jewish revolt against him.

On the upper slopes of the hillside, a fine ancient synagogue and an olive-oil press are open to view on the left of the access road. More than 20 catacombs were unearthed in the excavations. The largest of these had 24 chambers and over 200 stone coffins, many with inscribed art motifs or inscriptions (now open to the public). The chalk hills of Bet She'arim were ideal for excavating such caves, but the harder limestone for the four-ton coffins had to be brought from Mount Carmel some distance away. A common form of burial was in an *arcosolium,* an arch-roofed niche in the wall in which the body was laid. In addition to the stone coffins, or sarcophagi, clay and lead coffins and the nails of wooden ones were found as well. Some 250 funerary inscriptions were found on the coffins—mostly in Greek with the rest in Hebrew, Aramaic, and Palmyrene—indicating that a good number of the denizens of this necropolis had come from beyond the town, some from as far abroad as Yemen and Mesopotamia.

No sarcophagus escaped the attention of grave-robbers in later centuries, for the dead were often buried with some of their possessions. Still visible on the coffins is an astonishing range of art motifs, both Jewish and pagan. The adjacent cave, once a water cistern, is now a modest but well-organized museum. Among the displays is a nine-ton glass slab, the largest piece of glass from the ancient world, and strong evidence of the industrial activity current in Bet She'arim in this period.

Many catacombs were closed by beautifully wrought stone doors, which still move smoothly on their stone hinges. One cave in particular, more ornate than the rest, carried the inscribed names of Rabbi Gamliel and Rabbi Shimon, the sons of Yehuda Hanassi. People at once jumped to the conclusion that here at last the final resting place of Yehuda Hanassi had been found. But there is no evidence to support the conclusion, and it remains merely an assumption of the uninformed. The site has been superbly landscaped by the National Parks Authority, its lawns and little cafeteria making it a favorite rest-stop.

The main road (Route 75) heads for Nazareth, or, via Nahalal to Afula and Bet She'an. From Afula, another road reaches Nazareth in 15 minutes, but let us follow the Afula–Tiberias road (Route 65). Afula Illit (Upper Afula) is built on the slopes of the Hill of Moreh, and has outstripped the older part of the town below. A bit further on, off to the right, is a small Arab village with a church in it. This is Nain, of Luke 7, where Jesus restored the widow's son to life. On the left (at the gas station) is Dovrat's fine roadside cafeteria, justly renowned for its goulash soup and apple strudel.

Looming ahead is the dome-like shape of Mount Tabor, at 588 meters (1,911 ft.) one of the highest and certainly the most dominating peaks of the Lower Galilee. Somewhere near its base the Israelite army of Deborah the Prophetess/Judge, under her general, Barak, routed the Canaanite chariot formations of Sisera. The latter fled to the tent of the Kenite woman Ya'el (Ja'el in the unfortunate English transliteration) to rest a while, but he misread her allegiances, and while he slept she drove a tent-peg through his temple—brutal, but effective. "So perish all Thine enemies, O Lord! But Thy friends be like the sun as he rises in his might," ends Deborah's victory song of praise (Judges 4–5). Scholars believe that when Barak's men "went down from Mount Tabor," they perhaps succeeded in luring the Canaanite chariots into the marshy plain, thus neutralizing them and leaving them at the mercy of the Israelite infantry.

Opposite Mount Tabor, a road to the right leads to the modern kibbutz of Ein Dor. Three thousand years ago, on the eve of his fateful battle against the Philistines, King Saul sought to communicate with the spirit of the dead prophet Samuel through the medium of Endor: "I am in great distress; for the Philistines are warring against me, and God has turned away from me and answers me no more . . . tell me what I shall do." "The Lord has torn the kingdom out of your hand, and given it to your neighbor, David," cried Samuel, "and tomorrow you and your sons shall be with me; the Lord will give the army of Israel also into the hand of the Philistines." In the subsequent battle on Mount Gilboa, Saul and his sons, including David's close friend Jonathan, were slain, and David's lament over them produced some of the Bible's loveliest poetry: "Thy glory, O Israel, is slain upon thy high places! How are the mighty fallen . . . "

Mount Tabor

The turn-off to Mount Tabor is on the left, either through the village of Dabbouriya, or at the next turn-off two kms. (one-and-a-half miles) further on (the two roads meet anyway). From a clearing you begin your climb, but a word of warning: the climb up Mount Tabor is steep and narrow, with many hairpin bends; if two cars meet, one has to back off to a widening in the road to let the other pass. A Nazareth taxi company has the concession to convey pilgrims up the mountain, and you may often find them operating and utilize their services.

It is a hard climb, but the traveler is rewarded at the top by a panorama of almost unreal tranquillity. The hill has a historic past: it was the meeting point of three tribal areas in Old Testament times, those of Zebulun, Issachar, and Naftali. Here, at Deborah's call, Barak's troops assembled to fight the Canaanites. Josephus Flavius had a fortified position on the summit during the Great Revolt against Rome.

Early Christian tradition identifies Mount Tabor as the "high mountain apart" (Matthew 17) which Jesus ascended with his disciples Peter, James, and John. "And he was transfigured before them and his face shone like the sun, and his garments became white as light. And behold there appeared to them Moses and Elijah, talking with him." Peter's suggestion to make "booths" for Jesus, Moses, and Elijah served as the architectural inspiration for early churches built on the mountaintop plateau, incorporating three chapels. It is said that the altar of the present Franciscan Church of the Transfiguration, consecrated in 1924, is on the site of the early chapel dedicated to Jesus. Two chapels of later centuries (for Moses and Elijah) are incorporated in the present structure.

Two stunning views await you—one, from the terrace of the Franciscan Hospice Casa Nova, to the west and south, and the other (walk carefully, please), from a platform on the ruins to the left of the modern church, to the east and north. Refreshments and rest-rooms are available at the Hospice. There is also a Greek Orthodox convent and hospice on the mountain.

From Mount Tabor continue towards Tiberias. As you enter the large village of Kfar Tavor, a road to the right takes you via Kafr Kamma, Yavne'el, and Poriah, descending spectacularly to Kinneret on the Sea of Galilee. Kafr Kamma is one of two Circassian villages in Israel. These are Muslims from the Russian steppes, settled here by the Turks in the last century, and still preserving some of their traditional folklore and writing.

On the descent to Kinneret there is a place to pull off the road exactly at sea level. The view of the Sea of Galilee (still 210 meters—683 ft.—below you), Golan, and the Upper Jordan Valley is simply breathtaking.

If you stay on the main road to Tiberias you have 10 kms. (six miles) from Kfar Tavor to the Golani Junction, of which more later.

Nazareth

In the days of Jesus, Nazareth was merely a village, and an insignificant one at that, nestled in a hollow in the Galilean hills. Today it is a large town of almost 50,000 inhabitants, sprawling untidily up the slopes above its original core. It is an entirely Arab town—these are Israeli Arabs: this is not disputed territory—of whom approximately half are Muslim and half Christian (of a dozen different persuasions). On a hill overlooking the town is Nazareth Illit, Upper Nazareth, a Jewish development town founded in 1957 and a quite separate municipal entity. Its main attraction is the Elite chocolate factory and the view over old Nazareth below.

Nazareth is at its quietest on Fridays and Sundays, the Muslim and Christian Sabbaths respectively, but come Saturday and the town explodes in a frenzy of activity. Arab peasants flock into town to sell their produce or buy goods, Israeli families from the surrounding area come looking for bargains in the souk, and tourists pick their way through the crowds and the traffic jams, past vendors and donkeys, to discover the "spiritual Nazareth" behind all the very unspiritual hullaballoo. It is a noble mission, to be sure, but not one in which success is assured. Not a few Christian pilgrims have found the sights and sounds of the modern town too discordant with their Scripture-induced preconception of how Nazareth should look, and have retreated, somewhat bemused by the experience.

The Basilica of the Annunciation

According to the New Testament, "the angel Gabriel was sent from God to a city of Galilee named Nazareth, to a virgin . . . and the virgin's name was Mary. And he came to her and said, 'Hail, O favored one, the Lord is with you! . . . And behold, you will conceive in your womb and bear a son, and you shall call his name Jesus.' " This is the event known to Christianity as the Annunciation, and the cave where it is believed to have occurred has been hallowed by tradition and enshrined for at least 1,600 years. The Byzantines built a church here in the 5th century. The Crusaders rebuilt it in the early-12th century only to have it destroyed by the Mamluks in the 13th. The Franciscan church of 1730 was demolished in 1954 to make way for the present immense edifice, a decade in building, and consecrated in 1969. Both Byzantine and Crusader remains are included in the present church.

As you enter the courtyard of the Basilica, turn right. Along the courtyard's outer wall are mosaic panels depicting the Annunciation and related themes, donated by Catholic communities around the world. Look out for the unusual and exotic Oriental mosaics from countries like Thailand and Taiwan. The bronze doors at the main entrance of the church depict in simple and beautiful relief major events in the life of Christ, with other events depicted in the background. Enter the lower church, built around the cave-dwelling believed to have been Mary's house, and thus the place of the Annunciation. Note the remains of the Byzantine apse and the Crusader walls, and the vibrant colors of the modern Austrian-made stained-glass windows.

Ascend the spiral staircase (near the entrance) to the upper church. This section is huge—about 65 meters (210 ft.) long and 27 meters (90 ft.) wide—and here the cupola, the inside of the high dome, is seen in all its impressive height: some 60 meters (195 ft.) above the crypt, say the height of a 16-story building. It represents the chalice of a lily (a symbol of purity) rooted in heaven, and is inscribed with the recurring letter "M," for Mary. The basilica functions as a local Catholic parish church today, and so, as in most Catholic churches, you will find representations of the Stations of the Cross, here superbly-designed Italian ceramic plaques on the pillars. Note that the inscription at the bottom of each plaque is in Arabic, the language of the local parishioners. The huge mosaic at the very front of the basilica (behind the altar) has a cast of thousands. It features Jesus and Peter in the center, an enthroned Mary behind them, to our right the Hierarchical Church, to our left the Charismatic Church, and on the sides the local Holy Land Church with its principal sanctuaries.

The main attraction in this upper basilica are the so-called banners, large wall-panels, also gifts of the Catholic communities of different nations. Both the British and the Australian panels are vividly colored mosaics on the Annunciation theme. The Canadian panel is done in terracotta, showing Mary in the midst of Canada's lakes and forests. The American panel of Mary in silver relief against a background of

color is drawn from chapter 12 of Revelations: "And there appeared
a great wonder in heaven; a woman clothed with the sun, and the moon
under her feet, and upon her head a crown of twelve stars." Especially
worth noting are these three, all using the Mother-and-Child theme:
Cameroun (West Africa), where the stark lines of white, black, and
brick-red create a startlingly harmonious African motif; Japan, an
exquisitely gentle mosaic in which Mary's shawl is made of cultivated
pearls and inlaid gold; and Venezuela, a fine wood-carving set in a
niche.

Outside, at this level, is a glass-encased baptistry built over the
remains of what is thought to have once been a Jewish *mikveh,* a ritual
immersion bath. Up the steps, past the Terra Sancta College, is the
Church of St. Joseph, where a rock-hewn underground complex is
traditionally identified as Joseph the Carpenter's work-shop.

Souk and Synagogue

Coming out of the Basilica of the Annunciation, you can bypass the
souk and walk down the street to the main road where you left your
car. If you are feeling weary there is often a "Nazareth taxi" at the exit
of the Church, a donkey whose owner will offer to take you to the
bottom of the hill! (Where was he when you had to walk *up* the street?)
You are on Casa Nova street, but do not be alarmed—it has nothing
to do with the fabled lover. In the old days, the Franciscans had a
hospice in Nazareth to house pilgrims. When it began to deteriorate,
they built another and called it the New House, or Casa Nova, to
distinguish it from the old.

The tourist shops are not in the souk itself, where tourists seldom
venture, but along Casa Nova Street, and the main Pope Paul VI Road.
Here people sometimes stop to browse for eastern-style dresses, baubles, religious trinkets, blessed or unblessed beads. It is the merest echo
of the huge bazaar of Jerusalem's Old City, and more like that in Acre
where the souvenir-salesmen are on the tourist tracks, and the souk
itself is designed for local consumption.

Of course if you want to buy kitchen-ware, a chicken, a half-kilo of
pistachio nuts, or a cassette tape of Oum Kultoum, the souk is where
you will find it. But many a pilgrim will enter the souk looking for the
"synagogue." It is on the right-hand side of the main thoroughfare. If
the building is closed, the family in the apartment above the courtyard
has the key. They are Melkites, Greek Catholics, and wrested control
of the place from the Franciscans in the 18th century. The "synagogue"
is centuries-old but in no way original, nor in fact even a synagogue.
It is built on the site identified by tradition as that of the synagogue to
which Jesus went "on the Sabbath day. And he stood up to read; and
there was given to him the book of the prophet Isaiah." (Luke 4). Jesus
selected a prophetic passage which, in Christian tradition, he himself
was to fulfill. His rendition pleased his listeners, but his interpretation
did not, and they drove him out of town.

Mary's Well: A Rival Tradition

Christianity does not speak with a single voice in Nazareth, and the rivalry between different denominations has on occasion been fierce. The Franciscans most strongly represent Latin (Roman Catholic) interests, but there are in addition convents, hospices, and hospitals of the Carmelite Sisters, the German Sisters of St. Charles, the French Sisters of Charity, the Salesians, and others. The latter have the fine Salesian Church of the Boy Jesus, built on the hill behind the town. The view can be imagined, but you have to walk up there to enjoy it. Maronites of Lebanese origin have a small congregation where mass is celebrated in Arabic and Aramaic. Up a side street from Casa Nova is the Anglican Church, completed in 1871. And a kilometer further, near Mary's Well, is a Baptist Church and School affiliated with the Southern Baptist Convention.

The round, white, modern structure on the main road (towards Tiberias) is labeled Mary's Well, but is in fact no more than the outlet of Nazareth's only natural source of water, which is today within the Greek Orthodox Church of St. Gabriel across the square behind the structure. An "apocryphal gospel" relates that it was here that the angel Gabriel appeared to Mary and announced her coming motherhood. Evidence of at least a Crusader church dating from the 12th century is strong, though it is thought that the place may have been consecrated even earlier. The Church of St. Gabriel was built in 1750 and boasts a magnificent carved-wood *iconostasis,* or chancel-screen, and somewhat less-magnificent wall-paintings. The original spring can still be seen, and the old well by which its water was drawn out.

Of Water, Wine, and a Wedding

The Tiberias-bound road climbs out of Nazareth, offering occasional tantalizing views of the town. But there are no convenient places to park on this side of the road, and if you want a panoramic view, turn right at the big intersection at the top of the hill to Nazareth Illit, Upper Nazareth. Also at the top of the hill, Route 79 breaks off to the left to Acre and Haifa via the onetime Jewish centers of Tzippori (Sephoris—identified as Mary's birthplace), and Shefar'am.

Ten minutes' drive from Nazareth along the Tiberias road brings you to Cana, the Arab village of Kafr Kana today. Apart from the telephone lines, T.V. antennas, and derelict cars, the area looks much as it did in ancient times. Olive groves still dominate the landscape, villages are built on hillsides to free the valleys for farming, the asthmatic bray of a donkey rends the air, and fig-trees, grape-vines, and pomegranates remind one how much local color is reflected in the Bible. There are places to stop on the left side of the road—about eight kms. (five miles) out of Nazareth—from which to get a fine view of Cana. The spot itself is less than enchanting since the villagers, in defiance of official regulations, use it as the village dump.

Official orange signs in the village center and on the main road show the way to the traditional place where the marriage at Cana, attended by Jesus and his mother Mary, was celebrated. When the wine had run out, Mary turned to Jesus who, at first reluctant, miraculously turned jars of water into wine of superior quality. Cana is venerated by Christians as the place where, with this first miracle (John 2), Jesus emerged from his "hidden years" at Nazareth, and began his public ministry in the Galilee.

As elsewhere, so here too, rival Latin (Roman Catholic) and Greek Orthodox churches lay claim to being built on the spot of the miracle. The 19th-century Franciscan (Catholic) church is the one with the twin white towers, and is worth visiting. If you are in luck, the local priest might agree to show you around.

The Road to Tiberias

Just beyond the village, you meet up with Route 77; left to Haifa, right to Tiberias. Turn right. Six kms. (four miles) further on is the Golani Junction, one of the most important road junctions in the Galilee: behind you are Haifa and Nazareth; to the left are Safed (Zefat) and the Upper Galilee (Route 65); to the right are Mount Tabor, Afula, and the Jezre'el Valley; and ahead are Tiberias and the Sea of Galilee. A museum near the intersection is dedicated to the Golani Brigade which captured the cross-roads in the War of Independence of 1948.

On your right, flanking the Afula road, is a newly-planted forest of pine and cypress. The Jewish National Fund is dedicated to land reclamation, and has planted well over 170 million trees around the country in the last half-century to replace the forests uprooted in the centuries before. At this spot there is a do-it-yourself planting center ("Plant a Tree with Your Own Hands") where at $7 a tree, you can leave something living behind you in Israel. The Bible elevates the act of planting trees to a *mitzva,* an injunction: "When you come to the Land and plant all manner of tree" (Leviticus 19). The reference here is specifically to fruit trees, but other traditions speak of all trees. "What do you do," asks a pithy Rabbinic conundrum, "if you are busy planting a tree, and that moment the messiah comes? First finish planting the tree, and then get up to greet the messiah!"

Continuing towards Tiberias, you pass on the left the religious kibbutz of Lavi, with its fine guest house. One unusual source of income for the kibbutz is the design, manufacture, and export of synagogue furniture, a development of their do-it-yourself enterprise when they built their own synagogue years ago. Just beyond the kibbutz, also on the left, is a double-peaked rocky hill—these are the Horns of Hattin where, in 1187, the Crusader armies were routed by Saladin, bringing to an end the Latin Kingdom of Jerusalem. Although the Third Crusade succeeded in restoring some parts of the country to Christian control, they were never able to regain the lost glory of the first kingdom. Here you begin the descent to Tiberias and the Sea of Galilee.

PRACTICAL INFORMATION FOR THE JEZRE'EL VALLEY AND LOWER GALILEE HILL COUNTRY

TELEPHONE CODES. We have given telephone codes for all the areas in the lists that follow. These codes need only be used when calling from outside the area concerned.

RESTAURANTS. Restaurants here are not exactly thick on the ground. Little cafeterias are available at Bet She'arim and Megiddo, restaurants at Ma'ayan Harod and Sachne. Cafeterias and good felafel stands in Bet She'an, likewise in Afula. The Egged Central Bus Station cafeteria in Afula can be very satisfactory if the cook's in the mood. Eat lunch with the kibbutz members at **Kibbutz Megiddo,** just up the road from the tel. **Kibbutz Dovrat** runs a very good roadside inn, 8 kms. (5 miles) out of Afula on the Tiberias road (Rte. 65): their rich goulash soup has a national reputation. At the Ein Harod gas station (between Afula and Bet She'an) there is a cafeteria serving mostly local-type food. **Hanoked** in Kfar Tavor (Rte. 65) specializes in lamb dishes in a rustic atmosphere.

Youth Hostels. Kiryat Tivon, 18 kms. (11 miles) out of Haifa on the Migdal Ha'emek–Nazareth road (tel. 04–931482). 90 beds. Family rooms available, members' kitchen. **Ma'ayan Harod,** 11 kms. (7 miles) east of Afula off the Bet She'an road (tel. 06–531660). 150 beds. Family rooms available, members' kitchen, airconditioning, park, pool; beautiful surroundings.

Hospice. Franciscan Convent of Transfiguration, on Mount Tabor (tel. 06–767489). Book in advance.

Camping. Mobile Post Gilboa, Ma'ayan Harod (tel. 06–581660). In glorious, grassy grounds, with huge eucalyptus trees, Gideon's spring, pool, restaurant.

HOW TO GET AROUND. Egged buses serve this area as every other in Israel. The towns of Nazareth, Afula, and Bet She'an have fairly regular bus routes. Sites on these routes are thus easily accessible, though sometimes necessitate a bit of a walk (Megiddo, Ma'ayan Harod, Bet She'arim). Other sites have less frequent services (Bet Alfa, Sachne, Mount Tabor), and schedules should be checked with Egged.

Tours. No excursions originate in this area, but Nazareth, Megiddo, and Bet She'arim appear on the itineraries of several tour operators, leaving from Jerusalem or Tel Aviv—Galilee Tours, United Tours, and Egged Tours. Travel agents and hotels carry their brochures, and will make the necessary bookings.

MUSEUMS AND HISTORIC SITES. All the places listed below are treated in detail in the main text. Note that (N.P.) indicates a National Park. In general, you will find that this area of Israel is among the richest in places of interest.

BELVOIR (Kochav Hayarden), turnoff 13 kms. (8 miles) north of Bet She'an on Rte. 90. Powerful 12th-century Crusader **castle,** last to fall to Saladin. Spectacular view. (N.P.)

BET ALFA. On Kibbutz Heftziba, 8 kms. (5 miles) from Bet She'an. Finely preserved 6th-century A.D. **mosaic** synagogue floor. (N.P.)

BET SHE'AN. Bet She'an Museum, near Bet She'an Central Bus Station. Archeological artifacts and an enthusiastic curator. Open daily, approximately 8.30–3.30, Fri. 8.30–12.30.
  Bet She'an Roman Theater, in Bet She'an itself. Best-preserved example in Israel. 2nd–3rd century A.D. (N.P.)

BET SHE'ARIM, 21 kms. (13 miles) from Haifa, off Rte. 75 at Kiryat Tivon. A 2nd–4th-century A.D. Jewish **necropolis,** and a beautiful picnic spot. Small museum. (N.P.)

BET STURMAN, on Kibbutz Ein Harod (Me'uchad), 13 kms. (8 miles) from Afula on Rte. 71 to Bet She'an. **Museum** of natural and human history of the area, plus showcase for kibbutz artists.

CANA, 8 kms. (5 miles) northeast of Nazareth on the Tiberias road (Rte. 754). The modern village of Kafr Kanna, site of Jesus' first miracle. Franciscan (Catholic) and Greek Orthodox churches.

MA'AYAN HAROD, 11 kms. (7 miles) from Afula off Rte. 71 to Bet She'an. The place where Gideon's men were selected for battle. Spring, pool, park. (N.P.)

MEGIDDO, near intersection of Rte. 66 and Rte. 65 (Hadera–Afula road). The **tel** of 25 ancient cities, including one of Solomon's. Small museum, excavations, water tunnel. (N.P.)

MOUNT TABOR, about 16 kms. (10 miles) northeast of Afula (Rte. 65). Identified with New Testament transfiguration. Large church and magnificent view. Mount Tabor is always open; its church (tel. 06–767489) is open daily 8–12, 2–5. A Nazareth taxi company has the concession for servicing Mount Tabor (tel. 06–554745). (Nothing larger than a minibus can use the road up the mountain.)

SACHNE, just east of Bet Alfa. Park, natural warm springs, and a swimming area. (N.P.)

YIZRE'EL (Jezre'el), 7 kms. (4 miles) south of Afula on Rte. 60. **Kibbutz** with exhibition of local artists and craftspeople (ceramics, weaving, etc.). Small **tel** of King Ahab's ancient city.

SPORTS. Swimming is available at the two National Parks of Ma'ayan Harod and Sachne (see above). Mount Gilboa has fine **hiking** trails. For information, contact the Alon-Tavor Field Study Center (of the Society for the Preservation of Nature in Israel), located near the foot of Mount Tabor (tel. 06–767998).

PRACTICAL INFORMATION FOR NAZARETH

TOURIST INFORMATION. Government Tourist Information Office, Casa Nova St. (tel. 573003). Open Mon. to Fri. 8–5; closed Sat., Sun. and Christian holidays.

Telephone Code. The area code for Nazareth is (06).

HOTELS. Nazareth offers three officially listed hotels, all with prices inclusive of breakfast. All are partially airconditioned and have diningrooms, bar, and coffeeshop.

Galilee Hotel (M), Paulus VI St. (tel. 571311). 90 rooms, most with shower only. **Grand New Hotel** (M), St. Joseph St. (tel. 573020–1). 92 rooms, most with bath.

Nazareth Hotel (M), (tel. 577777). 87 rooms, most with bath.

Hospices. Mostly Catholic, they are plentiful in Nazareth: **St. Joseph Theological Seminary,** P.O.B. 99 (Greek Catholic); **Sisters of Nazareth,** Casa Nova St., P.O.B. 274; Casa Nova, P.O.B. 198.

Also **Betharam:** the **Franciscan de Marie** (White Sisters); and the **Christian Encounter Center.** For further information, contact the Tourist Office.

RESTAURANTS. Food in Nazareth tends to be less expensive than in larger cities. The emphasis is on Middle-Eastern cuisine, with the hotels and hospices generally serving European-type meals. Most restaurants, but not all, are found near the tourist-frequented intersection of Paulus VI and Casa Nova Sts.

Worth trying are **Astoria, El Amal** (The Hope), **Omar el Khayam, Riviera,** and **St. Joseph.** The **Holy Land Inn** opposite the Galilee Hotel serves excellent unelaborate, Italianesque meals. **Nof Nazareth** in Upper Nazareth is a good kosher spot.

SHOPPING. Near the old souk, on Casa Nova St., and down on Paulus VI St., there is a wide range of souvenir shops, some limiting themselves to cheap baubles and knick-knacks, others hoping for greater windfalls by selling expensive jewelry, some very good, others less so. **Massawi** on Paulus VI St. is in the latter range, but boasts a coffee-bar *and* the area's only clean toilet facilities. The **souk** itself has little to attract the tourist other than its atmosphere and human mosaic. The **pastry shop** near the Tourist Information Office on Casa Nova St. has superb Middle-Eastern delicacies. Especially good is the *bourma,* a sweet roll that resembles shredded wheat on the outside and is filled with whole pistachio nuts. Another cluster of similar stores can be found near the Greek Orthodox Church at Mary's Well.

Since many of the shopkeepers are Christian Arabs, many shops are closed on Sundays.

CHURCHES. The **Anglican Church,** off Casa Nova St. Dates from the 19th century. The **Baptist Church,** near Mary's Well, built earlier this century, can be visited by arrangement.

Basilica of the Annunciation. This vast Franciscan basilica was completed in 1969 over the remains of Byzantine and Crusader churches. Venerated as the site of Mary's home and of Gabriel's appearance to her announcing the birth of Jesus. Awesome edifice, impressive artwork, beautiful stained-glass. Open daily Apr. through Sept. 8.30–11.45, 2–5; Oct. through Mar. 9–11.45, 2–4.30; Sun. 2–5 only. Also on the site is the **Church of St. Joseph,** built over the workshop of Joseph the Carpenter.

Church of St. Gabriel, a kilometer north just off the main street. Greek orthodox church built over Nazareth's only spring—Mary's Well. One of the spring's outlets, on the main street itself, is enclosed within a modern, round, white structure. Open daily 8–12, 2–5.

Salesian Church of the Boy Jesus. Fine-looking, red-roofed building on the top of Nazareth's highest peak. Ascent is by foot!

Synagogue, in the souk, just a few minutes' walk from the Franciscan Basilica. Melkite (Greek Catholic) tradition. Closed Sundays. Key (if closed) at apartment above courtyard.

Religious Services. No regular Catholic mass is conducted in English in Nazareth, but often a pilgrim group will conduct their own service which the individual visitor might join. Information regarding services of all denominations can be obtained from the Tourist Information Office on Casa Nova St.

THE SEA OF GALILEE

The Waters of the North

How does the visitor familiar with the Great Lakes respond when he reaches the "Sea" of Galilee and finds it to be a freshwater lake 22 kms. (14 miles) long from north to south, and 12 kms. (seven-and-a-half miles) wide at its widest? Does he think of the Jordan River, the very name of which conjures up memories of such significant events, being as "deep and wide" as, say, the Mississippi, the Hudson, or the St. Lawrence? To the ancients, unfamiliar with the more imposing geographical features of the world, their vocabulary limited by narrow horizons, local streams, mountains, and bodies of water loomed larger in their minds than perhaps they do in ours today. Your whole world might exist right here in this basin. You might never leave it in your entire lifetime, and if you did it might be an expedition long-anticipated and long talked-over when you returned—if, God willing, you did return.

In Hebrew, the lake is known by its Biblical name of Kinneret. The poets say that the name derives from the shape of the lake, which resembles that of a *kinnor*, an ancient harp. But the real explanation is somewhat more prosaic. Kinneret was the name of an important city on the northwestern edge of the lake in the Canaanite and Israelite periods, and evidently gave its name to the body of water it dominated. By comparison, a later name, Lake Tiberias, derives from the prominent settlement of more recent times, and is already mentioned in the Gospel of St. John.

Although there are seasonal fluctuations in the water level of the Sea of Galilee, we are at about 210 meters (683 ft.) below sea level here, in that deep gash in the earth's surface, the Great Rift Valley, that extends all the way to Kenya. To the west, the rocky hills of the Lower Galilee rise irregularly, here almost sheer, there in rounded piles. To the east, the dark volcanic cliffs of the Golan Heights loom menacingly in an almost unbroken line high above the lake. In only three places around the lake does the shore widen to form a plain capable of extensive cultivation: Ginnosar (Gennasereth) on the west, Bethsaida on the northeast, and where the Jordan River leaves the lake in the south.

Tiberias

After the death of Herod the Great in 4 B.C., his kingdom was divided among his three sons. Herod Antipas, "the Fox" (this is the Herod who executed John the Baptist and who was in Jerusalem that first Easter), got the Galilee. In A.D. 18 he dedicated a new city on the shores of the Sea of Galilee, naming it in honor of his patron, the Roman Emperor Tiberius. From the outset, Herod Antipas planned a glorious Hellenistic-style city to emulate the cosmopolitan centers of the Roman Empire. He built grandly, including an extravagant palace and a huge theater. But it was not easy for Herod Antipas to find Jews to live in the town. They had no love for the House of Herod; in addition, Tiberias was built on the ancient cemetery of Biblical Rakat, making the site impure and unfit for settlement. Nonetheless, by a combination of coercion and incentives—housing and land, mainly—he began populating the town with builders, artisans, and even freed slaves. When it became the seat of Herod Antipas' court, the noble families moved in as well.

Only reluctantly and under duress did the city of Tiberias pay lip service to the Jewish Revolt against the Romans (A.D. 66–70) and when Vespasian appeared at the gates of the city it promptly surrendered without a fight, saving itself the destruction of other Galilean towns. Throughout most of the Roman period it was given autonomous status, ruling a substantial territory, and allowed to mint its own coins and reckon its own calendar from the date of the founding of the city. The proximity of the marvelous hot springs of Hammat brought it prosperity as well, and by the 3rd century it occupied an area of about 200 acres, approximately equivalent to the area of Jerusalem's Old City today, with a population of 30–40,000.

The Jewish population increased considerably during this time. In the 2nd century A.D., Rabbi Shimon Bar Yochai ceremonially purified Tiberias and declared it fit for settlement. After the failure of the Bar Kochba Revolt in A.D. 135, the nucleus of all Jewish communal activity in Israel moved from Yavne, on the Mediterranean, to the Galilee. Tiberias itself eventually became the capital of the Galilee, and the seat of the Sanhedrin, the Jewish High Court. The so-called Jerusalem Talmud—that vast compilation of rabbinic commentary on Jewish laws and customs—was completed here. This combination of circumstances was eventually to elevate Tiberias to the status of one of Judaism's four Holy Cities.

The Crusaders made Tiberias the capital of their Principality of Galilee in the 12th century, but it fell to Saladin when he crushed the knights at the Horns of Hattin in 1187. The city declined in the 13th century until the Turkish Sultan Suleiman I gave it to the well-connected Jewish nobleman Don Joseph Nasi in 1562. Don Joseph revived the Jewish community and planted mulberry trees, hoping to establish a silk-worm industry. But the enterprise was short-lived. In 1740, the Beduin ruler of the area, Daher el-Omar, sought to revive the city and invited Turkish Jews to settle in Tiberias. His motivation was partly economic; but politically he could not trust many of his local subjects, and needed citizens whose first loyalty would be to him personally. The leader of the group from Izmir was one Aboulafia, perhaps the best-known family-name in Tiberias even now. The community was joined in 1777 by a group of Hasidim, a devout, charismatic Jewish sect from Eastern Europe. Ibrahim Pasha, the Egypt-based rebel against the Turks, rebuilt the city wall in 1833, but just four years later a massive earthquake devastated the town, leaving death and destruction in its wake.

Tiberias slowly recovered, expanding beyond its traditional confines and up the hill behind the town. Arab violence against Jews in the town broke out in the years 1936–39, but the Jews responded more vigorously during the War of Independence in 1948, beating off their attacks. Between 1948 and 1952, when Israel was absorbing huge numbers of Jewish refugees, Tiberias quadrupled its population. Today it is a town of some 30,000 inhabitants, with tourism the base of its economy.

Water Skiing and the Tombs of Great Men

The development of tourist sites and the exposure of the old and the ancient go hand-in-hand in Tiberias. For instance, opposite the entrance of the Tiberias Plaza Hotel a piece of land was being prepared for construction, but the workers' shovels almost immediately hit ancient structures below ground. The site was excavated to expose Byzantine buildings, a Crusader wall, and a Turkish inn. The new building was canceled!

The majority of the walls and towers readily visible all over the downtown area are, for the most part, 12th-century Crusader, repaired in the 18th century, improved in the early-19th, and partly destroyed by the earthquake of 1837. At that point residents of the town gleefully pounced on the fallen stones and carted them off to effect their own domestic repairs.

Tiberias' most famous denizen was the great 12th-century sage, Maimonides, whose tomb, a short walk up from the town center on Ben Zakkai Street, can be visited. Born in Cordoba in Spain, Maimonides made a name for himself as a philosopher, the physician to the royal court of Saladin in Egypt, and, in the Jewish world, as the greatest religious scholar and spiritual authority since the Talmudic period of the 4th century A.D. After his death in 1204, his remains were interred in Tiberias. Nearby, and giving his name to the street, are the alleged remains of Yohanan ben Zakkai, the famous rabbi who, during the Roman siege of Jerusalem in A.D. 69, had himself carried out of that city in a coffin, and begged the general, Vespasian, to allow him to leave the stricken city and settle in Yavne on the coast. In so doing, he assured the uninterrupted continuation of Jewish life, law, and learning in Israel after the center in Jerusalem had been eclipsed. Further up the hill, one can visit the tomb of Rabbi Akiva, the spiritual leader of the Bar Kochba Revolt against the Romans, who, after his capture in A.D. 135, was tortured to death in Caesarea. And a few kilometers away, behind Hammat Tiberias, is the Tomb of Rabbi Meir Ba'al Ha-nes, the "Miracle Worker," a legendary personality who supposedly took a vow that he would not lie down until the Messiah came, and was therefore buried in an upright position. His name has become a sort of banner for charitable organizations, and many a miracle has been attributed to the power of prayer at his tomb.

In the short distance between the Tiberias Plaza Hotel and the main Rosh Pina–Metulla road, there is a cluster of interesting old synagogues, mosques, and a church. Some of the synagogues date from the Aboulafia period in the 18th century. One of the old mosques houses the Municipal Museum. The Franciscan Church of St. Peter commemorates the events described in John 21: Jesus entrusting Peter with the care of "his flock." One of the most evocative trips for the Christian pilgrim in the area is a boat ride on the Sea of Galilee where Jesus calmed the stormy sea (Matthew 8) and walked on the water (Matthew 14). For anyone who knows the area, the occurrence of a sudden storm rings true. Winds from the west are sometimes funneled through the hills and without warning whip up the calm waters of the lake. (For details of boat trips, see *Practical Information.*)

But such potential disturbances do nothing to deter the windsurfers and waterskiers whose numbers are on the increase. These are still far from being popular sports, but the facilities are there, both here in Tiberias and across the lake on its northeastern shore.

Once boating on the lake was not only the fisherman's means of livelihood, but a convenient way of commuting from one shore-side town to another. The New Testament mentions this often, and it was still true until better roads and swifter vehicles made the land alternatives preferable earlier in this century. A local treasure-hunt was mounted years back for the boat sunk in the lake while carrying Ottoman gold during the Turkish retreat in World War I. The Sea of Galilee has not delivered up its secret and the bullion still gilds the lake bed in an unknown spot.

From Tiberias to Tabgha

We leave Tiberias heading north, skirting the lake shore along the Rosh Pina road, Route 90: a series of fish restaurants-cum-swimming/boating spots, a tiny harbor, and we're out of town. Fishing on the Sea of Galilee is usually done at night, the main hauls being freshwater sardines and the indigenous St. Peter's fish. The latter make excellent eating straight off the bone; only a few restaurants will fillet it for you.

About four kms. (two-and-a-half miles) out of Tiberias, there is a small, white-domed building to the right, and a walled enclosure containing some ancient ruins just beyond. In the Second Temple period, this was the site of the village of Magdala, the home-town of Mary Magdalene, or, more properly, Mary the Magdalene. How curiously tenacious is the tradition that she had been a "fallen woman," a sinner who had repented of her ways and followed Jesus. There is no passage in the New Testament to this effect, only that she had been possessed of demons and had been cured (Luke 8). Magdala is the Aramaic form of Migdal, meaning tower, and a modern Jewish farming village bearing that name is slightly further along the road. Until a few generations ago, a small, wretched, Arab village sat here, a village that left a graphic impression on the American writer Mark Twain as he journeyed across the country on horseback in 1867. The sides of the houses, built in "the ungraceful form of a dry-goods box," he wrote, "are daubed with a smooth, white plaster and tastefully frescoed aloft and below with disks of camel dung placed there to dry. This gives the edifice the romantic appearance of having been riddled with cannonballs, and imparts to it a very warlike aspect." His other remarks about the village and the general area of his day are no less unflattering!

To the left of Migdal is a canyon, Wadi Hamam in Arabic, at the head of which is the most important shrine of the Druze community in Israel. Nebi Shuweb, the Prophet Jethro (Moses' father-in-law), is venerated by the Druze, and every year the community gather here in their thousands to pay their respects in a great festivity at his supposed tomb.

On the plateau above the canyon are the remains of the ancient town of Arbel, complete with ruins of a 3rd-century A.D. synagogue. In the Second Temple period, the town was reputedly the fiercest bastion of Jewish nationalism in the land. When the interloper Herod arrived in the country (39 B.C.) with the title King of the Jews bestowed upon him by grace of Rome, he was bitterly opposed by the Jews themselves, and nowhere more so than at Arbel. Failing to stop Herod's armed advance, the people of Arbel fled to the caves now visible high in the canyon walls. Herod resorted to the daring plan of lowering soldiers in cradles over the edge of the cliff, allowing them to gain access to the caves and destroy the opposition.

At Migdal, a turn-off to the left (Route 807) takes you up to join a new highway (Route 85), the most convenient route to Acre and Western Galilee. Remaining on our lakeside road, we pass Kibbutz Ginnosar on the right, with its guesthouse and picnic site.

Where the road climbs a small ridge, there is an electric power installation on your right. This provides power for the huge water pumps buried in the hill behind it. For water-poor Israel, the Sea of Galilee is the major freshwater reservoir, and here water is lifted to a sufficient height where it can begin flowing south through the pipes and canals of the National Water Carrier. This system, completed in 1964, integrates the country's water sources and redistributes them according to need as far south as the Negev. On the small ridge is the tel of the ancient city of Kinneret, yet another way-station on the great Via

Maris. Immediately beyond it is an intersection. To your right is the
road to Tabgha and Capernaum, to which we shall shortly return.

Above the Lake

The Rosh Pina–Metulla road now begins climbing in a series of
hairpin bends. A five-minute drive and a small road to the right takes
you to the Mount of Beatitudes. There is a hospice here kept by the
Italian Order of Franciscan Sisters, and a round, copper-domed chapel
designed by the same Barluzzi who built the Church of All Nations in
Jerusalem's Garden of Gethsemane. It was completed in 1937 under
the auspices, perversely enough, of Mussolini's Fascist regime, as an
inscription reminds you. The porch that encircles the church gives a
superb view of the Sea of Galilee and surrounding mountains, particularly in the late afternoon.

"Seeing the crowds, he went up on the mountain," writes the Evan-
gelist Matthew, "and when he sat down, his disciples came to him. And
he opened his mouth and taught them saying: 'Blessed are the poor in
spirit, for theirs is the kingdom of heaven . . . ' " This is the beginning
of the Sermon on the Mount (Matthew 5), its nine verses beginning
"Blessed are . . . " being the Beatitudes. Tradition has selected this spot
as the likely candidate for that great sermon. Although nothing in the
Gospel account allows one to identify the place, the Mount of Beatitudes, with its tranquil gardens and sweeping view, gives as good a
sense of the stage of Jesus' Galilean ministry as you will find anywhere
in the area.

A short way north on the main road, a turn to the right brings you
to the ancient synagogue of ancient Korazim. Although it has not been
as thoroughly prepared for viewing as other synagogues of the same
period (2nd–3rd centuries A.D.), the similarities in design and decoration to its contemporaries at Bar'am and Capernaum, for instance, are
readily obvious.

Tabgha: Of Fish and Fishermen

Heptapegon—Seven Springs—the Greek-speaking Byzantines called
it, and with the centuries the name was corrupted to the Arabic Tabgha
of today. Since the 4th century A.D., Christian pilgrims have been drawn
to the spot, believing it to be the "deserted" or "lonely" place where
Jesus miraculously multiplied five loaves of bread and two fish and fed
the vast crowd that had followed him. "And they all ate and were
satisfied. And they took up 12 baskets full of the broken pieces left over.
And those who ate were about 5,000 men, besides women and children." (Matthew 14).

A good part of the mosaic floor of an ancient Byzantine church has
survived, and is now incorporated in the Byzantine-style church completed by the Benedictine Order in 1981. The mosaic is lovely: the
motifs are of mostly water-related flora and fauna of the area, and
evidently of the Nile in Egypt as well! An even stronger indication of
the Egyptian influence is a "Nilometer" on the mosaic floor, a tower
with gradations on it found in the Nile River to measure its level during

the flood season. Undoubtedly the most famous part of the mosaic of this or any other Byzantine church in Israel is the depiction (right near the altar) of two fish and a basket of loaves. It is small, simple, and an eloquent reminder of the miracle here recalled.

Close by, though entered from the road by a different gate, is a simple, basalt church built on the lake-edge by the Franciscans in 1934, the Church of the Primacy. John's Gospel relates that after his resurrection, Jesus appeared to his disciples by the Sea of Galilee as they were coming in by boat after a frustrating night's fishing. He directed them to throw the net in again and they hauled it out of the water bulging with fish. Breakfasting on the shore with his disciples, Jesus thrice commanded Peter to "feed my sheep." Peter went on to become Bishop of Rome, making Tabgha a very special place for Pope Paul VI on his visit to the Holy Land in 1964.

Although the Scriptural passage also gives no geographical indication of where the events took place, there is an interesting curiosity here. The so-called St. Peter's fish, which is indigenous to the Sea of Galilee, dislikes the cold. Ask the local fishermen: at certain times of the year you will find the greatest concentration of fish near Tabgha where the warm springs spill into the lake.

At the water's edge are the carved rocks once part of the Byzantine structures, and revered as *Mensa Domini,* the Table of the Lord, recalling that breakfast long ago.

Capernaum

Three kms. (two miles) east of Tabgha is Capernaum, Kfar Nahum in Hebrew, once a substantial town on the Sea of Galilee. What stands out from afar is the white-washed and red-domed Greek Orthodox church; but what we have come to see lies within the Franciscan monastery grounds.

The ruins here were known, if not clearly identified, long before serious excavation of Capernaum began. The piecemeal exploration of the site in the 19th century had left much of its beautifully-carved masonry freshly exposed, an open invitation to pilfering by house-builders and vandalism by treasure-seekers. It was not until the site was acquired by the Franciscan "Custody of the Holy Land" in 1894 that it could be protected from these casual but persistent pilferers. Serious excavations began a decade later.

If we have used the word traditional to describe other Christian sites in the area, here at Capernaum we are on solidly historical ground. This town was nothing less than the headquarters of Jesus' three year ministry in the Galilee. Near here he called his disciples—"I will make you fishers of men"—preached in the synagogue, and performed miracles. Jesus performed more miracles in or within sight of Capernaum than anywhere else in the country. Nevertheless, the citizens of the town rejected Him, incurring His wrath and a venomous curse: "And thou, Capernaum, which art exalted unto Heaven, shall be brought down to hell!"

On the right, as you enter the site, is a line of decorated stones from Capernaum's 2nd- or 3rd-century A.D. synagogue. Rather than using the hard and rather crude local black basalt, the builders of the synagogue went further afield, importing better, whitish limestone. The stone-work is of exceptional standard, depicting typical Jewish motifs from the period—grapes, pomegranates, figs, olives, palm trees, lions, and geometric designs. On a lintel is a sort of covered wagon, thought to be the artist's depiction of the mobile Ark of the Covenant. A column carries an Aramaic inscription dedicated to "Alpheus the son of Zebedah the son of John" who contributed to the building of the synagogue. How modern that sounds!

The excavations a little further on display a sign explaining that this was the house of St. Peter. A 5th-century, octagonal church with a mosaic floor was found here built over much earlier buildings, with some evidence to suggest it had been a site of Christian devotion as early as the end of the 1st century A.D. Note the crudity of the village houses by comparison with the synagogue—the pride of the village—right above them.

The synagogue of Capernaum has long been regarded as the archetypical example of the Galilean, or early, synagogue, a category that includes the synagogues at nearby Korazim, Bar'am in the Upper Galilee, and Katzrin on the Golan. In general, these synagogues, built in the 2nd or 3rd century, more closely resembled a Classical Roman temple than the later Byzantine basilica. Additionally, their principal decorative emphasis was on *exterior* stone carvings and reliefs. Later synagogues on the other hand, as at Bet Alfa and Hammat Tiberias, generally dating from the Byzantine period, the 4th–6th centuries, are characterized by colorful and often elaborate mosaic floors; *interior* decoration, that is.

The building here was clearly an imposing edifice, well-built, and with a second story above the high main hall. Its stone benches recall the literal meaning of synagogue—a place of assembly, intended originally to hear the reading of the Torah, and teachings or interpretations based on it. Only later did synagogues come to be houses of worship as well. A further curiosity here is that the synagogue faces north, away from Jerusalem, rather than being aligned toward the Holy City. Was the idea that the gates opened towards Jerusalem, allowing the prayers to flow, as it were, towards the Holy City? Or was the Ark containing the Torah scrolls a moveable one that could be brought around to the synagogue's southern wall during the service? Or perhaps the traditional orientation had not yet become mandatory when the synagogue was built, which would hint at a very early date for its establishment.

The Franciscan Fathers, on the other hand, basing themselves in part on the dating of hoards of ancient coins unearthed here, argue that the synagogue was built only in the mid-4th century A.D., despite the architectural evidence to the contrary. Archeology is often inconclusive enough to allow such controversies to rage for years. But consider this: by the mid-4th century the Christianized Roman (i.e. Byzantine) Empire was already well-established, militant, and anti-Jewish in its first flush of victory. How would the Byzantines have allowed such a huge and impressive synagogue to be built overshadowing what was already a Christian holy site, the House of St. Peter?

An inscription adorns each of the synagogue's main columns. On the right an ancient one in Greek recalls that one "Herod" was a major contributor to the synagogue's building fund. The other inscription, on the left, is a dedication in Latin to the Franciscan Father Orfali, Capernaum's excavator and restorer, who died in 1926.

The identification of this monumental building as a synagogue is confirmed by the quintessentially Jewish symbols inscribed on the capital of a column displayed on the right between the synagogue and the exit: the seven-branched *menorah,* the ram's horn *(shofar),* and the incense-shovel.

As you leave, look out for an olive-oil press, plus a substantial rolling-stone, and flour-mills, made of the durable volcanic basalt stone. So good was this hard stone for milling that the export of "agricultural equipment" from the Sea of Galilee was evidently a lucrative business, and such "equipment" has been found as far away as Qumran, Jerusalem, and the Mediterranean coast.

It is possible to join a boat-ride (unscheduled) from Capernaum to Tiberias or vice versa (see *Practical Information* for Tiberias).

The Eastern Shore

Four kms. (two-and-a-half miles) east of Capernaum, you cross the Jordan River just above its entry into the Sea of Galilee. It is muddy here, and faster-flowing than at the southern end of the lake, where it leaves it. Two kms. (one-and-a-half miles) further, a road to the left (Route 88) takes you to the northern Golan and Mount Hermon via the Upper Customs House. A few moments' drive further along the shore road and you reach another intersection. Here you turn right (Route 92) and you're southbound on the eastern shore. This is the valley of Bethsaida mentioned in the New Testament. Although there was a Jewish town here in ancient times—Peter was a native of Bethsaida—many of the rich fields around the lake are now being cultivated for the first time.

The road skirts the lake, sometimes along a narrow strip between the Golan Heights now looming above you and the water's edge. The first road up the Heights to your left takes you to the Second Temple Period city of Gamla (see the *Upper Galilee and the Golan* chapter); the second to the village of Ramot with its holiday cottages; and the third, at the historical site of Kursi, is the main road to the southern Golan, Route 789. Along this northeastern section of the lake several new beaches and picnic areas have been developed.

Kursi was a prosperous monastery in the 5th and 6th centuries A.D., conveniently located to provide hospice facilities to the swarms of Christian pilgrims to the Sea of Galilee. This was in the heyday of the Byzantine Empire, and the buildings found here, including the fine church now partially restored, attest to a high level of craftsmanship and culture. The New Testament relates the story of Jesus curing a Gadarene (or Gerasene) demoniac by exorcism, the demons which possessed him then entering a herd of swine grazing nearby. The Byzantines identified Kursi as the site where these swine plunged to their destruction in the lake (Luke 8).

Kibbutz Ein-Gev, five kms. (three miles) south of Kursi, is well-known to Israelis for an astonishing variety of reasons: a prehistoric site was found here, and on a hill overlooking the kibbutz was the ancient Jewish town of Sussita, or Hippios in Greek; along with another half-dozen settlements further south, its vulnerable position below the Golan Heights made it a prime target for Syrian gunners until that threat was removed in the Six Day War of 1967; its fish restaurant supported by its own fishing industry, has become a famous and popular lunch-stop; it provides a range of holiday facilities (see *Practical Information*); it runs a scheduled ferry service across the lake to Tiberias and back, and charter boats between those two places and Capernaum; and it is the venue of the prestigious annual Ein Gev Spring Festival of music and dance, attracting the crème de la crème of performers.

Ten kms. (six miles) south, the road to Tiberias swings to the right No hurry, we'll get back on it. But meanwhile turn left onto Route 98 for Hammat Gader on the Jordanian border, and an unforgettable experience.

The Roman Empire's Number Two Spa

You may at first glance think this title presumptuous, but it was the considered opinion of the 4th-century A.D. Greek biographer, Eunapius and there is reason to believe he should have known. Indeed, in beauty and size the Roman baths of Hammat Gader were surpassed only by those at Baiae (Naples).

Built originally in the 2nd century A.D. to utilize the therapeutic hot mineral springs, the whole complex, and the neighboring town of Gadara which developed it, was hit by an earthquake in A.D. 363. The rebuilding which followed increased both the size and the beauty of the spa. It continued to be used throughout the Byzantine and Arab periods until the late-9th or early-10th century. The findings of archeologists working at Hammat Gader since 1979 eloquently complement and confirm the many historical references to the place.

The entrance to the baths was through an almost seven-meter (22-ft.) wide corridor, once covered and kept dim to dramatize the effect of first seeing the baths themselves. Entered through a high decorative colonnade (now restored), the warm pool of the Hall of Pillars was a pleasing introduction to the opulence of the spa. The enclosed hall was illuminated through numerous glass-paned windows and presided over by statues of Aesculapius, the god of medicine, and Hygieia, the goddess of health. Evidently the undoubted therapeutic benefits of the spa were not its only attraction: two of the springs were known respectively as Eros (the god of love) and Anteros (the god of mutual love). Part of the wall here has been preserved to a height of almost eight meters (25 ft.). In the adjacent large hall, once a pool itself, 35 inscriptions were found dedicated to wealthy "alumni" of Hammat Gader, who, having been cured by the waters, gratefully contributed to the beautification of the baths. The identification of the Lepers' Pool is still controversial, though it is clearly referred to in historical accounts.

Ah, at last, the Caldarium! There were several hot pools of differing temperatures—a large Oval Pool, a small Oval Pool, and a small round hot tub. The mineral spring which supplied them emerges from the bowels of the earth at 52° C (126° F), its waters cooled for the bathers by a system of lead pipes and fountains. And when you had finished taking the waters, you could refresh yourself in the cool Hall of Fountains, where the largest pool of the complex—31 meters (100 ft.) by 14 meters (45 ft.)—was filled by 32 fountains spouting through carved stone heads, both human and animal. Many of these heads have been found, mutilated by Muslim iconoclasts in later centuries, as well as elaborate inscriptions dedicated to royal personages.

Today the hot springs, suitably cooled to a caressing warmth, are again providing pleasure to thousands. The modern openair pool is set in a wonderfully landscaped park providing picnic areas, pool facilities, a restaurant, and an alligator farm! A substantial synagogue with an elaborate mosaic floor was excavated in the '30s, while a large Roman theater still awaits the archeologist's spade.

The road to Hammat Gader is an absorbing experience in itself. It is cut out of the southern slopes of the Golan Heights above the impressive gorge of the Yarmuk River, a tributary of the Jordan. A bridge across the gorge clearly shows the route of the disused Haifa–Damascus railway, built by the Turks. On the opposite bank is ancient Gilead, today in Jordan. Perhaps the proximity of Gilead, and the memory of its most famous son, suggested the name by which the springs were known to Jews and Christians in the Byzantine era: the Baths of Elijah.

Degania and Kinneret

Known as the Mother of the Collectives, Degania is the oldest kibbutz in Israel, founded in 1909 at the southern point of the Sea of Galilee. Here the Jordan River begins its long journey south. On its opposite bank, the second kibbutz, Kinneret, was established two years later.

Conditions were hard indeed. Although the soil was good and water plentiful, the newcomers were inexperienced farmers, rocks had to be cleared, the heat in the summer was enervating, malaria took its toll, and local Beduin bandits harassed the settlers. But they were no ordinary settlers, for if their physical means were limited, their spiritual resources were great. Many of them were Jewish intellectuals from Russian cities whose ideology motivated them not merely to return to their roots, to the land of their forefathers, but to do it on their own terms.

For centuries, in whichever country the wandering Jew had lived, he found himself forced off the land and into one or another commercial activity. Some prospered, many did not, but Jewish society gradually became almost completely middle class. This new breed of Jew left all that behind him—it was not merely the taming of the land that excited him, but "conquest of labor." The work ethic was not merely adhered to, it was passionately embraced. But even that was not enough. For the settlers also wanted to build a democratic society, one based on equality and mutual help. The community was the thing; and if the needs of the individual and those of the community conflicted, the latter would prevail. The kibbutz was born.

There are two Deganias today—Aleph (A), the original kibbutz, and Bet (B), established alongside it in 1920. A museum of natural history on Degania Aleph is named after A. D. Gordon, the spiritual mentor of the settlement in its first difficult years. The original farmhouses are being renovated as a history museum. One of Degania's founders was Shmu'el Dayan, whose son Moshe, born on the kibbutz, was to become one of Israel's military and political leaders. Levi Eshkol, prime minister of Israel in the 1960s, was a member of Degania Bet.

At the entrance to Degania Aleph stands a small and rusty French tank, of World War II vintage. On May 15, 1948, the day after Israel's Independence was declared, seven Arab armies invaded the new-born state. The Syrians came down the Golan and across the Tzemach Junction. Two kibbutzim en route—Massada and Sha'ar Hagolan— were overrun, but the attack on Degania was foiled at its very gate, the Syrian tanks stopped by small arms and Molotov cocktails. The tank was left as a memorial.

Cross the Jordan River (of which more in a moment), heading towards Tiberias. Barely a kilometer further on, on the right (the lakeside of the road) on a bend, is a low stone wall. This is the Ohalo cemetery, a beautifully maintained, tranquil place, the official cemetery, too, of Kibbutz Kinneret. The names of those buried there read like the index of a history of the country in its early days—Hess, Borochov, Katznelson, Syrkin. Enter through the upper (right hand) opening in the wall, and continue directly on the same path. You come to a small, cobblestoned clearing between the graves with a fine view of the Sea of Galilee and the Golan Heights. Turn left, and down a few steps to the next path. In front of you is a grave covered with small stones—a Jewish tradition of recalling one's visit and paying respects— with a small, stone bench attached. This is the last resting place of Rachel "Hameshoreret," the Poetess. That is how she is remembered. Every Israeli knows her poems, many of which have been put to music and become popular folk-songs; but not one in ten thousand can tell you her family name. (It was, in fact, Bluwstein.)

Her tombstone is eloquently devoid of biographical information: it carries the only name by which she is known, Rachel, and four lines from one of her poems: "Spread out your hands, look yonder: nothing comes. In the great expanse each man has his Nebo" (the mountain from which Moses looked into his "promised land" that he would never enter). In the stone seat is a recessed canister with a complete volume of her poems, just a few steps away from the palm trees where she once sat and wrote them.

The River Jordan

By contrast with the muddy movement of the river north of the Sea of Galilee, the Jordan south of the lake is almost still, the eucalyptus trees on its banks reflected in its waters. On a beautiful stretch of the river at the entrance to Kibbutz Kinneret, a pilgrim baptism site has been built, allowing safe access (including wheelchair access) to the water, and hot shower and changing facilities as well.

It was in the Jordan River that Jesus was baptized by John the Baptist, and all geographical indications (Matthew 3) point to the traditional site near Jericho. But since the river becomes the frontier between Israel and Jordan just 10 kms. (six miles) south of its Sea of Galilee exit, and remains so for the rest of its course to the Dead Sea, access has become impossible at the traditional site of the baptism. As a result pilgrims have for years come to a few convenient sites near the lake itself.

Tiberias Hot Springs

Two kms. (one-and-a-half miles) before Tiberias are the hottest mineral springs in Israel, gushing out of the earth at 60° C (140° F). It is surely no surprise that their therapeutic effects would have been known to the ancients. In fact there is written evidence of the place being known, and therefore presumably used, even in Old Testament times. But no archeological evidence earlier than the Hellenistic period, about the 3rd century B.C., has been found at the site. The Jewish town of the Second Temple period was called Hammat, meaning Hot Springs, but as the town was gradually overshadowed by its larger neighbor, Tiberias, it became known by association as Hammat (or Hammei) Tiberias, the Tiberias Hot Springs. A coin minted in Tiberias by the Emperor Trajan around A.D. 100 shows Hygeiea, the goddess of health, sitting on a rock with a spring gushing out from under it, evidence of the importance Hammat Tiberias had already gained as a health spa. The Jews saw in such waters the miraculous hand of God; the Romans added the hedonistic dimension.

Local legend relates the origin of these miraculous springs. The great King Solomon felt the need of a good hot bath. Whether it was for himself or his peoples' ills is not clear and opinions differ; but the authoritarian King commanded a bunch of young devils to descend into the bowels of the earth to heat the water. The waters gave such relief to those who bathed in them that their fame quickly spread abroad, bringing the lame, the sick, and the barren from many lands. Seeing such gladness, Solomon worried what would happen when he died and the devils stopped heating the water. In his wisdom he decided to afflict the unlucky devils with deafness. They *still* have not heard of his death, and out of the awe they hold him in unceasingly continue their labors. People vow that the waters' sulphur smell testifies to the truth of the tale, being a sure sign that Hell had a hand in the matter.

So special a place did Hammat Tiberias occupy in Jewish life in the Galilee in the period of the Mishna and Talmud (2nd to 5th centuries A.D.), that Rabbis even permitted the pious to bathe in the springs on the holy Sabbath. The sages were not unanimous on the point of cooking in the hot springs on the Sabbath, however, (cooking on the Sabbath by conventional means is forbidden by Orthodox Jewish custom), though many thought it permissible. You can cook a three-minute egg in about 10 minutes in the springs!

The Turks built a bath house here in the 18th century, now a tiny museum at the entrance to the historical site, and another in the 19th century, since incorporated in the modern spa complex. That, in turn, has been somewhat superceded by the ultra-modern facility opened in 1978 on the lakeside of the road. For the vacationer it offers marvelous warm pools, both indoor and outdoor, lawns, and a decent restaurant. For the sufferer from any of a wide range of ailments, the spa runs a Medical Clinic and Health Sanatorium comparable to Europe's best. (See *Practical Information* for further details).

A Superb Mosaic

The town of Hammat was devastated and rebuilt several times, but ultimately survived the eclipse of Rome and the retreat of Byzantium, and remained a vibrant Jewish town at least until the 8th century. The synagogue uncovered on the site and now open to the public was one of five built in successive periods on the same site. It was built in A.D. 341, and its superbly crafted mosaic floor should not be missed. The motifs are almost identical to those of the Bet Alfa synagogue in the Harod Valley—the classic Jewish symbols and the Wheel of the Zodiac —but the artistry is altogether superior. At Bet Alfa we discussed the question of such pagan motifs as the Zodiac with the Greek sun-god Helios at its center appearing in a synagogue, despite the prohibition of graven images. Here the conundrum is sharper yet. First, some of the human figures in the mosaic—Aquarius, for example—are nude; secondly, the synagogue was not in some remote, rustic community where perhaps, one could argue, an unorthodox tradition had taken root, but was a suburb of Tiberias, at the time the seat of the Sanhedrin, the Jewish High Court! Clearly the design was symbolic, probably representing, as we have suggested before, the orderly cycle of seasons. While the congregants recognized of course that all was in the hands of God, they could not represent Him graphically and thus resorted to an artistic convention of the time.

One of the three Greek inscriptions relates that one Severus, "the servant of the illustrious princes" (the heads of the Sanhedrin), was involved in the work, probably as chief builder. The Aramaic inscription contains this blessing: "Peace be upon him who performs charity in this holy place, and blessings upon him who will perform charity. Amen amen selah."

PRACTICAL INFORMATION FOR
THE SEA OF GALILEE

TELEPHONE CODES. The area code for the whole of the Sea of Galilee is (06). No area code is necessary when calling from within the area.

RESTAURANTS. There are reasonable eating places in a number of places around the lake, notably at the Guest Houses of **Nof Ginosar** and **Vered Hagalil.** Otherwise try the popular eateries on the Golan beach or at Ein Gev, both on the east side of the lake. There is also a cafeteria for lighter meals at the gas station at Tzemach at the southern tip of the lake on Rte. 90.

Youth Hostels. Poriya (the "Taiber" Hostel), in the hills above the Sea of Galilee, turn-off 5 kms. (3 miles) south of Tiberias, P.O. Box 232, Tiberias (tel. 750050). 140 beds, family rooms available, members' kitchen. Difficult location without a car. **Karei Deshe** (the "Yoram" Hostel), next to Tabgha, turn-off Rte. 90, 13 kms. (8 miles) north of Tiberias, Mobile Post Korazim (tel. 720601). 180 beds, airconditioning, swimming, family rooms available, members' kitchen. Glorious location among eucalyptus trees on shores of the Sea of Galilee.

Hospice. Mount of Beatitudes (Franciscan Sisters), tel. 20878.

Guest Houses. Nof Ginosar (M), 9 kms. (6 miles) north of Tiberias (tel. 792161/3). 170 airconditioned rooms, most with bath. An unequalled location amid lawns and huge eucalyptus trees on the Sea of Galilee itself. Bar, coffee-shop, dining room, and an absolutely superb dairy buffet. Swimming, waterski-ing, windsurfing. Lectures and tour of kibbutz. **Vered Haglil** (M), 18 kms. (11 miles) north of Tiberias on Rte. 90, Mobile Post Korazim (tel. 735785). Styled as a guest farm featuring horseback riding, its airconditioned cabins command a sweeping view of the area and of the Sea of Galilee below. Fine, American-style restaurant. Moderate cabins and inexpensive bunkhouse arrangements as well.

Kibbutz Lavi (M), 10 kms. (6 miles) west of Tiberias on the Nazareth road (tel. 799450). **Ramot Holiday Village** (M), on the slopes of the Golan above the Sea of Galilee's northeast shore (tel. 763636). 47 airconditioned rooms, 30 with bath. Dining room, bar, coffeeshop, pool. Fine view of lake. Some inexpensive rooms as well. **Ein Gev Holiday Village** (I), on Sea of Galilee's eastern shore (758027/8). 83 self-sufficient, airconditioned caravans with shower, kitchenette; sleep 4. Dining room, coffeeshop, beach.

Camping. Ein Gev, on the eastern shores of the Sea of Galilee (tel. 758027/8). **Ha'on,** on the southeastern shores (tel. 751144). **Kefar Hittim,** in hills above Tiberias (tel. 795921). **Ma'agan,** at the southern end of the lake (tel. 751172, 751360).

 HOW TO GET AROUND. Public buses run by Egged are reasonably frequent along the western shore of the Sea of Galilee from Degania via Tiberias to Tabgha and Vered Hagalil; less frequent up the east side from Tze-mach via Ein Gev to Ramot; and non-existent around the north from Ramot via Capernaum to Tabgha. A car is more useful! Roads in this region are good.

 MUSEUMS AND HISTORIC SITES. Capernaum, site of an ancient synagogue and Jesus' area HQ. Open daily 8.30–4.

DEGANIA "A" (Aleph). Bet Gordon. **Museum** of natural history, agricul-ture, and pioneering. Open Sun. to Thurs. 9.30–4, Fri. 8.30–1; closed Sat.

HAMMAT GADER. About 8 kms. (5 miles) east of Tzemach. Hot springs, elaborate ancient Roman **baths.**

KURSI. 5 kms. (3 miles) north of Ein Gev. With a Byzantine **church.** Summer months 8–5, winter 8–4. (N.P.)

MOUNT OF BEATITUDES. Site of the **Sermon on the Mount.** Open daily 7 A.M.—5.30 P.M. (church only closed 12.30–2).

TABGHA. Church of the Multiplication (of the loaves and fishes); **Church of the Primacy** (of Peter). Open daily 8–5.

YARDENIT. At entrance to Kibbutz Kinneret. Access to the Jordan River for the **baptism** site.

SPORTS. Water-sports at Nof Ginosar (see Guest Houses). Golan Beach, 9 kms. (6 miles) north of Ein Gev, provides a wide range of equipment (waterskiing, windsurfing, sailing) and entertainment (paddle boats, water-slides, etc.). Horseback **riding** at Vered Hagalil (see Guest Houses).

PRACTICAL INFORMATION FOR TIBERIAS

TOURIST INFORMATION. Government Tourist Information Office, 8 Elhadeff St. (tel. 720992).

HOTELS. With Tiberias at 210 meters (683 ft.) below sea level, vacationers are attracted here more by the mild winter climate than the summer heat. High season, however, is generally April through May (the spring Passover season) and late-September through October. Some hotel rates hardly change at this time, while others increase significantly. The summer heat being what it is in Tiberias, all hotels, even the most lowly, have full airconditioning in their rooms.

Although the term is not locally used, a downtown designation also implies a lakeside location, while other hotels are higher up the hillside on which Tiberias is built. All hotels have dining rooms.

Deluxe

Tiberias Plaza, located near the newly-developed tourism complex by the water, P.O. Box 375 (tel. 792233). 272 rooms with bath. All amenities, including health club, pool, beauty parlor, video room, T.V., waterskiing. Grill-room, bar, piano bar. The new **Fish On The Roof** fish-and-dairy restaurant is on the open promenade between the hotel and the lake (Apr. to Nov. only). Disco with live music on promenade Apr. through Nov., in hotel Dec. through Mar. Free walking tours of Tiberias 2–3 times weekly. AE, DC, MC, V.

Expensive

Galei Kinneret, Kaplan Ave. (tel. 792331). 127 rooms with bath, and the grande dame of the area's better hotels. Sedate and distinctive character, and lovely grounds right on the water's edge, including a terrace for afternoon tea.

Bar, coffeeshop, pool, and all other amenities. High season rates are in the deluxe range. AE, DC, MC, V.

Jordan River, Habanim St. (tel. 792950). 400 rooms with bath. Downtown location; heated pool, health club, sports facilities. AE, DC, MC, V.

Moderate

Ariston, 19 Sederot Herzl (tel. 790244/6). 75 rooms with bath. Bar, coffeeshop, synagogue.

Ganei Hamat, about 2 kms. (1½ miles) out of town on the lake road, Habanim St. (tel. 792890). 190 rooms, all with bath or shower. Rooms in the hotel tower are very good, those in the more rustic, tree-shaded annex somewhat more functional; the difference is reflected in the rates. All amenities, plus its own lakeshore beach over the road, and a special deal with the Tiberias Hot Springs spa next door. In high season annex rates double, while the tower rates *soar* into the deluxe category. AE, DC, V.

Golan Hotel, up the hill at 14 Achad Ha'am St. (tel. 791901/4). 72 rooms with bath. A most pleasant hotel with great views of the lake. Bar, piano bar, nightclub, pool. AE, DC, MC, V.

Hartman Hotel, 3 Achad Ha'am St. (tel. 791555). 69 rooms, most with bath. Bar, pool, sauna, T.V. on request. AE, DC, MC, V.

Ron Beach, on the edge of town heading north P.O. Box 173 (tel. 721418, 791350). 74 rooms. A great location, right on the water's edge, with lawns on the lakeshore. Good food.

Washington, 13 Zeidel St. (tel. 791861/3). 111 rooms with bath. Bar, coffeeshop.

Inexpensive

Arnon, 28 Hashomer St. (tel. 720181). 20 rooms with shower. Up the hill; bar.

Astoria, 13 Ohel Ya'akov St. (tel. 722351/3). 57 rooms, some with bath, most with shower. On the main Nazareth–Haifa road. Video room. AE, DC, MC, V.

Daphne, P.O. Box 52 (tel. 792261/3). 73 rooms, most with bath; up the hill.

Eden, 4 Ohel Ya'akov (tel. 790070/2). 82 rooms, most with bath, the rest with showers. Bar, video room; up the hill.

Eshel, Tabur Ha'aretz St. (tel. 790562). 18 rooms, most with bath or shower. Cheapest of all; up the hill.

Holiday, Gedud Barak Rd. (tel. 721901/3). 110 rooms with bath; all with lakeview. Terrific location by the shore (though separated by the main road). Bar, coffeeshop, nightclub, pool, sauna.

Menora Gardens (Ganei Menora), 3 kms. (2 miles) south of town (tel. 792770, 792769). 73 rooms, most with bath. A quiet resort hotel with extensive grounds.

Pe'er, 2 Ohel Ya'akov St. (tel. 791641/2). 70 rooms, most with bath. Bar, coffeeshop, nightclub, piano bar, T.V. on request. DC, MC, V.

Polonia, Hagalil St. (tel. 720007). 25 rooms with shower. Modest downtown hotel with bar and coffeeshop.

Quiet Beach, Gedud Barak Rd. (tel. 720602). 76 rooms, most with bath. On a prime waterfront site. Bar, coffeeshop; swimming, waterskiing. Rates loop into the moderate range in high season. AE, DC, MC, V.

Tiberias, 19 Ohel Ya'akov St. (tel. 792270). 72 rooms, most with bath. Health club, sauna; up the hill.

Tzameret Inn, P.O. Box 200 (tel. 794951/3). 80 rooms with bath. In splendid isolation at the top of the mountain. Pool. AE, DC, MC, V.

Hospices. Church of Scotland Center (Presbyterian), P.O. Box 104 (tel. 790144). Lovely gardens, friendly, downtown location. **Terra Sancta** (Franciscan, Catholic), P.O. Box 179 (tel. 720516). Near lake-edge; bed only. **YMCA Peniel-by-Galilee** (Protestant), P.O. Box 192 (tel. 720188). 3 kms. (2 miles) north of town on the lake. High rates.

Youth Hostel. Meyouhas Youth Hostel couldn't be more central—at the corner of Hayarden St. and Gedud Barak Rd., P.O. Box 81 (tel. 721775). 240 beds, airconditioned, family rooms available. Well-fitted and well-run.

Another, non-official, youth hostel exists in Tiberias; inquire locally.

RESTAURANTS. The specialty of the area is St. Peter's fish; compare prices. The better restaurants, like Tiberias Plaza's **Fish On The Roof** on the Promenade (tel. 792233), are likely to serve a far better fish (at a far bigger price). Several other Promenade restaurants offer seating right on the water where the sardines fight for scraps of bread thrown in. The resort places which offer swimming and water-sports also do good lake fish; try (north of town) **Blue Beach** and the **Ron Beach Hotel.** Also **Quiet Beach, Lido,** and **Shells Beach.** South of town is **Sironit** and **Valley Beach.** The spa at Tiberias Hot Springs has an immaculate restaurant. Sometimes the older restaurants on Habanim St. and the side streets connecting it to the Promenade will offer more for your money—plus a local atmosphere—than the better-situated, more tourist-oriented lakeside spots.

Chinese food has arrived in Tiberias, and **The House,** opposite the Lido on Gedud Barak Rd. (tel. 792353), is of international class. Reservations are advisable. Another is **Crimson Flower** on Mosque Square (tel. 790211).

If you are looking for a more Continental touch try **C'est Si Bon,** or splurge at **Donna Grazia,** a fine restaurant/bar/gallery with dancing at night. **Mitzpor** way up the hill above the town commands a stunning view of Tiberias and the Sea of Galilee. Hamburger joints and good pub/restaurants have recently opened near the new promenade.

Felafel stands abound, as do pizza and ice-cream joints, especially around the brash, video-blaring strip near the Promenade where the young set and the back-packers like to hang out.

TOURS AND EXCURSIONS. Walking tours of Tiberias led by a qualified guide leave from the Tiberias Plaza Hotel twice a week December through March, three times a week April through November—a valuable experience in a town where the street names evoke its history as much as the ruins.

Many tours come through Tiberias, but **Galilee Tours** on 10 Hayarden St. (tel. 720330, 720550) have tours of the Golan Heights, Upper Galilee, and Haifa/Acre beginning in Tiberias itself. Also try **Egged Tours** at the Central Bus Station (tel. 720474) for information. A wonderful experience is a boat ride across the Sea of Galilee. The **Kinneret Sailing Company** operates a scheduled service from their mooring at the Tiberias Promenade to Kibbutz Ein Gev around 11.15, leaving on the return trip at 12.45, with enough time for a leisurely St. Peter's fish lunch on the water at the Kibbutz's famous restaurant. This service is year round, but in summer is increased to 3–4 sailings in each direction per day. Chartered trips for organized groups keep these motor cruisers busy plying between Tiberias and Capernaum, and, less often, between

Capernaum and Ein Gev. Individuals can arrange to join such trips; the Company's office is on the Promenade (tel. 721831, 720248).

 MUSEUMS AND HISTORIC SITES. The hot springs and spectacular 4th-century A.D. mosaic synagogue floor of **Hammat Tiberias** should not be missed (see text), 2 kms. (1½ miles) south of the city center. Its grounds are in a National Park (and are therefore on the National Park Card), open daily 8–4 (until 5 in the summer); Fri. 8–2. The **tomb of Maimonides,** the great 12th-century Jewish scholar/philosopher/physician is on Ben Zakkai St., and nearby are the traditional **tombs of Yochanan Ben-Zakkai and Akiva,** sages of the Roman period. A walk around the downtown area reveals old buildings, towers, and walls of several medieval periods, and Jewish and Muslim structures of the Turkish era. The **Municipal Museum** tells part of the story, and free guided tours tell the rest.

 SPORTS. Tiberias' location invites water sports, though for most locals this does not extend beyond **swimming. Boating** and **waterskiing** are available, however, through several of the hotels (Tiberias Plaza, Galei Kinneret, Ganei Hamat, Quiet Beach) and beach resorts (Blue Beach, Lido, Sironit, Valley Beach).

 RELIGIOUS SERVICES. Tiberias has its fair share of synagogues, both old and new, Ashkenazi and Sephardic. Ask at your hotel or the Tourist Information Office. Catholic mass (in English) is celebrated in St. Peter's Church daily at 7 A.M., and on Sundays at 8.30 and 11 A.M. The Presbyterian Church of Scotland Center has a service at 8 P.M. every Sunday.

THE UPPER GALILEE AND GOLAN

Where the Past Is Present

This chapter covers one of the most beautiful and well-watered parts of Israel, a fascinating melange of spectacular scenery, historical sites, and places straight out of today's newspaper headlines. For the purposes of touring, the region can be taken as a whole, but in fact it is easily divided into three distinct areas.

First, Merom Hagalil, the Highlands, a rugged block of difficult and often magnificent mountain terrain. It tumbles down to the Mediterranean coast on the west, continues north across the border into an almost equally mountainous Lebanon, and presents a forbidding, wall-like face to the Lower Galilee in the south and the Hula Valley in the east. Many of its peaks exceed 1,000 meters (3,250 ft.), with the highest —Mount Meron—reaching 1,208 meters (3,926 ft.). Its sites include Safed (Zefat), Mount Meron itself, Bar'am, and Peki'in.

Secondly, the Hula Valley, a long rectangular valley dotted with modern agricultural settlements, mostly kibbutzim, and intensively cultivated. From vantage points overlooking the valley, you can easily pick out the contrasting lands—fish-cultivation ponds; orchards of oranges, apples, avocado, and pecans; cotton, wheat, and alfalfa fields.

258

At the northern end of the valley, the three main tributaries of the Jordan River combine, exiting through a gorge in the south towards the Sea of Galilee. Among the places of interest here are the tels of Hatzor and Dan, Tel Hai, and the nature reserves of the Hula, the Tannur, Dan and Banias (Caesarea Philippi).

Thirdly and lastly are the Golan and the slopes of Mount Hermon, areas that came under Israeli control after the Six Day War in 1967. But although travelers often pass through the Golan intent on understanding contemporary political issues, the area offers much more to the adventurous. There are canyon hikes to waterfalls and natural pools; historical sites like the Second Temple period city of Gamla and the medieval Nimrod's Castle; and the geological interest of this extinct volcanic region. And don't forget Israel's only ski slopes on Mount Hermon.

Three parallel routes approach the Upper Galilee from the west coast, the main one from Acre (Akko) to Safed, Route 85; one from Nahariya to Sasa, Route 89; and a third further north via Shlomi.

If you have your own car and plenty of time, the northern route via Shlomi will offer you wonderful mountain scenery. There are several northerly detours which touch the Lebanese border and rejoin the main route . . . just to add flavor to the expedition. A word of caution though: this is a narrow and winding road used by trucks and farm vehicles, and one should drive with more than usual care. The road joins the Nahariya road either four kms. (two miles) east of the town of Ma'alot, or, if you prefer, at Sasa, another nine kms. (five-and-a-half miles) further east.

Ma'alot and Peki'in

Ma'alot, 18 kms. (11 miles) east of Nahariya, was built from scratch in 1957 as a development town, designed to absorb some of the hundreds of thousands of Jewish refugees who had reached Israel that decade from Arab lands. The town was catapulted into the headlines in May 1974, when a P.L.O. terrorist squad, having infiltrated across the border from Lebanon, captured a school. There they found a group of high-school kids from the Galilee city of Safed. They were on an excursion, and had been given permission to camp out overnight in the school. The children were held hostage for a day. A rescue attempt at the 6 P.M. deadline failed, and 24 of the children were shot dead by the terrorists. The limelight in which Ma'alot found itself also illuminated the town's economic and social problems, stimulating a modest influx of "western" Israelis, mostly professionals, who felt called to show solidarity and help the community. Today Ma'alot enjoys a common local council with its close neighbor, the small Arab town of Tarshiha.

Just east of Ma'alot, a road heads off to the right, dropping via Peki'in to the Acre–Safed highway. Peki'in, or Buqeia in modern Arabic, is today a mixed Druze-Arab village, but is said to have had a continuous Jewish presence since the days of the Second Temple, 2,000 years ago. As late as the '30s, there was a small but significant Jewish community in the village. But most moved away, leaving just one family, that of Zinati, to maintain the token presence. The family's last patriarch died a few years ago, and his daughter has tenaciously tried to hang on in the face of official indifference and low-level harassment by neighbors. The old synagogue, with fragments of more ancient ones on the same site, is worth visiting, though is not often open. Above the village, and just below the road, is a small cave traditionally identified as the one in which Shimon Bar-Yochai, a rabbi of the 2nd century A.D., hid with his son from the Romans for 13 years, surviving on spring water and the bean of the carob tree. A new Jewish farming village of the same name is just up the road.

Bar'am

At the Sasa road junction east of Ma'alot, another lovely mountain road climbs northwards to the ancient synagogue remains of Bar'am and the northeastern part of the range. Although less famous than the ruins at Capernaum on the Sea of Galilee, Bar'am boasts one of the best-preserved early synagogues in Israel. Towns such as Bar'am dotted the Galilee and Golan in the late Roman period (2nd and 3rd centuries A.D.), when Judea to the south had lost its preeminence as the Jewish center, following the suppression of the Bar Kockba Revolt in A.D. 135 and the rebuilding of Jerusalem as the pagan Aelia Capitolina. Of the well-over 50 ancient synagogues uncovered around the country from this and the later Byzantine period (4th–7th centuries A.D.), a significant majority were found in the north. Built at a time of greater Roman tolerance of Jewish religious and communal life, the synagogue clearly shows the investment of time and money the community devoted to their most important building. A section of the lintel of the facade, now in the Louvre in Paris, contains the Hebrew inscription: "May there be peace in this place, and in all the places of Israel. This lintel was made by Jose the Levite. Blessings upon his works. Shalom."

Between the Sasa junction and the Acre–Safed road, a turn-off to the left takes you to the Arab village of Jish, the "Gush-halav" of the Second Temple period. Ask the locals for directions to the antiquities, especially the ancient tombs.

Botany and Bonfires

Mount Meron is not only the highest mountain in the Galilee (1,208 meters, 3,926 ft.), but its 25,000 acres of slopes are preserved as Israel's largest nature reserve. Coming from Nahariya on Route 89, the turn-off is three kms. (two miles) before the Sasa junction. A good road past the Nature Preservation Society's Field School takes you almost to the top. You can park and picnic here, but the major attraction is the walking trail which encircles the peak. The views are breathtaking in all directions. Stations along the way draw your attention to examples of the rich and varied flora of Mount Meron. There was human settlement on these slopes in the Israelite (Old Testament) and Mishnaic (late-Roman) periods; today the wild boar, marten, polecat, and dormouse have the area almost to themselves. Bear, leopard and antelope were once found here, but have been hunted to extinction.

The scene is quite different at the eastern foot of Mount Meron. The Acre–Safed road winds round it, passing near the tombs of several great rabbis of the Roman era. Here are buried Hillel, the preeminent sage of the Herodian period (late-1st century B.C.), and his contemporary, Shammai. Great teachers both, the differences between the stern and strict Shammai and the more compassionate and lenient Hillel hardened in the generations after them into two rival schools of thought. This is an oft-quoted example of this difference: a heathen came to Shammai with the demand that he would convert if Shammai would teach him the entire Torah while he, the heathen, stood on one foot. Shammai rebuked him for his impudence and sent him on his way. He then went to Hillel with the same request. "What is hateful to you, do not unto your neighbor," replied the great sage. "This is the entire Torah, all the rest is commentary. Let us sit down and discuss it."

Of greater significance even than the tombs of Hillel and Shammai is that of Shimon Bar-Yochai, survivor of the Bar Kochba Revolt and refugee from the Romans for 13 years. The 16th-century mystics who settled in Safed (see below) believed that Bar-Yochai had penned the *Zohar* (Book of Splendor), the central work of the mystical Kabbalah movement. That the book was actually written in 13th-century Spain they could not have deduced, but even today such an irrelevant fact is not allowed to interfere with the traditional annual pilgrimage to the great man's tomb!

For centuries now, the pilgrimage has become a celebration of Lag B'Omer, the festive 33rd day after the first day of Passover. Bonfires were lit, and eye-witness accounts describe the religious ecstasy and not-always-religious abandon which accompanied the celebrations. Rabbis over the years rumbled about the unseemly behavior, and on occasion even banned the festivities outright. Today things are a little tamer, but the convivial atmosphere has not been completely lost. The ultra-orthodox Hassidim still come to pray fervently at Rab Shimon's grave, while less zealous North African Jews just as fervently tend their barbequed shishkebab. It is traditional to give three-year-old boys their first haircut on this day; in times past their locks were consigned to the bonfire.

The Road to Safed

The highway from Acre eastwards—Route 85—forms the border between the hills of Lower Galilee and the mountains of Upper Galilee. It passes through a valley carpeted with olive trees, some believed to be 2,000 years old. In Biblical times, this was the territory of the prosperous tribe of Asher, which provided the finest olive oil in Israel, used in the Temple in Jerusalem.

Thirty-two kms. (20 miles) from Acre is a junction where the Safed road meets a new network of highways. From here you can reach Nazareth to the south, Tiberias and the Sea of Galilee to the southeast, and bypass Safed to the Hula Valley and Golan.

As you begin the climb towards Safed, you pass the village of Amirim on your right. The members of this moshav are all vegetarians, and some of the families in the community offer holiday accommodations and excellent home-cooked vegetarian/natural meals in an unsurpassed setting. The winding road continues through pine forests with designated picnic areas and fine hiking trails, past Mount Meron (see above), finally reaching Safed, at over 900 meters (3,000 ft.) Israel's loftiest city.

Safed: Crown of the Galilee

Old Safed was built on and around the hill known locally as Hametzuda, the Citadel. Although the modern town has expanded onto the neighboring peak of Mount Canaan, and along and down ridges adjacent to the original center, the Citadel, now draped in greenery, is still visible from afar as it thrusts above the city.

Although a natural sentinel on the highways crossing the Galilee, the site of Safed was uninhabited in Biblical times. During the Great Revolt against the Romans (A.D. 66–70), a Jewish stronghold was apparently built here, though no trace of it remains. The summit of the hill was a beacon in Talmudic times, 1,600 years ago or so, its bonfires informing the countryside around of the beginning of the New Month, according to which the Jewish calendar was determined. In the Middle Ages, the Crusaders erected a powerful citadel which was captured by the Arab ruler Saladin in 1188, soon after his decisive victory at the Horns of Hattin. It was regained and restored 50 years later by the Order of the Templars on a grand scale, making it the largest and most massive Christian fortress in the East. It was able to keep at bay for some time the besieging army of the Mamluk sultan Baybars, only to fall at last in 1266. Once covering an area of 10 acres, only fragments of the citadel's mighty walls remain today, surrounded by the pines and well-tended flower-beds of the municipal park.

A thriving settlement had grown up in the shadow of the Crusader castle walls. Though it declined with the eclipse of the Crusader presence in the Galilee, the town survived. In the early 16th-century, its Jewish community was joined by a stream of Sephardic Jews driven out of Spain by Ferdinand and Isabella in 1492. Among them were several great rabbis who were to leave their mark on the age, and no less on subsequent generations. Yosef (Joseph) Caro, whose synagogue is one of the most charming in the old Jewish Quarter, is esteemed to this day as the author of the *Shulchan Aruch,* an authoritative handbook of Jewish religious practice. Shlomo Alkabetz composed the beautiful Sabbath hymn *Lecha Dodi,* personifying the Sabbath as a "bride" and a "queen." But it was Isaac Luria, the Ari—an acronym for Adoneinu Rabbeinu Itzhak, our master and teacher Isaac—who was the towering personality of the period, evolving his own system of Kabbalah, Jewish mysticism. This flowering of Kabbalah and scholarship in the city's golden age has added the name of Safed to those of Jerusalem, Hebron, and Tiberias as one of Judaism's holy cities.

Many come to Meron and to Safed to draw their inspiration from the sages of bygone days. The Kabbalists tried to grapple with ultimate, existential problems. Why, for example, is there evil in a world supposedly created in God's perfect image? Every word, every letter of the Bible, it was believed, held a hidden and profound meaning. He who could find the key to unlock the code, to see behind the surface meanings, would be blessed indeed, for knowledge and wisdom and final understanding of those Ultimate Questions would surely be his.

A devastating earthquake in 1837, the deprivations of World War I, and the Arab riots of 1929 persuaded many survivors to leave the town, so that by 1948 the large Jewish majority of the 19th century had been reversed. The departing British army left the town's key strategic positions to the Arab forces who set about besieging the Jewish Quarter. Reinforced by a handful of Palmach men (part of the clandestine Jewish army at the time), the mostly elderly devout Jews of the Quarter resisted successfully. Once again the Citadel, with its strategic position above the heart of Safed, with its sweeping views and steep slopes, was the focal point of the battle, as it had been in Crusader times.

The Jewish Quarter

Access to the old Jewish Quarter is from Rehov Yerushalayim (Jerusalem Street), a road that encircles the Citadel. A square in the heart of the Quarter, the old Kohlenplatz, the "charcoal square," was once the social and economic center of the neighborhood. A two-story house on the square was the command post of the Quarter's defence in 1948. A stepped street takes you down to the Ari Synagogue on the right (the one on the left is relatively new). This one belongs to the Ashkenazi congregation; the Sephardic Ari Synagogue is much further down the Quarter.

Down the steps again and to the left, a cobbled street leads to the Caro Synagogue. The seating concept is different here. A cushioned bench runs around the synagogue wall, reminiscent of the days when people sat cross-legged on cushions on the floor. On request you can open the Ark containing Torah Scrolls; one is at least 400 years old. A glass-faced cabinet at the back of the synagogue is the *geniza,* where damaged scrolls or prayer-books are stored (but never destroyed since they contain the name of God). The turquoise paint here and elsewhere in Old Safed in believed efficacious in keeping away the evil eye. "It's the color of Heaven," they say.

More difficult to find, though worth the effort, is another 16th-century Sephardic synagogue, the Abouhav, one street further down the hillside from the Caro. The locals say that in the great earthquake of 1837, when most of the synagogue was ruined, only the wall containing the Holy Ark was miraculously spared. Two arks are, in fact, in use today; one is opened only on the High Holy Days and Shavuot (Pentecost, traditionally the Festival of the Giving of the Law), the other on lesser occasions. There is believed to be a curse on anyone contravening this custom, and that when the Torah Scrolls had to be removed temporarily from the special ark for renovation, 12 men shared the task. "All," declare the locals, "died within the year."

Two cemeteries, the old and the new, are on the hillside below Safed. The former resonates with the names and fame of the Kabbalists of old—Luria, Cordoviero, Alkabetz, Caro. Unknown ghosts lurk there, and, it is said, "if the legs of the devout are of a sudden tired, it is from walking over hidden graves." (In a separate plot of the new cemetery, bordered by cypresses, the 24 teenage victims of the terrorist massacre at Ma'alot in 1974 are buried.)

A stroll through the little-changed, narrow alleyways of the old Jewish Quarter, a pause under a fig tree in a crumbling stone courtyard, a quiet moment in a turquoise-daubed 16th-century synagogue, a sudden stunning view across to Mount Meron, a near-collision with a latter-day religious zealot hurrying through the streets—the visitor with a soul is captivated. The past is present in Safed.

The Artist's Quarter

The look and feeling of the old Arab Quarter has been kept alive. Now the Artist's Quarter, the winding alleyways and refurbished old dwellings are an enchantment all their own. Although little happens here during the winter—almost all the artists also have homes in the warmer coastal regions—come summer, the Quarter bursts out of its hibernation like some gorgeous butterfly. Potters, painters, and sculptors are at work and welcome the tourist who may enter a gallery or workshop with just curiosity, but leave two cups of coffee later with a purchase to treasure. (The hawkers of pictures and trinkets on the streets of the Jewish Quarter should not be seen as representative of Safed's Artist Colony.)

Right through the Artist's Quarter stands the renovated 200-year-old Austrian Post Office, dating from the Turkish period. The bar here was once the postmaster's private apartment; the dining room the stables. Later, rooms were added, and the building became a *khan,* a Turkish inn. Today it is the Rimon Inn, Safed's best hotel, an enchanting harmony of stonework and gardens, its different levels commanding a panoramic view of mountains and gorges.

Out of Safed, Route 89 heads up over Mount Canaan, and then drops rapidly, reaching Rosh Pina and the Tiberias–Metulla highway.

Rosh Pina—a Cornerstone

In December 1881, a Romanian Jew, one David Shuv, arrived in Palestine as the representative of a group of would-be pioneers. His mission: to find and purchase an area of land on which to build a village. The plot of land at the foot of Safed's mountain ridge seemed suitable, and, moreover, was for sale. The deal was almost soured by the arrival of representatives of a different Romanian organization. While Shuv and his companion hired donkeys, donned the raiment of the local inhabitants, and moved around the district without fuss, the newcomers rode in on horseback in European dress "looking for all the world," Shuv wrote, "like Englishmen and Americans on a Cook's Tour." The word spread like wildfire—these unbelievably wealthy (!) Europeans had come to buy land. Prices rose hand in hand with expectations.

Though the site was remote—not one road reached the area yet—and the land had to be cleared of boulders before any farming could be done, other advantages and the charm of the position prevailed, and Shuv bought the land. Thirty young families joined him that year, sailing from Romania to their ancestral homeland in a ship called, with exquisite irony, *Titus,* the name of the Roman general whose destruction of Jerusalem in A.D. 70 had begun the exile from which they were only now returning. The beginnings were hard, but when the rains came to soften the sun-baked earth, and the plow first bit into it, the settlers joyously celebrated that day (in December 1882) as the true foundation of their new home. They called the village Rosh Pina— "cornerstone"—from Psalm 118: "The stone that the builder has rejected has become the headstone of the corner."

The Safed road runs right through the heart of the village, but get into its backstreets, and especially the upper and older parts of the settlement, and your romantic imagination should have no difficulty recreating the sights and sounds of a bygone era. The old, red-roofed stone houses, cobblestone streets, olive groves, and orange orchards stand witness.

Hatzor: "Head of All Those Kingdoms"

Ten kms. (6 miles) north of the Rosh Pina junction, and about four kms. (two miles) past the turn-off to Route 91 and the Golan Heights, Route 90 enters a narrow pass. Ahead, dominating the pass, is a large, flat-topped mound, or tel. This is the site of the ancient city of Hatzor, and the road it still dominates is part of the Via Maris, the ancient highway that linked Egypt and Mesopotamia.

A metropolis of international stature, Hatzor was the only ancient city in Canaan, as Israel was then called, to earn frequent mention in Mesopotamian documents of the second millenium B.C. Joshua razed Canaanite Hatzor in the 13th century B.C. The Book of Joshua describes the city as being, in earlier times, "the head of all those kingdoms." Indeed, the area of the ancient tel, the artificial mound made up of successive levels of settlement, is some 210 acres, three times that of the country's next largest.

While Israelites settled Hatzor after Joshua's conquest, it was not to regain its former glory for a further 300 years, when Solomon rebuilt it as one of his great regional military/administrative centers, along with Megiddo and Gezer. It was finally destroyed by the invading Assyrians in the 8th century B.C., and its Israelite inhabitants were led off to exile in chains. Thereafter it was inhabited only sporadically, and was never to rise above the level of a small settlement or highway fortress.

A four-season archeological excavation began in 1955, led by Yigael Yadin, best-known for his excavation of Masada in the '60s. Twenty-one different strata of settlement were exposed, going back to the Early Bronze Age (circa 2,700 B.C.), and down to the Hellenistic period (2nd century B.C.). Simultaneous excavations were carried out in the "upper city," the bottle-shaped higher mound comprising some 10 per cent of Hatzor in its heyday, and in the "lower city," the huge rectangular plateau below it.

Little of the lower city remains today. But its finds were sometimes no less dramatic than those of the better-known mound above it. All of Hatzor—the upper and lower cities together—flourished in only two periods: the 18th and the 14th centuries B.C. In all other periods, the upper city alone was inhabited. Remains of royal palaces and tombs, temples and shrines, statues and stelae yielded to the spade in the lower city. And, at the 13th century B.C. level, evidence of destruction by fire, with an abundance of Mycenean pottery fragments to date that stratum, gave eloquent support to the Biblical description of Joshua's destruction of the city.

The upper city is open to visitors, with careful diagrams helping interpret the confusing array of archeological remains. Here, too, evidence of Joshua's conquest was found; of the modest Israelite settlement that followed it (fresh out of the desert, they were not yet city-builders); of Solomon's great city; of the ingenious and laboriously dug water system of the 9th century B.C.; of the 8th-century earthquake recorded in Amos; and of the Assyrian destruction soon to follow. Even the name of the last Israelite king, Pekah, was found inscribed on a wine jar, apparently part of His Majesty's stores.

Many of the artifacts found at Hatzor are on display at the special museum at the entrance to kibbutz Ayelet Hashachar just over the road, others are in the Israel Museum in Jerusalem.

Hula Valley: Conservation and Cultivation

Just about eight kms. (five miles) north of Hatzor, an orange sign points right to the former marshlands of the Hula (Huleh) Nature Reserve, recognized in the 1970s by the International Union of Conservation of Nature as a reserve of world importance. It began with the creation of a seven-mile canal network, finished in 1958, that crisscrossed 775 acres bordering Lake Hula. The reserve opened in 1964, but closed again and then reopened in 1979 after replanning and landscaping. Primarily a bird sanctuary today, it also boasts open water areas, swamp meadow, and a reed habitat where water buffalo were reintroduced and now wallow in the mud as in former eras. Throughout the reserve, there is impressive plant life, including papyrus thickets (nowadays scarcely found outside the Sudan). This is a paradise all year for birds of many species, flying to and from Europe, Asia and Africa: storks, pelicans, wild geese, ducks, and many migratory birds unfamiliar to Westerners. The waters abound with carp, catfish and perch, though fishing, like hunting, is strictly forbidden. The topminnow, an American fish that lives on mosquito eggs, played a big part in helping rid the area of malaria. Tourists can visit here daily, for minimal fees, and the regular free tours are highly recommended.

The next road to the left winds back up into the mountains. These are the Heights of Naftali, named after the Biblical Israelite tribe that once lived here. The modern fortress at the top was built by the British —similar fortresses dot the country, controlling important road junctions or vantage points—and is popularly known as Nebi Yesha, the "prophet Joshua" in Arabic. Muslim tradition accords Joshua that status and says that he had a religious college in the valley nearby! The fortress, now a military base, is known in Hebrew as Metzudat Ko'ach, literally, the Citadel of Strength; but the word "ko' ach" is made up of two Hebrew consonants, the numerical value of which is 28, and the place is named in memory of that number of Israeli soldiers killed in the fierce battles here in the 1948 War of Independence. The road continues north along the spine of the ridge, eventually returning to the Hula Valley at Tel Hai. On the way, near kibbutz Menara, it offers arguably the most spectacular view in Israel! The best time to appreciate it is in the afternoon.

The American writer Mark Twain, who rode through the Hula Valley in 1867, wrote: "There is not a solitary village throughout its whole extent—not for 30 miles in either direction . . . One may ride ten miles hereabouts and not see ten human beings." How different the scene is today! A town and 25 farming villages, mostly kibbutzim, have changed the face of the valley, tilling its rich and well-watered soil, once malaria-infested marshland, producing in some cases world-record yields (cotton and alfalfa).

Areas and Eras of Conflict

The town of Kiryat Shemona serves as the only urban center in an otherwise almost completely agrarian region. It takes its name—the Town of the Eight—from the eight settlers who fell in the defence of Tel Hai in 1920 (see below). Like Ma'alot, Kiryat Shemona made the headlines in 1974 when Arab terrorists crossed the Lebanese border by night, came down the mountain slope behind the town, and broke into an apartment at dawn, massacring an entire family. By 1982 the spate of terrorist attacks had again reached major proportions. In response, Israel invaded Lebanon, the first stage of Operation Peace for Galilee.

The conflicts in this area date back to the years immediately following World War I. While Great Britain and France argued over which should have final control of the upper Hula Valley, which bordered their respective holdings, bands of Beduins and Arab villagers roamed unchecked, harassing the tiny Jewish settlements and plundering when they could. The looked-for help from the south never materialized. One tiny settlement was destroyed; the veteran village of Metulla was temporarily abandoned; and the communal settlement of Tel Hai was overrun. Only Kfar Giladi successfully defended itself, going on to become a large and prosperous kibbutz.

The heroic stand of Tel Hai had two important consequences for the later history of the region, one psychological and one political. It was the first modern example of Jewish armed self-defense, and did much to change the local image of the Jew as timid and defenseless. Secondly, the survival of at least two of the Jewish settlements in this far northerly Galilee finger determined that when the final borders were drawn by the League of Nations in 1922, they would be included in the British mandated territory of Palestine, and thus, after 1948, in the State of Israel. The stockade of Tel Hai has been restored as a museum, and its black basalt walls and red roofs overlook the road just north of Kiryat Shemona.

Metulla is Israel's most northerly settlement. Founded in 1896 as a village of independent farmers with the aid of Baron Edmond de Rothschild, it has known hard times over the generations. The tenacity of its inhabitants has borne fruit (in the most literal sense), however, and despite its vulnerable position on the Lebanese border, it has prospered. A marvelously picturesque village, it has for long been a favorite vacation-spot for Israeli families.

Waterfalls and Nature Trails

The Hula Valley may be the one part of Israel that has more water than it knows what to do with. The main streams, the sources of the Jordan River, are perennial, but Nahal Iyon, a small and lovely canyon, is seasonal. The best time to visit is late winter or spring. Entering near Metulla, one can follow a good walking trail to view its four waterfalls. The lowest and finest is independently accessible by car. It is called the Tannur waterfall, the Oven, because the rock formation it has carved out is reminiscent of rustic Arab ovens. The entrance is between Tel Hai and Metulla, and the Tannur, when flowing, can be seen in the distance from the road.

An esoteric sidelight for the Bible scholor: just north of the Tannur is a long tel, that easily recognizable flat-topped mound that indicates the site of an ancient city. This is Abel of Bet-Ma'acah, the last refuge of a rebel against King David (II Samuel 20).

At the edge of Kiryat Shemona, the main road (Route 99) heads east to Dan, Banias, Mount Hermon, and the Golan Heights. Just before Kibbutz Hagoshrim, the road crosses the Hatzbani, one of the tributaries of the Jordan. Just beyond the kibbutz is the park of Hurshat Tal, developed to preserve the huge Tabor oaks, a rare example of trees this size surviving the centuries of armies, woodcutters, and nomads. There are lawns and a swimming pool fed by the cold waters of the River and Dan, and on a warm day you could do worse than to take off a couple of hours to relax here.

Certainly the queen of the Nature Reserves in the area is Tel Dan (turn off 10 kms.—six miles—from Kiryat Shemona). It owes its jungle-like vegetation to the fact that the River Dan, the Jordan's largest source, rises here not as a single spring, but as a cluster of springs creating myriad streams and rivulets which eventually combine. Apart from being a marvelous picnic spot—one can sit right on the banks of the main stream—Tel Dan offers a nature trail through idyllic surroundings. Soon after it begins, the trail divides into a short trail (about 30 minutes), and a longer one (about one hour). Do take the longer one if you have the time. You can purchase a leaflet in English detailing the Reserve, and specifically linked to several numbered spots along the way.

Dan: The City of the North

The tel of Tel Dan is not immediately identifiable as such to the untrained eye, so densely is it covered in trees and shrubs. Its area is huge—four times larger than Megiddo, and second only to Hatzor—an indication of its importance in ancient times. Founded as the Canaanite city of Laish some 5,000 years ago, it was captured by the tribe of Dan sometime in the period of the Judges, and renamed after their patronymic ancestor. The classical dimensions of the Biblical Israelite kingdom were often described as "from Dan to Beersheba." After the division of the Kingdom in 922 B.C., Jeroboam, the secessionist king, built religious centers at the northern and southern ends of his domain —Dan and Bethel—to substitute for the now-inaccessible Temple in Jerusalem. At Dan he raised a cultic golden calf, and altars from this period have, in fact, been found in excavations at the site.

The local Arabic name for the mound is Tel el-Kadi, the Hill of the Judge. "Dan" means just that in Hebrew, and Jacob's death-bed blessing on his son Dan was that he would "judge his people." But the Arabic legend has a different version of the name. Once there were three rivers, the Dan, the Banias, and the Hatzbani, the sources of the Jordan, which argued among themselves as to which was the most important. God was invited to judge the matter. He came down, sat on the tel (hence, Hill of the Judge), heard their arguments, and pronounced judgement: "Unite, and you will surely become the most important river!" They did, and became the Jordan.

The Greek God Pan and the Gospels

The road twists up to Banias. The stream here springs full-born from the foot of Mount Hermon, lazily in summer and fall, swollen in winter and spring. In the Hellenistic and Roman periods (at least 3rd century B.C. to 1st century A.D.) this was a cult center for the worship of Pan, the Greek god of the forests and "wild places," the shepherds' god. In the cliff-face behind the spring are several arched niches, some with small pedestals where a statue of Pan would once have stood. Greek inscriptions of dedication are still clearly legible. The shallow cave may once have been used in the ceremonies of the cult, but its shape and dimensions have been changed by the earthquakes of later centuries. The Greeks called the town here Panias, in honor of the god; in Arabic, which lacks the consonant "p," it has become Banias.

In 198 B.C., after a century of ruling Israel, the Hellenistic Ptolemies of Egypt were defeated by the Hellenistic Seleucid empire of Syria. In the late 1st century B.C., King Herod the Great built a temple here dedicated to Augustus Ceasar. His son, Philip, made it a city, dedicated to the Caesar of his day and called Caesarea Philippi, to distinguish it from his father's city of Caesarea on the Mediterranean. It is by this name we know it in the New Testament (Matthew 16). Here, in response to the question "And who do you say I am?", Peter confessed the true nature of Christ, a pivotal event in Jesus' ministry. Some scholars feel that Jesus may have deliberately selected the heartland of paganism for this great declaration of faith. A small, (closed) Greek Orthodox church nearby recalls the event. The Crusaders had a town here, too, and some remains can still be seen, but little is left of earlier periods.

Across the main road a path leads you along the river, depositing you a comfortable 45 minutes later at the powerful Banias Waterfall. A hundred meters along the path is a water-mill, still in use today; a small channel was led off the main stream to drive the basalt grinding stones. Alternatively, you can visit the waterfall without the hike: the turn-off is a kilometer back on the road to Dan.

Mount Hermon and Nimrod's Castle

Snow-capped Mount Hermon simply dwarfs all other peaks in the area. A huge mountain block, it looms over the Upper Galilee, but is not part of it. Its summit, at an elevation of over 2,800 meters (over 9,000 ft.), is in Syrian territory, but its lower southern slopes serve as an Israeli ski resort in the winter. Geologically distinct from the volcanic basalt of the Golan, its climate and vegetation are almost alpine in character. Just above Banias, Route 989 breaks off to the left to Nimrod's Castle, the village of Neve Ativ (which operates the ski slopes), the Druze village of Majdal Shams (highest in the country), and the ski slopes themselves.

No-one knows how Nimrod's Castle—Kala'at Namroud in Arabic —got its name, and its medieval history is the subject of some controversy. But nobody has any reservations about the interest to be found in the mammoth fortress (about 500 meters, 1,620 feet long), the impressiveness of its location on a mountain spur, or the beauty of its panoramic view. It guarded the route from Damascus via the Golan and Banias to Lebanon and the Mediterranean coast. It is generally believed that it was initially built by the Crusaders in the 12th century, and throughout that and the following century it changed hands several times as Christians and Muslims vied for control over the area. It was not a time of unrelieved warfare, however, and there is evidence of periods of peaceful co-existence between the two sides, with the flocks and herds of both mingling in the pastures. The donjon, or keep, the main tower of the fortress, faces east, the direction from which the Crusaders could expect an attack. Muslim rebuilding expanded the west-facing tower, and added some superb architecture and stone masonry. Stone inscriptions in Arabic still recall the period.

The castle boasts an intriguing curiosity: an extremist Muslim sect of the period held the fortress for some time. They were characterized by two things—they were cut-throats, and they smoked hashish extensively. The name by which they became known, Hashishin (the hashish users), has given us the English word assassin, expressing the violence associated with the sect. Marco Polo, the 13th-century Italian explorer, wrote in his diaries of being captured by the Assassin and held "somewhere between Damascus and Jaffa." We're a long way from Jaffa, but this could be a candidate for the place described.

THE GOLAN HEIGHTS

The Golan, as the area is simply known, is a sort of stretched half-moon in shape, about 60 kms. (38 miles) long from north to south, and between 15 and 25 kms. (9 to 16 miles) wide. The whole region was actively volcanic in the geologically not-so-distant past, and many symmetrical volcanic cones still dominate the landscape. Where the dark basalt rock has weathered or been cleared, the mineral-rich soil supports a wide variety of crops. The gentler terrain and climate of the southern Golan has attracted settlement far more than the less hospitable north. In the spring the region, already greened by the winter rains, comes alive with wildflowers; but when the summer heat has frizzled everything to a uniform yellow-brown, it seems a land of desolation—unless you know its hidden places. For the beauty of the Golan lies in its many deep canyons, with streams, 50-meter (over 160 ft.) waterfalls, luxuriant vegetation, and hiking trails.

There is evidence of very ancient burial on the Golan in the form of dolmens, funerary monuments about four millenia old, but no settlements until Herod the Great tamed the area in the 1st century B.C. For the next five centuries or so, many Jewish villages existed here, and remains of their houses and synagogues have been found in several places.

A more sinister period in the area's history began earlier this century. The Golan had been attached to Syria, then under French control, after World War I. During Israel's War of Independence in 1948, Syria became her most implaccable enemy. For the next 19 years, the Golan was turned into an armed camp, its deeply fortified positions on the edge of the Heights bristling with artillery and commanding the vulnerable Israeli villages of the Sea of Galilee region and the Hula Valley. There were 19 years of sporadic harassment, while below in the valley bomb shelters were converted into children's nurseries and tractors had armor-plating bolted around the driver's seat. On the fourth and fifth days of the Six Day War in June 1967, the Heights were taken by frontal assault, and though the cost in human life was high, the Galilee breathed freely for the first time in a generation.

There are two easily accessible old Syrian bunkers from which to get a gunners'-eye-view of the valley below, and an appreciation of the strategic value of the Heights. One is Tel el-Faher in the northern Golan, the turn-off to which is to the right just above Banias (off Route 99). The other is known as Mitzpeh Gadot for the kibbutz it overlooks, in the central Golan, just above the B'not Ya'akov Bridge (Route 91). It is easily recognized by the big triangular concrete memorial built there. An important word of caution: the sites are safe, but beyond the fences and clearly-marked paths are old Syrian minefields.

As you climb east from Banias on Route 99, the first and most picturesque of four Druze villages appears across a valley on your left. A kilometer to the left of the intersection at the top of the hill (in the Druze village of Mas'ada), and you reach a parking-lot and restaurant on the edge of a small, oval lake, Birket Ram, the High Lake. Although it looks like a crater—and the region was volcanic, after all—geologists believe it was formed by the collapse of a limestone cavern below the younger basalt layer. The historian Josephus Flavius of the 1st century A.D. tells of an experiment conducted by Philip, son of Herod, who threw wheat-chaff onto the lake and was able to watch it come out at Banias (!). Although there are absurdities in this account, Philip did have the right idea; seepage from the lake does merge as a spring—though not the Banias—further down the mountain.

Head back through Mas'ada and continue on the main road, Route 98, for 16 kms. (10 miles) where you then find yourself on a rise with a view to the east. Below you are the fields and orchards (excellent apples) of the nearby kibbutzim. Where the fields end is the frontier with Syria. The ruined town is Kuneitra, captured by Israel in 1967, lost and regained in the Yom Kippur War of 1973, and returned to Syria in the Disengagement Agreement that followed. It is now a demilitarized zone, and Syria has made no effort to rebuild the town. Next to it is the United Nations Compound, a cluster of white, silver-roofed buildings of the U.N. Disengagement Observer Force.

The road—Route 91—almost immediately swings west, away from the frontier, past Kibbutz Ein Zivan. About 14 kms. (nine miles) beyond Ein Zivan, Route 9088 heads off to the southern Golan, of which more in a moment. Two kms. (one-and-a-half miles) further, Route 888, to the left, will have you down at the Sea of Galilee in 10 minutes. The old, battered building at this intersection was a French customs house in the Mandatory period between the Wars. Ahead, the road winds down to the Jordan River, passing Mitzpe Gadot (Syrian bunkers) and crossing the river at the B'not Ya'akov Bridge on its way to Rosh Pina. There are ancient fords here, and in the Middle Ages the Crusaders took tolls from travelers crossing the river. When asked where their money was going, the Crusaders replied that it was sent to the Convent of the Sisters of St. James in Paris. James in Hebrew and Arabic is Ya'akov or Yakoub (Jacob); sisters somehow became daughters *(banot),* and so the bridge got its name.

Three kms. (two miles) down Route 9088 to the southern Golan, is the new town of Katzrin with its Museum of Antiquities. Beyond the town, an orange sign guides you to the ancient 2nd- or 3rd-century synagogue of Katzrin (a contemporary of Bar'am and Capernaum).

Gamla: Masada of the North

Our last stop is a particularly memorable one. Beyond Katzrin, turn left at the intersection and shortly afterwards, right on to Route 808. About 10 kms. (six miles) further, a well-marked road to the right takes you to Gamla. In the fields on either side of this access road are strange stone structures, stone "tables," as it were, reminiscent of the Greek letter "pi." These are dolmens, funerary monuments, apparently from the 2nd millenium B.C.

"Gamla had refused to surrender (to the Romans), relying on its inaccessibility," wrote the Jewish historian, Josephus Flavius, of the siege of Gamla in the early stages of the Great Revolt (A.D. 66–70). "On the face and both sides [of the hill on which the town is built] it is cut off by impassable ravines." Built on a hump-like spur resembling a camel in profile *(gamal* is the Hebrew for camel), the fortified town of Gamla was the last refuge for 9,000 Galilean Jews in A.D. 67.

Again Josephus: "Built against the almost vertical flank, the houses were piled on top of one another, and the town seemed to be hung in air and on the point of tumbling on top of itself from its very steepness." The terrain was almost the Romans' undoing. They were able to reach the town thanks to the engineering efforts of Vespasian's three legions, but in their zeal they overreached themselves, and when the defenders swung round and counter-attacked, the Romans were "swept down the slope and jammed inextricably in the narrow alleys." Panicking, the Romans climbed onto the roofs of houses, which, unequal to their weight, collapsed, adding to the devastation.

Rallied by their commander, Vespasian (whom Josephus ingratiatingly describes in almost superhuman terms), the Romans first by stealth and then by force were able to drive the last defenders to the summit, while the town was "deluged with the blood" of those slaughtered by the Romans. Seeing no escape, the survivors flung themselves to their death in the abyss below the town.

From a look-out point a few hundred meters to the left (south) of the parking lot, Gamla, with the Sea of Galilee in the background, appears dramatically below you. Every topographical detail of Josephus' description is clear. The archeological excavations of Shmaryahu Guttman have uncovered the breached city wall and stepped houses. Also uncovered was a synagogue, the oldest yet found in Israel. If you're the gung-ho type, a good trail descends from the parking lot to Gamla itself, but it's a stiff walk back.

At the look-out point, an unobtrusive memorial—a ground-level cut-out aluminum inscription against the black basalt rock background —remembers other fighters, members of modern Israeli settlements on the Golan killed in the Yom Kippur War of 1973.

Back on the main highway, and a kilometer to the south is another intersection. A right turn onto Route 869, and you begin the descent to the Sea of Galilee.

PRACTICAL INFORMATION FOR THE UPPER
GALILEE AND THE GOLAN

TELEPHONE CODES. We have given telephone codes for all the towns and areas in the lists that follow. These codes need only be used when calling from outside the area concerned.

HOTELS AND RESTAURANTS. There is not a wide choice of either hotels or eateries in this vicinity. Below we have listed a few of those you might look out for, however.

KIRYAT SHEMONA. 29 kms. (18 miles) north of Rosh Pina. The **North Hotel** (M), (tel. 06–944703). 90 rooms with bath and airconditioning. Bar, coffeeshop, nightclub, T.V. on request. AE, DC, V. **Tel Hai Youth Hostel,** about 2 kms. (1½ miles) north of Kiryat Shemona (tel. 06–940043). 200 beds, family rooms available, members' kitchen. Located on terrific grounds.

Restaurants. There are many small restaurants in the town mostly serving Middle-Eastern-style food, or "Western" with a Middle-Eastern touch.

METULLA. 7 kms. (4½ miles) north of Kiryat Shemona, this is the most northerly point in Israel and right on the Lebanese border. **Hotel Arazim** (M), (tel. 06–944143/5). 28 rooms. AE, DC, V. **Sheleg Halevanon** (M), (tel. 06–944615). 31 rooms. **Hamavri** (I) (tel. 06–940150).

Restaurants. Hotels can sometimes provide light lunches. There is a café/restaurant on the main street, and a good rustic grill/restaurant off to the right in a new neighborhood as you enter the village.

ROSH PINA. At the foot of the mountain, east of Safed. The old part of the village is very picturesque and good to poke around in. Good bus connections. **Youth Hostel,** tel. 06–937086. 100 beds and quite good, especially the family rooms.

Restaurants. There are a few roadside cafeterias which serve passing travelers.

Guest Houses. All are kibbutz-run and on kibbutz grounds, and are very comfortable, airconditioned, with bars, coffeeshops, pools. All provide evening lectures—usually with slides or video—on kibbutz life, and morning guided tours of the settlement. Superb settings, with much greenery and flowers, are very much the norm. Most credit cards are accepted.

Ayelet Hashachar (E), opposite Tel Hatzor, about 7 kms. (4½ miles) north of Rosh Pina (tel. 06–935364). 144 rooms with bath. Choice of full-course meal or à la carte daily. Pioneered the kibbutz guest house concept in the Galilee.

Kfar Blum (M), turnoff on Gonen road 24 kms. (15 miles) north of Rosh Pina (tel. 06–943666). 46 rooms, most with bath. Intimate, friendly; good food. Many members are former Americans or English. Tennis; pool. **Kfar Giladi** (M), above Tel Hai, a few kms. north of Kiryat Shemona (tel. 06–941414/5). 155 rooms with bath. Tennis, excursions, gymnasium. **Hagoshrim** (M), 6 kms. (4 miles) east of Kiryat Shemona on the road to Dan and Banias (tel. 06–945231). 121 rooms with bath. Tennis. À la carte dairy lunches available. **Neve Ativ** (M), high on the slopes of Mt. Hermon (tel. 06–944331). A holiday village with pool, tennis, billiards, restaurant, and all in a spectacular location. Though designed to serve the ski slopes in the winter months, it is necessary to check whether they are open during the summer.

Camping. At **Hurshat Tal,** just beyond Kibbutz Hagoshrim, some 6 kms. (4 miles) east of Kiryat Shemona. The site is characterized by huge Tabor oaks, and adjoins the Hurshat Tal park, with its lawns and swimming pool fed by the Dan Stream.

 HOW TO GET AROUND. Scheduled buses serve all sites and settlements in the area out of Safed, Rosh Pina, or Kiryat Shemona, but many routes are infrequent. Check times at Egged Central Bus Station in each town.

 MUSEUMS AND HISTORIC SITES. All places listed here are treated in detail in the main text. (N.P.) indicates a National Park.

BANIAS. 13 kms. (8 miles) east of Kiryat Shemona on Rte. 99. One of the sources of Jordan, **shrine** to the Greek god Pan, Caesarea Philippi of the New Testament.

BAR'AM. About 15 kms. (9 miles) northwest of Safed, above Sasa. Substantial remains of a 2nd-3rd-century A.D. **synagogue.** (N.P.)

GAMLA. Accessible via Rte. 869 from the Sea of Galilee, or via local roads from northern Golan. Labeled the Masada of the North, this is a **fortified city** of the Great Jewish Revolt against the Romans, which fell to Vespasian in A.D. 67 with great loss of life. Great overlook. Excavations.

HATZOR. Hatzor Museum. Across the road from the tel (see below), at the entrance to Kibbutz Ayelet Hashachar. A fine collection of artifacts and visual aids. (N.P.)

Tel Hatzor 7 kms. (4½ miles) north of Rosh Pina. Greatest Canaanite city of the 2nd millenium B.C., and a major regional center of King Solomon. Excavations. (N.P.)

KATZRIN. In central Golan between the Rosh Pina–Ein Zivan road (Rte. 91) and the Capernaum–Hushniya road (Rte. 87). Ancient **synagogue** and archeological **museum** of the area.

NIMROD'S CASTLE. East of Banias and above it on Neve Ativ road (Rte. 989). (N.P.)

Tel Dan. 10 kms. (6 miles) east of Kiryat Shemona, just off Rte. 99. Terrific wonderland of greenery and running water; large tel, and excavations. Open Sat. to Thurs. 8–4, Fri. 8–1.

Tel Hai. 2 kms. (1½ miles) north of Kiryat Shemona. Jewish communal settlement overrun in 1920, now restored as a museum of way of life and events of the time. Open Sun. to Thurs. 8–1, 2–5 (winter until 4), Fri. 9–1, Sat. 8–1.

SPORTS. There is a **swimming** pool in Safed; in addition, kibbutz guest houses have pools for guests, and some have **tennis** courts as well. There is a cold pool at Hurshat Tal. Large tennis center in Kiryat Shemona. Ski slopes in winter on Mt. Hermon, operated by Neve Ativ (tel. 06–944331/8); check in advance for opening dates and times. Good, easy **hiking** is available in the Banias and Tannur nature reserves. Longer hikes on the Golan Heights are advisable only when accompanied by someone who knows the way.

PRACTICAL INFORMATION FOR SAFED

TOURIST INFORMATION. Government Tourist Information Office, 7 Rehov Yerushalayim (Jerusalem St.), tel. 930633.

Telephone Code. The area code for Safed is (06).

HOTELS. Safed's hotel situation is unique in Israel. At an altitude of 950 meters (over 3,000 ft.).—the most elevated city in Israel—it is one of the few places in the country that is reasonably pleasant during the intense heat of July and August. As a consequence, some hotels raise their rates especially in August and over the Jewish holidays (Passover in the spring, and the late-September/October period). Some charge a minimum rate that includes half-board, giving you a choice of lunch or dinner, as well as breakfast.

The hotels are situated in two sections: on Mt. Canaan, above the town, and in Safed itself.

There are no deluxe hotels in the area, and rates tend to be lower than in the major cities.

Moderate

Central Hotel, Jerusalem St. (tel. 972666). 54 rooms, half with bath, half with shower. Bar. Excellently located. Rates up by 50% in high season. MC.

David Hotel, on Mt. Canaan (tel. 930062, 971662). 42 rooms with bath; partly airconditioned. Bar.

Nof Hagalil, on Mt. Canaan (tel. 931595, 970880). 34 rooms, 24 with bath, 10 with shower. Bar; sweeping views of the area. MC, V.

Rimon Inn, Artists' Colony (tel. 930665/6). 36 rooms. Once a post office when the Turks ran the country; today's dining room then stabled horses. Restored in 1967, most of it is some 200 years old, with a new wing following the graceful stone architecture. Fruit grows for guests to pick in a flower garden. Timeless atmosphere; a unique "away-from-it-all" sort of place on the fringe of the Artists' Quarter. Pool. AE, DC, MC, V.

Ron, Hativat Yiftach St. (tel. 972590/1/2). 50 rooms. Bar, coffeeshop, pool, nightclub in season. Good location.

Zefat Hotel, on Mt. Canaan (tel. 930914, 972579). 36 rooms. Bar.

Inexpensive

Berinson House, tel. 972555, 972382. 38 rooms with bath. Doubles its rates in high season.

Motel Canaan, on Mt. Canaan. (tel. 970929). 21 rooms, kitchenettes, bar, and coffeeshop.

Pisgah, on Mt. Canaan (tel. 930105, 970044). 55 rooms, most with bath. Bar, coffeeshop.

Ruckenstein, on Mt. Canaan (tel. 930060, 971007). 26 rooms. Well-run, family-owned hotel with bar, coffeeshop, T.V. on request, in-house movies. Rates jump 66% in high season. V.

Youth Hostel. Bet Benyamin, (tel. 931086). 120 beds, family rooms, members' kitchen. Not Israel's best.

Guest House. Moshav Amirim, 14 kms. (9 miles) out of Safed towards Acre (tel. 89571). Not a conventional guest house; some residents offer family accommodations, others exceptional home-cooked vegetarian/natural meals.

RESTAURANTS. Pinati, on Jerusalem St., looks like nothing much but has good Middle-Eastern food at moderate prices. **Milo,** in the artists' quarter, is a gathering place for the local fraternity. Kosher **Hamifgash** is a top and popular restaurant on Jerusalem St., not far from non-kosher **Azmon.** There's good food at **Batia** (Oriental/European), also on Jerusalem St., as well as at the restaurant in the Egged Bus Station.

MUSEUMS AND HISTORIC SITES. The Artists' Quarter is a colorful conglomerate of old buildings in the former Arab Quarter, where artists and craftspeople live and work. The General Exhibition at the entrance to the Quarter has examples of the work of most artists, and is open Sun. to Thurs. 9–6, Fri. 9–noon, Sat. 10–1.

Citadel (Metzuda), once a Crusaders' stronghold, is now a park with fine views.

Glickenstein Municipal Museum, on the Metzuda, or Citadel Hill. Houses art and Judaica. Open daily 9–noon, 4–6; Fri. 9–noon only.

Ha'ari Ashkenazim, a synagogue with an odd and interesting Ark dating from the early-19th century.

Ha'ari Hasephardi, near the cemetery. One of the few synagogues to have withstood intact the earthquake of 1837.

Museum of the Art of Printing. Safed boasted the first Hebrew press in Israel (16th century). Open daily 10–noon, 4–6; Fri. 10–noon only.

Synagogue of Rabbi Joseph Caro. Author of the magnum opus, the *Shulchan Aruch.* A pronounced medieval atmosphere.

NIGHTLIFE. As such, this exists only during the summer. Outdoor dancing at the **Metzuda,** a pleasant café at the top of Metzuda Park. Several hotels have dancing in the evenings. There are three nightclubs: the nightclub at the **Ron** hotel; **Leilot Kanaan** is in the basement of a medieval house; and **Moadon Hashaot Haktanot,** in a vaulted cave, was formerly a Turkish hammam. Also, the **Rimon Inn** has a marvellous little bar room.

THE NEGEV AND EILAT

Deserts and Discos

Encompassing about half the land mass of Israel, though home to only a small part of its population, the vast empty spaces of the Negev —vast by Israeli standards anyway—retain something of the pioneering mystique of the early days of the modern State of Israel. Yet though much of the area remains virgin, large tracts of what was once wilderness have now been developed, extensively so in many cases, and burst with crops to such an extent that, measured simply as desert, it can be difficult in places to determine the borders of the region.

Roughly speaking, however, the Negev comprises the southern half of Israel, an inverted triangle with the Jordanian and Egyptian borders marking its eastern and western sides respectively, and Eilat on the Red Sea its southernmost tip. The northern border—the base of the triangle —lies approximately 27 kms. (17 miles) north of Beersheba, the only large city in the region and its capital. Though predominantly desert, the landscape is varied. There is sand in the Negev, to be sure, though not sand dunes, and a good deal of dust, too, come to that, but there are also mountains and canyons, and, surprisingly perhaps for so barren and dry a land, a wide variety of animal and plant life.

An Ancient Land

The Negev may well have changed more in the years since the foundation of the modern State of Israel in 1948 than in the entire period since the end of the Roman Empire. Nonetheless, its recorded history is long and varied. The ancient Israelites had fortifications here, as did the Nabateans and the Romans after them. These early settlers developed irrigation techniques that are remarkably sophisticated, even by modern standards. Between these periods of permanent settlement, the entire area was home to bands of Beduin nomads (their voracious herds of black goats have long been the bane of farmers here). The Beduin are still very much a distinctive presence in the Negev, though very much less than they once were. Indeed, a clear pattern has emerged over the centuries of retreat by the Beduin in the face of strong central government, and northern advance in times of weak government. Today, of course, the former conditions apply. To a considerable extent, however, the Beduin are now giving up their wandering life and beginning to make permanent homes for themselves, the signs of which can be easily recognized as you drive through the region: seemingly random collections of tents, tin shacks and concrete homes marking different stages in this gradual process. A number of tribes have refused to give way and under considerable pressures have stuck to their old wandering ways.

Possibly the most dramatic change to have occurred in the Negev in the past few years, however, has been the building of huge new army bases, constructed after Israel's withdrawal from Sinai in 1982. These in turn have encroached further on the traditional Beduin lands, and have tended to increase the pressures on them to abandon their traditional way of life.

Beersheba

Beersheba is a modern, bustling city of 130,000 people. Though an ancient city, it has been transformed since 1948, the result of a determined and deliberate effort to expand and settle this, the southernmost large city of Israel. The camel caravans that still stride down the main street ensure that the place retains at least a flavor of a Wild West frontier town, but a brand new university, a fine orchestra and theater companies, and some of the most striking modern architecture in the country have placed the city firmly in the 20th century. It is undeniable that here more than anywhere in the Negev there has probably been more change in the last 40 years than in the 3,000 years of settlement that preceded them.

The most recent event of note before the capture of the city by Israeli troops in October 1948 from the Egyptians, who had installed themselves there as the British left, was probably Abraham's visit 3,800 years ago. The town Abraham visited was located at the tel—the characteristic mound formation that invariably marks the site of an ancient city—some eight kms. (five miles) east of the present city. Elsewhere, along the bank of a wadi, or dry river bed, archeologists have found traces of human habitation dating back 6,000 years. Many of the finds from this and other nearby sites are now in the small municipal museum in the town center, in a building that once served as a morgue.

In later years, the city's significance lay in the fact, still pertinent to some degree today, that it marked the border between the settled agricultural lands to the north and the arid barren regions of the Beduin to the south. In addition, it also constituted an important way station on the caravan route to Egypt.

You can of course still visit the old town in Beersheba, with its stone buildings erected by the Turks, who made it an administrative center. It was here that Lawrence of Arabia, disguised as a Beduin, was imprisoned by the Turks in World War I. He crept into the town to spy out its defences and his capture and probable torture by the Turks has long remained a mysterious and enigmatic event in a mysterious and enigmatic life. Try to imagine the buildings a little more dilapidated, the streets unpaved and without sidewalks, camels and donkeys instead of cars, and you will be coming close to the atmosphere of those times. For that matter, you can even visit Abraham's Well, which is certainly ancient, even if its link to the patriarch is a matter of conjecture.

For a taste of the ancient and the modern, visit Beersheba on its regular Thursday morning Beduin market—it's worth making a special effort to see. The market now exists as much for the benefit of the tourists as for the locals, and everyone is very much aware they are putting on a show. Nonetheless, it remains a vital part of life in the region, with Beduins and farmers congregating to conduct their business and to exchange gossip and news. Plastic kitchenware, ancient coins, the latest in brass trinkets and, of course, camels, all feature prominently among the goods for sale. The Beduins mingle and haggle, with more recent immigrants from Soviet Georgia or veteran immigrants from Romania or Morocco chipping in for good measure. The language of trade is Hebrew, with a generous mixture of Arabic thrown in.

For a very different picture of Beersheba, visit the futuristic buildings of Ben Gurion University. David Ben Gurion was Israel's first prime minister and the architect of the modern state, playing a leading role in the development and settlement of the Negev, which he believed to be a key to Israel's future stability and prosperity. Recently, the university has played a part in the fulfillment of another dream as one of the sites for negotiation between Egypt and Israel.

Into the Heart of the Negev

Drive south from Beersheba on Route 40. The first sign of life comes some 30 kms. (19 miles) from Beersheba, at the Bir Asluj crossroads. A small grove of eucalyptus trees marks the graves of Israeli soldiers killed fighting the Egyptians in 1948 in the battle for the Negev. The modern Kibbutz Mashabbei Sadeh and Moshav Telalim are nearby. A further 13 kms. (eight miles) down Route 40 brings you to Kibbutz Sde Boker, founded by a group of young pioneers in 1952, today renowned for its peach and olive groves. A year later the original settlers found themselves joined by a much older and far more distinguished member, the 67-year-old David Ben Gurion himself, who had that year resigned as prime minister, an office he had held since 1948. The acceptance to kibbutz membership of a man well beyond his physical working life was unprecedented, and has remained a unique example. Some of Sde Boker's members were at the time opposed to the move despite (or perhaps because of) Ben Gurion's awesome prestige. A few years later, however, the political differences which had culminated in his resignation were patched up and he returned to office. In 1963, however, he again resigned and returned to the kibbutz which he made his home until his death in 1973. The simple shack in which he lived has been kept as it was at his death, and has become something of a place of pilgrimage. Ben Gurion and his wife Paula are buried a few miles to the south of the kibbutz at the Sde Boker Institute overlooking the gorge of Nahal Zin.

Among its other facilities, the campus includes the prestigious Desert Research Institute, where top scientists in fields such as solar energy, biology and agriculture work to enhance man's quality of life in the desert by using as their starting point the desert's own unique features and the need to preserve them.

From the Sde Boker Institute a gravel road snakes down to Ein Avdat, a wondrous chalk canyon where a desert spring has created cataracts and pools amid a riot of vegetation. In the afternoon especially you may be lucky to see ibex come down the cliffs to drink.

Ten kms. (six miles) or so south of Sde Boker is the hilltop site of ancient Avdat. It was founded by the Nabateans, a powerful desert people who flourished from the 3rd century B.C. to the 1st century A.D., as a station for spice caravans coming from Arabia to the east, via their capital Petra (in modern-day Jordan), to the Mediterranean market ports. The Nabateans developed an ingenious system of trapping the flood-waters of the winter rains, and exploiting them for extensive farming. From the top of the hill you can see green patches of fields and orchards, the successful project of botany professor Even-Ari to prove that the Nabatean farms were not mythical, by restoring parts of their irrigation systems, working the fields with primitive implements, and waiting for the rains! Though many ruins of Nabatean Avdat can still be seen, most of the prominent structures on the site are from the later Roman and, especially, Byzantine settlements here (the latter perfected the Nabatean farming methods in the valleys below). Especially noteworthy are the Roman tower, Byzantine acropolis complete with churches, and dwelling caves in the cliff-face below it.

Continuing south a farther 22 kms. (14 miles) from Avdat you come to the new town of Mitzpe Ramon, perched on the edge of the giant crater, Makhtesh Ramon, 40 kms.- (25 miles) long, nine kms.- (five miles) wide and 400 meters-(1,250 ft.) deep. The town was established in 1953, but, isolated in the middle of the Negev, it has had a tough time of it. Having no natural resources to speak of, it has proved difficult to attract industry here, so far from the center of the country. And with the construction of a new road to Eilat bypassing Mitzpe Ramon a few years ago, the town became even more isolated, a process which has happily been halted by the opening of a new geological park, highlighting the many unusual rock formations of the crater. There is an impressively futuristic visitors' center at the entrance to the town with a panoramic view of the crater, displays of regional geology, flora and fauna and a 15-minute audio-visual program. A winding road descends into the crater itself, signs by the road-side giving explanations of the different rock-types and rock-formations you pass on the way. Carved out by water action over many eons of time, the crater—technically a "cirque"—serves as a window onto the country's geological history. In addition, several unique fossil specimens have been found of dinosaur-like animals that once roamed the region.

The road—still Route 40—crosses the crater—and continues south through varied desert landscapes to join Route 90, 96 kms. (60 miles) later, just 45 minutes north of Eilat.

A couple of miles west of the town is an observatory, built to take advantage of the altitude, the clear unpolluted air and the relative absence of surrounding lights in the area.

Toward Sinai

Backtracking from Mitzpe Ramon five kms. (three miles) brings you to the junction of Route 40 and Route 171. Turn left, west, for the Sinai and the Israeli-Egyptian border 34 kms. (21 miles) away. The border itself is marked by painted oil drums. A soldier at the entrance will ask you to fill out a form, the intention being simply to ensure that no cars are left stranded here at night. The border road is a new one, and somewhat narrow, and has been carefully laid out to follow the contours of the hills and blend into the landscape. Anyone in search of natural wilderness will find it here in abundance.

As you drive north along the border there are several lookout points with marvelous views over the Sinai. The ancient city of Kadesh Barnea, one of the Israelites' major halts on their way from Egypt to the Promised Land, can also be seen, though not visited. At the northern end of the road, about an hour's drive later, at the junction with Route 211, another soldier will check you out. Here Egyptian and Israeli soldiers, equally bored, stand guard, their respective flags flapping in the breeze.

Driving eastward along Route 211 towards Route 40, the main north–south highway, you arrive at Shivta, another ancient city which, like Avdat, was founded by the Nabateans, reaching its peak under the Byzantines. The remains of three large churches constitute the principal attraction here.

Just before reaching Route 40, you come to a curious stone building with a round tower next to it. This is all that remains of a rail station built by the Turks just before World War I. The rail line was intended to run all the way to Mecca, today in Saudi Arabia. The war, and defeat by the British, ensured that the line was never completed.

Eastern Negev and the Arava

Passing through Beersheba's industrial zone, pick up Route 60 heading northeast. Just out of town, on a hill to your left, is the monument to the Negev Brigade which secured the region for Israel in the War of Independence in 1948. Each concrete structure represents something reminiscent of the time—a water-tower, a trench, a tent-flap, and so on. The view from the tower is worth the climb. Opposite, a road strikes off to Tel Sheva, the excavated and partially restored site of Biblical Beersheba. An adjacent museum relates not only to the archeological site, but also the folklore of the neighboring Beduin tribes. Passing Omer, Beersheba's garden suburb, you soon reach the Shoket Junction. Route 60 continues north entering the Judean Mountains towards Hebron and Jerusalem. Route 31 to the left joins the Beersheba-Tel Aviv highway, while to the right it is 32 kms (20 miles) to Arad.

This is an area where the transition of the Beduin from tent-dwelling nomads to villagers is most in evidence. Indeed the area has long since produced its first crop of university graduates and a Member of the Knesset. About 22 kms. (14 miles) from the Junction, a turn to the left takes you to Tel Arad, site of that most ancient town. Of particular interest in this well-presented excavation is the sanctuary in the Upper City, complete with altar (now in the Israel Museum), dating from the days of the Kingdom of Judah. It was presumably just this type of regional temple, detracting from the centrality and uniqueness of that in Jerusalem, that aroused the wrath of the Old Testament prophets.

Modern Arad is a very young, well laid-out town whose clean mountain air and dry desert climate have made it an ideal haven for asthma sufferers. Its several modest hotels serve not only vacationers seeking a change from muggy Tel Aviv, but tourists using it as a jumping-off point: the west side of Masada (Roman ramp path) is a half-hour's drive away (secondary road Route 3199), and even less time is needed to reach the Dead Sea by continuing east on Route 31. Just before the last descent of Route 31 to meet Route 90, two observation points on the left side of the road give marvelous views of the gorge of Nahal Zohar and its small ancient forts, once a major highway fording the shallow southern end of the Dead Sea towards the land of Edom. (For the continuation north or south, see page 126.)

The main road from Beersheba to Eilat is Route 25 southeast via Dimona, descending to join Route 90 near Sodom, and thence via the Arava to Eilat. Dimona, 36 kms. (23 miles) from Beersheba, is another of the Negev's several development towns founded in the 1950s expressly to absorb the huge influx of Jewish immigrants—many of them refugees—at the time—a fact which explains the heterogeneous population drawn from lands as diverse as India, Morocco, the Soviet Union and North America. About five kms. (three miles) beyond Dimona, a turn to the right leads to Mamshit (Kurnub), the best-preserved of the Negev's ancient Nabatean towns. 37 kms. (19 miles) separate you from the Arava Junction.

From here the road runs monotonously south to Eilat, 195 kms. (122 miles) away, following the Arava, the southern part of the Jordan Rift, and the northernmost reaches of the Great Rift Valley. Ranged along its length are numerous small agricultural settlements, some established only in the last decade. The climate here is ideal for fruit, flowers and vegetables, much of it early ripening, grown both for local consumption and export. Many of these little settlements operate small restaurants, snack bars and service stations. Here, too, are two kibbutzim affiliated with the Jewish Reform Movement.

A better known kibbutz is that of Yotvata, 41 kms. (25 miles) to the north of Eilat. The kibbutz has its own dairy which not only supplies Eilat with dairy products, but also competes successfully with the dairies of the north. You can sample its products in the well-run snack bar which it maintains just off the highway. There's also a visitors' center just behind the snack bar that graphically and imaginatively charts desert life: plants and animals, rock formations, and residents both past and present are covered. Nearby there's a holiday village, complete with swimming pool, run by Kibbutz Gerofit.

Just south of Yotvata is the entrance to the Hai Bar Nature Reserve, dedicated to preserving rare species of animals mentioned in the Bible. A good number of the animals here had become extinct in Israel many centuries ago and had to be imported from neighboring countries, through sometimes devious means. A rare species of donkey was flown out from Iran only hours before revolutionaries closed the airport. You can either drive through the reserve in your own car or take a tour.

A few miles south of the Nature Reserve, a road running off to the right from Route 90 leads to Timna Park, the site of ancient copper mines said to have been run by King Solomon. The park also contains a series of impressive red rock formations—King Solomon's Pillars— that rise dramatically skyward. Not far from the Pillars are a series of inscriptions made by ancient Egyptian, Israelite, Nabatean and Beduin caravan drivers. Not all those who left inscriptions could write and so they left their stories in pictures. A small artificial lake and grove of trees are also being planned for the park. Closeby are the modern Timna copper mines. The recent drop in the world price of copper has raised significant doubts as to their future, however.

Eilat

All this is minutes, and worlds, away from Eilat, with its beaches, hotels, restaurants and nightclubs. The location of Israel's southernmost town, on the Red Sea, has made it a favorite winter vacation spot for Europeans, many of whom come for a week or two without ever seeing the rest of Israel. For some, the only distraction, after a hard day of working on their tans, is a night of disco dancing. But Eilat has much to offer those for whom a vacation is not complete without some serious sightseeing.

Though tourist guides like to equate Eilat with the biblical Etzion Geber, King Solomon's outlet to Africa, where the Queen of Sheba is said to have landed, the actual site of the ancient port was probably closer to the present Jordanian town of Akaba, whose lights twinkle across the bay at night. Until 1949, when it was taken in a lightning campaign by a small Israeli army force, which used a sheet marked with ink for their flag, Eilat was nothing more than a square stone building, once a Turkish police post, with the name of Umm Rashrash. Though a road was laid a few years later, the town did not begin to develop until the Red Sea was opened to Israeli shipping after the Suez campaign in 1956.

Since that time it has had its ups and downs. The doubt surrounding the future of the Timna copper mines, once one of the mainstays of the local economy, has hit the town badly. Similarly, the opening of the Suez Canal to Israeli shipping, a condition of the Camp David agreement, has also had serious repercussions in Eilat. Whereas before Israeli shipping from the Far East docked at Eilat, from where their cargoes were sent overland to the heart of the country, today of course, using the Suez Canal, ships are able to dock directly at the northern ports of Ashdod and Haifa. As a consequence, tourism has become increasingly important to the town, and is rapidly becoming its principal source of revenue.

The town is laid out with the hotels and beaches all along the shore, except for the chunk of shoreline occupied by the port and the navy. Most of the residents of Eilat live in the hills overlooking the sea and it is here that the schools, hospital, offices and supermarkets are also located. Dividing the two is the airfield. Local planners are hoping to have it moved northward, both to remove the roar of planes from the beach and to develop the airfield area and make it a link, rather than a dividing line, between the two parts of town. Meanwhile, because of the limitations of the present airfield, many of the charter flights from abroad land at the Uvda military airfield north of the town.

In addition to the Timna Park and Hai Bar Nature Reserve, both just a short drive north of the town, Eilat offers a wonderful view into the underwater world of tropical fish and coral. No visitor will want to miss the Underwater Observatory, where you can walk down a stairway into the sea and view the coral formations and the fish, with their amazing shapes and colors, from a series of windows in the wall. The observatory also has its own aquarium with an extensive collection of tropical fish on view.

Nearby is the Coral Beach Nature Reserve where you can rent a snorkel and flippers (or bring your own). Far more demanding is deep-sea diving, with air tanks and full gear, and those who want to spend more time will find diving centers offering lessons and rental equipment. Another way of viewing the fish and the coral is through one of the glass-bottomed boats which make regular excursions. The more athletically inclined will find plenty to occupy them with windsurfing, swimming and waterskiing.

Daily yacht excursions leave from the marina at the north beach, often including either a gourmet dinner or evening dancing. Depending on the political situation with Egypt, the yachts sometimes anchor for swimming and diving off Coral Island, in Egyptian territory, which has the ruins of a Crusader fortress built out of granite. According to a recent agreement with the Egyptians, visitors can also tour the island itself.

From Eilat, tours are also available to Egyptian Sinai, especially Mount Sinai and the nearby St. Catherine's Monastery, a wilderness refuge which, as a result of its isolation, has succeeded in preserving rare early-Christian art treasures. An Egyptian visa is obtainable at the border. The crossing point into Sinai is at Taba, a small section of beachfront which was the object of a border dispute between Egypt and Israel. At the time of writing, the luxury Aviya Sonesta Hotel and Rafi Nelson's Village at Taba, a favorite beach hideaway for Eilat residents, were still in Israeli hands. Similarly, seaside and diving resorts which were developed during the Israeli occupation of Sinai include Dahab, Nueiba and Sharm e-Sheikh, all of which were still functioning at the time of writing. Negotiations on the future of Taba have so far proved inconclusive.

PRACTICAL INFORMATION FOR THE NEGEV AND EILAT

TOURIST OFFICES. There are **Israel Government Tourist Offices** in Arad, Commercial Center (tel. 057-958144); Beersheba, 120 Herzl St. (tel. 057–36001); and Eilat, New Tourist Center (tel. 059–72268). Information on special events is posted on special bulletin boards in hotels, while in Eilat there is also a local newspaper in Hebrew and English which lists special events. The **Voluntary Tourist Service,** whose members usually remain on duty for a few hours every evening, to give help and advice to visitors, is also active in Eilat.

Telephone Codes. We have given the telephone codes for all the areas in the lists that follow. These codes need only be used when calling from outside the dialling area concerned.

HOTELS AND RESTAURANTS. The hotels listed below in Beershaba, Arad and Eilat are all clean and comfortable and have all the facilities a visitor can expect. However, with the exception of a few youth hostels or camp sites, there are no places to stay outside these urban areas. Restaurants are also few and far between in the Negev, and, again with the exception of Eilat, Beersheba and Arad, few are open in the evening. There are three, however, on **Route 40**—at Ben Gurion's Hut on Kibbutz Sde Boker; at Avdat, below the antiquities; and in Mitzpe Ramon—and on **Route 90**—next to the gas stations at Hatzeva, Ein Yahav (particularly good), and Yotvata.

ARAD. Masada (M), P.O. Box 62 (tel. 057–957140). 104 rooms. Swimming pool. DC, MC, V. **Margoa** (M), Moav St. (tel. 057–957014). 160 rooms. Swimming pool, health club. V. **Nof Arad** (M–I), Moav St. (tel. 057–957056). Swimming pool. **Arad** (I), Hapalmach St. (tel. 057–957040). 51 rooms.
Restaurant. Galit (I), Commercial Center. Simple food.

BEERSHEBA. Desert Inn (M–E), P.O. Box 247 (tel. 057–424922). 164 rooms. Swimming pool, tennis courts. AE, DC, MC, V. **Arava** (I), 37 Histadrut St. (tel. 057–78792). 27 rooms.
Restaurants. Chinese Restaurant (M), 97 Histadrut St. (tel. 057–70050). **Papa Michel** (M), 95 Histadrut St. (tel. 057–77298). Middle Eastern dishes. DC,

v. **Tel Beersheba** (M), east of town (tel. 057–30100). Beduin-style dining in a tent; don't miss it if you're in the area. Closed Friday night and Saturday.

EILAT. Aviya Sonesta (L), Taba (tel. 059–76191). 326 rooms. Informal luxury with pool, private beach, tennis courts, children's activities, water sports. AE, DC, MC, V. **Neptune** (L–E), North Beach (tel. 059–73131). 267 rooms. Two pools, health club. AE, DC, MC, V. **Club In** (E), Coral Beach (tel. 059–75122). 168 villas, self-contained units with two bedrooms, lounge and kitchenette. Swimming pool, tennis courts, minimarket, restaurants. AE, DC, MC, V. **King Solomon's Palace** (E), North Beach Lagoon (tel. 059–76111). 460 rooms. The newest hotel in Eilat with a pool, tennis courts, pub, yacht, daily activities for adults and children. AE, DC, MC, V. **Moriah** (M), North Beach (tel. 059–72151). 190 rooms. Swimming pool, tennis courts. AE, DC, MC, V. **Adi** (M), Tzofit St. (tel. 059–76151). 32 rooms. AE, DC, MC, V. **Queen of Sheba** (M), North Beach (tel. 059–72121). 92 rooms, tennis courts. AE, DC, MC, V. **Caravan Sun Club** (M), Coral Beach (tel. 059–73145). Swimming pool, tennis courts. AE, DC, MC, V. **Edomit** (I), New Tourist Center (tel. 059–73103). 85 rooms. Newly built, centrally located. AE, DC, MC, V.

Restaurants. Le Bistro (E), Elot St. (tel. 059–74333). French cuisine, informal atmosphere. AE, DC, MC, V. **La Coquille** (E), North Beach. Very pricey, but some claim it's one of the best restaurants in the country. AE, DC, MC, V. **Last Refuge** (E), Coral Beach (tel. 059–72437). Seafood, a favorite of local residents. AE, DC, MC, V. **Haleluyah** (M), New Tourist Center (tel. 059–75752). North African specialties. DC, V. **Lalo** (M), North Beach (tel. 059–76085). Moroccan dishes. **Red Coral** (M), Coral Beach (tel. 059–75787). French cuisine, seafood. **Oasis** (I), North Beach (tel. 059–72414). **Pundak Habira** (I), Almogim St. Eastern European dishes, lunch only. **Shrimp House** (I), Hatmarim St. (tel. 059–72758). All-you-can-eat dinners.

Youth Hostels. Hostels are often filled up far in advance and distances between hostels are considerable, so it is always a good idea to make reservations well in advance.

Beit Blau Weiss, P.O. Box 34, at Arad (tel. 057–97150). 250 beds. Family accommodations. **Beit Noam,** P.O. Box 2, at Mitzpe Ramon (tel. 057–88443). 160 beds. Family rooms. **Beit Yatziv,** 79 Haatzmaut, at Beersheba (tel. 057–77444). 300 beds. Family accommodations. **Eilat,** P.O. Box 152, in Eilat (tel. 059–72358). 160 beds. Very popular. If this one is full, try: **Max's Hostel,** near the central bus station in Eilat. Recommended by tourists.

Camping. Public Camping, opposite Coral Beach, in Eilat (tel. 059–73105). Simple facilities for tents. **Ramon Geological Park,** at Mitzpe Ramon. Guarded outside area with running water and lavatories. **Sun Bay,** North Beach, in Eilat (tel. 059–73105). Hook-ups for mobile homes and tents. Cooking and washing facilities. **Ye'elim,** Kibbutz Yotvata, Arava highway, north of Eilat (tel. 059–74362). Well-tended lawns, swimming pool, mini-market, children's playground; accommodation in bungalows and mobile homes.

HOW TO GET AROUND. By Plane. *Arkia,* tel. 03–413222, Israel's inland airline, has several flights daily from Tel Aviv, Jerusalem and Ben Gurion Airport to Eilat. The flight takes less than an hour.

By Bus. There is a regular service from Beersheba to all points in the Negev, but buses are sometimes infrequent and it is as well to enquire about schedules in advance. **Egged,** tel. 03–432414, runs regular buses during the day and at night from Tel Aviv and Jerusalem to Eilat. **Galilee Tours,** 142 Hayarkon St., Tel Aviv (tel. 03–225817), offers a daily luxury airconditioned bus from Tel Aviv to Eilat.

By Car. Roads in the Negev are fair to satisfactory. Drivers must take care to stay awake on long desert stretches and to watch out for other drivers. Take plenty of drinking water. Service stations are fairly frequent, but it is a good idea always to have at least half a tank of gas. Be sure to check your radiator often in hot weather.

Although most Israelis are helpful and friendly, you should *not* hitchhike in the Negev, *especially* women traveling alone.

Tours. Tours of the Negev desert sites are available from Tel Aviv and Jerusalem; enquire at your hotel or at **Egged Tours,** 15 Frishman St., Tel Aviv (tel. 03–244177); **Galilee Tours** and **United Tours** in either city. In Eilat, there are regular tours to the Timna Park and the Hai Bar. Glass-bottomed boat tours, for viewing the coral reefs and tropical fish, leave regularly from the dock near the Coral Beach.

For desert tours, in open vehicles, contact **Johnny Tours** in the Richter Tourist Center, Eilat (tel. 059–76777) or **Neot Hakikar** in Jerusalem, 36 Keren Hayesod St. (tel. 02–636494). There are walking tours of the bird sanctuary in Eilat which leave every Tuesday and Thursday morning at 8 from the Sun Bay Hotel.

 MUSEUMS AND HISTORIC SITES. National Parks are indicated as N.P.

ARAD. Tel Arad. Excavation of remains from the biblical period. N.P.

AVDAT. Ein Avdat. A desert spring with waterfall, pools and tropical vegetation; in a spectacular canyon.

Ancient Avdat. A reconstructed city from the Nabatean and Byzantine period. N.P. Open daily 8–5 (winter 8–4); Fri. 8–4.

BEERSHEBA. Abraham's Well. Hebron Rd. and Keren Kayemet St. Open daily 8–7; Fri. 8–1.

Beduin Market. Hebron Rd., every Thurs. from sunrise until about noon.

Negev Museum, Haatzmaut St. Shows objects from nearby excavations. Open Sun., Mon., Tues. 8–1.30; Wed., Thurs. 8–4.30; Fri. 8–1; Sat. 10–1.

Tel Sheva. Biblical Beersheba. Excavations. Has a restaurant in a Beduin tent and a gift shop with local handicrafts. Open 9–11; no lunch on Sat. Excavations open all day. N.P.

EILAT. Bird Sanctuary. Near North Beach, this is the resting point for thousands of migratory birds on their way between Europe and Africa. Has marked paths and blinds.

Coral Beach. A nature reserve with corals and tropical fish.

Hai Bar. Near Kibbutz Yotvata; this is a nature reserve with rare wild animals mentioned in the Bible. Open daily 7.30–2; Fri. 7.30–1.

Timna Valley Park. Off the highway north of Eilat. Has inscriptions by ancient caravan drivers, copper mines from the Biblical period, impressive red sandstone columns. Open daily 7.30–2; Fri. 7.30–1.

Underwater Observatory. Near Coral Beach. This is an absolute must. Here you can view fish and coral in the sea from windows in an underwater tank. There is also an impressive aquarium. Snack bar. Open daily 8.30–4; Fri. 8.30–3.

Yotvata Visitors Center. A display of local sights, with maps and an audio-visual program. Open daily 7.30–2; Fri. 7.30–1.

MAMSHIT. Ancient Nabatean town. Open daily 8–5 (winter 8–4); Fri. 8–4. N.P.

LAHAV. Joe Alon Museum of Beduin life and folklore. Off the Tel Aviv–Beersheba highway. Open daily 9–3; Fri 9–1.

MITZPE RAMON. Mitzpe Ramon Visitors Center. Explanations of rock formations, suggested tours of the area, a film, and a magnificent view of the Ramon crater itself.

Ramon Geological Park. A vast crater with unique stone formations and the remains of ancient civilizations. Open daily 9–4.30; Fri. 9–1.

SDE BOKER. David Ben Gurion's Hut. Last home of Israel's first prime minister. Open Sun. to Thurs. 8–3.30; Fri., Sat. 8–1.

Ben Gurion's Grave. At the nearby Desert Research Institute, overlooking the canyons of Nahal Zin.

SPORTS. Visitors to Eilat in particular can keep active all day long. Many of the hotels have **tennis** courts and most have **swimming** pools. **Surf boards** and **wind-surfing** equipment may be rented at several spots along the beach and from most of the hotels. Equipment for deep-sea **diving** is also available. For further information, enquire at hotels and at the IGTO.

INDEX

INDEX

The letter H indicates Hotels & other accommodations. The letter R indicates Restaurants & other eating facilities.

FODOR'S TRAVEL GUIDES

Here is a complete list of Fodor's Travel Guides, available in current editions; most are also available in a British edition published by Hodder & Stoughton.

U.S. GUIDES

Alaska
American Cities (Great Travel Values)
Arizona including the Grand Canyon
Atlantic City & the New Jersey Shore
Boston
California
Cape Cod & the Islands of Martha's Vineyard & Nantucket
Carolinas & the Georgia Coast
Chesapeake
Chicago
Colorado
Dallas/Fort Worth
Disney World & the Orlando Area (Fun in)
Far West
Florida
Forth Worth (see Dallas)
Galveston (see Houston)
Georgia (see Carolinas)
Grand Canyon (see Arizona)
Greater Miami & the Gold Coast
Hawaii
Hawaii (Great Travel Values)
Houston & Galveston
I-10: California to Florida
I-55: Chicago to New Orleans
I-75: Michigan to Florida
I-80: San Francisco to New York
I-95: Maine to Miami
Jamestown (see Williamsburg)
Las Vegas including Reno & Lake Tahoe (Fun in)
Los Angeles & Nearby Attractions
Martha's Vineyard (see Cape Cod)
Maui (Fun in)
Nantucket (see Cape Cod)
New England
New Jersey (see Atlantic City)
New Mexico
New Orleans
New Orleans (Fun in)
New York City
New York City (Fun in)
New York State
Orlando (see Disney World)
Pacific North Coast
Philadelphia
Reno (see Las Vegas)
Rockies
San Diego & Nearby Attractions
San Francisco (Fun in)
San Francisco plus Marin County & the Wine Country
The South
Texas
U.S.A.
Virgin Islands (U.S. & British)
Virginia
Waikiki (Fun in)
Washington, D.C.
Williamsburg, Jamestown & Yorktown

FOREIGN GUIDES

Acapulco (see Mexico City)
Acapulco (Fun in)
Amsterdam
Australia, New Zealand & the South Pacific
Austria
The Bahamas
The Bahamas (Fun in)
Barbados (Fun in)
Beijing, Guangzhou & Shanghai
Belgium & Luxembourg
Bermuda
Brazil
Britain (Great Travel Values)
Canada
Canada (Great Travel Values)
Canada's Maritime Provinces plus Newfoundland & Labrador
Cancún, Cozumel, Mérida & the Yucatán
Caribbean
Caribbean (Great Travel Values)
Central America
Copenhagen (see Stockholm)
Cozumel (see Cancún)
Eastern Europe
Egypt
Europe
Europe (Budget)
France
France (Great Travel Values)
Germany: East & West
Germany (Great Travel Values)
Great Britain
Greece
Guangzhou (see Beijing)
Helsinki (see Stockholm)
Holland
Hong Kong & Macau
Hungary
India, Nepal & Sri Lanka
Ireland
Israel
Italy
Italy (Great Travel Values)
Jamaica (Fun in)
Japan
Japan (Great Travel Values)
Jordan & the Holy Land
Kenya
Korea
Labrador (see Canada's Maritime Provinces)
Lisbon
Loire Valley
London
London (Fun in)
London (Great Travel Values)
Luxembourg (see Belgium)
Macau (see Hong Kong)
Madrid
Mazatlan (see Mexico's Baja)
Mexico
Mexico (Great Travel Values)
Mexico City & Acapulco
Mexico's Baja & Puerto Vallarta, Mazatlan, Manzanillo, Copper Canyon
Montreal (Fun in)
Munich
Nepal (see India)
New Zealand
Newfoundland (see Canada's Maritime Provinces)
1936 . . . on the Continent
North Africa
Oslo (see Stockholm)
Paris
Paris (Fun in)
People's Republic of China
Portugal
Province of Quebec
Puerto Vallarta (see Mexico's Baja)
Reykjavik (see Stockholm)
Rio (Fun in)
The Riviera (Fun on)
Rome
St. Martin/St. Maarten (Fun in)
Scandinavia
Scotland
Shanghai (see Beijing)
Singapore
South America
South Pacific
Southeast Asia
Soviet Union
Spain
Spain (Great Travel Values)
Sri Lanka (see India)
Stockholm, Copenhagen, Oslo, Helsinki & Reykjavik
Sweden
Switzerland
Sydney
Tokyo
Toronto
Turkey
Vienna
Yucatán (see Cancún)
Yugoslavia

SPECIAL-INTEREST GUIDES

Bed & Breakfast Guide: North America
Royalty Watching
Selected Hotels of Europe
Selected Resorts and Hotels of the U.S.
Ski Resorts of North America
Views to Dine by around the World

AVAILABLE AT YOUR LOCAL BOOKSTORE OR WRITE TO FODOR'S TRAVEL
PUBLICATIONS, INC., 201 EAST 50th STREET, NEW YORK, NY 10022.